Understanding Leadership

Lao Tzu, Marx, the Buddha, Ibsen, Machiavelli—these are just a few of the world's great thinkers who have weighed in on the subject of leadership over the centuries. Yet, the contemporary student of leadership often overlooks many of these names in favor of more recent theorists hailing from the social sciences. *Understanding Leadership: An arts and humanities perspective* takes a different angle, employing the works of the great philosophers, authors, and artists found in world civilization and presenting an arts and humanities perspective on the study of leadership.

The authors build their conceptual framework using their *Five Components of Leadership Model*, which recognizes the leader, the followers, the goal, the environmental context, and the cultural values and norms that make up the leadership process.

Supporting the text are a wealth of case studies that reflect on works such as Ayn Rand's novella *Anthem*, Eugène Delacroix's painting *Liberty Leading the People*, Charlie Chaplin's film *Modern Times*, Athol Fugard's play *"Master Harold" . . . and the Boys*, Lao Tzu's poetic work *Tao Te Ching*, and Antonín Dvořák's *New World Symphony*. The authors also introduce studies from various world cultures to emphasize the role that cultural values and norms play in leadership. This illuminating framework promotes the multidimensional thinking that is necessary for understanding and problem solving in a complex world.

Understanding Leadership: An arts and humanities perspective will be a valuable textbook for both undergraduate and postgraduate leadership students, while leadership professionals will also appreciate the book's unique liberal arts and cultural approach.

Robert M. McManus is the McCoy Associate Professor of Leadership Studies and Communication at the McDonough Leadership Center at Marietta College in Ohio. He co-edited *Leading in Complex Worlds* (Jossey-Bass) and has served as the Chair of the Leadership Education MIG for the International Leadership Association.

Gama Perruci is the Dean of the McDonough Leadership Center at Marietta College in Ohio. He also serves as a consultant for the *New York Times* (nytimesinleadership.com) and leadership session facilitator for Dartmouth College's Rockefeller Center for Public Policy and the Social Sciences.

'There are thousands of books on leadership that answer some of the critical leadership questions. This is the only leadership book that addresses ALL of them. McManus and Perruci tackle the complexity of leadership, including the role of followers and context. They examine leadership from cultures ranging from West to East and from all continents, and they deal in depth with the critical question of "Leadership for what?" This is a must read for any true scholar of leadership.'

Ronald E. Riggio, Ph.D., Associate Dean of the Faculty, Kravis Leadership Institute, Claremont McKenna College, USA.

'This book opens the door to understanding leadership for students, scholars, and practitioners alike. The authors present a wide array of theories and ideas that challenge us to gain our own insights on how these can work together, and help us to become effective leaders and followers in our complex world.'

Sadhana Hall, Deputy Director, The Nelson A. Rockefeller Center for Public Policy and the Social Sciences, Dartmouth College, USA

'In this much needed text McManus and Perruci extend the injunction to 'know thyself' by inviting us to know our wider world more fully. Readers will be informed, challenged and inspired through an artful examination of 'I'/'We' leadership paradoxes.'

Dr Ralph Bathurst, Massey University, New Zealand

Understanding Leadership

An arts and humanities perspective

**Robert M. McManus and
Gama Perruci**

Routledge
Taylor & Francis Group

LONDON AND NEW YORK

First published 2015
by Routledge
2 Park Square, Milton Park, Abingdon, Oxon OX14 4RN

and by Routledge
711 Third Avenue, New York, NY 10017

Routledge is an imprint of the Taylor & Francis Group, an informa business

© 2015 Robert M. McManus and Gama Perruci

The right of Robert M. McManus and Gama Perruci to be identified as authors of this work has been asserted by them in accordance with sections 77 and 78 of the Copyright, Designs and Patents Act 1988.

Every effort has been made to contact copyright holders for their permission to reprint material in this book. The publishers would be grateful to hear from any copyright holder who is not here acknowledged and will undertake to rectify any errors or omissions in future editions of this book.

Excerpts from An Enemy of the People by Henrik Ibsen, adapted by Arthur Miller, copyright 1950, 1951, renewed © 1979 Arthur Miller. Used by permission of Viking Penguin, a division of Penguin Group (USA) LLC.

Excerpts from Enemy of the People, Copyright © 1950, 1951, 1978, 1979 by Arthur Miller, used by permission of the Wylie Agency, LLC. (Electronic rights.)

Excerpts from "Master Harold . . . and the boys" by Athol Fugard, copyright © 1982 by Athol Fugard. Used by permission of Alfred A. Knopf, an imprint of the Knopf Doubleday Publishing Group, a division of Random House LLC. All rights reserved. Any third party use of this material, outside of this publication, is prohibited. Interested parties must apply directly to Random House LLC for permission.

Excerpts from "Master Harold . . . and the boys" reprinted by permission of ICM Partners. (UK and Commonwealth; eBook; Worldwide). Copyright © [1982] by Athol Fugard.

Trademark notice: Product or corporate names may be trademarks or registered trademarks, and are used only for identification and explanation without intent to infringe.

British Library Cataloguing in Publication Data
A catalogue record for this book is available from the British Library

Library of Congress Cataloging in Publication Data
McManus, Robert M.
   Understanding leadership: an arts and humanities perspective/
Robert M. McManus and Gama Perruci.
   pages cm
   Includes bibliographical references and index.
   1. Leadership. I. Perruci, Gama. II. Title.
   HM1261.M395 2015
   303.3′4—dc23   2014036222

ISBN: 978-0-415-72872-0 (hbk)
ISBN: 978-0-415-72873-7 (pbk)
ISBN: 978-1-315-85152-5 (ebk)

Typeset in Bembo by Florence Production Ltd, Stoodleigh, Devon, UK

MIX
Paper from
responsible sources
FSC
www.fsc.org   FSC® C013604

Printed and bound by CPI Group (UK) Ltd, Croydon, CR0 4YY

For my parents,
Roger and Rita McManus—RMM

To my mother (Areli) and wife (Kathleen)
for their continuous support of
my leadership journey—GP

Contents

Figures

Tables

Foreword

What would a word cloud on leadership look like?

This word cloud was generated by doing a content analysis of the conference presentations at an International Leadership Association Inc. (ILA) global conference.

It looks messy—much like the study and practice of leadership in today's unpredictable and ever changing world.

In recent years, the ground has shifted in virtually every important sphere of life—economic, political, cultural, and environmental. The world is being reshaped by scientific and technological innovations, global interdependence, and changes in the balance of economic and political power.

The challenge we face is that we can never fully understand our world in the linear way laid out by reductionistic science. Today's problems are ambiguous and complex. The idea of knowing the future exactly and preparing for it perfectly is, of course, not feasible. The idea of making a complex system do just what we want it to do is, of course, not possible.

The world is turbulent and nonlinear. And yet, there is something in the human mind that draws us toward a linear way of thinking. We often think in straight lines rather than a word cloud. We like to think in whole numbers rather than a metric cube.

There is, however, a part of us that is attracted to an opposite set of tendencies. We appreciate the beauty of art, the beauty of music, the beauty in nature, and what we can learn by studying them. We learn that there is an underlying order to the disorder of Mozart's beautifully dissonant Symphony No. 40 in G minor. We learn that there is a series of interconnecting systems in nature when we pay attention to the interrelational characteristics that surround us every day.

We can get stuck in our own normal way of doing and thinking. When that happens, we develop a neural lockstep—a mind rut. The deeper the rut, the harder it is to break free. But our strange attraction to both linear and nonlinear ways of thinking can get us out of our mind ruts. We can think differently and learn from different viewpoints and disciplines—from the scientists and the humanists.

How does leadership address today's complex problems and interdependencies? We are learning, more and more, that differing views and perspectives are not a problem but an opportunity to flourish—because, in a complex world, multiple perspectives are required.

Studying leadership from an arts and humanities perspective gives us the tools, the insight, and the understanding to ask questions, challenge underlying assumptions, and think critically to understand the complexity and interconnection between and among disciplines. McManus and Perruci's book does just that—studying some of the great artists and thinkers from around the world over the span of history. They give us a dynamic perspective on the study and practice of leadership through multiple viewpoints.

As a student, McManus and Perruci note, you have a wonderful opportunity to explore leadership through the lens of the arts and humanities, furthering your understanding of leadership concepts and theories to support your journey to, ultimately, become an effective leader.

McManus and Perruci describe leadership through a framework that they call the Five Components of Leadership Model, which includes the leader, the follower, the goal, the environmental context, and the cultural values and norms. Most importantly, they look at leadership as a process that deems all five components equally valuable. The process is core to the framework.

This book is peppered with wonderful case studies using works of art, pieces of music, plays, and books of well-known historical figures, musicians, writers, and artists such as Henrik Ibsen, Eugène Delacroix, Charlie Chaplin, and Miguel Ángel Asturias. Allow me to add one more: Robert Berks, sculptor of world-renowned scientist and humanitarian Albert Einstein.

This bronze bust of Einstein is located in Princeton, New Jersey, and sits on a granite pedestal inscribed with a quote from him that reads: "Imagination is more important than knowledge. Knowledge is limited, whereas imagination embraces the world."

Albert Einstein was born in Ulm, Germany, in 1879. Before he left Europe in 1933, he was known as the "wandering professor," traveling extensively to give speeches and take short-term appointments at various universities in Europe. One of those appointments was at the University of Prague.

In 2009, the ILA held its global conference in Prague, where we had the opportunity to listen to the Prague Chamber Orchestra in the stunning Lichtenstein Palace. The palace was not always a place of music. It was built in the sixteenth century and often served as military headquarters where battle plans were developed. During World War II, it was converted to the Czechoslovakian Communist Party political center. It was not until after the war that the space was reimagined to its current function of hosting beautiful music.

Lichtenstein Palace is now home to the world-class Prague Chamber Orchestra, which is remarkable for one practice in particular: Since its inception over 50 years ago, it has performed without a conductor. During the conference concert, we experienced music that spoke to our hearts, our minds, and our souls. The evening was a lesson in imagination. The transformation of the Lichtenstein Palace illustrated how something old with a purpose dedicated to war can be redesigned into something new with a purpose dedicated to experiencing music.

The evening was also a lesson in leadership. Beautiful music can be created by a group of musicians without a conductor, without one leader. It taught us four main points:

- Process is at the core of leadership.
- Everyone has the capacity to lead and all members must contribute their leadership to the success of the music.
- Leadership is shared.
- Leadership requires passionate dedication to a shared purpose.

And there was a fifth lesson from that evening of leadership and music. It was what our host, Harvey Seifter, called the "suspension of disbelief," which involves a willingness to embrace ideas that are different from—and may even contradict—one's own. It is at the nexus of these differences—at these intersections—that innovation emerges.

This book takes the time to explore the intersection of ideas and concepts from disparate viewpoints and many different disciplines. In the first section of the book, McManus and Perruci describe the five components of their model through the use of case studies and stories, weaving them together into the process of leadership. Knowing both of the authors, I can visualize their interactive and probing Socratic teaching of these leadership concepts. They use an arts and humanities perspective to derive lessons from works such as Emanuel Leutze's painting *Washington Crossing the Delaware*, Charlie Chaplin's film *Modern Times*, and Hermann Hesse's book *Siddhartha*, as well as from the writings of Plato and Aristotle, which illuminate the historical foundations of leadership.

In the second section, McManus and Perruci emphasize the importance of our global society and the complexity of our world. The authors take the reader on a journey around the globe to illuminate the different cultural values and norms that influence effective leadership.

In the final section, they ask the probing meta question: "Leadership for what?" Here, I would encourage you to use your imagination to think about how today's complex problems can be solved by exploring effective leadership for positive change—which brings me back to our friend Albert Einstein.

Einstein was a person who imagined the impossible. He was driven by an imagination that broke from the limitations of knowledge. He made imaginative leaps. His theories were astonishing, mysterious, and counterintuitive.

Think about the quantum revolution that he helped to launch. The relativity of space and time, the bending of light beams, the warping of space, and, of course, $E = mc^2$.

It took great knowledge for Einstein to conclude $E = mc^2$. But it also took great imagination to understand what the splitting of the atom meant to the world.

I am not arguing for the reader to split the atom—that has already been done—but there are real global problems that need solutions and leadership.

Einstein was a Nobel laureate in physics. He was also a philosopher and an educator, who left a lasting imprint on the world. His fingerprints are all over today's technologies, such as photo cells, lasers, fiber optics, and space travel.

He was also a humanitarian, an immigrant, and a citizen of four different nations. Talk about someone who cut across disciplines, sectors, *and* geography.

Imagine what you can do by reading this book to get a better understanding of leadership through this provocative lens of the arts and humanities.

My hope for you is that you discover a heightened sense of imagination by reading, discussing, understanding, and applying the concepts in this book—and that your discoveries along the way give you a broader and deeper understanding of leadership.

What will you discover by reading this book?

What will your leadership word cloud look like?

Cynthia Cherrey
President, International Leadership Association
Vice President for Campus Life, Princeton University

Acknowledgments

This book is a product of several years of scholarship and curriculum development while we were serving at the McDonough Center for Leadership and Business at Marietta College in Ohio. The McDonough Center was one of the first comprehensive undergraduate leadership programs established in the United States, and it is an honor to be a part of that institution's long legacy to the field of leadership studies.

All our students at the McDonough Center have been instrumental in helping us shape and articulate our thoughts about leadership. Several sections of our LEAD 101 Foundations of Leadership course commented on early drafts of the manuscript, and our LEAD 203 Global Leadership students were some of the first to hear our ideas about the importance of culture and leadership. All of these students provided valuable feedback. In particular, we thank the four students who were a part of the senior capstone in leadership studies course in the spring of 2014 for commenting on early drafts of chapters: Luke Badaczweski, Alex Martin, Brett Notarius, and Mary Roberts. Our office assistant, Jenna Skoglund, was also particularly helpful in helping to proofread the manuscript for style form. Other faculty, staff, and students at the Center supported us in various ways as we developed the manuscript. We thank Heather Eichner, Megan Hendrich, Christy Hockenberry, Arielle Jennings, Alexandra Perry, Tanya Judd-Pucella, and Cristie Thomas for their support in myriad ways throughout this project.

Many of our other colleagues at Marietta College were also extremely helpful in reviewing versions of the manuscript, giving feedback on key concepts, and providing technical, research, and writing support. They include: Janet Bland, Chaya Chandrasekhar, Beverly Hogue, Mark Miller, Janie Rees-Miller, Beverly Renner, Linda Roesch, and the staff of the Legacy Library at Marietta College. We also thank the faculty and administration at Marietta College who provided Robert with a sabbatical to work on the manuscript and supported this endeavor.

David Brown deserves particular mention. David proofread the entire manuscript over an 18-month period and assisted in forming our style and tone. His keen eye and ear helped us create a much better manuscript. It was particularly helpful to hear from a person outside of the field of leadership studies to test our ideas for transparency and accessibility as well as scholarship. Gama's wife, Kathleen Perruci, was also helpful in this regard. Her copy-editing training proved to be a valuable contribution to the success of this project. We thank them both for their generosity and their commitment to our work.

Our colleagues at other institutions also provided valuable feedback on drafts of chapters throughout the book. In particular, we thank: Mohammed Al-Rwali (Hamad bin Khalifa University), JoAnn Barbour (Gonzaga University), Ted Goertzel (Rutgers University), Dennis C. Roberts (Qatar Foundation), Matthew Sowcik (Wilkes University), and Naaman Wood (Duke University). Gama also received helpful feedback from the students and staff at Dartmouth College's Rockefeller Center for Public Policy and the Social Sciences. He presented many of the concepts developed in this book while serving as a session facilitator at Dartmouth's Global Leadership Program and the Management and Leadership Development Program (MLDP). In particular, we would like to thank Sadhana Hall, Vincent Mack, and Thanh Nguyen.

Consistent with our arts and humanities perspective, artist Charles Atkins, Jr. created the line drawings found at the beginning of each chapter. We thank him for being able to articulate our vision for each chapter in an artful form. We also thank Ryan Zundell who was instrumental in providing graphics that visually illustrate the concepts presented in this book.

We also thank our production team at Routledge for their support, comments, and assistance in bringing this project to fruition. Likewise the anonymous reviewers who read and commented on the original prospectus for the book were very helpful and their assistance is appreciated.

Finally, we owe a debt of gratitude to our family and friends who provided the emotional support needed to sustain us as we worked on this long-term project: David Brown and Jolene Powell were particularly gracious with their time and support for Robert. Gama thanks Kathleen Perruci for her encouragement and enthusiasm for this scholarly project.

Introduction

Plato, Lao Tzu, Marx, the Buddha, Machiavelli, Ibsen, Mohammad—these are just a few of the world's great thinkers and artists who have weighed in on the subject of leadership over the centuries. Yet, the contemporary student of leadership often overlooks many of these names in favor of more recent theorists hailing from the social sciences. This book takes a different approach. Employing the works of the great philosophers, authors, and artists found in world civilization, we present an arts and humanities perspective on the study of leadership.

This perspective is built around a framework of what we refer to as the Five Components of Leadership Model. We developed the Five Components Model at our home institution, the McDonough Center for Leadership and Business at Marietta College in Ohio. We designed this book to address the unique aspects of each of the components identified in the model: the leader, the follower, the goal, the environmental context, and cultural values and norms. When we look at leadership as a *process* rather than simply the ability of specific *leaders*, the other components of leadership become equally important in our understanding of how leadership works.

We hope readers will come away with an appreciation for the long history of leadership thought and the various ways leadership is demonstrated in the arts and humanities. In addition, we have designed our book with an international focus to incorporate perspectives of leadership from diverse cultural traditions such as Western, Latin American, Islamic, African, Buddhist, and Taoist cultures. Thus the book is designed to not only look at leadership from an arts and humanities perspective, but also through a global lens.

We have carefully chosen works from areas representing a wide range of the arts and humanities including: fine art, history, philosoph, theatre, film, politics, dance, literature, poetry, sculpture, and religion. We hope that this approach will highlight the ubiquity of leadership thought demonstrated throughout the arts and humanities. We have purposely chosen to include classic works that can be easily accessed through the internet, the public domain, or at a very small cost in hopes that our readers will take the opportunity to encounter these primary texts for themselves. This will provide a much richer experience for our readers. At the end of each chapter, we have prepared a few questions to help guide the reader's thinking and provide an opportunity for readers to reflect on the leadership concepts and artifacts discussed in the chapters. We have also highlighted a few resources at the end of each chapter to help readers further pursue those concepts addressed therein.

We wrote this book with undergraduate and graduate students who desire to study leadership in mind. The book may be used as a primary textbook in a class in leadership studies, or paired with a more theoretical source and used as a supplemental text. However, we hope all students, as well as leadership practitioners, will find what we have written here helpful to their understanding of leadership.

Studying leadership through the arts and humanities helps meet two needs of the contemporary student of leadership, regardless of their level of study. One, it provides for the development of the type of multidimensional thinking that is necessary for understanding and problem solving in a complex world. Two, it helps the student of leadership to find meaning and purpose for their own lives as they learn to lead themselves as well as others.

Within this framework, we seek to: (1) explore the historical and contemporary tradition of commentary about the subject of leadership and its importance; (2) encourage critical thinking and reasoning to be applied to the study of leadership in a multidisciplinary context; (3) present the importance of understanding roles, context, complexity, and culture; (4) consider the ethical implications of leadership; and (5) encourage students to apply what they learn in these pages to develop themselves and others as they work for the greater good of humankind.

The book is divided into three parts. Part I presents our Five Components of Leadership Model. This section concentrates on the first four elements of the model—the leader, the followers, the goal, and the environmental context. This section also goes into detail regarding the ways theorists have historically presented these fundamental elements of the leadership process. Part II of the book focuses on leadership in a global context to examine the way a culture's values and norms affect its views about leadership. Each chapter presents a particular culture and addresses the way the culture views leaders and followers, as well as the way the culture views its moral foundations and the way in which decisions should be made. This part is not intended to be a detailed analysis of the cultures we address, but rather to illustrate the way in which different cultures may view leadership. In Part III, we examine the question "Leadership for what?," that is, what is the purpose for understanding leadership and developing one's leadership ability. Yes, knowledge and skill can help promote one's self, but, more importantly, such an understanding can develop the whole person in such a way that she or he can give back to others.

In Chapter 1, we introduce the reader to the field of leadership studies and present our model. We also present a brief contemporary history of the field while introducing the reader to the different methodologies used to study leadership. Finally, we familiarize the reader with our arts and humanities approach as we examine the famous painting "Washington Crossing the Delaware" by German American artist Emanuel Gottlieb Leutze.

Chapter 2 presents the foundations of leadership thought found in thinkers such as Plato and Aristotle and places the focus of leadership on a continuum between the primacy of the individual and the primacy of the group. We highlight two brief case studies in this chapter: Karl Marx and Friedrich Engels' *The Communist Manifesto*, to discuss the primacy of the group, and Ayn Rand's novella *Anthem*, to illustrate the primacy of the individual.

Chapter 3 examines the importance of effective followership and the responsibilities followers have in the leadership process. Even the most passive follower is implicitly involved in a group reaching, or not reaching, its common goal. This chapter uses Arthur Miller's adaptation of Henrik Ibsen's classic play *An Enemy of the People* to highlight different approaches to followership and the importance of followers finding their voice and contributing to the leadership process.

Chapter 4 continues the course of the Five Components Model and focuses on the ways in which leaders and followers go about achieving goals. We explore the broad continuum of ethics ranging from Kant's categorical imperative to Mill's utility principle while examining Eugène Delacroix's painting "July 28: Liberty Leading the People" in the context of the French Revolution.

The next chapter (Chapter 5) focuses on the environmental context. Leadership is situational. The specific context in which leadership is practiced has a dramatic influence on the leadership process. An organization's culture and setting has vast implications on the ways leaders and followers approach their goals. In this chapter, we examine Charlie Chaplin's famous film *Modern Times* to see how the immediate environment affects the leadership process.

Chapter 6 presents leadership in Western cultures. Leadership in the West is often viewed as a prize. Followers may see themselves as "paying their dues" until they can obtain their own position as a leader. Leaders are expected to be rational, efficient, and results oriented while basing their decisions on secular ethical principles. Our case study here is Niccolò Machiavelli's *The Prince*. Because many of our readers will be from the West, we compare other cultural approaches of leadership we address in the book to the Western perspective in order to draw attention to these differences.

The next chapter (Chapter 7) explores leadership in Latin American cultures. Latin America's history and cultural legacies color the way in which it views leadership. Leaders are expected to show their charisma and boldness in exchange for their followers' loyalty and reverence. The culture's respect for the "natural order" of the role and the Judeo-Christian traditions so important to Latin America also affects the perception of ethics and decision making. In this chapter, we highlight Guatemalan author Miguel Ángel Asturias' Nobel Prize-winning novel *El Señor Presidente* (*The President*).

In Chapter 8, we examine leadership in an Islamic context. One cannot understand leadership in the Islamic world without understanding the centrality of the Muslim faith. Leadership in this culture is seen as a sacred trust. The moral implication is for one to be a "good" leader and a "good" follower one must be obedient and unified as one dynamically pursues Allah's will. We use Moustapha Akkad's 1977 film *The Message* as a way to understand the importance of history and religion to an Islamic view of leadership.

Leadership in African cultures is addressed in Chapter 9. Africa's indigenous tribal history, coupled with the slave trade and colonization, makes it difficult to define a distinctly "African" style of leadership. Nevertheless, some common themes can be identified such as the African concept of *umbutu*, or the African ethic of finding one's self in community. In this chapter, we examine the practice of the African circle dance and the meaning its implications have on a collaborative approach to leadership.

Chapter 10 considers leadership in Buddhist cultures. Leadership in Buddhist culture is viewed as a personal journey towards obtaining wisdom and enlightenment. The Buddhist teaching of the Four Noble Truths and the Eightfold Path guides this journey. Leaders are to be role models for their followers, and the followers are to defer to the leader's wisdom. We will use Herman Hesse's *Siddhartha* as a text to consider the implications that a Buddhist worldview may have on the leadership process.

In Chapter 11, we consider leadership in Confucian and Taoist cultures. The idea of "servant leadership" has made an indelible impact on leadership literature and thought. This concept can be traced back to the Taoist idea of "leader as servant" and the concept of *wu wei*, or doing without forcing. The leader in this system sees his or her purpose as to guide the follower to the goal in a way that is in keeping with the Tao and the paradoxical tensions of the universe. In this chapter, we examine the ancient poetic text *Tao Te Ching* by Lao Tzu.

In Chapter 12, we look at leadership to develop one's self. Author Bill George observes that those who fail to lead have first failed to lead themselves. The importance of self-awareness and mindfulness are essential for one to lead ethically and with passion and purpose. We use the Bohemian/Czech composer Antonín Dvořák's famous *New World Symphony* to explore this theme.

Chapter 13 features the idea of leading for the purpose of developing others. Studying leadership to develop one's self is noble, but it is not enough. The student of leadership must seek ways to develop their followers to reach their own potential, find their own passion, and lead others. Here we highlight Author Fugard's *"Master Harold" . . . and the Boys* as an example of transformational leadership that encourages both the leader and the followers to higher levels of motivation and morality.

Finally, in Chapter 14, we examine the idea of leadership to contribute to the greater good. Altruism, compassion, kindness, benevolence—these ideas are often not the first to come to mind when one thinks of "leadership." True leaders look beyond their own self-interests. They should consider the implications of their decisions and the way they may affect others in hopes of creating a better world. In this final chapter, we take a multi-textual approach to understanding leadership and discuss Jesus of Nazareth's parable of the Good Samaritan, François-Léon Sicard's "Statue of the Good Samaritan," and Camille Pissarro's painting "The Garden of Tuileries on a Spring Morning" to illustrate these concepts.

Leadership cannot be reduced to a few easy steps or principles. It is an ever evolving process with myriad variables. We hope this book helps the student of leadership to consider the various components of leadership that this knowledge not only further develops the reader's understanding of leadership, but ultimately assists the student to become a more effective leader. Understanding leadership and developing one's leadership abilities is a lifelong journey. We hope that what we have provided in these pages aids the reader in this quest.

Part I

How to think about leadership

Leadership, as a field of study, has expanded dramatically in recent years as more organizations (higher education institutions, businesses, nonprofits, and even the public sector) have recognized the importance of leadership development in the twenty-first century. We are clamoring for more (and better) leaders who are capable of leading our societies in more effective ways. As challenges become more complex, and solutions seem more elusive, we call on more wise leaders to step up. But, how do we develop those leaders? Where do they come from?

They come from societies that promote, first and foremost, a deeper understanding of leadership. In this section, we review the intellectual history of the field and then introduce a simple definition of leadership, which is centered on five components—leaders, followers, goals, the environmental context, and the cultural context. This definition will guide our journey through this book.

Part I is dedicated to the first four components of our definition—leaders, followers, goals, and the environmental context. These are the building blocks of leadership. By investigating each component through separate chapters, you will be able to analyze their individual peculiarities. We saved the fifth component for Part II since the world offers a wide variety of cultures; therefore, it deserves more extensive treatment. Part III shifts our focus from the study of leadership to its practice. It will be your opportunity to connect the dots and see how the five components work together in an applied context.

Leadership, as a field of study, has three "branches"—leadership education, leadership training, and leadership development. In the 1980s, as the proliferation of leadership programs took place in American and European universities, Dennis Roberts provided a pioneering framework for the field.[1] He acknowledged the importance of skill building (leadership training), but also highlighted the need for providing emerging leaders with an understanding of leadership concepts (leadership education). The combination of the two (education and skill building) contributes to "leadership development."

Some leadership programs emphasize the curricular side of leadership studies, offering classroom-based courses that stress different aspects of leadership—e.g., organizational leadership, leading change, and global leadership. These courses

Figure P1.1 The three branches of leadership

cover the *knowledge* side of the field. We see very few practitioners seeking a leadership program for the sake of learning about different theories and models. From that standpoint, leadership studies is dissimilar to fields such as political science. Many students take courses from the latter because they enjoy the subject in its own right—as an intellectual exercise in expanding their knowledge of politics, and not because they want to become a better politician. Leadership studies students may find more affinity with those from psychology, for example, who aside from enjoying the intellectual field, also see direct application to their professional plans and personal lives.

Most practitioners participate in leadership programs because they want to become better leaders, often defined as someone who possesses strong leadership skills. Most leadership programs are based on the co-curricular side—the ability of aspiring leaders to expand their leadership skills through hands-on activities. These programs emphasize the *action* component of leadership studies with a stress on specific skills, such as facilitation, decision making, teamwork, and conflict resolution.

Leadership programs in both higher education and organizations (business and nonprofit) organize a variety of activities, such as workshops and day-long challenge courses, in order to offer aspiring leaders an opportunity to practice their leadership skills. As the global marketplace has become fiercely competitive, these skills are prized additions to an aspiring leader's résumé and professional development.

A growing trend in leadership studies programs is to offer a comprehensive combination of *knowledge* (leadership education) and *action* (leadership training), because the two together lead to *growth* (leadership development). Simply offering a "toolbox" (leadership training) is not enough. We must also engage our aspiring leaders in critical thinking and deep analytical thought processes that take place on the *knowledge* side. Leadership development is the product of putting *knowledge* to the test through *action*. It takes us beyond the intellectual mastery of theories and models and connects knowledge to experience.

In non-Western societies, this combination is often referred to as *wisdom*. Prasad Kaipa and Navi Radjou argue that we limit ourselves when we focus only on developing smart leaders.[2] Instead, they argue for a change in our mindset—moving from smart to wise leaders. Wisdom leadership calls for noble purpose, role clarity, discernment, flexible fortitude, and enlightened self-interest.

Leaders, therefore, cannot simply seek to develop their leadership skills without understanding first the theories and models that explain (and guide) leadership development. Sometimes, emerging leaders are eager to start "doing leadership" in the same way novice piano players might want to sit down and bang on the keyboard in order to master their musical skills. Piano teachers actually discourage too much playing before the fundamentals are fully understood at the theoretical level; otherwise, the novice piano players may pick up bad habits that will be difficult to shake along the road.

And so it is with leadership development. As John W. Gardner argued in his classic, *On Leadership*, "The first step is not action; the first step is understanding. The first question is how to think about leadership."[3] Part I, therefore, serves as your first steps into your deeper understanding of how leadership works.

Notes

1   D. Roberts, ed., *Student Leadership Programs in Higher Education* (Carbondale, IL: American College Personnel Association, 1981).
2   P. Kaipa and N. Radjou, *From Smart to Wise: Acting and Leading with Wisdom* (San Francisco: Jossey-Bass, 2013).
3   John W. Gardner, *On Leadership* (New York: Free Press, 1990), p. xiv.

1 Understanding leadership

The first step is not action; the first step is understanding. The first question is how to think about leadership.[1]

John W. Gardner

Any individual who aspires to become better at an endeavor must first acquire a certain level of knowledge related to it. While we may be eager to move into action, the first step—as the quote above reminds us—should be understanding. This chapter is designed to lay the groundwork as you seek to gain a deeper appreciation for how leadership works.

Leadership seems to apply to so many facets of life that we are left with the sense that it is impossible to put our intellectual arms around it. Philosophers and practitioners have debated the nature of leadership for millennia. As an intellectual concept, leadership is so expansive that in order to create meaningful insights about it, we have to take on an interdisciplinary approach, borrowing languages from many different disciplines. While many scholars view this as positive, others decry the inability of the field to coalesce.[2] We are all speaking different languages, while claiming to be capturing the essence of leadership. In the process, we are left with a cacophony of languages—a true Tower of Babel.

The tower metaphor can help us understand the real challenges that leaders face when seeking intellectual guidance from the leadership studies' literature. As the story goes in the book of Genesis, King Nimrod initiated a project to build a tower by the banks of the Euphrates River, in what became Babylon in the ancient world (present-day Iraq). This massive and ambitious tower was supposed to be so tall that it would reach to the heavens. Alarmed by the effectiveness of the project, God intervened. His strategy was simple—mix up the languages so the tower builders could not effectively communicate. Once communication broke down, the project came to a halt. Simple, yet brilliant! The fastest way to undermine a project is to take away the participants' ability to communicate with one another (see Figure 1.1).

Figure 1.1 Gustave Doré (1832–1883), "The Confusion of the Tongues," 1897
From a private collection
Photo credit: HIP/Art Resource, New York

There is a leadership lesson in this story—achievement has as its foundation the use of a common means of communication. A cursory look at recent leadership book titles suggests a wide variety of approaches, theories, and models. The studies of leadership are rich in allusions to other disciplines—psychology, political science, economics, sociology, even biology, to name but a few. We praise the interdisciplinary nature of leadership studies as a source of intellectual strength in the field. The drawback, however, is that we have collected many bricks for this construction project, but they seem scattered around the worksite, and no one seems to know how to bring them together under a single architectural plan in order to build the tower. There are so many different "models" of leadership that a tower builder would be perplexed at the idea that they are supposed to all converge together and form an elegant structure.

The first order of business in a book that seeks to elucidate our understanding of leadership is to simplify language. Rather than offering a complex theory that only a few practitioners will find useful—thus becoming yet another "brick" in this tower—we propose a simple architectural design to which bricks can be added. This book offers a sketch of a language—what we refer to as the Five Components of Leadership Model to be used in building our leadership tower.[3] The project is not so ambitious as to offer a definitive general theory of leadership. Instead, we offer a simple structure that will help emerging leaders make sense of leadership in the twenty-first century.

Our approach to understanding leadership

Throughout this book, we will explore the five components of leadership by introducing works from the arts and humanities. Our artifacts for study are artistic in nature, such as novels, paintings, and music. This research method is broadly referred to as "textual analysis." The term "text," as used here, simply means any sort of artifact that is created for an intended audience.[4] The term "analysis" refers to *reading* and *interpreting* the themes found in the artifact and the context in which the artifact was originally produced.[5] Each chapter in this book analyzes a different artifact to illustrate the leadership concepts contained therein.

The idea of reading an artifact may seem odd to someone who is not familiar with this sort of methodology. In reality, you do it all the time. Whenever you have shared with a friend the meaning you found in a book or a film, for example, you were analyzing an artifact. It may be helpful to consider this approach as *interpretive*, because it is, quite literally, interpreting the meaning of the artifact.[6] Of course, scholars are much more systematic about the process. Often, researchers using this approach are advancing a particular theory. Other times, they are simply looking for the implications and meanings that may be found in the artifact as a way to understand the artifact itself better.

Indeed, sometimes there may be competing interpretations and arguments that can be made about a single artifact, and *both* interpretations may be equally valid. Textual analysis is a more *humanistic* and *qualitative* approach to understanding. The practice is in keeping with the type of research methodology used by scholars in the arts and humanities, such as the visual and performing arts, literature and rhetoric, history, philosophy, and religion.

However, many of the leadership theories and models referenced in this book actually have their roots in the social sciences—fields such as psychology, sociology, political science, and management. This type of research is usually carried out by means such as performing experiments or collecting surveys.

This is referred to as a *quantitative* approach to research. As the term connotes, a quantitative approach is concerned with *measuring* a phenomenon and using a *deductive* form of reasoning to apply the general to the specific. For instance, if 99 out of 100 people surveyed say "power" is an attribute associated with those in leadership positions, chances are power is an attribute you also attribute to those in leadership.

Qualitative or humanistic research, by way of contrast, is more *inductive*. One may be able to understand more about power and its use and misuse from analyzing Shakespeare's *Julius Caesar*, for example. By using an inductive approach to reasoning, one would apply the specific to the general and say that one needs to understand power as displayed in *Julius Caesar* to be a wise and effective leader. Alternatively, a scholar could simply analyze *Julius Caesar* to see what Shakespeare's play seems to say about leadership and power without even attempting to apply the lessons learned to other situations. All these broad approaches to research and the methodologies they employ are found in the field of leadership studies.

Figure 1.2 depicts a continuum of the way in which researchers may go about understanding leadership and forming their theories and models. This book marries the two approaches of qualitative and quantitative research in an effort to provide readers with a more holistic understanding of the field. Students studying the arts, humanities, social sciences, natural sciences, and various other professions all stand to gain a great deal through studying leadership. By blending these approaches, students are more likely to see the broader implications of their knowledge about leadership.

Studying leadership through the arts and the humanities also helps to meet two other needs of the contemporary student of leadership. First, it provides for the development of the type of multidimensional thinking that is necessary for understanding and problem solving in a complex world. Second, it helps the student of leadership to find meaning and purpose for their own lives as they learn to lead themselves as well as others. We hope that the reader of this book seeks not only to use the lessons learned herein as "equipment for leading," but also to use them as "equipment for living" throughout their life.[7]

Figure 1.2 Research methods used to understand leadership

Case study: Emanuel Leutze's "Washington Crossing the Delaware" (1851)

For our first artifact, we analyze the oil-on-canvas painting, "Washington Crossing the Delaware" (1851). This famous artwork by the German-born artist, Emanuel Leutze (1816–1868), captures the moment at which the Continental Army and the militia are crossing the Delaware River in order to confront the Hessian garrison in Trenton, New Jersey, on December 25, 1776.[8] It is designed to serve as a patriotic and inspirational piece. We can derive several insights about leadership from this piece of art by connecting the historical context and the images portrayed in the painting. Before we delve into the analysis of the painting, however, we need to provide a background from which to build our understanding of the five components of leadership.

Background on the painting

The painting depicts a surprise attack in the middle of the winter. After several failures in the summer and fall, the Continental Army was ready to take a break for the winter season. Morale was low. Faced with the grim prospect of another season of defeats in the spring, General George Washington developed a bold plan—to surprise the German mercenary forces in Trenton in order to shift the momentum of the Revolutionary War. They entered New Jersey in the middle of the night on Christmas Day and then marched nine miles to defeat the Hessians. On the morning of December 26, the Patriots quickly overwhelmed their opponents and took the town.[9]

This heroic act became a turning point in the revolution. The capture of Trenton had no intrinsic strategic value for the war effort. Its true significance laid in the symbolic effect that it had on the Continental Army. It lifted morale among the troops and rekindled the vision of independence and victory against the British. As morale increased, so did the number of new recruits who joined the cause.

Leutze picked a topic that would clearly resonate with an American audience.[10] The painting not only represented a historic event in the New World, but it also had a German context. Less than 100 years after General Washington crossed the Delaware River, Europe in the 1840s was awash with unrest as liberals battled conservatives for political supremacy.[11] The 1789 French Revolution had pushed the liberal cause throughout the continent—including Germany.[12] An economic downturn threw masses of unemployed urban workers into the streets, fueling the sentiment that the Industrial Revolution had brought misery and suffering. In France, the 1848 uprisings meant the end of the monarchy of Louis-Philippe and the establishment of the Second Republic. In the German Confederation, where Leutze was living at the time, the starving poor took to the streets and challenged the authority of the princes.[13]

Leutze saw parallels between the liberal aspirations in Europe in the 1840s and the American experience in the 1770s. His earlier experience living in the United States when he was a child had a deep influence on his hopes for unity within the German Confederation. His painting, therefore, became a tribute to the American Revolution but also a statement about the liberating spirit of a grand vision—unity under a single ideal.

Leutze eventually returned to the United States in 1858 and two years later was commissioned by the U.S. Congress to paint a mural in the United States Capitol, Washington, D.C. ("Westward the Course of Empire Takes Its Way"). He settled in Washington, which he called home until his death in 1868.

Leutze's painting "Washington Crossing the Delaware," currently in the Metropolitan Museum of Art, is actually a second version—the first having been damaged in a fire in his studio in 1850. The second version, completed a year later, was eventually displayed in New York to rave reviews. A private collector bought it, and later the painting was gifted to the museum in 1897 where it hangs to this day.[14]

Description of the painting

This painting (Figure 1.3) is monumental in size—3.78 m × 6.48 m—and displays a dramatic moment in the crossing of the Delaware River. We have to suspend judgment of the historical inaccuracies in order to fully appreciate the artifact. If the artist had tried to be historically accurate, he would have had difficulty showing the boats crossing on a rainy night in the dead of the winter, with no light source. Instead, we see bright colors and a glow in the background. Amid the ice chunks, the small patch of land to the left, and the flotilla in the

Figure 1.3 Emanuel Gottlieb Leutze (1816–1868), "Washington Crossing the Delaware," 1851

Oil on canvas, 837.5 × 647.7 cm
Gift of John Stewart Kennedy, 1897 (97.34)
Metropolitan Museum of Art, New York, NY, USA
Photo credit: Image copyright © Metropolitan Museum of Art
Image source: Art Resource, New York

background, our eyes are drawn to the forefront where we see the "flagship" with General Washington, the American flag, and his crew.

Leutze was very intentional in his placement of every individual in the flagship. The variety of crew members suggests the diverse ethnic and socio-economic composition of the rebellious colonies. The main boat can be divided into three groups. In the front, we see three crew members—including Prince Whipple (an African American freed slave who participated in the Revolutionary War) and a Scot rowing. A steersman in the very front, wearing a raccoon skin cap, uses a long pole to move the ice blocks out of the way. In the back of the boat, we see five figures: an oarsman in red; another in green, suggestive of Native American heritage; a sick soldier with a bandaged head; a farmer; and an officer holding his hat against the wind.

The center of attention belongs to the general, the flag held by a militiaman, and the young James Monroe, another Founding Father of the United States. They capture our attention as a glow frames their position of importance. In the background, on the left side in the sky, one sees a faint star. Considering that the attacking flotilla started their journey on December 25, the parallels are clear, as one observer notes, "Washington and his men move toward the light of hope, guided by the morning star—which, given the Christmas connection, suggests the Star of Bethlehem."[15]

Analysis: A working definition of leadership

What can this painting teach us about leadership? It clearly shows a common image of leadership—a courageous leader in charge. So powerful is this image that at times we use the words "leader" and "leadership" interchangeably. For instance, we often hear references to the leadership of an organization—meaning, those with decision-making powers. We make a direct association between those in positions of authority and the word "leadership."

We quite often adopt this connection between positional power and leadership when we talk about leadership. We play "leadership roles" in our communities and organizations and see ourselves as leaders; therefore, we are engaged in leadership. A related image that we often find in the popular media—and it is clearly depicted in this painting—is the connection between leadership and traits commonly associated with successful leaders: courage, passion, vision.

In a way, Leutze's painting represents a longing for this type of courageous leadership as exemplified in the General's daring attack. Washington not only exhibited heroic leadership but he also inspired his followers to work with him to achieve an incredible feat.[16] Biographies and memoirs often reinforce these images of extraordinary leadership. We find inspiration in reading about leaders' heroic leadership as models to be emulated. Even the ruthless warriors Genghis Khan and Attila the Hun have yielded "leadership secrets" to the modern leader.[17] When studying these famous lives, we hope somehow to catch motivational glimpses of greatness. Every year, dozens of books are published expounding practical leadership "lessons" that can be derived from studying great leaders' lives and actions—the titles related to George Washington are a good example.[18]

Leutze did not disguise his focus on Washington (including the glow of light around him) as the central figure of the painting. There is no question about who the leader is in this painting. Whenever we have traveled outside the United States and introduced this image to a non-American audience that is unaware of Washington and his role in the December 1776 surprise attack, he is quickly identified as the leader. We seem to make a natural assumption that leaders are the most important figure in leadership. After all, the very word *leadership* suggests the higher status of those in position of authority.

Leutze's painting reinforces this image. The enormous size of the painting can be taken as an expression of the grandeur of the task before the Continental Army. However, it also represents the placement of General Washington on a pedestal. In the way it is displayed, as well as the central focus on Washington in the painting, one has to look up to see the general. In a way, this is representative of how we tend to view leaders in a Western context—larger-than-life figures to be emulated and revered.

The painting creates a clear image of leadership that resonates in most Western countries—the leader as a hero figure, endowed with superior powers, calm under pressure, resolute. These are all the qualities that we associate with successful leaders. Despite the hostile environment, the calm hero inspires followers to work hard and remain focused on the task at hand. At the same time, followers are relegated to an inferior (subordinate) position—bringing about the successful implementation of the leader's vision.

If we imagine the boat as an organization, clearly the leader has set the goal, and he is standing tall, facing it. However, who is doing the "work" according to this painting? While the lighting in the painting makes them less visible compared to the flag and the General, the followers seem to be doing the brunt of the work associated with achieving this common goal. They are rowing, moving the ice chunks to the side, and carrying the flag.

Aside from the battle they are about to face, there is an ultimate goal depicted in this painting—independence (as represented through the flag). Again, the glow surrounds both the flag and the leader, as if the two are intimately connected. The message that the painter conveys, therefore, is that the leader is closely associated with the ultimate goal.

The followers—below both the leader and the flag—play a supportive role, helping the leader achieve this ultimate goal. That seems to be the recurring image of leadership in Western societies—a larger-than-life leader, standing tall, and guiding hard-working followers, who deeply believe in the leader's vision, but do not receive the same level of recognition. In reality, the title of this painting is misleading. Washington was not the only one who crossed the Delaware River on that boat that cold night.

"Great leaders" can teach us much about the nature of leadership. As a complex human phenomenon, however, leadership is viewed in the following chapters as a process made up of individual components each contributing to the whole picture. Rather than putting the spotlight on the leader—as in Leutze's painting of Washington—we seek to widen the "glow" to encompass the whole landscape, including the other shipmates, the frigid waters of the Delaware River, and the battle that they are all getting ready to face.

The five components of leadership

When we look at leadership as a *process* instead of simply the heroic ability of leaders, other components become equally important in our understanding of how leadership works. In this book, we offer a working definition of leadership based on five components: leaders, followers, goal, environmental context, and cultural context. There is no denying that leaders play an essential role in leadership. They often provide the energy and vision that guide followers' actions. Leaders, however, come in many different forms.

The image of the larger-than-life leader—as illustrated in Leutze's painting—often discourages people from taking on the leader role. This book seeks to demystify this role and describe other ways for leaders to contribute to the leadership process. The first step in demystifying the image of the leader is to conceptualize leadership as a separate category that exists beyond the leader.

One of the ways to demystify the image of the leader as synonymous with leadership is to take a closer look at the role the followers play in the leadership process. It makes little sense to talk about leaders without considering their followers. In Leutze's painting, the followers are portrayed as subordinates—below the leader and outside the spotlight. In reality, we live in a very different environment. The twenty-first century has witnessed the rise of "followership" as a major consideration in our understanding of leadership, as Chapter 3 will discuss. Followers are now empowered by education, technology, and new means of communication, which allows them to play an active role in negotiating their space in the leadership process.[19] While we have not seen any institutions developing followership studies programs, we have come a long way when followers are perceived as equally important as leaders in our conceptualization of leadership. How would Leutze's "Washington Crossing the Delaware" painting have looked if painted from the followers' perspective?

We need to recognize the power and influence of followers in the relationship. After all, the followers carried muskets in Leutze's painting. While we do not presume that those muskets were ever intended to be used against General Washington, leaders across Europe were well aware of the revolutionary potential of starving unemployed workers. Being a follower does not mean being powerless and disengaged from the process. Rather, the leader–follower roles are constantly being renegotiated again and again. Leaders cannot assume that followers will be passive bystanders in an organization—or even a country.

Followers are partners in the pursuit of the third component of leadership in our model—the goal. In the study of leadership, scholars pay close attention to the ways in which leaders and followers work together and develop goals. James McGregor Burns' *Leadership*, for instance, makes the distinction between "transactional" and "transformational" leadership. In the former case, leaders and followers establish a relationship based on an exchange—the supervisor promises pay raises in exchange for higher productivity from his/her workers. In transformational leadership, leaders and followers work together to elevate themselves to a higher level of motivation and morality.[20]

Leutze had a transformational leadership model in mind when he drew parallels between the American revolutionary experience and the German revolution of 1848–1849. The goal—to unite the colonies under a single government serves as the same aspiration of liberals in Germany. In the American case, regardless of the nature of the relationship between leaders and followers, they worked together because they had a goal in mind— independence.

We often assume that leaders shape the goals of an organization, even a country. True, leaders do have more power to set the agenda, but the followers also influence how far leaders can push. Followers shape the legitimacy of goals through their acceptance or rejection of a leader's vision. Followers also often have aspirations that leaders cannot ignore. Divided followers also can have a disastrous impact on the attainment of goals, as we noted earlier with the collapse of the German revolution under the divisions between the middle and working classes.

The relationship between leaders and followers in pursuit of a goal (or goals) does not take place in a vacuum. Leadership is essentially situational—and that is what complicates matters. What works in one situation does not ensure success in another. If it did, we would be able to develop a leadership "field manual" for you with the formula for success. After memorizing the formula, you would be prepared for any circumstance. If only the real world could be that simple.

Leaders who are effective in one situation find themselves trounced in another. In studying leadership as a process, we must understand the organizational and historic forces that are shaping decision making. General Washington's daring attack was based on the premise that the Hessians would be caught off guard because of the Christmas festivities. There was also the expectation that all sides in the fighting had retired into their respective encampments in order to face the rigors of winter. The element of surprise not only included the time of day, but also the season in which the attack took place. General Washington, in this case, took advantage of the context in order to regain the momentum in the Revolutionary War.

Finally, just as leadership cannot be divorced from context, we cannot discount the importance of values and norms in shaping the leaders' and followers' worldviews. We often see leadership books that tout the "ten steps" to successful leadership. When delving into the details, we find recom- mendations that fail to consider a leader's cultural background. Leaders and followers are socialized into specific cultural norms. The very depiction of the General standing, as opposed to rowing along with everyone else, is part of a cultural assumption that leaders are somehow "separate from" or even "better than" their followers.

Defining leadership

Once these five components (leaders, followers, goal, environmental context, cultural context) are taken into consideration, a simple definition of leadership emerges (see Figure 1.4.):

> Leadership is the process by which leaders and followers develop a relationship and work together toward a goal (or goals) within an environmental context shaped by cultural values and norms.

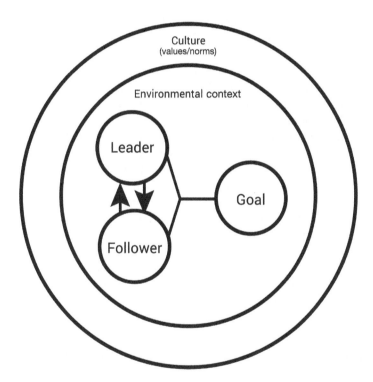

Figure 1.4 The Five Components of Leadership Model

This book is structured around the five components from this definition of leadership. As we explore each component in depth, we will examine the theories and models associated with each. We will also discuss ethical considerations derived from each component. At the same time, consistent with our arts and humanities approach, we will connect artifacts to these components and examine fundamental questions that leaders must address.

Part I of the book focuses on the first four components—leaders, followers, goals, and the environmental context. We treat the fifth component, cultural values and norms in Part II. This section has several chapters, because there are many different values and norms to be considered. Globalization has heightened the importance of viewing leadership as a cross-cultural phenomenon. As national borders become blurred, communication technology expands, and human mobility grows, leaders and followers must be prepared to deal with conflicting cultural assumptions about leadership. In Part II, we investigate six cultural frameworks: Western, Latin American, Islamic, African, Buddhist, and East Asian. Our interest here is not so much to expose you to the different characteristics of each cultural framework, but to relate them to our leadership model.

The last part of the book (Part III) applies a critical question—Leadership for what?—to the first three components of leadership. For the leader, we focus on "leadership for developing oneself." For the follower, we explore the role that leaders play in developing others. As for the goal, we discuss the importance of leaders and followers contributing to the greater good. The other two components (environment and culture) serve as the contexts from which to better understand how leaders and followers go about answering the "leadership for what?" question.

Ultimately, the value of this book will be found in your ability to connect the insights of the following pages with your own experience. By raising your awareness of how leadership works, we hope that you will become a better leader *and* follower, better able to navigate difficult situations, anticipate cross-cultural challenges, and learn to apply the different theories and models connected to the five components of leadership.

The use of artifacts allows you to reflect on the different creative expressions related to leadership themes. In Leutze's case, for instance, you were challenged to consider the heroic view of leadership—the leader standing tall above the followers. In subsequent chapters, you will be introduced to different ways of seeing the leader–follower relationship, and the impact that different environmental and cultural contexts have on leadership in general.

The intellectual context of the contemporary study of leadership

As we introduce each of the five components in separate chapters, we will highlight some of the leadership theories and models associated with each. In keeping with the tower metaphor introduced in the beginning of the chapter, the five components of leadership will serve as the architectural framework to which we will attach the "bricks" (the theories and models from the leadership literature). For this chapter, however, we need to provide an overview of the intellectual history of the leadership studies field so you will have this chronology in mind when examining these theories and models.

Today, we refer to leadership as an intellectual field of study. Leadership studies certainly has a history of development, a codified body of knowledge, common constructs, academic journals, scholars, professional organizations, and all the requirements necessary to garner standing as its own "discipline" in the larger academy. However, scholars are not in agreement as to whether it constitutes an academic discipline.

Leadership as "purposeful interaction"

Insights gained from one discipline can certainly be applicable to multiple fields, and that is common in higher education. When the Swiss developmental psychologist Jean Piaget probed the nature of childhood, he was not limiting himself to a single discipline. His theory of cognitive development resonated in many disciplines such as philosophy and psychology. Today, the field of education uses Piaget's theories to develop appropriate curricula for different grade levels. In other words, insights from one discipline can find expression in other intellectual camps.

What makes a discipline intellectually distinct are the types of question that the scholars in that field propose to explore (and, it is to be hoped, answer). They may not all agree on the answers, but they draw from the same set of questions. In economics, for instance, we see disagreements over models and assumptions, but economists can agree on the fundamental premises of the field. Keynesians, the disciples of the British economist John Maynard Keynes, are still calling for an activist government in the marketplace, while the followers of the American economist Milton Friedman extol the virtues of supply-side economics. They diverge deeply on macroeconomic policy prescriptions, but they are both anchored in the same question—how should values be exchanged?

For leadership studies, we propose that the central intellectual focus revolves around human beings' *purposeful interaction*. This focus invites debates about ethics and power relations. On the ethical side, purposeful interaction suggests choices to be made—forks in the road to be confronted. Those choices help clarify intent. Leaders and followers bring to the relationship certain values that guide their behavior. Intentionality becomes an expression of those values. In the natural world, events happen (e.g., two stars colliding in space). We do not assume intent in those events.

In leadership, we make a distinction between motion and action. Leaders and followers engage in a relationship that involves action with implicit and explicit intent. We assume human beings have free will—the ability to make choices based on their own volition. As humans interact, they form social structures, which define power relationships. In leadership, we are concerned with the way individuals come together and develop a relationship with a purpose in mind. We can all argue whether the purpose is ethical or not, or who should have the ultimate decision-making authority. However, *purposeful interaction* is the overarching language that organizes our thinking about leadership.

The empirical study of leadership

Many ancient and classical sources have investigated the dynamic of leadership from a leader's standpoint through the millennia. However, the beginning of the empirical study of leadership in the West is traced back to the late nineteenth century and the beginning of the twentieth century with its focus on a leader's traits. The Great "Man" Theory is an example of the intellectual thinking that the field faced in its infancy when it equated *leadership* with the characteristics of a *leader*.

Scholars from the period focused on the development of a list of traits that characterized successful leaders. Historian Thomas Carlyle popularized the notion that in order to understand the history of the world, one only had to study the biographies of "great men."[21] In fact, Leutze's depiction of General Washington fits closely with this conception of leadership. Leaders possess special qualities that define history itself.

Despite considerable effort, scholars could not come up with an agreed on list of these special qualities. As a result, this approach became largely discredited by the 1930s. Leadership scholarship shifted away from traits and turned instead to a leader's desirable behavior—particularly in the ways leaders motivated followers in the pursuit of a goal. By the 1940s, leadership theories tended to take into consideration the first three components (leader, follower, goal) of our model. The contingency and situational theories that emerged in the 1950s and 1960s posited the optimal motivational strategies that leaders might adopt in order to maximize organizational goals.[22] In other words, we had to look at the *context* (the fourth component in our leadership model) in order to understand the main actors' behavior.

By the early 1970s, leadership scholarship paid increasing attention to the influence relationship between leaders and followers. If we were to draw an arrow between leaders and followers, the traditional view of leadership saw the direction of the arrow going from the leader to the follower. Scholars such as James McGregor Burns and Joseph Rost changed this view to a mutual influence with the arrow going in both directions.[23]

Recent theories have expanded our perspective beyond context and introduced values and norms as shaping the main actors' behavior. Globalization has drawn our attention to the cross-cultural dynamic of leadership.[24] This emerging subfield, global leadership, was pioneered by Dutch researcher Geert Hofstede in the 1980s. Based on survey data from more than 50 countries, Hofstede identified five dimensions of culture: power distance, individualism, masculinity and femininity, long- or short-term orientation, and uncertainty avoidance. [25]

Building on Hofstede's findings and the contributions of other scholars interested in intercultural leadership competence, in 1991 a group of researchers led by Robert House launched the Global Leadership and Organizational Behavior Effectiveness (GLOBE) research program—a massive undertaking that enlisted contributors from many different countries to empirically investigate the cultural dimension of leadership.[26] Describing each culture's conception of leadership based on specific dimensions, the GLOBE research program was able to demonstrate that people's ideas of "good leadership" varied across cultures. For a practitioner, the GLOBE research posed two challenges: (1) Building teams that encourage diversity of thought and capitalizing on cultural differences; but, at the same time, (2) making sure that cultural differences do not undermine the effectiveness of the organization. Leaders must develop their intercultural leadership competence in order to face these two challenges.

The end of the century and the beginning of a new one has seen a multitude of approaches and definitions of leadership. As we survey the leadership studies landscape today, it may feel daunting for an emerging leader seeking intellectual guidance from the literature. Drawing back to the tower metaphor, this book is designed to offer a simple work plan that should help you take your first steps in understanding leadership.

Summary and concluding remarks

This chapter has served to introduce the reader to the overall approach we will be using throughout this book, as well as present a brief snapshot of the diverse field of leadership studies. The Five Components of Leadership Model presented here is intended to offer a common language to discuss the process of leadership. The following chapters in this book will focus on the individual components that make up this model of the leadership process. These components include the leader, the followers, the goal, the environmental context, and the values and norms of the culture in which the leadership process is functioning. Part I will focus on the first four components of the model, while Part II will examine the ways several different cultures view leadership; finally, Part III will examine the purposes of leadership to develop one's self, to develop others, and to contribute to the greater good. We propose that our definition of leadership should not be intended simply as an intellectual exercise, rather it should be an important first step in better understanding leadership. We have provided a framework for this important work by examining various artifacts found in the arts and humanities to elicit what they have to say about the leadership process. This is just one approach among many found in the academically diverse field of leadership studies. As we progress through the book, we will call on many of the theories and models used to describe aspects of the leadership process. The rich intellectual history and the various approaches used to understand the process of leadership all boil down to one question, "How do humans purposefully interact?" This is the central question of the field of leadership studies. At the end of each chapter, we will provide readers with questions to hone their thinking as well as a few additional resources to develop their further understanding of leadership.

Before we begin our study, however, we encourage the readers to hold a few questions in mind throughout our time together: How have you traditionally conceived leadership? How is your understanding of leadership evolving as you proceed through the following chapters? What is the importance of followers? Are you an effective follower? What can you do to become more effective as a leader *and* as a follower? What is the goal you have in mind for your own leadership? What is the goal for the organizations to which you belong? Do you know? Is there a clear vision? Are the means of achieving the goal as important as the goal itself? How does the situation affect the leadership process? Can anyone ever reduce leadership to a formula or "easy steps" or "irrefutable laws"? How does your culture affect your view of what leadership should—or should not—be? Would you be as successful as a leader if you were operating in a culture other than your own? What would you have to do to adapt to be successful? Finally, why do you want to become a leader? To whom much is given, much is expected. What responsibilities as well benefits will you incur by developing your understanding and skills as a leader? We do not mean to overwhelm the reader with a list of questions. However, we do want to point out that the study of leadership often yields more questions than it does answers. But answers are available. As we noted in the beginning of the chapter, the first step in leadership should not be action; rather, it should be understanding. We invite you to begin that process with us.

Questions for discussion

- Before reading this chapter, did you view leadership in terms of Leutze's depiction of General George Washington? Why, or why not?
- What are your assumptions about the ideal partnership between leaders and followers? Do these assumptions fit with the image presented in Leutze's painting?
- From an ethical standpoint, do positive ends (goals) justify unethical means (how goals are accomplished)? Many of Washington's troops were sick, hungry, and exhausted. Yet, he called on them to go the extra mile. If the surprise attack had been a terrible failure, do you think his judgment would have been questioned?
- Have you considered how your culture might affect your view of leadership? What might the image of "the perfect leader" be in your culture?

Additional resources

The following are just a few helpful resources for the student of leadership to develop a broader understanding of the field of leadership studies, its history, theoretical models, and research approaches:

B.M. Bass with R. Bass. *The Bass Handbook of Leadership: Theory, Research, and Managerial Applications*, 4th edn., New York: Free Press, 2008.
K. Grint, *Leadership: A Very Short Introduction*, Oxford: Oxford University Press, 2010.
B. Kellerman, *Leadership: Essential Selections on Authority, Power, and Influence*, New York: McGraw-Hill, 2010.

Notes

1 J. W. Gardner, *On Leadership*, New York: Free Press, 1990, p. xiv.
2 This argument is further explored in G. Perruci and R. M. McManus, "The State of Leadership Studies," *Journal of Leadership Studies*, 6, 3 (2013): 49–54. See also M. Harvey and R. Riggio, eds., *Leadership Studies: The Dialogue of Disciplines*, Cheltenham: Edward Elgar Publications, 2011.
3 The Five Components of Leadership Model was originally referred to as the "McDonough Model" in reference to the setting in which we first developed and refined it, the Bernard P. McDonough Center for Leadership and Business at Marietta College, Ohio. The model was also explained in "Leadership Education Across Disciplines: The Social Science Perspective," *Journal of Leadership Studies* 7, 4 (2014): 43–47. The authors wish to acknowledge J. T. Wren and M. J. Swatez who helped form their thinking with their "The historical and contemporary contexts of leadership: A conceptual model," in J.T. Wren, ed., *The Leader's Companion: Insights on Leadership Through the Ages*, New York: Free Press, 1995, pp. 245–252.
4 The terms "text" and "artifact" may be used synonymously.
5 For an excellent resource on reading artifacts, see S.K. Foss, *Rhetorical Criticism: Exploration and Practice*, 3rd edn., Long Grove, IL: Waveland Press, 2004.
6 E. Griffin refers to the continuum between quantitative and qualitative research as a continuum between objective and interpretive research in much the same way. See E. Griffin, *A First Look at Communication Theory*, 7th edn., Boston, MA: McGraw-Hill, 2009, pp. 20–24.
7 The term "equipment for living" is attributed to rhetorician Kenneth Burke. See K. Burke, "Literature as equipment for living," in *The Philosophy of Literary Form*, 3rd edn., Berkeley: University of California Press, 1973, pp. 293–304.
8 For a historical account of this key event in the American Revolution, see D.H. Fischer, *Washington's Crossing*, Oxford: Oxford University Press, 2006.
9 Not all American troops crossed the Delaware. Supplies were low.
10 The painting became a huge success once displayed in New York in the 1850s. This success also enhanced the painter's reputation in the United States.
11 See C.E. Maurice, *The Revolutionary Movement of 1848–9 in Italy, Austria–Hungary, and Germany*, New York: Haskell House Publishers, 1969.
12 See K.H. Jarausch and L.E. Jones, eds., *In Search of a Liberal Germany: Studies in the History of German Liberalism from 1789 to the Present*, New York: St. Martin's Press, 1990; W. Siemann, *The German Revolution of 1848–49*, C. Banerji, trans., New York: St. Martin's Press, 1998.
13 To forestall calls for republicanism, the German princes appointed prominent liberals to their cabinets. A unified national assembly representing all Germany was created in Frankfurt. The new parliament set out to develop a new federal system under the authority of a single emperor. Once no German monarch claimed the crown under the liberal constitution, including King Frederick William IV from the powerful German kingdom of Prussia, the revolutionary movement fizzled out. By the summer of 1849, troops loyal to the princes crushed the rebellion, including the hopes for a representative government. See T.S. Hamerow, *Restoration, Revolution, Reaction: Economics and Politics in Germany, 1815–1871*, Princeton, NJ: Princeton University Press, 1958.
14 B.L. Scherer, "A Narrative of Heroism in Crisis," *Wall Street Journal*, December 20, 2013, p. C13.
15 Ibid.
16 Leutze's experience with the Revolution of 1848 also brings to light his own disappointment with Germany's failure to unite under a liberal leader and advance the patriotic aspirations of all Germans.

17 For examples, see J. Man, *The Leadership Secrets of Genghis Khan*, London: Transword Digital, 2010; W. Roberts, *The Leadership Secrets of Attila the Hun*, New York: Grand Central Publishing, 2007.

18 Our fascination with Washington's leadership skills has garnered him a remarkable list of recent books on this topic, including: M.J. Flynn and S.E. Griffin, *Washington & Napoleon: Leadership in the Age of Revolution*, Dulles, VA: Potomac Books, 2012; G.M. Carbone, *Washington: Lessons in Leadership*, New York: Palgrave Macmillan, 2010; R. Brookhiser, *George Washington on Leadership*, reprint edn., New York: Basic Books, 2009; S. McDowell, *Apostle of Liberty: The World-Changing Leadership of George Washington*, Nashville, TN: Cumberland House Publishing, 2007; J.C. Rees and S. Spignesi, *George Washington's Leadership Lessons*, Hoboken, NJ: Wiley, 2007.

19 See R. Riggio, I. Chaleff, J. Lipman-Blumen, eds., *The Art of Followership: How Great Followers Create Great Leaders and Organizations*, San Francisco: Jossey-Bass, 2008; B. Kellerman, *Followership: How Followers are Creating Change and Changing Leaders*, Boston, MA: Harvard Business School Press, 2008.

20 See Burns, *Leadership*, pp. 19–20.

21 T. Carlyle, *On Heroes, Hero-Worship and the Heroic in History*, London: Oxford University Press, 1928.

22 P. Hersey and K.H. Blanchard, *Management of Organizational Behavior*, Englewood Cliffs, NJ: Prentice Hall, 1969; B.M. Bass and J.A. Vaughan, *Training in Industry: The Management of Learning*, Belmont, CA: Wadsworth, 1966; B.M. Bass, *Leadership, Psychology, and Organizational Behavior*, New York: Harper & Brothers, 1960; F. Fiedler, *Leader Attitudes and Group Effectiveness*, Urbana: University of Illinois Press, 1958.

23 See Burns, *Leadership* and J.C. Rost, *Leadership for the Twenty-First Century*, New York: Praeger, 1991.

24 See G. Perruci, "Millennials and Globalization: The Cross-cultural Challenge of Intragenerational Leadership," *Journal of Leadership Studies*, 5, 3 (2011): 82–87.

25 G.H. Hofstede, *Culture's Consequences, International Differences in Work-Related Values*, Thousand Oaks, CA: Sage Publications, 1980.

26 This project resulted in two impressive volumes: R.J. House, P.J. Hanges, M. Javidan, P.W. Dorfman, and V. Gupta, *Culture, Leadership, and Organizations: The GLOBE Study of 62 Societies*, Los Angeles: Sage Publications, 2004; R.J. House, P.W. Dorfman, M. Javidan, P.J. Hanges, and M.S. de Luque, *Culture and Leadership across the World: The GLOBE Book of In-Depth Studies of 25 Societies*, Los Angeles: Sage Publications, 2014.

2 The leader

The man who lets a leader prescribe his course is a wreck being towed to the scrap heap.[1]

Ayn Rand

Workers of the world, unite! You have nothing to lose but your chains![2]

Karl Marx

It is no coincidence that we begin our discussion of leadership by focusing on the leader. In our definition of leadership, introduced in the previous chapter, the leader plays a key role in the process. However, this role is much more complex than simply detailing the attributes of a person with an important title. As this chapter will show, a more complex view of leadership will take us beyond the leader as the individual "in charge."

As we examine the relationship between leaders and followers, we have to take into consideration the way they influence one another. On the one hand, we can conceive of a relationship based on the expectation that whatever the leader decides goes. That would suggest a "command and control" (directive) approach under which the leader should be free to make decisions without the influence of the followers. On the other hand, we can also imagine an organization whose followers are empowered to make decisions. The leader, in this case, plays a facilitative role.

These two contrasting views are explored through the works of two philosophers—Ayn Rand (representing the directive approach) and Karl Marx (representing the facilitative approach). The two offer utopian worldviews, under which the former treats followers as subordinates and the latter calls for followers to rise up and lead the way. These extremes form the basis for a leadership continuum, which can give us the full range of leader–follower relationships. The chapter ends with a representative sampling of leadership theories and models that cover different places on this continuum—from the leader-focused traits approach (popular in the early decades of the twentieth century) to the servant leadership approach (popular at the turn of the twentieth century).

Case study: Karl Marx and Friedrich Engels' *The Communist Manifesto* and Ayn Rand's *Anthem*

As the dates of their lives reveal, Karl Marx (1818–1883) and Ayn Rand (1905–1982) were not contemporaries, but, had they ever met, we would certainly have witnessed an epic battle. In fact, we did. Much of the Cold War during the second half of that century centered on these competing forces— one espousing the primacy of the group (collectivism), the other celebrating the primacy of the individual (individualism). For this section, we contrast two of their intriguing works—Marx's *The Communist Manifesto* and Rand's novella *Anthem*.

Background on Marx's The Communist Manifesto

Before investigating this artifact, we must first introduce the historical context from which it emerged. Marx was born in Trier, Prussia, in 1818, to a comfortable middle-class family and during a time of rapid industrialization in Europe. As peasants moved to cities in search of economic opportunity and became urban workers, business owners benefitted from considerable cheap labor. Working conditions were deplorable, and workers were accorded little legal protection. The rise of socialism in the nineteenth century was no accident. Workers demanded political rights in an environment that supported the protection of capitalism and the power of the rising merchant class—the bourgeoisie. The continent was ripe for revolution.

Within this environment, "A specter [was] haunting Europe—the specter of Communism." So begins Karl Marx and Friedrich Engels' famous political pamphlet *The Communist Manifesto*. Marx and Engels created the *Manifesto* to systematically summarize communist thought for the general public. Although Karl Marx was the *Manifesto's* primary author, Engels provided support and an early draft on which the work was based. However, it is Marx who further developed and is most associated with communist thought, even to the point that the terms "Marxism" and "communism" are often used synonymously.

While the *Manifesto* was written in 1848, it is surprising to see that the specter of communism still haunts the world's collective conscious today, although many have never read Marx and Engels' work. This is no doubt due—at least in part—to the atrocities committed by infamous leaders who so heinously abused communist thought, such as in the cases of Joseph Stalin's Great Purges, Mao Zedong's Cultural Revolution, and Pol Pot's Khmer Rouge. No doubt, both Marx and Engels would have been horrified to see how their political ideology was polluted to the point of poison. However, if one were to actually read *The Communist Manifesto*, many would find they resonate with at least some of the basic assumptions and values proposed. If we were to place these abuses aside for a moment, and concentrate simply on the *Manifesto's* core concepts, we would see that Marx and Engel's work stands as a representative of the extreme end of the continuum that privileges the primacy of the group.

Synopsis of the Manifesto

The Communist Manifesto is broken into four separate sections: I: bourgeois and proletarians; II: proletarians and communists; III: socialists and communist literature; and IV: position of the communists in relation to the other existing opposition parties.

I. Bourgeois and proletarians

In the first section, Marx and Engels argue that the whole history of human society can be boiled down to an economic struggle between classes. At this particular point in history, there are two major groups, the bourgeoisie and the proletarians—the "haves" and the "have-nots." The bourgeoisie are the capitalist owners who control the means of production, such as those who operate factories, control railroads, and own land. The proletarians are the wage laborers who struggle to eke out an existence, such as those who operate the machines in those factories, labor on those railroads, and pay rent to those landlords.

The authors argue that in the bourgeoisie's insatiable quest for more money and power they have altered the basic structure of all human relationships and have reduced them to mere exchanges of economic value. No relationship—not even those as fundamental to human society such as the State, religion, and family—have escaped the bourgeoisie's indelible mark of personal self-interest:

> The bourgeoisie has stripped of its halo every occupation hitherto honored and looked up to with reverent awe. It has converted the physician, the lawyer, the priest, the poet, the man of science, into its paid wage laborer. The bourgeoisie has torn away from the family its sentimental veil, and has reduced the family relation to a mere money relation.[3]

The very essence of humanity has been reduced to a constant cycle of production and consumption controlled by the bourgeoisie.

Then comes the good news: Marx and Engels argue that the bourgeoisie have committed a fatal flaw—they have overproduced. The rise of the Industrial Revolution and mass production has led to a special point in history that will enable the proletariat to rise up and create a more equitable society through communism.

II. Proletarians and communists

Marx and Engels argue that communism is the party of the proletariat. If the proletariat hopes to obtain power and create a better life for everyone, they must revolt against the bourgeoisie and embrace the single driving tenet of communism—the abolition of private property. By this, Marx and Engels do not mean the personal property earned by one's own labor, but rather the *capital* that is created by the labor and exploitation of others. Property belongs to the individual. Capital, contrariwise, belongs to the group. Capital is only produced by the united efforts of all people.

For example, a person who "owns" a factory that makes widgets cannot "own" the *capital*, or the profit it creates. That profit is not a direct result of his or her personal labor. Those widgets are only possible because of the collective effort of those workers producing and selling them. Thus, the factory should be owned by all of the workers who make and sell those widgets, and the profits created shared among everyone in the factory. Communism takes this line of thought to its logical conclusion. *All capital* should be communally owned.

Marx and Engels argue that the communal sharing of capital would lead to a much more important adjustment to the division between the bourgeoisie and the proletariat—that is, the elimination of social class that leads to social unrest and exploitation. To possess capital is to possess a social status. Once capital is communally owned, status disappears. Although some may argue that such an adjustment would violate the individual, the authors argue that the present system of capitalism only favors the few who have the *wealth to be individuals*, whereas all others are left behind. The authors argue that communism, by way of contrast, would offer everyone the opportunity to fully participate in all society has to offer. After Marx and Engels answer some of the objections of their detractors, they propose the path to reach their communal goal.[4] Once Marx and Engels have put forth the basics of communism, they detail the way their view is different from socialism.

III. Socialists and communist literature

Many people mistakenly equate socialism with communism. Marx and Engels take the time to differentiate between the two. Although, to be sure, both socialism and communism favor the primacy of the group, the difference is a matter of degree. The authors present three basic types of socialism: reactionary socialism, conservative or bourgeois socialism; and critical-utopian socialism and communism.

Reactionary socialism is simply that—a reaction—a fear of the bourgeois that the proletariat may indeed rise up against them and remove them from their positions of power. They exclaim to the proletariat: "We feel your pain," but they make little effort to change the basic system of exploitation that keeps them in power. It is as if the bourgeois move to the front of the mob to make the impeding revolution appear to be more of a parade with themselves as the grand marshals. Such approaches fail to take into account the specific historical contexts that led to the unrest in their particular situations. This reactionary socialism creates a "petty bourgeois" class that fails to recognize the major issues that can lead to substantive change.

Conservative socialism also recognizes the unrest among the proletariat. However, conservative socialism attempts to address the proletariat's unrest and injustice simply as a means to appease them so that the bourgeois can maintain their power. We may see conservative socialism take such forms as minimum wage laws, philanthropic and humanitarian efforts to help the poor, charitable organizations and social justice programs, or even administrative reforms to address inequality. Marx and Engels have two issues with this type of socialism: (1) It does not go far enough to address the inequalities that do exist in society; and (2) the motivation behind it is simply to keep the bourgeois in power and to prevent too much unrest among the proletariat that might lead to a revolution and bring about real and substantive change. This is often the kind of socialism seen practiced in the West. Marx and Engels put a fine point on it when they say "the bourgeois is [still] a bourgeois—[even if it is] for the benefit of the working class."[5]

Finally, Marx and Engels present critical-utopian socialism and communism. Those who fall into this camp realize the disparity between the bourgeoisie and the proletariat and clearly articulate the need for substantive change. Their one fatal flaw, however, is that "they reject all political, and especially all revolutionary action; they wish to attain their ends by peaceful means."[6] Because of this, they are "necessarily doomed to failure," impotent to bring about the reforms needed to truly change society.

IV. Position of the communists in relation to the other existing opposition parties

The fourth and final section of *The Communist Manifesto* is by far the shortest and is quite simple. Marx and Engels say that communists will work with any party to bring about their goals, even those who do not quite hold up to their ideals such as those already mentioned. Specifically, they will support any revolutionary movement that seeks to uproot the social structures that create inequality among classes. They will support any movement that seeks to address their fundamental concern of private property. They will support any movement that will eventually lead to the uprising of the proletariat to overthrow the bourgeoisie. At the end of *The Manifesto*, Marx and Engels call their readers to action with their famous rallying cry echoed by revolutionists since their time—"Workers of the world, unite! You have nothing to lose but your chains!" It is a compelling vision for those who value the primacy of the group.

Background on Rand's novella Anthem

If Marx can be viewed as a product of his historical period, Rand is no exception. In a way, Marx's work deeply shaped Rand's life. Ayn Rand (1905–1982) was born in St. Petersburg, Russia, as Alissa Rosenbaum before she emigrated to the United States when she was 21. She lived through both the Kerensky and the Bolshevik Revolutions in Russia, which led to her family losing their business and finding exile and famine in the Ukraine. Her early history provides a rich psychological context to understand her later work. She is known for her popular novels such as *Atlas Shrugged*, *The Fountainhead*, and *Anthem*—the subject of our case study here. However, the heart of Rand's work is her philosophical system, which she identified as "objectivism."

Rand was fond of telling a story about being asked to summarize her philosophical thought while standing on one foot. She responded: "Metaphysics: objective reality. Epistemology: reason. Ethics: self interest. Politics: capitalism."[7] But Rand presented her philosophical positions in her novels long before she attempted to present her ideas more systematically. She once said "Fiction is a much more powerful weapon to sell ideas than non-fiction."[8] If we were to base the accuracy of Rand's assertion solely on the popularity and influence of her novels, she was undoubtedly correct. In one survey, Rand's book *Atlas Shrugged* was identified as second only to the Bible in its impact on reader's lives.[9] Her reception in formal academic and philosophical circles, however, has historically been less enthusiastic.[10]

Whether found in Rand's popular fictional writings or in her subsequent philosophical musings, such as in *The Virtue of Selfishness*, the individual reigns supreme. Her unwavering embrace of free market economics and egoist ethics earned her the title among libertarians as the "Goddess of the Market." Her influence can still be seen in economic thought and policy. Although at her zenith in the 1960s, her popularity resurged some years later with members of the Tea Party in the United States who still claim her as a sort of secular patron saint. Her reoccurring theme of the primacy of the individual is often presented with her version of the "Ideal Man" triumphing over the imposing will of the collective as is seen in her work *Anthem*.

Anthem provides a concise introduction to Rand's themes and philosophical thought. The book was originally titled *Ego*—that part of the conscious Freud attributed to producing a sense of self. Rand later changed to the title to reflect a more sophisticated hymn of praise to the ego, hence the name *Anthem*.[11] The book succinctly and yet artfully distills Rand's philosophy of the primacy of the individual.

Synopsis of the book

The cardinal sin in the world of *Anthem* is to see oneself as a discrete individual apart from the group. The inhabitants refer to themselves as "we" rather than "I"—the "Unspeakable Word"—a literary device that can cause some confusion to those first encountering Rand's story. Even to whisper the word "I" is punishable by death. Children are removed from their biological mothers at birth and raised by the government; the State practices eugenics. The State's goal is to create a society in which all men and women love and care for each other equally. Even acknowledging a preference for a particular friend or lover is forbidden. Mysterious councils determine all social class, professional vocations, and mates. Those grouped into like vocations and sexes live together in sterile communal dormitories called "Houses." Before retiring each night, every House recites a collective pledge encapsulating their society's values:

> We are one in all and all in one.
> There are no men but only the great "We."
> One, indivisible and forever.[12]

Rand does not provide an apocalyptic reason or date that has led to the creation of her nightmarish communal world, but later in the novel we do learn that our own time was the height of civilization for the individual—what the current society refers to as the "Unmentionable Times."

Rand's protagonist is Equality 7–2521. We first meet him as he scribbles in his diary while hiding in a subway tunnel preserved from the Unmentionable Times. Rand's entire novella is written as entries into Equality 7–2521's diary. He is a young man of 21 whose intellectual curiosity and physical form is beyond his assigned vocation in the House of the Street Sweepers. He stumbles on the subway tunnel while working with his friend International 4–8818, and he has secretly spent his evenings alone there ever since. He steals slips of paper and bits and pieces of trash found in the City Cesspool to conduct primitive science experiments and keep his journal by candlelight.

As he searches for a word to describe his newly found autonomy, his mind turns to his childhood when he witnessed a man burned alive in the city square for uttering the Unspeakable Word. The "Transgressor" calmly stared Equality 7–2521 in the eyes as he met his death and marked him for his future destiny when he too would discover the Unspeakable Word.

Equality 7–2521's individuality begins to grow, and he meets a young woman, Liberty 5–3000. Her spirit and beauty match his own, and they find themselves inextricably drawn to each other. He refers to her as "the Golden One," and she dubs him "the Unconquered." She is 17 and is slated for the City Palace of Mating—a thought that fills Equality 7–2521 with dread. Although he loves her, he is powerless to pursue her.

One day, while experimenting in the ancient subway tunnel, he rediscovers electricity. He is able to reconnect the wires of a light fixture found from the Unmentionable Times. Astonished at his discovery, he is convinced that his invention will secure for him a place in the House of the Scholars. The last invention seen in their society was the development of the wax candle, which was created by a group of 20 men 100 years previously. Before he can share his discovery, however, he himself is discovered. He is sent to the Palace of Corrective Detention where he is beaten for being found alone—a crime in his world—and refusing to answer questions about his actions or whereabouts.

He escapes from the Palace of Corrective Detention and rushes his invention to the World Council of Scholars to share his discovery, but he is immediately met with suspicion and contempt. The Scholars are not so much fearful of his invention as they are outraged that Equality 7–2521 has discovered it on his own. Fearing the Scholars will once again imprison him and destroy his precious light, he flees to the Uncharted Forest outside the city.

In the Uncharted Forest Equality 7–2521 finds food and shelter, but he also finds his love—the Golden One. She followed him into the forest after she heard he had fled for his life. Together they stumble on a home from the Unmentionable Times. They make their home and discover a library full of books. It is here that Equality 7–2521 finally discovers the Unspeakable Word—"I."

Rand's story takes a sudden turn as the couple discovers their ability to *name* and *claim* their individuality. It is also here where they can finally articulate their individual love for one another. Equality 7–2521 renames himself "Prometheus"—the Bringer of Light—and renames Liberty 5–3000, the Golden One, Gaea—the Great Mother of the Earth. He vows to rescue his friends from their collective State and together build a new society as a testament to the primacy of the individual. In the final pages of the book, we realize the full implications of Rand's title, *Anthem*, as the newly christened Prometheus "sings" a song of praise to his newfound sacred word—EGO!

Analysis: Between Prometheus and the Bolsheviks

The two artifacts serve as representative allegories of contrasting worldviews. If we take the bourgeoisie as another word for the leader and the proletariat as the followers, Marx conceived of a world in which the followers would be free from the leader telling them what to do. Under this worldview, the leader–follower relationship is defined in terms of oppression—the use of followers as a commodity in order to achieve the goals set out by the leader who, in turn, gets all the glory for accomplishing the goals. For Marx, the overthrow of the bourgeoisie was nothing short of giving the followers their rightful place as rulers of their own destiny. The 1917 Bolshevik Revolution in Russia built on Marx's call to action and brought down the Tsarist regime long associated with autocratic oppression.

In contrast, Rand saw Russia's Bolshevik regime as representative of the oppression associated with the collective controlling the fate of the individual. In *Anthem*, we see a group-based society stifling individuality with dramatic effect on creativity and progress—Prometheus' work. As a leadership allegory, we can conceive Rand's work as calling us to free the individual leader to be in charge of his/her own organization—unimpeded by the collective.

These contrasting worldviews assume different power distribution between leaders and followers. In the previous chapter, when we introduced our definition of leadership, the figure representing the leader (L) and the followers (F) had circles of about equal size. Suppose the diameters of these circles represent how much power they each have over the other. A representation of leadership in action would not assume symmetry—an equal distribution of power between a leader and his/her followers. Taken as a dyadic relationship, we can conceive of two extremes—one in which the leader holds all the power

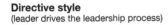

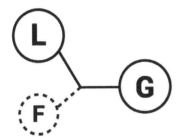

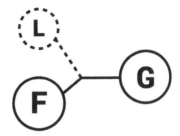

Figure 2.1 Contrasting dyadic leader–follower relationships

over the followers, and the reverse under which all power is accorded to the followers (Figure 2.1). Under the first perspective, the leader drives the relationship and defines the goals, as found in a directive leadership style, while the second possibility places the leader under a facilitative role—subservient to the followers and their goals.

A complete view of leadership must take power into consideration. Many scholars have paid close attention to the concept of power and authority when studying the role of the leader in the leadership process. John R.P. French, Jr., and Bertram Raven wrote an influential piece in 1959, titled "The Bases of Power," which has become a standard taxonomy in the field.[13] They defined power in terms of influence—the latter associated with change in behavior, opinions, and attitudes. French and Raven identified five bases of power: reward power (the promise of a positive benefit), coercive power (the threat of punishment), expert power (the power earned through knowledge or skill), legitimate power (the power that a title confers to allow decision-making authority), and referent power (the power based on the relationships developed between leaders and followers). But power is not simply in the purview of leaders; followers can also wield considerable power in a situation. One leadership scholar, Ron Heifetz, makes an apt distinction between "leading with authority" and "leading without authority."[14] While the former involves the use of power associated with one's position, the latter entails more complex influence relationships. As we can observe in Figure 2.1, the relative size of the diameter containing the leader or the follower indicates the power the parties have in the leadership process.

But power does not have to be *exclusively* accorded to either one of the parties involved—leaders *or* followers. It rarely is, and many would argue that it never should be. Many would argue that the relationship between leaders and followers should be one of "power with" rather than "power over."[15] Some would even argue that when the power in a relationship is grossly unbalanced such an arrangement should not even be defined as "leadership." James MacGregor Burns referred a gross imbalance of power as "power wielding"; such a use of power takes away individual choice. By taking someone's freedom to choose whether or not to follow a person, the power wielder does not exhibit the characteristics of a leader, and such an action should not be considered "leadership." Burns' distinction between leaders and power wielders is important because it sets individuals—such as Adolf Hitler—apart from others—such as Mahatma Gandhi. Such a view suggests there is no such a category as a "bad" leader—only "good" leaders and power wielders. Burns, therefore, argues, "All leaders are actual or potential power holders, but not all power holders are leaders."[16]

We can place these contrasting worldviews on a continuum in order to better understand the possible variations of the leader–follower relationship (see Figure 2.2). On the one end of the continuum, we can place Rand's Prometheus as the all-enlightened decision maker with the followers playing a secondary role. This leader-focused perspective defines a more directive style of leadership. Leaders set the goals, and followers are charged with helping the organization achieve them. In fact, *Anthem* ends with Prometheus developing the new goal for his future society—to liberate others from ignorance.

On the other end of the continuum, we find a more group-focused arrangement, under which the followers hold power over the leader. The leader plays the role of "facilitator," helping the group achieve common goals. The Bolsheviks, as the vanguard party of the proletariat in Russia, played this role of facilitators—bringing about the empowerment of the working class through their revolutionary fervor and collectivist goal.

While a detailed critique of each worldview falls outside the scope of this book, we can derive some leadership lessons from these contrasting perspectives. Throughout the twentieth century, we witnessed some of their limitations. On the Promethean side, the leader's "freedom" to pursue his/her creative passion became associated with the "command and control" style of leadership.[17] By ignoring the input and participation of followers in the decision-making process, the leader-focused approach came to be associated with an autocratic mindset. There is an irony in this dynamic. In the name of individual liberty (the leader's freedom to pursue his/her goals), the leader ends up taking away the followers' own liberty. Again, we see this irony in *Anthem*'s closing pages, as Equality 7–2521 renames Liberty 5–3000, the Golden One, Gaea—the Great Mother of the Earth. In the same breath that he sang praises to individuality, Equality 7–2521 managed to take away Liberty 5–3000's own power to name her own self.

On the collectivist side, we also see an irony at play. While the Bolsheviks' role was to facilitate the rise of the proletariat, in reality, Joseph Stalin hijacked

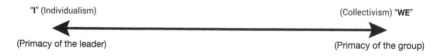

"I" (Individualism)   (Collectivism) "WE"

(Primacy of the leader)   (Primacy of the group)

Figure 2.2 The leadership continuum

the collectivist goals of the 1917 Revolution and established a totalitarian state that made a mockery of Marxist views. But this abuse has often been seen by those claiming to "sacrifice the individual or the few for the greater good of the group." You may remember George Orwell's classic story, *Animal Farm*, served as a simple, yet powerful critique of the way such a "facilitator" ended up replicating the autocratic practices of the farmer—a symbol of the bourgeois class. Unfortunately, although we would like to think that all animals are equal, when in power, some animals seem to become "more equal than others."

These two extremes serve as reminders of the utopian perspectives of a world dominated by either side. In reality, our everyday life is marked by the constant power negotiations between leaders and followers. Some scholars, such as Joseph Rost, argue that the industrial age, popular in the twentieth century, focused more on a command and control paradigm ("I"). As followers have become more educated and have come to expect a more visible role in the leadership process, the group-focused side of the continuum ("WE") has become more prominent in the new millennium.

We should not jump to that conclusion too quickly. As subsequent chapters will show, the environmental context also influences the optimal distribution of power between leaders and followers. In other words, which distribution is ideal? Well, it depends on the situation. That, however, does not take away the fact that leaders may be predisposed to operate best on one side of the continuum at the expense of the other side. We all have seen leaders who like to exert control over situations (directive leadership style), even though the environment calls for a more facilitative role. Conversely, we also have seen leaders fail miserably because they were unable to "take charge" when the environment called for that leadership style.

Most of us can identify our "comfort zone" within the continuum—a spot in which we are most secure leading. Our individual personality traits help shape our placement in this zone. Some leaders are comfortable playing the authoritative role, while others find comfort leading from behind. We may argue that we can adapt to different places in the continuum based on the situation, but that does not mean that we are comfortable adopting that style. After all, according to Rand, Equality 7–2521 was born with a "curse"— curiosity. He did not fit in with the "WE" world and longed for the "I" side of the continuum.

Part of the challenge in a leader's personal development is to widen this "comfort zone," in order to be effective in a wider variety of circumstances. For a leader who is comfortable with the directive approach ("I"), a move to the group-led side of the continuum ("WE") will test his/her ability to adapt. Conversely, a leader who is comfortable playing the role of a facilitator may find himself/herself in situations that demand a directive style of decision making. Expanding one's knowledge of different theories and models along the continuum, as the next section shows, can help the leader see the factors that influence the leadership process. That is a first step in developing self-awareness, which, in turn, challenges one's "comfort zone."

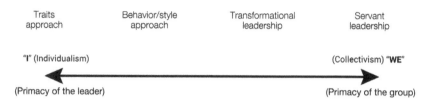

Figure 2.3 Representative theories/models along the leadership continuum

This wide array of placements on the leadership continuum can be found in the study and practice of leadership. In the previous chapter, we introduced the intellectual history of leadership studies as a way of giving you a sense of the evolution of the field. In this section, we build on that history and highlight some of the theories and models in the past century that have assigned different power levels to the leader along the leadership continuum.

Figure 2.3 highlights four theoretical approaches to leadership that span the full range of the continuum—moving from the traits approach on the "I" side of the continuum to Robert Greenleaf's servant leadership, which is representative of the "WE" side.

Starting from the left side of the continuum, our first theory/model is the traits approach. The traits approach is based on the idea that certain "individuals of superior ability" are naturally inclined toward leadership.[18] Leaders are born, not made. There were many scholars pursuing a traits approach to leadership in the early part of the twentieth century. The American historian, W.E.B. Du Bois, argued that invariably only a few in a group rise to prominence —what he referred to as "the talented tenth."[19] Leadership, viewed from this perspective, produces a clear division between leaders and followers. Leaders naturally rise to the top, as complexity and conflicting interests demand individuals with special ability.[20] As the power of these individuals grows, institutions are formed around the privileged few. The outcome of this social dynamic is the institutionalization of leadership.

Ralph Stogdill summarized the traits research of the early part of the twentieth century as part of the famous Ohio State University leadership studies and noted that leadership is not so much based on a universal set of traits as much as it is on particular behaviors—that is, leadership is not about who you are, but is more about what you do. Stogdill argued, "A person does not become a leader by virtue of the possession of some combination of traits, but the pattern of personal characteristics of the leader must bear some relevant relationship to the characteristics, activities, and goals of the followers. Thus, leadership must be conceived in terms of the interaction of variables which are in constant flux and change."[21] This moved the thinking about leadership towards a behavioral, or style, approach, which focused on two factors: a concern for the relationship between leaders and followers and a concern for the task to be accomplished. The two categories of behavior—relationship behavior and task behavior—become equally important in our understanding of leadership. As we move away from the extreme "I" side, leaders begin to cede power to followers.

While subsequent chapters will investigate these aspects—such as the relationship between leader and followers and the influence of environmental factors—in more depth, it is important here to highlight that Stogdill helped move the focus of the leadership literature in the direction of behavioralism (how the leader's actions contribute to success in leadership) and contingency (how the situation influences leadership outcomes). As he argued in his 1948 study, "The evidence suggests that leadership is a relationship that exists between persons in a social situation, and that persons who are leaders in one situation may not necessarily be leaders in other situations."[22] In other words:

> [L]eadership is not a matter of passive status, or of the mere possession of some combination of traits. Rather leadership appears to be a working relationship among members of a group, in which the leader acquires status through active participation and demonstration of his or her capacity for carrying cooperative tasks through to completion.[23]

Despite the move away from personality traits as the main determinants of leadership, the study of leadership remained leader-centric through the 1960s. By introducing the leader–follower relationship into our understanding of leadership, scholars at least began to pay attention to the middle range of the leadership continuum. Two patterns of leader behavior emerged as central to our understanding of leadership styles in the second half of the twentieth century —a leader focused on the task versus a leader focused on people. The former proposed a goal-oriented style, while the latter paid close attention to the relationship between leaders and followers. Popular theories and models of leadership such as Blake and Mouton's Leadership Grid, Hersey and Blanchard's Situational Leadership, and Fielder's Contingency Model all broadly address this tension.[24]

This tension illustrates the difficult tradeoffs that leaders have to consider when facing a particular situation. Sometimes, the leader will be better off spending time on building relationships (concern for people) and making the goal attainment as secondary. Other times, the leader will guide followers to focus on the task and place relationship building to the side for the moment. Effective leaders are able to decide the proper combination of the two factors based on the peculiarities of the situation and the environmental context—a topic further explored in subsequent chapters.

As we move further to the right in the continuum, we find transformational leadership as a model that stresses the importance of the relationship between leaders and followers. Burns' second conception of power use involves transactional leadership, which is viewed as a simple exchange—a bargain between leaders and followers. A leader provides a follower with an incentive for him or her to complete a task. The central criterion of transactional leadership is that "the bargainers have no enduring purpose that holds them together."[25] Burns, however, thought leadership could be—and, indeed, should be—more than a mere exchange. Rather, Burns thought leadership at it best is a transformational process in which leaders and followers engage each other in such a way as to raise one another to higher levels of motivation and morality.[26]

By "motivation" Burns was suggesting that such leadership fuses the leader and the followers in a "mutual and continuing pursuit of a higher purpose"[27]— that is, something that is transcendent to either the leader's or the follower's immediate goal. By "morality" Burns was referring to the human and ethical conduct of both the leader and the led. In short, Burns proposes that transforming leadership helps both the leader and the follower reach their full potential and go beyond either of their immediate self interests.[28] This is why we have placed this towards the "WE" end of the continuum.

As we move toward the end of the right side of the continuum ("WE"), we can explore a model of leadership that puts an emphasis on the follower. A model of leadership that best exemplifies this focus is Robert Greenleaf's servant leadership, in which he proposed that a true leader is a servant first.[29] Greenleaf questioned the command and control model of leadership and suggested that leadership should focus on the needs and aspirations of the followers, including a commitment to their growth and building a community.[30] The purpose of leaders is simply to assist followers reach their full potential and goals.

This radical conception of leadership completely rejects the notion that the leader should be the center of the leadership process. For many leaders, this approach is challenging. Are leaders not rewarded with authority because they possess superior abilities? Further, does positional power give the leader the legitimate means to pursue goals that he/she deems the most appropriate? The leadership continuum gives us the wide range of approaches that leaders can take when approaching their relationship with their followers.

Rand would agree with this assumption that leaders have demonstrated superior ability; therefore, they should be free to lead. Followers are considered subordinates because they do not have the same intellectual capacity as the leader. This view of leadership, which is common in the West, places the leader at the top of the hierarchy. The position of leader represents a prize earned through superior qualities. Rand's protagonist (Equality 7–2521) would be representative of this perspective—a lone hero single-handedly shaping the history of the world. Marx, however, would counter that once at the top, a leader uses this position to keep others from climbing and sharing power. The leader uses followers merely as a tool to achieve his/her individual interests as opposed to the interests of the collective. Thus, followers should hold the power and be the driving force of the leadership process. These two positions represent the far ends of either side of the leadership continuum.

Summary and concluding remarks

In this chapter, we have examined the first part of the Five Elements of Leadership model—the leader. In so doing, we have presented a leadership continuum spanning the primacy of the individual and the primacy of the group. We have illustrated these positions on the continuum with Ayn Rand's *Anthem* and Karl Marx and Frederick Engels' *The Communist Manifesto*. The placement on the continuum affects the perceived power relationship between leaders and followers. Depending on a person's view of the world, he or she may gravitate towards one end of the continuum or the other. This will affect a person's comfort with different styles of leading. Those resonating more with the primacy of the individual may be more comfortable with a command and control style of leadership. Whereas those embracing the primacy of the group may be more comfortable viewing the leader as a facilitator that assists followers to reach their goals. Four leadership theories and models were used to represent various points on this continuum, specifically a traits approach, a behavioral/style approach, transformational leadership, and servant leadership. The field of leadership studies contains many additional approaches to understanding the leader's role in the leadership process that can be placed at various points on the leadership continuum.

Leadership is not just about the leader, but the leader is essential to the leadership process. The leader's view of his or her proper place on the leadership continuum has vast ramifications for the leader's style, the means of obtaining the goal, and—not the least—the leader's relationship with his or her followers. Many leaders fail to understand that their followers and the particular situation in which they find themselves may call for a vastly different approach to leadership than the one with which they are most comfortable. They refuse to adapt—at their own peril. The lesson to be learned here—and which is in keeping with the general theme of this book—is that one must *understand* leadership before one can lead effectively. To blindly forge into the fray without first considering the different approaches to leadership is to invite failure. The first step must not be action, but understanding. We have taken that first step, and continue our journey in the next chapter, the followers.

Questions for discussion

- With which side of the leadership continuum do you resonate—the primacy of the individual or the primacy of the group?
- Where is your "comfort zone" on the leadership continuum?
- Which of the four approaches to leadership presented at the end of the chapter best fits with your own approach to leadership?
- Do you agree with James MacGregor Burns's distinction between power wielding and leadership? Why, or why not?
- Discuss the concept of power in leadership. Do you agree with the notion that leaders invariably use power to protect their own individual interests and, in the process, oppress their followers?

- Should leaders be free to make decisions regardless of their followers' opinions and interests? Why, or why not?

Additional resources

J.T. McMahon, *Leadership Classics*, Long Grove, IL: Waveland Press, 2010.

P. Northouse, *Leadership: Theory and Practice*, 6th edn., Los Angeles: Sage Publications, 2012.

J.C. Rost, *Leadership for the Twenty-First Century*, Westport, CT: Praeger Publishers, 1991.

Notes

1 A. Rand, *Atlas Shrugged*, New York: Signet/Penguin, 1957/1994, p. 934.

2 This is a popular paraphrase of Marx and Engels' final words in their work, *The Manifesto of the Communist Party*, originally published in 1848 by the Communist League. The original reads: "The proletarians have nothing to lose but their chains. They have a world to win. Working men of all countries, unite!" We have used the paraphrase here because it has become more well known and is most likely familiar to readers. We have used the English edition from 1888, F. Engels, ed., *The Communist Manifesto*. Available at www.gutenberg.org/ebooks/61. Published January 25, 2005. Accessed June 26, 2014.

3 Marx and Engels, *The Communist Manifesto*, I: Bourgeois and proletarians.

4 Marx and Engels suggest the following: 1) Abolition of property in land and application of all rents of land to public purposes; 2) a heavy progressive or graduated income tax; 3) abolition of all rights of inheritance; 4) confiscation of the property of all emigrants and rebels; 5) centralization of credit in the hands of the state, by means of a national bank with State capital and an exclusive monopoly; 6) centralization of the means of communication and transport in the hands of the State; 7) extension of factories and instruments of production owned by the State; 8) the bringing into cultivation of wastelands, and the improvement of the soil generally in accordance with a common plan; 9) equal liability of all to work; 10) establishment of industrial armies, especially for agriculture; 11) combination of agriculture with manufacturing industries; 12) gradual abolition of all the distinction between town and country by a more equable distribution of the populace over the country; 13) free education for all children in public schools; 14) abolition of children's factory labor in its present form, and 15) combination of education with industrial production. Ibid, II: Proletarians and communists."

5 Ibid, "III: Socialist and communist literature."

6 Ibid.

7 A. Rand, *Atlas Shrugged*, Signet/Penguin, 1996, pp. 1074–1075. For a primer on Ayn Rand's philosophy, see A. Rand, *The Virtue of Selfishness*, New York: Signet/Penguin, 1963.

8 Quoted in C.R. Pierpont, "Twilight of the Goddess," *The New Yorker*, July 24, 1995, 70–81.

9 Survey conducted by the Library of Congress and The Book-of-the-Month Club, November 20, 1991, 1. Survey based on 2032 responses. See www.nytimes.com/1991/11/20/books/book-notes-059091.html. Accessed August 12, 2014.

10 There are exceptions to this. See C.M. Sciabarra, *Ayn Rand: The Russian Radical*, University Park: Pennsylvania State University Press, 1995.

11 Some have noted the striking similarities between Rand's novella and Yevgeny's Zamyatin's novel *We*, published in 1921, long before Rand's *Anthem*, which was first

published in 1938—but Rand never acknowledged Zamyatin's influence. Both novels are set in futuristic dystopias in which all human beings must surrender their self to the collective State.

12 A. Rand, *Anthem*, London: Cassell, 1938. Available at www.gutenberg.org/ebooks/1250. Published March 1998. Accessed June 26, 2014.

13 J.R.P. French, Jr., and B. Raven, "The bases of social power," in *Studies in Social Power*, Dorwin Cartwright, ed., Ann Arbor: University of Michigan, 1959, pp. 150–167.

14 R.A. Heifetz, *Leadership Without Easy Answers*, Cambridge: Belknap Press of Harvard University Press, 1994.

15 Barbara Kellerman makes this observation in her commentary on Mary Parker Follett. See B. Kellerman, *Leadership: Essential Selections on Power Authority and Influence*, New York: McGraw-Hill, 2010, p. 102.

16 Burns, *Leadership*, p. 18.

17 For a critique of this approach, see M.J. Wheatley, "Good-bye, Command and Control," *Leader to Leader*, 5 (1997): 21–28.

18 E. Munford, *The Origins of Leadership*, Chicago: University of Chicago Press, 1909, p. 77.

19 W.E.B. Du Bois, *The Philadelphia Negro: A Social Study*, New York: Oxford University Press, 2007.

20 The traits approach continues to influence leadership thought. For example, see D. Goleman, *Emotional Intelligence*, New York, Bantam, 1995; and *Working With Emotional Intelligence*, New York, Bantam, 1998.

21 R.M. Stogdill, "Personal Factors Associated with Leadership," *Journal of Psychology*, 25 (1948): 35–71. Reprinted in B.M. Bass, *Bass and Stogdill's Handbook of Leadership: Theory Research and Managerial Applications*, 3rd edn., New York, Free Press, p. 76.

22 Ibid, p. 65.

23 Ibid, p. 77.

24 For a broad discussion of this topic, see P. Northouse, *Leadership: Theory and Practice*, 6th edn., Los Angeles: Sage Publications, 2012.

25 Burns, *Leadership*, p. 20.

26 Ibid.

27 Ibid.

28 Burns later softened his position on the extreme dichotomy between transformational and transactional leadership and suggested that leaders operate on both sides of the spectrum and combine the two approaches. J.M. Burns, foreword to *Reflections on Leadership*, R.A. Couto, ed., New York: University Press of America, 2007, viii.

29 Robert K. Greenleaf, *The Servant as Leader*, Cambridge, MA: Center for Applied Studies, 1970. In 1985, the Center was renamed the Robert K. Greenleaf Center.

30 Robert K. Greenleaf, *Servant Leadership: A Journey into the Nature of Legitimate Power and Greatness*, New York: Paulist Press, 1977. Greenleaf identified ten characteristics of the servant leader: listening, empathy, healing, awareness, persuasion, conceptualization, foresight, stewardship, commitment to the growth of people, and building community.

3 The followers

A community is like a ship; everyone ought to be prepared to take the helm.[1]
Henrik Ibsen, from *An Enemy of the People*

We turn our attention now to the role of followers and the relationship created between leaders and followers in the leadership process. As we articulated in Chapter 1, followers are a key component of leadership. Nevertheless, most people recoil at the idea of being referred to as a "follower." As a point of fact, however, we are all followers in multiple contexts—as citizens, as employees, as students, as members of clubs, committees, and religious organizations, and in countless other situations. Why is one's identification with this role met with such resistance? The reasons are most likely twofold. The first is that the term "follower" connotes a hierarchy, and, thus, a presumed lesser importance. This has led some scholars to suggest alternative terms for the role, such as "constituent" or "participant."[2] This does not negate the fact that we are all, indeed, still followers in many of the contexts in which we find ourselves. The second is that many people associate the idea of being a follower with passivity and lack of personal exigency. However, this need not be, and neither is it, the case. Followers can, and do, play a vital role in the process of leadership; that is, achieving a common goal.

Many times, the line between leaders and followers can be difficult to discern. Where followership stops and leadership begins is a gray area at best. As we shall see in our case study, there is a political leader, a mayor of a town, with the legitimate authority to make a key decision, and yet it is a follower who actively attempts to influence change and lead the people. There is often a great deal of flux between leadership and followership, and, in reality, leaders and followers have a great deal of influence on one another. Refusing to acknowledge or define the differences that do exist, however, does little to provide an understanding or the working vocabulary needed to investigate and articulate this crucial piece of the leadership process. Although several authors have offered definitions of followers and followership,[3] we broadly define a "follower" as a subordinate in any group in which one operates, and a "leader" being the person(s) formally recognized as holding the legitimate superior role and authority in the group. "Followership" then is the response of subordinates to their superiors.[4] To say followers are in subordinate positions, however, does not mean they are unimportant to the leadership process.

Many historical luminaries have weighed in on the power and importance of followers.[5] Unfortunately, much of this wisdom has been overshadowed by leader-centric models such as those we examined in the previous chapter. But recently the field of leadership studies has witnessed a booming recognition of the importance of the follower's role in the leadership process. In this chapter, we will present some of the key contemporary literature surrounding the study of followership and ultimately illustrate the ideas contained therein through our case study, Arthur Miller's adaptation of *An Enemy of the People* by Henrik Ibsen.

Case study: Arthur Miller's adaptation of Henrik Ibsen's *An Enemy of the People*

Norwegian playwright Henrik Ibsen (1828–1906) wrote *An Enemy of the People* in 1882. The play centers around a small town that has recently invested in building an elaborate spa to support its economy, but the town's doctor threatens to reveal the that springs that feed the spa are contaminated. Some say the play was based on an actual incident in which a Hungarian scientist was stoned in the 1830s because he had reported an outbreak of cholera in his resort town, thus ruining the tourist season and the town's economy.[6] The play provides a vivid illustration of the tension between the primacy of the individual and the primacy of the group we explored in the previous chapter.

Table 3.1 List of characters in *An Enemy of the People*

Dr. Thomas Stockmann	The town doctor for Kirsten Springs (protagonist)
Mayor Peter Stockmann	Dr. Thomas Stockmann's brother (antagonist)
Mrs. Catherine Stockmann	Dr. Stockmann's wife
Petra Stockmann	Dr. Stockmann's daughter and a school teacher
Morten and Ejlif	Dr. Stockmann's sons
Hovstad	The editor of the newspaper, *The People's Daily Messenger*
Aslaksen	The publisher of *The People's Daily Messenger*
Billing	An assistant editor for *The People's Daily Messenger*
Morten Kiil	Dr. Stockmann's father-in-law
Captain Horster	Dr. Stockmann's friend

Background on the play

The play's protagonist, Dr. Stockmann, acts as a voice for Ibsen's own thoughts and a response to the situation in which he found himself at the time. Ibsen was no stranger to controversy. He was then, and is now, known for his plays addressing pertinent social issues. At the time Ibsen wrote *An Enemy of the People*, he was still reeling from the public outcry he received from his previous play *Ghosts*, which dealt with the scandal of syphilis in the Victorian era, and was, more specifically, a social commentary about the moral hypocrisy of the late nineteenth century. His earlier play, *A Doll's House*, perhaps Ibsen's most famous work, was a proto-feminist piece that argued for the equality of women in a time when such a view was extremely unpopular. At the time Ibsen wrote and produced *An Enemy of the People*, he was considered somewhat of a social pariah himself and the play was certainly, in part, Ibsen's response to his detractors. So, Ibsen did use his play as a way to address his critics, but more generally he used it to advocate for the voice of the minority, regardless of the unsavory nature of the truth.[7]

The play's timeless theme of the tyranny of the majority found a new audience in the United States in 1950. American playwright Arthur Miller (1915–2005) adapted the play as a response to the growing Communist witch-hunt and the silencing of leftist voices in the United States spawned by the House Un-American Activities Committee during the Cold War. (We will return to this event in Chapter 5.) Miller was eventually called to testify before the committee but refused to cooperate. In a personal letter to a friend, Miller wrote: "My main interest in [*An Enemy of the People*] . . . is that through the guise of Ibsen—ssssh!—I have managed to say things I wouldn't dare say alone."[8] In this way, Miller's use of the play to speak truth to power and address his critics was not unlike Ibsen's own. When Miller adapted Ibsen's play, he was responding to a situation of his time. He wrote:

> I believe this play could be alive for us because its central theme is, in my opinion, the central theme of our social life today. Simply, it is the question of whether the democratic guarantees protecting political minorities ought to be set aside in time of crisis.[9]

The theme has not faded with time. Neither will it. As discussed in Chapter 2, there will always be the question of the extent the individual should subordinate himself or herself to the group or the "authorities who are in charge of the general welfare."[10] Thus, Ibsen's play remains as timely today as it did when it was first written. Although the specifics of the situation may change, the central question remains the same.

Synopsis of the play

Ibsen sets his play in a sleepy Norwegian hamlet at the end of the nineteenth century. The town has recently constructed a health institute and baths, Kirsten

Springs, fed by a water system connected to a local river. They hope the newly created spa will "put the town on the map" as a tourist destination. However, Thomas Stockmann, the town doctor and the medical officer of Kirsten Springs, suspects that they are the cause of a recent outbreak of typhoid and other diseases in early visitors to the baths. He has samples of the water sent to the university to be analyzed and discovers that the springs are, indeed, fouled. A tannery located upstream of the town is polluting the water. Dr. Stockmann dispatches his report to the town mayor, Peter Stockmann, who is also the Chairman of the Board of Directors for Kirsten Springs and also happens to be Dr. Thomas Stockmann's brother. Dr. Stockmann had warned the board not to source the springs downstream and he has been proved right. The doctor, his wife, Catherine, and children—their adult daughter Petra, and two young sons Morten and Ejlif—are sure the news will be met with welcome relief and that the doctor will be hailed as a hero for saving the town from ruin (Act 1, Scene 1).

The news of the doctor's report travels quickly. Catherine's father, Morten Kiil, is one of the first to hear the rumor of the poisoned springs. However, Kiil believes his son-in-law, Dr. Stockmann, is scheming to ruin and humiliate the town mayor. The play is set in a time before the public readily accepted the presence of microorganisms and bacteria, and his daughter and son-in-law are unable to convince Kiil otherwise. While waiting for a response from the mayor, Aslaksen, the publisher of the town's newspaper, *The People's Daily Messenger*, and its editors, Billing and Hovstad, are preparing to print the doctor's report and his proposal that the town build a water waste disposal plant and a new water system to feed the baths. The doctor starts to worry as he sees the story growing, but the publisher, Aslaksen, assures him that he will see to it that the majority of the town will support the doctor and his proposal. The mayor finally arrives to respond to the doctor's allegations and proposal. He has discovered that it would take 300,000 crowns to reconstruct the water system for the springs—an unimaginable amount of money at the time. The mayor accuses his brother of trickery and creating a hoax to humiliate him. He offers a compromise, however, and assures the doctor that if the water is indeed poisoned, he and the board will quietly work to reconstruct the springs over time. The mayor also forbids the doctor from reporting the news of the poisoned water, and even insists he retract his statements, or he will see to it that the doctor loses his job as the medical officer of the springs. The doctor refuses and the mayor accuses him of being a traitor and trying to ruin the town. As the curtain closes, the doctor vows to report the news of the poisoned springs to the people of the village (Act 1, Scene 2).

The second act opens in the office of *The People's Daily Messenger*. Aslaksen, Hovstad, and Billing are preparing the doctor's article for publication. Dr. Stockmann arrives and boasts of standing up to the mayor. We learn that one of the newspaper's editors, Hovstad, does, indeed, hope to use the story as fodder for a revolution to remove the mayor and the town's other elected officials from power. We also learn that Billing has his own political motivations for printing the story and is going to run for an elected office. The doctor leaves to attend to his patients, and then the mayor makes a surprise visit to the *Messenger* and demands to see the doctor's article. He warns the publisher and editors that if they print the story, the town will be taxed to pay for the doctor's proposal. If the newspaper supports the proposal and the new tax, they will lose their subscribers and they, too, will be out of a job. The doctor returns to find the mayor and learns the paper's officials now refuse to print his story, so he declares he will call a town meeting to report his news (Act 2, Scene 1).

The doctor convinces his friend Captain Horster to allow him to use his home for a town meeting because no one in town will rent him a hall. The people of the town do attend the meeting, but they refuse to let the doctor speak. They "vote" for the meeting to be moderated by the *Messenger*'s publisher, Aslasken, and he promptly gives the mayor the stage. When the doctor finally gets a chance to plead his case, his friends turn on him. The townspeople bully him off the platform and the mayor declares the doctor "an enemy of the people" (Act 2, Scene 2).

The curtain opens on the final act of the play with Dr. Stockmann and his wife Catherine gathering rocks that have been thrown through the windows of their home. They are evicted and the townspeople sign a pledge not to do business with them. Their daughter, Petra, is also fired from her teaching position at the local school, and their boys are beaten by the other children in the town. The mayor arrives and accuses Dr. Stockmann of falsifying the information for his own financial gain because his father-in-law, Morton Kiil, Catherine Stockmann's father, has used the story to purchase stock in the springs from the town's investors at a lower price—an investment that Dr. Stockmann's wife and he will eventually inherit. We also learn that Morton Kiil owns the tannery upstream that is causing the problem. The mayor and the newspaper publisher, Aslaksen, give the doctor one final chance to retract his story and be reestablished in the town, but he again refuses. The Stockmann family hopes to travel to America to begin a new life, but their friend Captain Horster loses his position as the captain of his ship and so they are left stranded in their little town. The foreboding final scene of the play depicts an angry mob descending on the Stockmann family. As the incensed crowd gathers, the doctor huddles his family and tells them:

> [R]emember now, everybody. You are fighting for the truth, and that's why you're alone. And that makes you strong. We're the strongest people in the world, and the strong must learn to be lonely.[11]

As the curtain falls, the crowd begins to thunder and another rock is thrown through the remaining window of the family's home. The family's future is anything but certain (Act 3).

Analysis: The role and responsibility of the follower

We turn now to the analysis of the play and what it has to say about the role of the follower and importance of effective followership. In so doing, we will examine the interplay between the roles of leader and follower, the importance of the leader–follower relationship, the various types of followers found in the play, and finally the ethical responsibilities of followers in the leadership process.

One of the most noteworthy aspects of the play for our purposes is that it offers a poignant example of the indistinct line between leaders and followers. This gray area can readily be seen in the interchange between the play's protagonist, Dr. Thomas Stockmann, and the play's antagonist, Mayor Peter Stockmann. The doctor is a leader in the sense that he is attempting to convince the mayor and his fellow citizens that the town's springs are poisoned and that they should fix the problem. In another sense, however, he is a follower. He is a citizen of the town and, thus, is in a subordinate position to the mayor. Also, he is an employee of the springs and serves at the discretion of the board, and, in that sense, he is a follower as well.

The relationship between the doctor and the mayor illustrates the dynamic between leaders and followers that is such an important part of the leadership process. Both Dr. Stockmann and the mayor desire the success of Kirsten Springs. They do indeed have a common goal. However, their assessments on the means of achieving that goal are very different. This illustrates the idea that leaders and followers are accountable to one another. Both are responsible for achieving the *common* goal and both leaders and followers are responsible for the *ethical implications of the means used* to achieve that goal. However, we must ask ourselves, is Dr. Stockmann a leader if the town does not choose to follow him? This leads us to the problem of follower motivation.

Let us consider for a moment that Dr. Stockmann *is* a leader simply in the sense that he is attempting to influence others on a path to take to reach their common goal. Although the doctor's intent is quite probably noble, and the springs are most likely poisoned, he is ultimately unsuccessful in leading people to his desired end. In attempting to lead the townspeople to reconstruct the springs, the doctor threatened his fellow followers' most basic needs. (Again, we will return to this subject in Chapter 5 when we discuss the context of the leadership situation.) This is not to suggest that the doctor should not have continued to pursue his goal, but had he considered his followers' motivation and how to simultaneously meet their needs, he may have been more successful. Leaders are wise to consider their followers' motivation and the best way to influence them to reach their goal. As one of our friends likes to say, "To be a leader, you have to have *at least one* follower!"[12]

Throughout the play, the doctor is given the opportunity to adjust his strategy. Perhaps he could have worked to purify the water of the springs in the short term as was suggested, and then ultimately have the opportunity to reconstruct the water system. Contrarily, he could have directed his potential followers' anger toward the tannery upstream that was causing the problem and create a new goal of shutting down the plant, or at least preventing it from poisoning the town's water supply. However, because he did not consider his followers' motivation and only focused on his personal goal of reporting the poisoning and reconstructing the water system, he lost sight of the common goal, which was the success of the springs and the welfare of all the stakeholders. Followership is ultimately a choice. Leaders and followers are co-producers of leadership. By choosing to follow, or not to follow, the followers give their leaders the authority and power to lead.

This leads us to more deeply consider the relationship between Dr. Stockmann and the mayor. Many theories of leadership place the process of leadership centrally in the relationship developed between leaders and followers. This poses a particular challenge for Dr. Stockmann and his brother, the mayor. The brothers have a tumultuous history fraught with sibling rivalry. As seen throughout the story, the mayor is hardly the ideal leader. He is arrogant, manipulative, deceitful, and abuses his power. He feels as though his brother, Dr. Stockmann, owes him his loyalty and silence for helping him and his family out of a difficult situation in the past. Likewise, although Dr. Stockmann presents himself as the noble lone steward of the truth, he is also arrogant, unyielding to compromise, and possesses his own jealous motives for desiring leadership. In the end, all parties involved suffer—not the least of whom are the visitors to the springs and the people of the town. The truth will ultimately be revealed, sooner or later, when the visitors to the springs become ill. One is left to wonder if all parties could have found a happier end to this story had the relationship between this leader and follower been better. The tragic relationship between one leader and one follower led to tragic consequences for everyone and demonstrates the significance of the leader/follower relationship.

But Dr. Stockmann is by no means the only follower in the play. Many of the play's characters illustrate various theories of followership. Of particular note is Robert Kelly's typology of leadership that he proposes in his work "In Praise of Followers."[13] Kelly presented one of the first theoretical models for the study of followers in which he identified five types of followers along an axis of participation (active/passive) and along an axis of critical thinking (independent/dependent).[14] (See Figure 3.1.) Depending on where a follower falls on the participation and critical thinking axes, Kelly identifies them as sheep, yes people, alienated followers, survivors, and effective followers:

- *Sheep* are passive followers possessing low critical thinking skills. They unquestioningly perform what is required of them, but no more. They are completely dependent on their leaders for direction.
- *Yes people* actively support the leader and the goal, but contribute little to no critical thought to the process. Never do they question the authority or the direction of their leaders.
- *Alienated followers* possess high independent critical thinking skills, and they are capable of contributing to the leadership process, but they are often disgruntled and cynical so they refuse to do so.

- *Survivors* adapt to the needs and desires of their leaders and situation. They are capable of critical thought and participation if called on. However, their goal is not so much to achieve the common goal of the group as it is to achieve their personal goal of surviving in the organization.
- *Effective followers* are strong critical thinkers, committed, and actively pursue the common goals of the group. They challenge their leaders if the situation warrants it or if a leader's direction threatens to distract from the common goal.

Figure 3.1 shows various characters from the play plotted on the two axes of participation and critical thinking that Kelly described.

Each of these types of followers can be seen in the play. First, there is the character of the newspaper publisher, Alasksen. He may be best described as one of Kelly's sheep. He is loath to make a commitment, and in the end, he simply does what is asked of him. When he is prevailed on to lead the town meeting in which Dr. Stockmann is to report the truth about the springs, Alasksen simply becomes a puppet of the people and prohibits Dr. Stockmann from presenting his evidence. Kelly describes ineffective followers as "buying into the hierarchy and seeing themselves as subservient, vacillate between despair over their seeming powerlessness and attempt to manipulate leaders for their own purposes."[15] This describes Alasken's followership well.

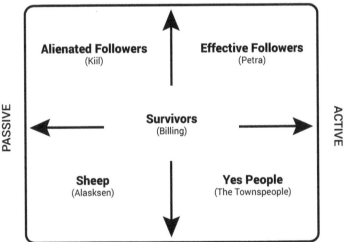

Figure 3.1 Characters in *An Enemy of the People* and Robert E. Kelly's five followership patterns

Reprinted by permission of Harvard Business Review. R.E. Kelly, "In Praise of Followers," Harvard Business Review, 66, 6 (1978): 142–148.

Likewise, there is Kelly's alienated follower, Morton Kiil, who holds a deep resentment against the town mayor for removing him from Kirsten Springs' Board of Directors. He is capable of assisting the leadership of the town; he even owns the tannery that is the cause of the pollution and could address the problem directly, but he refuses to do so. He removes himself from effective followership.

Similarly, Billing, one of the editors of the *Messenger*, starts out as an effective follower seeking to promote the good of the town, but in the end, he too abandons his conviction to protect his own interests. He is a survivor.

The townspeople represent Kelly's "yes people" well. They actively pursue the mayor's goal and refuse to critically examine the evidence against the mayor's position. In the end, the mob of "yes people" actively participate in silencing—and what appears to be murdering—the doctor and his family.

Finally, there is Petra, Dr. Stockmann's daughter. She understands the nature of the problem her father has exposed, and she actively supports her father in pursuing a solution. Miller describes her as "Ibsen's clear-eyed hope for the future—and probably ours. She is forthright, determined, and knows the meaning of work."[16] In short, she is an example of Kelly's effective follower.

Kelly's model as seen here comports well another typology of followership developed by Ira Chaleff in his book *The Courageous Follower*.[17] Chaleff groups leaders and followers around a common purpose, not unlike the Five Components of Leadership Model presented in this text (see Figure 3.2). In his

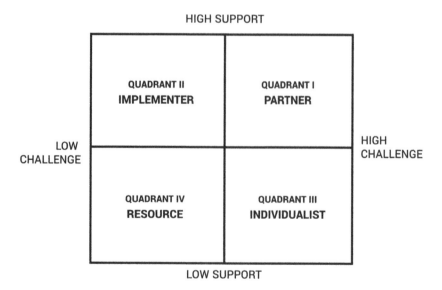

Figure 3.2 Chaleff's followership quadrants

model of followership styles, Chaleff creates a classification of followers based on 1) "the degree of support a follower gives a leader," and 2) "the degree to which the follower is willing to challenge the leader's behavior or policies if these are endangering the organization's purpose or undermining its values."[18]

Much like Kelly's typology, Chaleff identifies four styles of followership: partner, implementer, individualist, resource:

* *Partners* offer high support and high challenge.
* *Implementers* offer high support and low challenge.
* *Individualists* offer low support and high challenge.
* *Resources* offer low support and low challenge.[19]

Chaleff identifies ideal followers as *partners*—those who offer high support for their leader, but who are also willing to challenge their leaders and the process by which they achieve the group's goals. There is an absence of these types of follower in the play, and this absence is the main reason for the dire consequences for the Stockmann family, as well as the town and its visitors. Dr. Stockmann does fit Chaleff's definition of an *individualist* well. He challenges his brother, the mayor, but offers him no support in achieving the common goal. No, Dr. Stockmann is not the ideal follower, but it also seems that the town's leader, the mayor, discourages any kind of healthy followership. There is a brief interchange between the doctor and the mayor that illustrates this:

> *Dr. Stockmann*: Peter, don't you think it's a citizen's duty to share a new idea with the public?
> *Peter Stockmann*: The public doesn't need new ideas—the public is much better off with old ideas [. . .] I told you the stakes you are playing for here, and now I am going to give you an order. And I warn you, you had better obey it if you value your career.
> *Dr. Stockmann*: What kind of order?
> *Peter Stockmann*: You are going to deny these rumors officially
>
> [. . .]
>
> *Dr. Stockmann*: My convictions come from the condition of the water. My convictions will change when the water changes, and for no other reason.
> *Peter Stockmann*: What are you talking about convictions? You're an official, you keep your convictions to yourself.
> *Dr. Stockmann*: To myself?
> *Peter Stockmann*: As an official, I said. God knows, as a private person that's something else, but as a subordinate employee of the Institute, you have no right to express any convictions or personal opinions about anything connected with policy.
> [. . .] I forbid you as your superior, and when I give orders you obey.[20]

This exchange between the mayor and the doctor illustrates an essential aspect of Chaleff's scheme: Leaders have the responsibility to encourage effective followership and create a safe atmosphere for creative dissent.

In the mayor's case, however, he keenly seeks to create followers who are simply *implementers* who will actively support him with little challenge, or at the very least *resources* who will do what they are told and dare not question his authority. He aggressively seeks to suppress any follower who challenges his authority and will use any means necessary to do so, even such means as threatening to fire the doctor, intimidating the publishers and editors of the newspaper, and threatening the townspeople with an unbearable tax. Perhaps the best reason for the lack of effective followers in the play is because the mayor does not want or encourage them. There is a brief exchange between Dr. Stockmann and his wife, Catherine, that illustrates this point. Pleading with her husband to use caution she asks him, "Without power, what good is the truth?"[21] Although she is chastised for her candor, Mrs. Stockmann has a point. Leaders must be willing to relinquish some of their power if they desire their followers to be effective. Likewise, there are times when followers must seek to remove their leaders from power if they hope to ethically obtain the common goal. Nevertheless, it must be pointed out that the mayor's intimidating and toxic style of leadership and his purposeful grooming of ineffective followers does not release his followers from their ethical responsibility to hold their leader accountable. As Chaleff notes:

> Healthy followership is a conscious act of free will. When we no longer believe that what we are doing is the best thing or the right thing, we must review our options and their respective consequences. Otherwise, we are in danger of becoming automatons with a dulled sense of responsibility for our actions, who serve neither ourselves, the leader, the common purpose nor society well.[22]

Both Kelly and Chaleff provide the foundation for one of the most recent models of followership developed by Harvard professor Barbara Kellerman (see Figure 3.3). In her book *Followership*, Kellerman presents another typology of followers, but rather than plotting her types of follower on two axes, she places them on a single continuum according to their level of engagement.[23] It is important to note, according to Kellerman and her typology, that followers can be those who either *support* or *oppose* their leaders and their goals. She identifies and defines five types of followers: isolates, bystanders, participants, activists, and diehards:

- *Isolates* are entirely disengaged from the leadership process. They neither know nor do they care about their leaders or their goals.
- *Bystanders* are aware of their leaders and goals, but make the conscience choice to disengage, thus supporting the status quo.
- *Participants* display at least a modest degree of support or opposition to their leaders and their goals.

- *Activists* are highly engaged in either supporting or opposing their leaders and their goals.
- *Diehards* are willing to, quite literally, die in support of or opposition to their leaders and their goals.

Figure 3.3 Kellerman's followership continuum

Kellerman argues that although followers "have less power, authority, and influence, than do their superiors," they are by no means without these resources. But Kellerman also notes, with the followers' power comes the responsibility to hold leaders accountable: "Those who are immediately responsible for bad leadership include bad followers just as much as bad leaders."[24] Even in their silence or refusal to act, Kellerman argues, followers such as her *isolates* and *bystanders* are tacitly implicated in supporting the status quo of their leaders and the consequences of their goals.[25] This allegation has weighty implications. Unseen townspeople or silent characters who never make their way to the printed page in Ibsen's work are as responsible as the mayor and board for the sickness and perhaps death of visitors to the spring, as well as the fate of the Stockmann family. Even the most passive follower bears a responsibility for leadership, whether he or she acknowledges it or not.

Most of the characters we see in *An Enemy of the People*, however, are prime examples of Kellerman's *participant, activist,* and *diehard* followers (see Figure 3.4). Captain Horster who allowed the doctor to use his home to call a town meeting to report his news of the springs is a prime example of a *participant*. The captain paid a weighty price for his participation, but he is the most consistently supportive and ethical follower found in the play. Other characters, such as Hovstad, one of the editors of the newspaper, fit the definition of Kellerman's *activists*. He begins by aggressively supporting the doctor, opposing the mayor, and working to publish the news of the poisoned springs. When the mayor pressures him, however, and his own living is threatened, he quickly changes course to actively suppress the doctor's news. Finally, there is Dr. Stockmann, who is perhaps the most vivid example of Kellerman's *diehard* follower type found in dramatic literature. He is, quite literally, willing to die for his cause, and at the end of the play it appears that he will.

Unfortunately, the doctor's opposition to the mayor and his cause affects not only him, but also the lives and livelihood of his family and friends. Followers may pay a hefty price for their refusal to follow. As painful as thoughtful followership may be, if followers abdicate the responsibility of their role in the leadership process, they forfeit their ability to create change. No longer can followers defer to the romantic idea that leaders are wholly

Figure 3.4 Kellerman's followership continuum with characters from *An Enemy of the People*

responsible for the good, or bad, outcomes of the common goal. They are complicit with the leadership process, willfully and wittingly or not. Many people do not consider the ethics of followership until they are placed in a position in which they have to make a choice to courageously take a stand. Given the gravity of the problem and the context in which Dr. Stockmann was operating, he very well may have made the only ethical choice available to him. Sometimes the only *right* choice for followers is to choose *not* to follow. Such is the case of whistleblowers—those who draw attention to the unethical practices of a leader or organization to protect the common good. In the end, perhaps the most important lesson of the play is the ethical obligation of healthy followership and the responsibility that all followers must bear.

Summary and concluding remarks

In this chapter, we have examined the role and responsibilities of followers and their importance to the leadership process. Ibsen's play *An Enemy of the People* provides us with a prime example of followership. It also explores the value of follower motivation, the significance of the relationship between leaders and followers, and provides examples of the various typologies of followers created by scholars in the field of leadership studies, such as Kelly, Chaleff, and Kellerman. Finally, it raises important questions about the ethical responsibilities of followers and when they must make the choice *not* to follow. It also, however, forces us to examine our own followership. How often have any of us been swept along with the majority for fear of the consequences of speaking truth to power? Perhaps there comes a time in all followers' lives when they must say "NO!"

As the area of followership has continued to evolve, some have asked the question, "To what extent do followers really need leaders?" Such is the case with those who propose notions such as shared and dispersed leadership.[26] Others would argue that there is and will always be a need for leaders. There is a brief but humorous exchange between two minor characters in the play that illustrates this balance well. One of the newspaper publishers, Billing, addresses Captain Horster. Billing says: "Society, Captain, is like a ship—every man should do something to help navigate the ship." Captain Horster replies, "That may be all right on shore, but on board a ship it doesn't work out so well."[27] In fact, both observations are true. Followers need leaders and leaders need followers, and it is our responsibility to play both of these roles well.

Questions for discussion

• There is a line in the play in which the mayor, Peter Stockmann, tells his brother the doctor:

"God knows, in ordinary times I'd agree a hundred per cent with anybody's right to say anything. But these are not ordinary times. Nations have crises, and so do towns. There are ruins of nations, and there are ruins of towns all over the world, and they were wrecked by people who, in the guise of reform, and pleading for justice, and so on, broke down all authority and left only revolution and chaos"[28]

Are there times when a follower *should* be silent in order to protect the larger community? If so, when and in what circumstances?
• After reading the play, what are some key lines that stand out to you as being particularly insightful to understanding good followership?
• In Chapter 2, we discussed the tension between the primacy of the individual and the primacy of the group. How is this tension seen in *An Enemy of the People*? What are some moments in the play that illustrate this tension?
• Do capable and motivated followers need leaders? Why or why not?
• Think of a situation in which you were a follower. What could you have done to increase your effectiveness?

Additional resources

R.E. Riggio, I. Chaleff, and J. Lipman-Blumen, *The Art of Followership: How Great Followers Create Great Leaders and Organizations*, San Francisco: Jossey-Bass, 2008.
B. Shamir, R.I. Pillai, M.C. Bligh, and M. Uhl-Bien, *Follower-Centered Perspectives on Leadership: A Tribute to the Memory of James R. Meindl*, Greenwich, CN: Information Age Publishing, 2007.

Notes

1 H. Ibsen, *An Enemy of the People*, R.F. Sharp trans. Available at http://www.gutenberg.org/files/2446/2446-h/2446-h.htm. Accessed August 13, 2014.
2 J.C. Rost, *Leadership for the Twenty-First Century*, Westport, CN: Praeger, 1991, p. 107.
3 For encyclopedic summaries and references of the literature on followership, see M.C. Bligh, "Followership and Follower-centered Approaches," in A. Bryman, D. Collinson, K. Grint, B. Jackson, and M. Uhl-Bien, eds., *The Sage Handbook of Leadership*, Los Angeles: Sage, 2011, pp. 425–436; B.M. Bass and R. Bass, "Followers and Mutual Influence on Leadership," in *The Bass Handbook of Leadership: Theory, Research, and Managerial Applications*, 4th edn., New York: Free Press, 2008, pp. 400–436.

4 We are basing our definition here in part on B. Kellerman, *Followership: How Followers are Creating Change and Changing Leaders*, Boston, MA: Harvard Business Press, 2008; and J.W. Gardner, *On Leadership*, New York: Free Press, 1990.

5 For example, see Chapter 11 in which we discuss Confucius and Lao Tzu and their recognition of the importance of followers in their writings *Analects* and the *Tao Te Ching*. Aristotle also noted the importance of followers in his *Politics*.

6 H. Heiberg, *Ibsen: A Portrait of the Artist*, J. Tate trans., Coral Gables, FL: University of Miami Press, 1969, p. 220.

7 There has been some controversy about Ibsen's original play and scenes in which Ibsen seemed to provide racist arguments about "individuals bred to a superior apprehension of truths . . . and who have the natural right to lead." Miller addressed these passages in his adaptation, and argued "But *An Enemy of the People*, it seems to me, is really about Ibsen's belief that there really is such a thing as truth and it bears something like holiness within it, regardless of the cost its discovery at any one moment entails. And the job of the elite is to guard and sustain that holiness without compromise or stint." See A. Miller and H. Ibsen, *An Enemy of the People*, New York: Penguin Books, 1970, p.10.

8 Quoted in M. Gottfried, *Arthur Miller: His Life and Work*, Cambridge, MA: Da Capo Press, 2003, p.163.

9 Miller and Ibsen, *Enemy*, p. 8.

10 This is a line from the play that is spoken between Dr. Stockmann and Mayor Stockmann. See ibid, p. 27.

11 Miller and Ibsen, *Enemy*, 124–125.

12 B. Kellerman, author of *Followership*, often emphasizes this point in her lectures on the subject. Available at https://www.youtube.com/watch?v=kgLcAF5Lgq4. Accessed August 13, 2014.

13 R.E. Kelly, "In Praise of Followers," *Harvard Business Review*, 66, 6 (1988): 142–148.

14 Ibid; R.E. Kelly, *The Power of Followership: How to Create Leaders People Want to Follow and Followers Who Lead Themselves*, New York: Doubleday, 1992; R.E. Kelly, "Rethinking Followership," in R.E. Riggio, I. Chaleff, and J. Lipman-Blumen, eds., *The Art of Followership: How Great Followers Create Great Leaders and Organizations*, San Francisco: Jossey-Bass, 2008, pp. 5–15.

15 Kelly, "In Praise of Followers," p. 144.

16 Miller and Ibsen, *Enemy*, 30.

17 I. Chaleff, *The Courageous Follower: Standing Up To and For Our Leaders*, 3rd edn., San Francisco: Berrett-Koehler Publishers, 2009.

18 Ibid, p. 39.

19 Ibid, p. 40.

20 Miller and Ibsen, *Enemy*, pp. 55–56.

21 Miller and Ibsen, *Enemy*, p. 59.

22 Chaleff, *The Courageous Follower*, pp. 150–151.

23 Kellerman, *Followership*, pp. 84–86, 91–93.

24 B. Kellerman, *Bad Leadership: What It Is, How It Happens, Why It Matters*, Boston, MA: Harvard Business School Press, 2004, p. 13.

25 Kellerman, *Followership*, pp. 86–93. Kellerman alleges that this this is true of both her types of isolates and bystanders.

26 C.L. Pearch and J.A. Conger, *Shared Leadership: Reframing the Hows and Whys of Leadership*, Thousand Oaks, CA: Sage, 2003; P. Gronn, "Distributed Leadership as a Unit of Analysis," *Leadership Quarterly*, 13, 4 (2002): 423–51; T. Ray, S. Clegg, and R.A. Gordon, "A New Look at Dispersed Leadership: Power, Knowledge and Context," in J. Storey, ed., *Leadership in Organizations*, London: Routledge, 2004.

27 Miller and Ibsen, *Enemy*, p. 30.

28 Miller and Ibsen, *Enemy*, p. 89.

4 The goal

A revolution is an idea which has found its bayonets.
Napoleon Bonaparte

So far, we have covered two of the five components of leadership—leaders and followers. We have explored their relationship and how they contribute to the leadership process. In this chapter, we investigate the third component— the common goal. We challenge the notion of a division of labor where leaders are expected to define the goal, while the followers implement it. Followers can also participate in decision making. The Leadership Continuum, introduced in Chapter 2, helps us consider the wider range of possibilities—from leader-directed to follower-directed approaches and their role in setting and implementing goals.

Leaders are often the focus of our attention when we are discussing the goals of an organization because we tend to associate goal setting with the person "in charge." We certainly saw this in Chapter 1 with the image of General George Washington's resolute gaze in Emanuel Leutze's painting "Washington Crossing the Delaware." This leader-centric approach to leadership falls under the "I" side of the leadership continuum, as discussed in Chapter 2. That is the traditional view of how the goal fits within leadership. However, as Chapter 3 demonstrated, followers also matter. They can contribute to the development of goals in an organization.

When leaders and followers come together under a common goal, we call that point in time the "leadership moment." Goals are part of a specific historical context. In order to understand the dynamic of goal setting and the work that is to be done to achieve it, we also need to understand the events and forces that influence the leader–follower relationship. By recognizing the importance of historical perspective in our understanding of how leadership works, we also set the stage for the next chapters, which will discuss the immediate environmental and broader cultural contexts of leadership.

Before we introduce the case study, we need to differentiate between small "g" and big "G" goals. When you arrive at the office on Monday morning, you can establish your personal goals for the week—finishing a report, cleaning your desk, answering those emails clamoring for your attention. Those are goals that you have established for yourself, often at your own discretion. Even your decision on the priorities among that list often falls under your purview. That is the small "g" stuff that occupies our daily life.

In this chapter, we are focusing on the big "G"—the institutional goals that compel leaders and followers to work together and mobilize resources toward achieving their goal. For the big "G" goals, we consider two key questions: Who defines them? Who claims them as their responsibility? To begin answering these questions, let us go back to our definition of leadership, first introduced in Chapter 1:

> Leadership is the process by which leaders and followers develop a relationship and work together toward a goal (or goals) within an environmental context shaped by cultural values and norms.

This definition simply states that leaders and followers work together toward their goals, but it does not assume who developed them and who owns them.

The case study in this chapter, Eugène Delacroix's "July 28: Liberty Leading the People," clearly introduces an example of a big "G"—the revolutions that engulfed French society in the late 1700s and early 1800s. This case helps us understand in a deeper way the dynamic between goal setting and goal implementation. What happens when the leadership moment provides opportunities for both leaders and followers to articulate their own goals? Who "wins"? What are the ethical considerations of goal implementation? These are some of the questions that we will investigate in this chapter using the painting and the French revolutions as the backdrop.

Case study: Eugène Delacroix's "July 28: Liberty Leading the People"

We recently had the opportunity to accompany a small delegation of students to a leadership conference hosted by a prestigious military service academy in the United States. One of the undergraduate students in our group was majoring in art, and was herself developing into a fine artist. A cadet from another institution who was also attending the conference could not understand why someone would study art *and* leadership. What could one possibly have to do with the other? "You don't understand," our student replied. "The way an artist places her paint on a canvas can be an act of leadership."

The French romantic artist Eugène Delacroix (1798–1863) would have been proud of our student's response to her critic. On seeing the July 1830 Revolution in France, Delacroix was so moved by the people's passion that he was inspired to paint his famous "Liberty Leading the People" (Figure 4.1.). His painting eventually became a symbol for the people of France and, more broadly, for people fighting for liberty all around the world. As he was working

Figure 4.1 Eugène Delacroix (1798–1863), "July 28: Liberty Leading the People,"1830

Oil on canvas, 260 × 325 cm
Musée du Louvre, Paris
Photo credit: Erich Lessing/Art Resource, New York

on the painting, he wrote his brother to say, "If I haven't fought for my country, at least I'll paint for her."[1] Indeed, Delacroix's painting serving as the image of revolution has proved to be a more powerful act of leadership than he ever could have accomplished by taking up arms.

Background on the painting

Before delving into a description of the painting, it is important to discuss events in the late 1700s and early 1800s that shaped Delacroix's thinking. It is important to note that the painter is trying to capture the main elements of a dramatic historical event, while adding his artistic interpretation to it. Today, France's political system is part of the Fifth Republic, which was brought about under Charles de Gaulle's leadership and the enactment by referendum of a new constitution in 1958.[2] To say that France is under its fifth republic is to invite the question about the other four. While a full description of each republic falls outside the scope of this book, we can at least discuss the first one (1792–1804), which sets in motion the issues and ideals that shaped the events depicted in Delacroix's 1830 painting.

From its glory days as a merchant and military powerhouse, France had declined in the 1700s to the point of near bankruptcy.[3] During this critical period of economic crisis, the absolute monarch, Louis XVI (1754–1793), continued to engage in a lavish lifestyle while the general population experienced severe economic hardship.[4] He convened the Estates-General (a representative body of different segments of society) in Versailles in hopes of finding a solution to the country's dire financial situation. Among policy considerations was the revamping of the tax code, which might include tax increases even for the landed aristocracy. For Louis XVI, the convening of the Estates-General at Versailles served as a way to gain the support of the main representative groups in order to implement tough policies.

Instead of leading to a peaceful resolution to the economic crisis, the political gathering opened a "can of worms." In retrospect, Louis XVI sowed his own demise by convening the very forces that would challenge his absolute power. However, did he have a choice? The economic situation was untenable, and he needed a way out. By extracting more resources from his followers, he hoped to buy time.

Once convened, the Estates-General brought to light the deep divisions and resentments brewing in French society in the late eighteenth century. The political gathering could not even agree on the voting procedures. The Third Estate, representing the middle class and poorest citizens, declared itself a National Assembly and demanded the curtailing of monarchical powers.[5]

Although members of the clergy and nobility eventually joined the cause, fears that a coup backed by the aristocracy was imminent led the masses to take to the streets in Paris in open revolt. On July 14, 1789, an incensed mob stormed the Bastille in Paris—the symbol of royal oppression—in search of munitions, and in the process ignited what came to be called the French Revolution.[6] Today, the event is still celebrated in France as a national holiday.[7]

The storming of the Bastille, while significant in releasing revolutionary energy, did not constitute an organized movement with leaders at the national level. In the countryside, the peasantry led its own uprising (the "Great Fear") against the landed aristocracy, which still clung to a feudal order. The Bastille, therefore, represented the explosion of pent-up frustrations by myriad groups—a starving peasantry suffering under the steep rise in bread prices, a growing urban merchant class (the bourgeoisie) clamoring for political power, a demoralized aristocracy fearful that a weak monarch would lead to lost power and prestige, and an intellectual class espousing the political ideas of the Enlightenment (e.g., political equality, popular sovereignty, freedom of speech).[8]

The royal family was forcefully brought from Versailles to Paris and eventually acceded to France's first constitution, which established a constitutional monarchy. The National Assembly issued the Declaration of the Rights of Man and of the Citizen, which reflected many of the revolutionary ideals under the Enlightenment. The violence was far from over, however. The poor continued to demand the end of the privileges that the nobility enjoyed. While they had successfully gained "liberty" from monarchical oppression, they also hoped for "equality."

The revolutionaries themselves were divided between the Jacobins (radical liberals who wanted the goals of the revolution to be implemented more aggressively) and the Girondins (moderates who favored the constitutional monarchy).[9] The balance of power between these two groups helped shape the direction that the revolution would take. In between them laid the *sans-culottes* (the militants who came to symbolize the bayonets of the revolution— as expressed in Napoleon's quote in the beginning of the chapter).[10]

The *sans-culottes* presented themselves as the leaders of the common people— leading the uprising. While this suggested a possible affinity with the Jacobins, the real challenge during the revolutionary period was assessing who controlled the *sans-culottes*. On many occasions, their rage seemed to run unchecked. For the middle classes (the bourgeoisie), those uncontrolled bursts of revolutionary anarchy seemed threatening and unproductive.

When the king and his Austrian-born queen, Marie-Antoinette, attempted to flee in June of 1791, they were captured near the Austrian border. On September 22, 1792, the newly named National Convention declared the end of the Bourbon monarchy and the advent of France's First Republic. The king and queen were tried and eventually executed on the guillotine—the king in January of 1793 and the queen nine months later.[11] France degenerated into a cycle of extreme violence, not only domestically, but also with many of its neighbors—Austria and Prussia, in particular—that feared the spread of revolutionary fervor beyond French borders.

Eventually the Jacobins gained the upper hand under the leadership of Maximilien de Robespierre.[12] Through the Committee of Public Safety, he ushered in the Reign of Terror (1793–1794)—the massive slaughter of perceived opponents of the revolution; in particular, the aristocracy and the clergy. In the meantime, the poor continued to rebel, sensing that the bourgeoisie was now in control of the government and protecting its own economic interests at the expense of the underclass. The *sans-culottes* themselves became the target of the Committee of Public Safety. Rather than leading the country to order and stability under a single leader, the Reign of Terror caused a backlash, which eventually led to Robespierre's own downfall.

The succeeding five-man directory had Robespierre executed and enacted yet another constitution. This group proved just as corrupt and incompetent as the previous monarchies, opening the door for the rise of Napoleon Bonaparte as the military dictator ("first consul") in 1799, the official end of the French Revolution. Order was established, but at the cost of the political ideals that had motivated the spirit of the revolution in the first place.[13]

Between Napoleon's coronation in May of 1804 (ending the First Republic) and his downfall in 1814–1815, the ideals of the French Revolution remained alive. The Bourbon Restoration (1814–1830) under the Charter of 1814 brought back to power Louis XVI's heirs (first Louis XVIII, and later his brother Charles X), this time under a constitutional monarchy. Some of the gains of the revolution—such as equality before the law, press freedoms, and representative government—were incorporated into the new constitution.

The balance between centralization of power around the monarch and popular sovereignty under a representative government remained tenuous under the Bourbon restoration. Charles X was part of the absolutist wing of Louis XVI's court when the French Revolution first broke out in 1789. He had fled to England and waited until Napoleon had fallen from power in order to return and rejoin the Bourbon's family rule. Once crowned the new king in 1824, Charles X surrounded himself with supporters of absolutism and waited for the opportunity to dismantle the constitutional monarchy.

While the king had a clear goal (centralization of power), the parliament proved deeply divided. Two powerful forces clashed over control of the parliament. On one side, the ultraroyalists hoped to work with Charles X and maintain the supremacy of the king as the head of the state. On the other side, the liberals favored a more powerful parliament as a check to the king's power.

As the country faced economic crisis once again in the late 1820s, the deadlocked parliament gave the king his opportunity to act. In 1830, he issued the "July Ordinances"—a series of measures, which included the dissolution of the parliament, restriction on press freedoms (long associated with the liberal movement), restrictions of suffrage to the nobility alone (which would favor the ultraroyalists), and the call for new parliamentary elections under the new rules (which would restrict the liberals' access to the political process).

At the core of the July Revolution, the subject of Delacroix's painting, was Charles X's attempt to centralize more power around the monarchy.[14] The outbreak of violence in the streets in 1830 served as the "second act" of the French Revolution.[15] Riots and looting eventually led Charles X to flee Paris in August, and the Chamber of Deputies declared the throne vacated and appointed Louis-Philippe (the Duke of Orleans) as the "King of the French." The constitutional monarchy was restored, and the July Ordinances declared invalid. The Orleans house would rule France until 1848, when yet

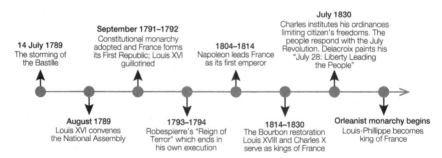

Figure 4.2 Timeline illustrating the historical context surrounding Delacroix's painting "July 28: Liberty Leading the People"

another revolution dethroned the monarchy and established the Second Republic. This was the context in which Delacroix painted his famous work (see Figure 4.2).

Description of the painting

Delacroix's painting is large in scale measuring 260 cm × 325 cm. He completed the painting in an astonishing three months, the haste of which can be seen in the painting's rough brushstrokes. Delacroix's romantic style was itself a kind of leadership and a rejection of the neoclassical style that was popular at the time.[16] The style and subject were deliberately intended to shock the viewer.

Subjects of the painting can be viewed as a large pyramid, the apex being the French *tricolore* and the base being the cobblestone barricade littered with corpses. The major subject of the painting is, of course, the goddess at the center, an allegorical representation of Liberty.

Unlike previous depictions of gods and goddesses, however, Liberty is not hovering over the people, watching them from afar. She is among them. Fighting with them.

She is captured mid-stride, hair and sash flying, as she leads her followers to battle. Her breast is bare and dirty with the filth and grime of war. She carries a rifle and bayonet and tramples on the corpses of her enemies. She harkens to the role of women in the Revolution who took up arms beside their male counterparts and fought in the streets. The goddess wears the red Phrygian cap that was typically associated with the pursuit of liberty and freedom in the days of Ancient Greece and Rome and again later in revolutionary France. This goddess is a street fighter.

To her left is a wild-eyed street urchin, pistols in hand, and carrying an ammunition pouch, likely stolen off the corpse of a Royal Guard. To her right, Delacroix painted himself into the scene as a young bourgeois—his top hat rakishly tipped. Although not a member of the street life surrounding him, he too has taken up arms for Liberty's cause. The painting, therefore, can be interpreted as the artist using his craft to make a personal political statement. He identifies with the revolutionary goal—liberty. Beside him is another man—most likely from a poorer class than his foil, but equally fearful and desperate. He brandishes a saber, in all likelihood stolen from a dead member of the infantry.

A woman clutches Liberty's leg out of hope and fear. A child grips a stone and poses ready to strike. The mob swarms the scene. Rich and poor, men and women, young and old, all follow Liberty's call. In the background, smoke and flames engulf the homes of Paris and the flying buttresses of Notre Dame. In the distance, a tiny *tricolore* waves from the famous church's bell tower. The naked and looted bodies of members of the Royal Guard lie at the feet of Liberty and the mob. The viewer is forced to confront the harsh reality that the road to liberty is often paved in blood.

After ascending to the throne, Louis-Philippe purchased Delacroix's painting, but ultimately banned its display, fearing that the painting would continue to incite riots and revolution, which would weaken the legitimacy of the Orleans monarchy. For him, the fight was against the excesses of Bourbon rule and not against constitutional monarchy itself. The idea of the Royal Guard being trampled in the streets was seen as incendiary and a subversive threat to the crown.

For years the painting disappeared and was hidden from public view. Only in 1874, 44 years after it was painted and 11 years after Delacroix's death, was it finally purchased by the Louvre Museum where it hangs to this day. Since that time, "Liberty Leading the People" has become an icon and symbol of France. It serves as an idealized symbol of a common goal and the invisible force that unites people to pursue something larger than themselves.

Analysis: Goal setting and implementation

The revolutionary period in the first half of the nineteenth century in France represents a powerful illustration of the tug-of-war between the forces of centralization around the monarch (the "I" side) and the various groups (bourgeoisie, working class, peasants) clamoring for a voice in the political process (the "WE" side). On the one hand, we see the absolute monarch claiming sovereignty and power over his subjects—the image of the leader "in charge." On the other hand, the people rise up and claim for their right to shape their own destiny.

This epic struggle shows what we call a "leadership moment" in French history—that point in the leadership process under which leaders and followers struggle to work together (or in competition) while influenced by an uncertain environment (the rise of representative democracy) and changing cultural norms and values (popular sovereignty). In reality, this struggle is not uncharacteristic of what leaders and followers face in most organizations as they are trying to define the common goal—albeit, hopefully, without the chaotic violence and bloodshed.

As Figure 4.3 shows, the leadership moment is that time period when leadership is "happening." We cannot divorce leadership from the historical developments taking place in an organization, in society, or even around the globe. Note in Figure 4.3 that the leadership moment is identified as independent of whether the goal has been attained. In other words, we do not define leadership in terms of goal attainment. Can leadership take place *before* goals are attained? Certainly! Based on our definition of leadership, we can observe the leadership process regardless of whether the goal has been attained.

In "Liberty Leading the People," Delacroix suggests a radical proposition—the goal itself plays the leader role. As you probably noticed in the historical background above, the revolutionary fervor during that period in French history did not yield the type of larger-than-life leader guiding the people toward democracy. When Napoleon came to the scene, he was not associated with

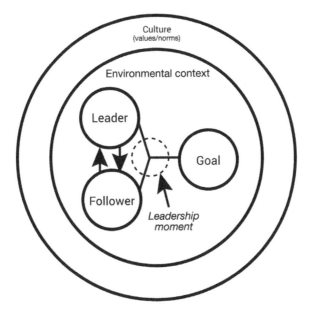

Figure 4.3 The leadership moment

advancing the revolution. Rather, he represented the effort to put the "brakes" on the excesses of the revolutionary hysteria. The power-wielding monarchs came to represent the "I" side seeking to subjugate their followers. Liberty, therefore, served as the unifying ideal that brought people together under a common goal.

This concept has been referred to as the "invisible leader"—the common purpose that brings leaders and followers together. One scholar, Mary Parker Follett, writes: "Loyalty to the invisible leader give us the strongest possible bond of union."[17] This is exactly what Delacroix captured in his metaphorical depiction of Liberty quite literally 100 years before Follett was writing. It was the invisible leader, Liberty, who motivated the followers and eventually led to the establishment of France as a constitutional republic. As we mentioned in Chapter 1, leadership is about much more than simply the leader. It is the Goal—the invisible leader—that brings leaders and followers together.

Directly related to the importance of the goal to the leadership process is the importance of developing a compelling vision. There must be a reason for the leaders and followers to come together. There must be a destination at the end of the journey. In our case study, personal liberty and a desire for a better life provided the vision for the future. In France's case, the path to obtain that vision was one of revolt.

Here we can draw an interesting parallel between Emanuel Leutze's "Washington Crossing the Delaware" (introduced in Chapter 1) and Delacroix's painting. They both place the goal as the central focus of their paintings. They both have a surreal glow in the background that draws our attention to those goals (the American flag and Liberty). They differ, however, on the depiction of leaders and followers in their interaction with the goal. In Leutze's case, Washington is clearly identified with the goal by standing next to the flag, while his followers are in a lower state outside the glow.

For Delacroix, the followers are more important than the leader. Followers are directly associated with the goal. The leaders were linked to abuses of power, lack of virtues, and were an impediment to the accomplishment of their true goals. The symbol of the leader's power—the Royal Guard—is relegated to the bottom of the painting, depicted as a defeated army. Their power is stripped from them (symbolized by the naked body on the ground) and transferred to the people carrying the bayonets.

Notice that Liberty is carrying a bayonet, as well. In other words, the goal in itself also has power. While in earlier chapters we discussed power in terms of the relationship between leaders and followers, we also must consider the power of goals to mobilize people. Ideas galvanize leaders and followers.

Big ideas serve as the larger-than-life players in the leadership moment. Big ideas inspire people to follow them and compel them to take up arms and even die for them. For Delacroix, the goal was much more important than the leaders and followers. Therefore, Liberty is carrying the flag, and the followers are standing by her—ready to serve that cause.

Since goals are so central to leadership, we can use this painting to explore two related questions: 1) Who sets the common goal? and 2) who drives goal implementation? In goal setting, we traditionally assume that leaders develop the goals. Once goals are set, leaders and followers move toward their implementation with the followers doing the brunt of the work. We all know that the real world is a lot messier than this neat model. Delacroix presents a different proposition: Followers set the goal (Liberty) and their unleashed revolutionary energy guided goal implementation.

As we know from the historical background presented earlier in the chapter, this revolutionary explosion did not lead to liberty. Instead, the excesses of the revolts eventually led to a backlash. Should we take from this leadership moment in French history that in the absence of leaders, follower-driven goals are doomed? Not necessarily. We are suggesting that leaders have to play a constructive role in the leader–follower relationship in order for the goals to be accomplished. While the painting may be an inspiring symbol of liberation, we propose that it also serves as a reminder that followership run amok is not an ideal outcome, either.[18]

Who should set the goal in leadership? For Charles X, the answer was obvious—the leader (the king). For the bourgeoisie, the working class, and the peasants taking up arms and following Liberty, a different answer was called for—the people (the followers). The leadership continuum helps us visualize the contrasting distribution of power between leaders and followers (see Figure 4.3). The Bourbon monarchy—a hierarchical structure with leaders at the top

"I" (Individualism)

Primacy of the leader

(Collectivism) "**WE**"

Primacy of the group

Hierarchical organization
(Leader-focused goal setting)

Flat organization
(Follower-focused goal setting)

Figure 4.4 Hierarchical vs. flat organizations on the leadership continuum

and followers as subordinates—centralized the goal setting responsibility with those at the top.

Most hierarchical organizations tend to use this top-down goal-setting model. They adopt clear decision-making responsibilities and organizational charts, which allow for consistency and efficiency. The command and control approach discussed in previous chapters assumes that the leader is in charge of goal setting. Followers may be consulted, but leaders have the ultimate authority to set organizational goals.

The top-down approach is not limited only to large hierarchical organizations. Small businesses, for instance, may still be hierarchical and controlled by the vision of the founding entrepreneur. The leader who started the business has more latitude to set the organizational goals, and the employees understand that the leader is "in charge" and has the legitimacy to define the priorities. While some entrepreneurial leaders may seek input from their followers while developing the goals, they tend to have a clear vision of what they would like to accomplish and see themselves ultimately as responsible for the success or failure of the organization (see Figure 4.4).

This top-down approach can also be a function of the leader's leadership style, regardless of the organizational structure. Some leaders feel more comfortable centralizing the decision-making process in order to retain control of the goals. We would not want to leave the impression that you should consider this top-down goal-setting model as unreasonable. There may be circumstances under which we do turn to our leaders for goal setting. For instance, in crisis situations, we seem to naturally defer to the leader and expect them to "take charge" and establish a goal for the organization. The environmental context, therefore, helps shape when this model is particularly applicable.

Leaders should approach goal setting in crisis leadership with caution, however. Louis XVI sought to be more consultative and ended up on the guillotine. For Charles X, the economic crisis served as an opening for him to centralize power, which led to a backlash and exile. In both cases, they misread the leadership moment and overplayed their hand. They fixated on their individual goals (enhancing the power of the absolute monarchy) and ignored the aspirations of their followers. In those leadership moments, the leaders should have attended to the grievances of their followers and incorporated their aspirations into the development of a common goal. In other words, Louis XVI and Charles X should have moved to the middle of the leadership continuum.

Also, as we shall see in the next part of this text, there may be some cultural and normative circumstances that give rise to the preferred use of the top-down goal-setting model. Some cultures, in fact, expect that the leader be the one who sets the goal. Failure of the leader to act on that expectation may lead to a loss of "face." In other words, we cannot divorce the two contexts, environmental and cultural, from influencing when the leader uses the top-down goal-setting model. When you lead a group, you have to pay attention to those contextual clues before participating in goal setting.

If we move to the "WE" side of the continuum, we see another goal-setting model, which emphasizes a "bottom-up" decision-making process. Flat organizations are particularly prone to use this model. Followers shape the priorities, which help define the goals of the organization. Leaders in flat organizations facilitate goal setting. They do not have the power to impose their preferred goals. Rather, they depend on the followers to express their preferences. Idealized democratic organizations are often characterized as a "bottom-up" goal-setting model, as opposed to the "top-down" view on the "I" side of the continuum.

In reality, most leadership moments in organizations fall in between these two extremes. Goal setting is the outcome of constant negotiating between leaders and followers—oscillating between top down and bottom up. The distribution of power within the organization provides the mechanism through which goals are set. As a leader, your main challenge then becomes one of assessing where the leader–follower relationship is in the continuum and then adjusting goal setting accordingly.

One of the cardinal sins of the absolute monarchs of the 1700s in Europe was to see a directive approach as the only acceptable leadership style of a "real" leader. All the while, the ground below them was shifting, as new social groups (urban working class, bourgeoisie, and peasants) demanded a move toward a more participative leadership style. The world had changed, but the monarchs failed to fully understand those changes. Once the Bourbons balked, the revolutionaries "fired" the leaders and sought to redraw the leadership map.

When moving to a participative role, leaders have to be careful to understand the leadership moment. Louis XVI lacked the political leadership skills to successfully navigate the firestorm that the convening of the Estates-General in his attempt to solve the economic crisis in the late 1700s brought about. Once the Third Estate set the new goal—constitutional monarchy—and the king resisted, the revolutionary keg exploded with consequences that reverberated into the 1830s and were captured by Delacroix's painting.

We cannot assume, however, that in a flat organization the followers will speak in one voice. In a brilliant essay, Karl Marx interpreted Napoleon's rise as the bourgeoisie's betrayal of its own democratic aspirations for the sake of stability, which would ensure the continuity of the capitalist order and its economic benefits.[19] The deep divisions within French society made it difficult to fully implement the original goals of the revolution—a topic to which we now turn.

After goals are set, leaders and followers turn to the question of who will drive the process. In other words, who will sit in the "driver's seat?" It might be reasonable to assume that whoever sets the goal should also claim its ownership. Delacroix's painting seems to suggest that the followers were driving the process since they were holding the bayonets. However, goal implementation is a separate dynamic that may involve a new set of expectations. The leader may adopt a top-down approach during the goal-setting phase and later relinquish power to the followers during goal implementation.

If we look back to the painting in Chapter 1, Emanuel Leutze's "Washington Crossing the Delaware," it was easy to discern that General Washington was directly associated with the big "G" goal implementation, which was the United States' independence from Great Britain—he is standing up. What if the painter had painted the general sitting down and paddling with his followers—leaving the flag alone under the glow? Would that have changed your perspective of goal ownership? (See Figure 4.5.)

Leutze's painting reflects the traditional Western perspective of the leader's close association with goal implementation, as Chapter 6 will discuss. In this perspective, the leader is charged with developing the goals, persuasively articulating them to his/her followers, and harnessing the resources and stamina to accomplish them. Followers are treated as commodities, "foot soldiers," in goal implementation. Indeed, in Leutze's painting, their main function is to clear the ice chunks and row. While the leader is in charge of goal implementation, he/she does not do the "dirty work."

In Delacroix's painting, the followers are in charge of goal implementation; that is a revolutionary concept. They are standing, moving forward with the goal (Liberty), while the leader, represented symbolically by the Royal Guard, lies on the ground, defeated. They are still charged with the "dirty work," but so is Liberty, the street fighter. While the image in itself has a romantic overtone—thus reflecting Delacroix's own association with the romantic movement of the period, there is no guarantee that the followers will succeed. Their faces seem apprehensive, as if trampling through uncharted grounds. Indeed, they were.

When contrasting the apprehension on their faces with Washington's face in Leutze's painting, we see a much different expression and one we often assume leaders are supposed to take during goal implementation. Big "G" goals are often associated with dramatic changes and risk taking. The traditional image of larger-than-life leaders is that they are resolute, courageous, and embrace risk with gusto. They remain calm as the world seems to be falling apart around them. In looking at General Washington's face, one is hardly aware that he is standing on a boat. We can probably deduce that the followers were not too keen on anyone standing up in such a small craft, as they are trying to cross

Figure 4.5 Leutze's "Washington Crossing the Delaware" and Delacroix's "Liberty Leading the People"

an ice-filled river. Yet, he is portrayed as an image of solid determination working to accomplish a worthy goal.

In contrast, followers are often portrayed as lacking the necessary traits that would make them heroic figures in goal implementation. After all, that is what makes them followers, as opposed to leaders. Delacroix challenges our perspective of followers and provides a true tribute to followership, as we examined in Chapter 3. Liberty inspires them to take up arms and become the heroes in this leadership moment. They gain confidence by keeping their eyes on the goal. This association may involve romance and innocence, as represented by the child next to Liberty, but they are willing to die for this cause.

How far should the followers go in fighting for their common goal? In Delacroix's painting, the fact that they are carrying weapons and trampling on dead bodies would seem to suggest that they are willing to pay—and demand—the ultimate sacrifice. The brutality and excesses of the French Revolution and the violence in the streets during the 1830 Revolution, however, bring to light another important issue—the ethical dilemmas that leaders and followers face when pursuing a goal. While the outcome may be noble (liberty), should there be restrictions on the means used to achieve it?

Philosophers have pondered this question through the ages with no discernible consensus. Niccolò Machiavelli, for instance, did not draw a moral connection between the goals and the means to attain them. He claimed that one should not attempt to define whether the means are moral. Leaders should use a power calculation in order to assess whether the means can do the job. Machiavelli's reasoning reflected the prevailing thinking that has become the foundation for modern Western leadership thought, as we will discuss in Chapter 6.

Under this perspective, the most important focus for a leader should be on the attainment of his/her goals. If the goals are met, Machiavelli argued, history will judge the means as acceptable—not necessarily moral, but justifiable. That was certainly the hope of Robespierre when he sent thousands of counter-revolutionaries to the guillotine in the name of liberty. However, for the people, the morality of the means did matter. We cannot kill the ideal (Liberty) in order to save it. Once they rejected his means, Robespierre's legitimacy as the moral leader of the revolution was undermined, which brought down his reign.

We can contrast Machiavelli's amoral perspective with the one presented by German philosopher Emmanuel Kant (1724–1804) who rejected the notion that the ends justify the means. Under his "categorical imperative" framework, leaders and followers should make sure that the means and ends are always morally defensible. Kant's *deontological perspective* (doing what is right unconditionally) establishes a high bar. Moral laws are to be followed unconditionally.[20] If liberty is morally right, we should fight for it to the very end. We should not compromise those ideals—no matter what. In a way, Robespierre took this approach when refusing to compromise the goals of the revolution—protecting its "purity."[21] However, the "no matter what" takes him to a morally tenuous position. Was it morally defensible to send thousands of opponents to the guillotine in the name of protecting the purity of the revolution?

British utilitarianism offers yet a third possible answer to the ethical dilemma involving the means in goal implementation. Jeremy Bentham (1748–1832) and John Stuart Mill (1806–1873) proposed the notion that leaders and followers should pursue goals that would ensure "the greatest benefit for the greatest number of people."[22] They propose a *teleological perspective*, or *consequentialism*, under which the end determines whether the means are morally right. In fact, Delacroix's depiction of the 1830 Revolution is an example. The population is presented as defeating oppression by liberating the masses. Certainly, under this perspective we are inclined to accept that the revolution brought about the end of feudalism in the countryside and the rise of representative democracy in the capital, not to mention press freedoms, which benefited society in general. Therefore, those benefits far outweighed the loss of lives in the streets.

The utilitarian perspective serves as a "happy medium" between Machiavelli's amoral stand and Kant's categorical imperative. Louis-Philippe's response to the situation demonstrated this type of accommodation. While he represented a constitutional monarchy, he was willing to respect many of the gains of the revolution. Order, however, was important, as demonstrated by his initial reluctance to display Delacroix's painting. Revolutions stir radical feelings among leaders and followers who often are not willing to compromise their position. This rigidity leads to ideological stand offs and further violence. The French Revolution showed episodic shifts that included all three perspectives (see Table 4.1).

Charles X engaged in a power play with his July Ordinances, albeit a miscalculation. The same can be said of Louis XVI when convening the Estates-General in order to address the economic crisis. Robespierre resisted compromising, which caused a backlash and his own loss of power. In contrast, Louis-Philippe extended his dynasty by accommodating the goals of the revolution, such as a representative government.

Contemplating Delacroix's painting in this historical context highlights a difficult issue for leaders and followers: How far are you willing to go in order to fight for the common goal? When do you choose to compromise in order

Table 4.1 Ethical perspectives expressed in the French Revolution

Machiavelli	*Bentham/Mill*	*Kant*
Amoral framework	Teleological ethics	Deontological ethics
Ends justify the means	Cost-benefit calculus	Categorical imperative
Power politics	"The greatest good for the greatest number"	"Follow your values regardless of the consequences"
Charles X	*Louis-Philippe*	*Robespierre*

to secure some gains, while not being able to fully realize the ideals contained in a common goal? Is compromise a sign of failure in reaching the common goal? For leaders and followers, addressing these ethical dilemmas constitutes the biggest challenge in the leadership moment.

Summary and concluding remarks

Delacroix's painting serves as an excellent artifact to examine the dynamic of goal setting and goal implementation in leadership. When the goals of the French Revolution were halted through the Bourbon restoration, it only represented a delay by the leaders (Louis XVIII and Charles X) of the seemingly inevitable implementation of goals set by the followers. This chapter has shown the importance of leaders and followers understanding the leadership moment they are facing—the historical forces that are shaping goal setting and goal implementation. In the case of the French Revolution, the ideas under the Enlightenment had significantly undermined the legitimacy of the absolute monarchy. Facing an economic crisis, the leaders sought ways to preserve their lifestyle, while demanding more sacrifices from their exhausted, yet empowered, followers. They were empowered by revolutionary ideas that told them that they did not have to accept the status quo and remain subservient and oppressed.

This chapter also showed that a common goal can be powerful. This notion of power takes us beyond the perspective that leaders are the ones associated with the ability to compel others to follow. In Delacroix's painting, the followers are focused on the common goal, while the leaders lie on the floor, naked and defeated.

When developing, and afterward implementing, common goals, leaders and followers must understand where they sit in the leadership continuum. While they may have the freedom to choose their placement in the continuum, they cannot ignore the influence of the environment and cultural norms in shaping their choices—a topic that we will turn to in the coming chapters.

Questions for discussion

- To what ethical "school of thought" do you most ascribe? Deontological? Teleological? Machiavellian? Why?
- To what extent should leaders or followers go to achieve their goal? Should violence—or any kind of coercive power for that matter—ever be a means to obtain a goal? Under what circumstances?
- What do you believe was the monarchy's fatal flaw that led to the French Revolution? What lessons can you learn from this failure in leadership?
- What is the "invisible leader" in your life or in the life of an organization to which you belong?
- Is there ever a time for a "command and control" style of leadership? If so, when?

Additional resources

S.R. Komives, W. Wagner, and Associates, *Leadership for a Better World: Understanding the Social Change Model of Leadership Development*, San Francisco, Jossey-Bass, 2009.

B. Nanus, *Visionary Leadership: Creating a Compelling Sense of Direction for Your Organization*, San Francisco: Jossey-Bass, 1992.

Notes

1 For example, J. Jones, art critic for *The Guardian* says of Delacroix's painting, "It is *the* image of revolution in art. There is no other painting that so sums up and distills the idea of revolution." In "The Private Life of a Masterpiece," Disc 3, *Masterpieces 1800–1850*, DVD, directed by J. Winnan, L. Donahue, M. Burke, M. Gold, and C. Lynch, London: BBC Home Entertainment, 2008.

2 H. Gough and J. Horne, eds., *De Gaulle and Twentieth-Century France*, New York: Edward Arnold, 1994.

3 G. Rowlands, *The Financial Decline of a Great Power: War, Influence, and Money in Louis XIV's France*, Oxford: Oxford University Press, 2012. Part of the economic crisis, aside from disastrous harvests that depleted the country's grain reserves, was due to France's financial support of the American Revolution.

4 A.A. Caiani, *Louis XVI and the French Revolution, 1789–1792*, Cambridge: Cambridge University Press, 2012.

5 The clergy represented the First Estate, while the nobility constituted the Second Estate. The Third Estate, in essence, was a residual category, the "leftovers" in French society. Each of these estates had one vote. Although the Third Estate constituted the great majority of the population, they were only permitted one-third of the vote.

6 A. Soboul, *The French Revolution 1787–1799: From the Storming of the Bastille to Napoleon*, A. Forrest and C. Jones trans., Boston, MA: Unwin Hyman, 1989.

7 C. Prendergast, *The Fourteenth of July*, London: Profile Books, 2008.

8 M.E. Gregory, *Freedom in French Enlightenment Thought*, New York: Peter Lang, 2010.

9 P. Higonnet, *Goodness Beyond Virtue: Jacobins during the French Revolution*, Cambridge: Harvard University Press, 1998.

10 The term *sans-culottes* refers to the outfit that the militants wore. Instead of the silk knee breeches (*culottes*) that the nobility wore, the militants wore long pants. Therefore, *sans-culottes* literally means "without knee breeches."

11 N. Plain, *Louis XVI, Marie-Antoinette and the French Revolution*, New York: Benchmark Books, 2002; R. Furneaux, *The Last Days of Marie Antoinette and Louis XVI*, New York: Dorest Press, 1990.

12 M. Linton, *Choosing Terror: Virtue, Friendship, and Authenticity in the French Revolution*, New York: Oxford University Press, 2013; J.M. Eagan, *Maximilien Robespierre: Nationalist Dictator*, New York: AMS Press, 1970.

13 M. Lyons, *Napoleon Bonaparte and the Legacy of the French Revolution*, New York: St. Martin's Press, 1994.

14 V.W. Beach, *Charles X of France: His Life and Times*, Boulder, CO: Pruett, 1971.

15 M.B. Cartron, *La Deuxième Révolution Française: Juillet 1830* [The Second French Revolution: July 1830], Paris: Artena, 2005; P. Pilbeam, *The 1830 Revolution in France*, London: Macmillan, 1991; C.H. Church, *Europe in 1830: Revolution and Political Change*, Boston, MA: Allen & Unwin, 1983.

16 G. Néret, *Eugène Delacroix: 1798–1863; The Prince of Romanticism*, C. Miller trans., London: Taschen, 1999.

17 M.P. Follett, "The Essentials of Leadership," in P. Graham, ed., *Mary Parker Follett— Prophet of Management: A Celebration of Writings from the 1920s*, Boston, MA: Harvard Business School Press, 1995, pp. 168–173.

18 There is another interesting parallel between this painting and a previous case study, *The Communist Manifesto*. Ironically, the rise of the bourgeois in Europe during the 1800s fueled the resentment of the working class, which led Marx and Engels to draft the manifesto, calling for the workers of the world to unite. The Bolshevik Revolution became the "third act" of the French Revolution—but played in a different country. Once again, the followers (the proletariat) rose up against the leaders (this time, the bourgeois) and brought about the birth of the Soviet Union. The bourgeois, which had participated in the French Revolution as oppressed followers in the late 1700s, came to be considered the oppressor under the Industrial Revolution of the 1800s.

19 K. Marx, *The Eighteenth Brumaire of Louis Bonaparte*, Toronto: Norman Bethune Institute, 1977.

20 E. Kant, *Foundations of the Metaphysics of Morals*, L.W. Beck trans., Upper Saddle River, NJ: Prentice-Hall, 1997; C. Chalier, *What Ought I to Do? Morality in Kant and Levinas*, J.M. Todd trans., Ithaca, NY: Cornell University Press, 2002.

21 R. Scurr, *Fatal Purity: Robespierre and the French Revolution*, New York: Metropolitan Books, 2006.

22 J.S. Mill, *Utilitarianism*, Mineola, NY: Dover Publications, 2007; J. Bentham, *The Principles of Morals and Legislation*, Amherst, NY: Prometheus Books, 1988.

5 The environmental context

More than machinery, we need humanity.
More than cleverness, we need kindness and gentleness.
Without these qualities, life will be violent and all will be lost.[1]

Charlie Chaplin

We move now to examine the next element of the Five Components Model—the context—the specific environment in which the leader and followers pursue their common goal. When we pose a leadership question to our students, we often receive the reply: "It depends. Leadership is situational." Of course it is. However, that does not mean that we cannot examine the nuances of a situation to understand or predict the success or failure of a leadership approach or endeavor.

Throughout this chapter, we will examine the ways in which the context affects the leadership process. There are many elements that make up the specific context of the leadership situation. As we saw in Chapter 4, significant forces such as the historical, economic, and political situation at the time can have enormous consequences for leaders and followers. Likewise, there are other, sometimes less evident, aspects of the context that can also have a dramatic impact on the leadership process. Factors such as the particular industry, an organization's unique culture, or the way in which an organization faces change can have an equally dramatic bearing on leaders and followers reaching a common goal. In this chapter, we will examine many of these factors and the way they interact to create and shape the specific context of the leadership situation.

To examine this aspect of the Five Components Model, in this chapter we will analyze a classic film of the American cinema, Charlie Chaplin's *Modern Times* (1936).[2] Chaplin's film presents his loveable and mischievous "Little Tramp" character as a factory worker attempting to adapt to the rapidly changing environment of the 1930s. When most people think of Charlie Chaplin today, they think of the endearing little clown with his diminutive mustache and derby hat. But there was more to Charlie Chaplin than just the

Little Tramp. And there was more to his films than lighthearted amusement. In *Modern Times*, Chaplin says a great deal about leadership and what leadership should and should not be.

Case study: Charlie Chaplin's *Modern Times*

Modern Times, released in 1936, was the last feature length film in which Charlie Chaplin portrayed his Little Tramp character. Times were changing, and the Tramp's silent pantomime, for which Chaplin was famous, was beginning to seem anachronistic as sound made its way to the silver screen. The film itself is a hybrid of sorts between a silent film and a "talkie" and has been aptly described as "a sound film with a silent film aesthetic."[3] Chaplin fought the advent of sound in film, in part because he thought it was less poetic and sophisticated than its silent predecessor, and in part because he knew it would sound the death knell of his beloved Tramp character. Thus, in the final moments of *Modern Times*, Chaplin gives his Little Tramp a voice for the first and last time.

The film mirrors the changing times Chaplin himself was facing and gives the film its title. The subject for the film itself was based on Chaplin's response to the Ford Motor Company's assembly line process and the debilitating effects the repetitive nature of the work was having on its workers.[4] To fully understand the implications and meaning of the film, however, we have to have a deeper understanding of the broader context in which the factory and its Little Tramp were operating.

Background on the film

The decades of 1920s and 1930s played host to a rapid rise in technology that we now take for granted. The Industrial Revolution had paved the way from hand production to machine manufacturing and the process of mass production was in full swing. Inventions such as the internal combustion engine, electrification, and the assembly line fundamentally altered the way people interacted with their environment. But the progress made and the economic growth during this time was not completely without its detractors. Notably, the influential late nineteenth and early twentieth-century sociologist Max Weber warned about the negative effects industrialization and its accompanying bureaucracy could have on the human spirit and creativity.[5] Nevertheless, by the early twentieth century, the world had seemed to embrace industrialization and bureaucracy that led to the economic boom in the 1920s.

The "golden age" of the 1920s hosted unprecedented growth in the United States and in many Western economies. However, this prosperity ended abruptly with the crash of the American stock market in 1929 leading to the Great Depression of the 1930s. The world economies were sufficiently tied together for the crash to reverberate around the globe. The Depression led to many banks failing and a skyrocketing unemployment rate. Many people lost their savings and found themselves penniless and homeless. Those who had jobs were often faced with unscrupulous labor practices, hazardous working conditions, and painfully meager wages. Bread lines and picket lines were both common.

The 1930s were also a volatile time politically. Although the 1920s were a time of prosperity for some, others were not so fortunate. Germany's demise after its defeat in the Great War led to its own economic collapse and the rise of Hitler, who was seen by many at the time as a savior for the devastated country. British colonialists were violently responding to Gandhi's non-violent Satyagraha movement to gain India's independence. Meanwhile, the Bolsheviks in Russia established the Soviet Union and embraced Marxist-Leninist Communism. Many hopeless people were unaware of the abuses taking place under Stalin's regime, such as his great purges, and saw communism as a possible answer to their own desperate situation. The popularity of communist and socialist ideas in the United States lead to the "Red Scare," which culminated in the House Un-American Activities Committee, which placed many in Hollywood—including Chaplin—on the U.S. government's blacklist. This was the context in which Chaplin produced his film.

Description of the film

In *Modern Times*, Charlie is a factory worker trying to adapt to modern life during the Great Depression. The film begins with Charlie working on an assembly line in a stylized futuristic factory in which Charlie turns bolts for hours on end as they speed past on a conveyer belt. In the end, Charlie is driven to a nervous breakdown by his demanding bosses and the monotonous and mindless nature of the work. He is committed to an asylum and ultimately fluctuates between prison and homelessness. (Of course, Chaplin's comic style affects the telling of the story, but the tragic plot remains.)

No sooner is Charlie discharged from the mental asylum and cautioned by his doctor to avoid excitement when he inadvertently gets swept up in a mob of workers protesting the labor conditions of the day. In a scene comically reminiscent of Delacroix's "Liberty Leading the People," Charlie is mistaken as the leader of the group of communist malcontents and is thrown into jail.

While in jail, Charlie thwarts a jailbreak and saves the day—all the while unknowingly high on cocaine! In appreciation for his valor, the officers provide him a comfortable little "home" in the jail—a welcome reprieve from the life of destitution he faces on the streets without a job. Unfortunately for Charlie, he is pardoned in honor of his bravery in thwarting the prison break. The warden provides him with a letter of reference, and Charlie finds a job in a shipyard, but after he accidently sinks a ship he finds himself once again homeless and hungry.

His wanderings lead him to the waterfront where he meets a young woman—a mischievous gamine stealing bananas and bread to feed her family. Her father is shot while striking, and she and her sisters are orphaned. Charlie is smitten with her. The police and the welfare officers try to corral the girl, but Charlie intervenes—in part to find a way back to prison and the comforts of a soft bed and a full belly. However, Charlie's plan separates him from his new love. When he is released from jail once again, Charlie finds his love waiting for him and he secures a job as a night watchman in a department store. He and the gamine think they have found a future for themselves, but the store is burgled and Charlie, once more, mistakenly winds up in jail. When he is released, his love is waiting for him once again and helps him secure a job as a singing waiter in a cabaret where she has found work as a dancer. Their new hope for happiness is placed in jeopardy when the authorities catch up with the girl and attempt to take her to a welfare home. Charlie, however, saves the day. After all they have been through, their future finally looks bright.

Analysis: The context and its effect on leadership

The first shot in Chaplin's film pictures a clock about to strike 6:00. The credits begin and dissolve into the title card. It reads: "*Modern Times*. A story of industry —of individual enterprise—humanity crusading in the pursuit of happiness." The clock dissolves into a herd of sheep running through a gate and then morphs into a crowd of people pouring out of a subway on their way to work at a larger than life factory. The juxtaposition of these shots draws a direct parallel between what Chaplin considered the treatment of workers in his day and sheep being led to slaughter.

In the next scene, a muscular and shirtless man in what appears to be the control room of the oversized factory pulls a lever and flips a switch to begin the day. Meanwhile, the president of the factory—Electro Steel Corp.—sits behind his palatial desk completing a jigsaw puzzle and reading the funny papers. He turns to a massive screen behind his desk and scans the factory's cameras to view the workers on the factory floor. He rings a bell and tersely shouts to the shirtless man in the power room "Section Five. Speed her up!" The man responds by flipping a few levers and turning a few dials on the great machine. We can hear the behemoth start to whirr and accelerate. We then see Chaplin's Little Tramp for the first time as he repetitively turns bolts on widgets as they whizz by on a conveyer belt.

Although Chaplin's film is intended to be a comedy, his depiction of factory life was not too far from the truth at the time. Low wages, poor work-ing conditions, breakneck assembly line speeds, and capricious layoffs were all common. One of the most influential leadership theorists writing at this time was Frederick Taylor (1856–1915). He made famous his idea of scientific management that emphasized a command and control style of leadership, and the style became extremely influential in modern industry in the early part of the twentieth century.[6] Scientific management—or Taylorism as it came to be called—took its cue from the environment of mass production. Taylor suggested that people could be led and managed in the same way widgets were produced on a machine. Taylor developed his famous time–motion studies in which he would design and measure the most precise and efficient way to complete a task—even the simplest of tasks such as turning a bolt. Once this was done, workers would be selected and trained to complete the task precisely as it was designed. They were then monitored to make sure they were working as quickly and efficiently as possible. Leaders were to do the thinking. Followers were to do the grunt work.

This is certainly the case with the president of Electro Steel and Charlie. These first scenes begin to establish one of Chaplin's major criticisms of the leadership in his day, specifically the mindless obedience demanded of followers and the inequality between them and their leaders. The student of leadership watching the film today may have a difficult time taking seriously the style of leadership portrayed in the film. There is a gross inequity between the president of Electro Steel who sits behind his palatial desk and fidgets with jigsaw puzzles while his workers are driven to the point of insanity.

But there is another criticism Chaplin levels against this command and control form of scientific management—it is dehumanizing to followers. When the president of Electro Steel orders Charlie's section to speed up production, Charlie is unable to attend to his simple everyday needs that are an essential part of being human. Scratching an irritating itch or shooing a pesky buzzing bee becomes a time waste. Any such action causes production to slow down, and Charlie is firmly chastised for attending to such human needs. When Charlie does get a chance for a break, he is so accustomed to the repetitive movements required of his job that he develops a twitch. When he takes a break in the factory restroom and attempts to smoke a cigarette, the president appears on a mammoth screen and scolds Charlie for loitering.

Even the most basic biological functions are seen as suspect. An inventor arrives and attempts to market a "feeding machine" designed to feed workers while they work so they can continue to be productive during their lunch hour. Poor Charlie winds up with soup in his lap and pie in his face! In the outlandishly demanding and fast paced environment, Charlie mindlessly places himself on the assembly line attempting to turn the bolts whirring past him. He gets caught, quite literally, into the gears of the great machine—a deliberate social statement of the common man being treated as a mere cog in the machine of modern industry (Figure 5.1). Charlie has finally had too much. He suffers a nervous breakdown and begins using his wrench to tighten everything in sight—including the buttons on a rather foreboding looking woman's blouse. In his manic rampage, he destroys the factory. Finally, he is sent to the asylum.

Chaplin's commentary about the state of leadership in his day had its basis in real life. Factory life in the 1920s and 1930s could, indeed, be dehumanizing. The leaders in *Modern Times*, such as the president of Electro and his foremen, make assumptions about their employees that affect their approach to leadership and have direct implications on their followers—in Charlie's case, it drives him to madness. A prime example of this in the film is the placement of cameras throughout the factory, including in the lavatory, to constantly monitor the workers to make sure they are being productive. Likewise, the timecard

Figure 5.1 Modern Times, Charles Chaplin—Charlie caught in the machine
Photo credit: Photo by Max Munn Autrey/Sid Avery & Associates. DBA mptv (mptvimages.com)

machine that Charlie must continually punch, and the feeding machine designed to make sure workers are being constantly productive, are examples of the leader's assumptions that the followers are naturally lazy and must be prodded to produce.

This view has also its roots in leadership theory. Leadership scholar Douglas McGregor summarized two basic views leaders held about the nature of their followers—the conventional view, which he termed "Theory X," and a new view, which he termed "Theory Y." McGregor summarizes the Theory X view: "Without the active intervention by [leaders,] [followers] would be passive, even resistant to organizational needs. They must therefore be persuaded, awarded, punished, controlled. Their activities must be directed."[7] Whereas McGregor describes the Theory Y view as: "People are not by nature passive or resistant to organizational needs. They have become so as a result of experience in organizations."[8]

Again, we can see these theories on display in Chaplin's film. When Charlie does get some relief from the monotony of the factory, he dallies in returning to his job. It seems he will find any excuse to prevent his return to the assembly line—he stretches, files his nails, distracts his co-worker, brushes lint off his sleeve—anything to avoid getting back to work. McGregor would ask what made Charlie act this way? Was Charlie really lazy, or was it the stifling environment in which he found himself to blame? But Douglas McGregor was not the first or the last to ask this question (see Table 5.1).

A key event that challenged the Theory X way of thinking was seen in the now famous Hawthorne Studies conducted in the 1920s at the Western Electric Plant in Chicago—in a context that was probably not unlike the factory Chaplin portrays in *Modern Times*. Researcher Elton Mayo was interested in the way Taylor's ideas affected the workers in the plant and wanted to know the precise lighting that best enabled the workers to perform their jobs effectively and efficiently. When his team of researchers lowered the lights, production went up. When they raised the lights, production went up. When they left the lights alone . . . production went up again! This led Mayo and his team to conclude that the workers were not so much assisted by the level of the lighting in the plant, but rather they were motivated by the idea that someone in a position of leadership actually cared about them. Mayo theorized that a happy worker is a productive worker and his studies led a revolution away from Taylorism to a more humane model of understanding the importance of the leadership context—what became known as the human relations approach. Unfortunately, for Charlie, this was not the thinking at the time.

Just as the Industrial Revolution had influenced Taylor's approach to leader–follower relations, the larger historical context played an important role in developing the human relations approach. The Great Depression, accompanied by worker unrest and the class struggles that reached a pitch in the 1930s, paved the way for a more humane way of viewing leader–follower relations. This was also the time when Roosevelt instituted public sponsored relief efforts in the United States and many other national governments began adopting and practicing socialism and communism, as we discussed in Chapter 2. The human relations approach reimagined what leadership *should* be and embraced the more cooperative ideas of decentralization and participatory

Table 5.1 "Theory X" vs. "Theory Y" understandings of human nature

Theory X	Theory Y
People dislike work and are naturally lazy	People need to work to find meaning. Given the right environment, people can enjoy work
People must be forced to or coerced into making an adequate effort to achieve the common goal	People are capable of directing themselves toward the goals they choose and accept
People avoid responsibility and desire to be told what to do	People will embrace responsibility to achieve a goal if given the right conditions
People are motivated by money and fear of punishment	People can be motivated by their desire to reach their full potential
People lack creativity and avoid improvement and change	People are naturally creative, but they must be given the opportunity and environment to pursue their creativity

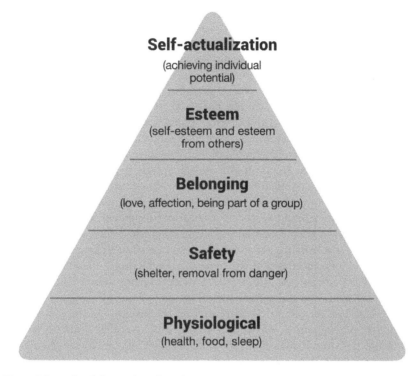

Figure 5.2 Maslow's hierarchy of needs

decision making. Rather than viewing followers as automatons, followers were conceived as adding value and intrinsically self-motivated if treated as fully functioning and thinking human beings. This is much more in keeping with McGregor's Theory Y that forces leaders to consider followers as fully functioning actors in the leadership process.

Consider a now widely familiar classic theory of follower motivation that also grew out of this time, Abraham Maslow's hierarchy of needs (Figure 5.2).[9] Maslow argued that in order for followers to reach the higher levels of motivation, their basic needs must be met. Before a leader can hope to motivate his or her followers to meet their self-esteem and self-actualization needs found at the top of Maslow's pyramid, for example, he or she must first find a way to meet their followers' more basic needs found at the base of the pyramid, such as the followers' physiological and safety needs.

What would be the scene in Chaplin's factory if the president of Electro ascribed more to a Theory Y view of followers and Maslow's approach? Leaders would not bark orders at the followers to complete impossible tasks, but would rather consult them in the best way to get the job done. Charlie would have time to attend to his physiological and mental health needs, and well as his safety needs, which would prevent him from his accident of falling into the machine and his nervous breakdown. The president and foremen of Electro Steel would consider *Charlie*'s needs. They would value him for his contribution to the company and praise him for a job well done. They would provide him with opportunities to grow and develop and he would not have to spend the rest of his days turning bolts on a massive conveyor belt. In short, the leaders of the factory would help Charlie to achieve all of the needs on Maslow's pyramid.

Although they may seem extreme, both of these approaches possess potential benefits and liabilities and may be better suited for different situations. Some environments, such as a factory, may indeed call for a more structured approach. Quality and efficiency can be much more carefully managed in such a controlled environment as Electro Steel. On the other hand, there are obvious liabilities, such as limiting human creativity and agency, which can be stifling and lead to poor morale and personal dissatisfaction. The human relations approach provided a healthy counterweight to scientific management. It focused on the needs of the followers and offered particular insight into follower motivation. Its emphasis on decentralization and participatory decision making usually results in better decisions and stakeholder ownership of decisions. Likewise, its stress on follower needs and dignity creates a more humane world. By the same token, decentralization and participatory decision making take much more time than does a "command and control" style of leadership. This may not be an option when timeliness is of extreme importance. Another criticism leveled against the human relations approach is that leaders may not always be able to trust their followers to make the best decisions. Some followers may take advantage of such an approach to the detriment of everyone reaching the common goal. Both approaches to leadership can still be readily seen practiced in all kinds of organizations today. Most organizations find themselves on a continuum between the two approaches and attempt to mix the benefits of both (see Figure 5.3).

These competing approaches enabled leaders to start to realize that they must attend to the purpose of the task at hand *as well as* the needs and wishes of the followers helping to accomplish that task. They paved the way for more complete ways of viewing leadership, such as the contingency approaches developed in the mid-portion of the twentieth century that encouraged leaders to balance their leadership style. Still, some organizations are more autocratic, leading to a more scientific management approach, whereas other are more democratic and are, thus, more in keeping with a human relations model. Depending on where an organization finds itself on this continuum, it builds a distinct culture all its own.

Figure 5.3 Continuum between scientific management and human relations approach

An organization's "culture" is its way of doing things. It entails many different aspects that collectively make up the broader context—such as the industry or field in which the organization is operating, the mission and values of an organization, and the leaders and followers, but an organization's culture is much more than just the sum of these parts.

Edgar Schein is one of the most well-known authors to write about organizational culture, specifically as it applies to leadership. He describes three levels of culture: artifacts, such as the actual physical space that houses the organization; espoused values, such as the organization's mission, goals, or formal philosophy; and the culture's basic underlying assumptions, such as those ideas about reality or truth, or even basic assumptions about human nature. Schein contends that the culture of the context determines the leadership style that is used.[10]

We can clearly see these ideas illustrated in our case study. Let us begin with the first of Schein's levels, the artifacts that are visually available for analysis. We can do this with our case study by examining two of the organizations found in Chaplin's film, the factory that we have been studying and the restaurant in which Charlie finally obtains a job as a singing waiter—quite a feat for a silent film star!

First, simply consider the physical environment of the two different organizations—a factory and a restaurant. The factory workers' dungarees are replaced with the waiters' bowties. The factory floor is replaced with the dance floor. Take into account the different industries portrayed in the film, manufacturing and service. It stands to reason that such different industries would have different environments. Whereas the factory is structured and mechanistic, the restaurant is a cacophony of humanity. Whereas the factory is run with precision and order, the restaurant is filled with chaos. Both are places of business and the outside environment is the same, but the internal environment is very different. Just as there are different internal environments, these environments may have different values.

We can infer the different values of these organizations by examining what is important to the leaders in each of these settings. The president of Electro Steel conveys his values by monitoring production on the factory floor and steadily increasing the speed of production. Every minute of every day is monitored. Employees punch in and punch out at a time clock, the assembly line is sped up throughout the day, and employees are closely monitored to make certain they are being as productive as possible. Whereas the manager of the restaurant is concerned with making sure all of the customers have a good time. Customers and wait staff sing and dance, patrons are allowed to bring their pets into the restaurant, drunken fraternity brothers are even permitted to play football with a roasted duck. (The only person who doesn't appear to be happy in Charlie's restaurant is the diner whose roasted duck is mistaken for a football.) Although the restaurant's manager still barks orders to the wait staff, the values in the café are very different from the steel factory. If we were to reduce these values to easily digestible clichés, we might summarize them with the maxims: "Time is money" and "The customer is always right."

This leads us to question the basic assumptions of the two different organizations presented in the film. The workers in the factory are thought to possess little to no ability to think for themselves. They are certainly not encouraged to be creative. As we mentioned earlier, the leader considers them in the Theory X camp—followers are considered indolent, lazy, and must be monitored to make sure they are doing their jobs. Conformity is rewarded, and deviation is punished. By way of contrast, the singers and waiters in the café are expected to like their work. Their creativity is applauded. This is the case when Charlie loses the lyrics to his song and has to make up his own tune. The customers love Charlie's improvisation, and so does his boss. He even pushes Charlie to take a bow. The manager provides a space for Charlie to do what he does best—perform—and that makes the customer happy and achieves the goal of the organization. This is much more in keeping with a Theory Y assumption that we discussed earlier. These artifacts, values, and assumptions all work together to create a unique culture in each of these organizations. Thus, as Schein contends, the culture of the organization determines the leadership style to be used.

There is another part of the context of *Modern Times* that can shed more light on this concept of culture, that is Chaplin's own response as a leader to the environmental context in which he was working. Although the United States was in economic turmoil in the 1930s, the film industry was booming. It was the beginning of the "golden age" of filmmaking. Chaplin was a wildly successful film personality by this point, and he had founded his own production company—United Artists—and owned his own studios. That kind of star power was unprecedented at the time. The first sound film, *The Jazz Singer*, was released in 1927 and the film industry was changing. "Talkies," as they were called, were in demand by audiences. This demanded that Chaplin also change to adapt to his environment. In part, *Modern Times* was a response to that demand. What does a silent film star do when he is forced to speak? Chaplin was resistant to change. When he first heard sound in films, he thought it was a fad. He reportedly said, "I give it another three years."[11] He was wrong. One author notes: "Looking into the future, Chaplin saw a crass, dehumanized sameness as a result of this supremacy of the machine [the subject for *Modern Times*] which might have brought to mind the brutal damage the arrival of sound signaled for his art."[12] In part, it is understandable that a silent film star like Charlie Chaplin would resist the change signaled by sound in film. His success was built on his silent pantomime. But it is a leader's business to foresee change and to embrace it. It took Chaplin 10 years to use sound reluctantly in his films and by that time the industry had already transformed.

But the changing film industry was not the only shifting aspect of the context in which Chaplin was operating. The political environment was also dramatically changing. Chaplin was one of the few filmmakers at the time who was openly critical of world politics and social issues. His films addressed topics such as childhood homelessness (*The Kid*), hunger and poverty (*Gold Rush*), and even the rise of Hitler (*The Great Dictator*). The themes of unemployment and the treatment of workers found in *Modern Times* were items on a long list of societal ills that Chaplin satirized in his films. His criticisms did not endear him to many people in positions of power.

Although he was once the most beloved film star in the world, by the time *Modern Times* debuted Chaplin was coming under increasing attack on all fronts. His detractors in the United States labeled him a communist for his criticisms of the economic inequality and the soulless capitalism of the 1930s. His Soviet audiences, however, were equally disturbed by his condemnation of uniformity and mass production. Stalin had just told his workers to increase production. Likewise, Chaplin's criticisms of autocracy resulted in his film being banned in Mussolini's Italy and Hitler's Germany.[13] By implication, if Chaplin was criticizing the mindless droning of American workers, he was equally criticizing the mindless uniformity communist and fascist systems required of their citizens.

What is the responsibility of a leader and an organization to address the larger context in which they are operating? Chaplin could have very easily continued to make the kind of Keystone slapstick type comedies that originally made him very wealthy and very famous. But rather, he chose to comment on the social ills of his day, ultimately to his own detriment. Chaplin's desire to address the broader context in which he was operating reflects the belief that a leader's context extends far beyond the boundaries of the direct environment in which he or she is leading.

In the corporate world, the difference between these views is articulated as the difference between a shareholder view and stakeholder view of the context (see Figure 5.4). A shareholder view of the context would contend that Chaplin's first and only responsibility was to himself, as the owner of his own film production company, and to any investors in his films; that is, Chaplin should make films that are popular and earn as much box office revenue as possible. Economist Milton Friedman argued, "There is one and only one social responsibility of business—to use its resources and engage in activities designed to increase its profits."[14] A stakeholder view of the context, by the same token, contends that a leader and organization must take into account the many parties that are affected by their actions: employees, customers, the community, governments, as well as the owners and investors: That is leaders and organizations are responsible to "individuals and constituencies that contribute, either voluntarily or involuntarily, to [an organization's] wealth-creating capacity and activities, and who are therefore its potential beneficiaries and/or risk bearers."[15]

In recent years, more people have demanded that leaders and their organizations be responsible to their many constituents. Likewise, many organizations and leaders have embraced their corporate responsibility. (We will return to this topic in Chapter 14.) It should be noted, however, that this view may come at a cost—in some cases resulting in lower profits, and in some cases resulting in personal sacrifice. This was certainly Chaplin's fate for

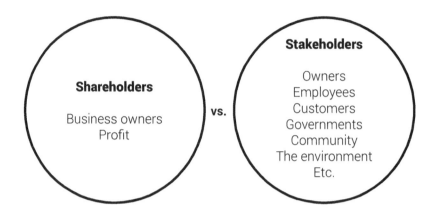

Figure 5.4 Shareholder vs. stakeholder models

viewing his responsibility extending beyond the doors of his studio and the box office.

Some were suspicions about Chaplin's patriotism because of his practice of infusing social criticism of the United States into his films. This practice earned him the watchful eye of the Federal Bureau of Investigation.[16] *Modern Times* was considered by some to be "red propaganda"—a pejorative term at the time for films critical of American policies that may be perceived as sympathetic to leftist ideology. One writer notes, "If there were any remaining doubts about the nature Chaplin's social attitudes, they were dispelled by *Modern Times*."[17]

Chaplin's outspoken commentary may have been tolerated in the 1920s and 1930s, but the political context changed after World War II. President Roosevelt had assisted Hollywood in the 1930s and exempted films from war censorship while providing them with valuable financial and political support.[18] But political conservatives started to more closely scrutinize and criticize Roosevelt's New Deal policies after the war. Chaplin had used his platform as a popular personality to make social commentary and that had earned him political enemies at home and abroad. Chaplin denied being a communist, but as the Cold War between the United States and the Soviet Union heated up, Chaplin was caught in the crossfire.[19] He made a few films after *Modern Times*, but they were never received as well as his earlier films. Certainly this was in part because of his retiring of the Little Tramp, but it was also in part because of his criticism of United States' policies. This did not stop Chaplin. In 1947 Chaplin released *Monsieur Verdoux* in which he criticized the production and use of weapons of mass production. Keep in mind that this was only two years after the United States dropped two atomic bombs on Japan. In 1952 Chaplin released his final American film, *Limelight*. He was a British citizen and had obtained an exit visa to promote the film abroad. The U.S. Attorney revoked

Chaplin's re-entry permit on his first day out of the country. Chaplin lived in exile in Switzerland and did not step foot into the United States again until 20 years later, after the political context changed once again in his favor. Chaplin learned that a leader's commitment to addressing the surrounding context can cost a great deal more than profits.

Summary and concluding remarks

Charlie Chaplin's *Modern Times* provides us with an opportunity to see how the context in which leaders and followers operate affects the leadership situation. This chapter and the previous chapter have vividly illustrated the consequences the political and economic environment may have on the leadership context. Important ingredients of the context include the nature of the task that is to be accomplished, the industry or the field in which the leader and followers are operating, the views that leaders and followers hold about the nature of leadership, and the culture of the organization. Many argue the leadership context extends far beyond the simple give-and-take between leaders and their followers within an organization. All of these factors have an effect on leaders and followers reaching their goal. Likewise, these factors change over time. Leaders and followers are wise to understand and adapt to the changes they face. This chapter has presented the significance of understanding the broader context of the leadership situation.

In the case of the factory depicted in *Modern Times*, the popularity of mass production influenced the way leaders perceived their followers and the way they related to them. Historically, the atmosphere created by this way of thinking caused followers to revolt against their leaders and demand more equality and better working environments and living conditions. The dialectic created between leaders and followers led to an important evolution in thinking about leadership, that is, both the task to be accomplished and the relationship between leaders and followers are vital aspects of the leadership process. What might be considered "good" leadership in one circumstance might be considered completely inappropriate in another.

We have also illustrated here that organizations create their own unique cultures and ways of reaching their common goals though the artifacts, values, and assumption leaders and followers share. We also considered how leaders and followers adapt to a changing environment. Again, this unique ordering of experiences that create the context of the leadership process defies the logic that leadership can be reduced down to a formula or "ten easy steps." After all, *leadership is situational*, and leaders and followers must examine the situation to determine the best way to reach their goals.

Finally, we considered the boarders of the leadership context. Are the lines drawn around the context of the leadership situation tightly constrained to limited parties, or do these lines demand a much larger understanding of those affected by a leader their followers' actions and the goals they pursue? In the next part of this volume, we expand these lines to encompass an even broader understanding of the leadership context, that is, the entire culture in which leaders and followers are operating and their collectively shared values and norms.

Questions for discussion

- In what situations might a "scientific style" of leadership be most effective? Contrarily, when might more of a human relations approach be more called for?
- What is your view of human nature? Do you resonate more with a "Theory X" view or a "Theory Y" view? Why?
- Do you think leaders and organizations should take a stakeholder view or a shareholder view of the context? Why?
- Do you think celebrities, such as Charlie Chaplin, have a responsibility to speak out on the social issues of their day? Are celebrities leaders?

Additional resources

G. Morgan, *Images of Organizations*, updated edn., Los Angeles: Sage, 2006.
P. Senge, *The Fifth Discipline, The Art and Practice of the Learning Organization*, rev. edn., New York: Doubleday/Random House, 2006.
M.J. Wheatley, *Leadership and The New Science: Discovering Order in a Chaotic World*, 3rd edn., San Francisco: Berrett-Koehler Publishers, 2006.

Notes

1 *The Great Dictator*, motion picture, Charles Chaplin Film Corporation, Los Angeles, 1940.
2 *Modern Times*, motion picture, Charles Chaplin Film Corporation, Los Angeles, 1936.
3 K. Harness, *The Art of Charlie Chaplin: A Film-by-Film Analysis*, Jefferson, NC: McFarland & Company 2008, p. 150.
4 J. McCabe, *Charlie Chaplin*, Garden City, NY: Doubleday, 1978, p. 182; C. Chaplin, *My Autobiography*, London: Bodley Head, 1964, p. 411.
5 M. Weber, *The Protestant Ethic and the Spirit of Capitalism*, translated by Stephen Kalberg. London: Routledge, 1930/2012.; M. Weber, *The Theory of Social and Economic Organization*, London: Oxford University Press, 1947.
6 F.W. Taylor, *The Principles of Scientific Management*, New York: Harper & Brothers, 1913.
7 D. McGregor, "The Human Side of Enterprise," *Management Review*, 46, 11 (1957): 22–24, 88, 89, 91. Excerpt reprinted in T. McMahon ed., *Leadership Classics*, Long Grove, IL: Waveland Press, 2010, p. 181.
8 Ibid, p. 183.
9 A.H. Maslow, "A Theory of Human Motivation," *Psychological Review*, 50, 4 (1943): 370–396.
10 E.H. Schein, *Organizational Culture and Leadership*, 4th edn., San Francisco: Jossey-Bass, 2010.
11 D. Robinson, *Chaplin: His Life and Art*, New York: McGraw-Hill, 1985, p. 389.
12 Harness, *The Art of Charlie Chaplin*, p. 150.

13 McCabe, *Charlie Chaplin*, p. 186.
14 M. Friedman, "The Friedman Doctrine: The Social Responsibility of Business is to Increase its Profits," *New York Times Magazine*, September 13, 1970. Available at http://query.nytimes.com/mem/archive-free/pdf?res=9E05E0DA153CE531A15750 C1A96F9C946190D6CF. Accessed August 14, 2014.
15 H.J. Smith, "The Shareholders vs. Stakeholders Debate," *MIT Sloan Management Review*, 44, 4 (2003): 85–90.
16 Robinson, *Chaplin: His Life and Art*, pp. 750–756.
17 D.A. Cook, *A History of Narrative Film*, 2nd edn., New York: W.W. Norton, 1980, p. 214.
18 Ibid, pp. 456, 472; also see R. Maltby, "Made for Each Other: The Melodrama of Hollywood and the House Committee on Un-American Activities," in P. Davies and B. Neve, eds., *Cinema, Politics and Society in America*, Manchester: Manchester United Press, 1981.
19 Robinson, *Chaplin: His Life and Art*, pp. 539–543.

Part II

The cultural context of leadership

In Part I, we looked at the first four components of our definition of leadership (leaders, followers, goals, and the environmental context). Now, we turn our attention to the last component—the cultural context of leadership. Our basic premise is that leadership by its very nature is culturally bounded. Our behavior as leaders and followers, as well as our social and organizational structures (the environmental context), are shaped by cultural norms and values. And that is why in our graphic representation of leadership, we place the last component as an all-enveloping circle around the other components. In other words, we cannot separate any of the other components from the cultural context.

Interest in this link between culture and leadership has grown in recent years because of the intensification of globalization.[1] As different cultures come into closer contact, leaders and followers need to gain a deeper understanding of how leadership works in a variety of cultural contexts. In particular, leaders should not assume that their followers operate under the same cultural norms and values. Globalization has made possible more communication and collaboration across national borders—a positive development.[2] However, globalization also has brought about intense conflicts, in what Samuel Huntington famously called the "clash of civilizations."[3]

As we begin our exploration of the links between culture and leadership, we need to define at the outset what we mean by this social phenomenon. In a nutshell, culture refers to the beliefs, customs, and traditions of a group of people. In computer terms, culture may be seen as the "software" of individuals within a collective. As long as the hardware is turned on, the software is telling us what to do, and how to do it.

Culture is a collective product—passed down from generation to generation. It is reinforced through repetition and in many cases "updated" through new information, experiences, and interpretations of reality. As a social phenomenon, culture is dynamic and ever changing. Some argue that with globalization, change will be even more the norm than in previous decades.[4]

Leadership is closely linked to culture because the latter provides the script that leaders and followers use individually and collectively. Culture helps us make sense of the tension between the "I" and the "WE" in the leadership continuum. Some cultures show preference to one side over the other—

Western culture focusing on the "I" compared to the strong reliance on the "WE" in Asian cultures. However, we need to guard against oversimplification. Once we dig deeper, we also see many elements of the "WE" side in Western culture, as well as the "I" in Asian cultures.

This section of the book highlights only some of the many different variations—leadership in Western, Latin American, Islamic, African, Buddhist, and East Asian societies. A more exhaustive study would be able to provide hundreds of cultural approaches to leadership. The purpose of the section, however, is to give you an entry point into these complex cultures through the lens of leadership.

We invite you to explore the following chapters with three considerations in mind. First, these chapters can be an excellent opportunity for you to understand your own cultural map and see how it influences your behavior as a leader and a follower. Second, they can also be an opportunity to expand your understanding of how leadership works in different cultural settings— different from your own. Third, they can help you reflect on themes from different cultures that resonate with you personally. They may lead you to incorporate some of those new values into your own mindset.

Following the same arts and humanities approach used in the previous section, each chapter in Part II will present a case study drawn from historical experiences that have shaped a particular culture. We must offer a disclaimer here that no single case study can reveal all of the values and norms associated with an individual culture. Rather, we will use these artifacts to suggest certain cultural patterns associated with the behavior of leaders and followers.

Finally, before charging ahead with the chapters on different cultures, we need to offer a word of caution. First, there is always a danger in making generalizations about a certain culture. We will be walking a thin line between descriptive statements and stereotypes. These chapters are designed to give the reader a broad overview of leadership in particular cultures—what Richard Lewis calls "a first best guess."[5] However, the reader should keep in mind that each person is unique and may or may not reflect the cultural values and norms we describe. Second, observers of a culture (other than their own) need to guard against misperceptions—drawing conclusions about other cultures based on their own cultural values. Sometimes we infer "facts" based on our own cultural perceptions. Third, we seek to offer a descriptive account of leadership in different cultures, as opposed to a prescriptive posturing—analyzing cultures with a judgmental eye. With those caveats in mind, we move onward.

Notes

1   See, for instance, D.A. Rondinelli and J.M. Heffron, eds., *Leadership for Development: What Globalization Demands of Leaders Fighting for Change*, Sterling, VA: Kumarian Press, 2009, J. Canals, ed., *Leadership Development in a Global World: The Role of Companies and Business Schools*, New York: Palgrave Macmillan, 2012; R.S. Bhagat, H.C. Triandis, and A.S. McDevitt, *Managing Global Organizations: A Cultural Perspective*, Northampton, MA: Edward Elgar, 2012. For a useful introduction to

globalization, see R. Mansbach and E. Rhodes, eds., *Introducing Globalization: Analysis and Readings*, Thousand Oaks: CQ Press, 2013; W. Coleman and A. Sajed, *Fifty Key Thinkers on Globalization*, New York: Routledge, 2013.

2   A. Cerra, K. Easterwood, and J. Power, *Transforming Business: Big Data, Mobility, and Globalization*, Hoboken, NJ: Wiley, 2013.

3   In fact, he saw these clashes as the most critical challenge for international relations with the end of the Cold War in the early 1990s. See S. Huntington, *The Clash of Civilizations and the Remaking of World Order*, New York: Simon & Schuster, 2011.

4   S.N. Mohammed, *Communication and the Globalization of Culture: Beyond Tradition and Borders*, Lanham MD: Lexington Books, 2011; G. Spindler and J.E. Stockard, eds., *Globalization and Change in Fifteen Cultures: Born in One World, Living in Another*, Belmont, CA: Thomson/Wadsworth, 2007.

5   R.D. Lewis, *When Cultures Collide: Leading Across Cultures*, 3rd edn., Boston, MA: Nicholas Brealey International, 2006.

6 Leadership in a Western cultural context

A prudent man should always follow in the path trodden by great men and imitate those who are most excellent, so that if he does not attain to their greatness, at any rate he will get some tinge of it.[1]

Niccolò Machiavelli

What does it mean to be a Western leader/follower? How do Western norms shape the relationship between leaders and followers? How are Western values found in goal setting and implementation? How do Western values shape the environmental context? Western culture seems ubiquitous in the twenty-first century. Everywhere we turn—no matter where we are in the world—we come into contact with some of the symbols associated with the West, particularly brands from popular culture (rock 'n' roll music, fast food outlets, movies, and television shows, to name a few).[2] While those symbols do carry certain messages about what it means to be a Westerner, in this chapter we want to dig a little deeper using the Five Components of Leadership Model developed in Part I. In this chapter, we seek to uncover some of the values and norms that shape the behavior of leaders and followers in Western societies and organizations.

What we mean by a "Western" perspective is actually the result of centuries of social change that gave rise to certain values and norms that we come to associate with the West today. In this chapter, we explore a brief history of this social change as a way to identify some of the themes that link Western values to leadership. In particular, we link Western leadership to five major historical periods—Ancient Greece (5th century BCE); Rome (spanning both its republic and empire periods from 509 BCE to 393 AD); the Renaissance in Europe (fifteenth and sixteenth centuries); the Enlightenment (eighteenth century); and the Industrial Revolution in Europe and North America (nineteenth century).

Our interest here is not to provide a detailed account of each historical period.[3] Rather, we are interested in drawing your attention to some of the cultural themes associated with each historical period that helped shape leadership in Western societies.[4] Consistent with our arts and humanities approach, we introduce a case study drawn from one of the great periods in Western civilization—the Renaissance. Niccolò Machiavelli's *The Prince* (1513) is often highlighted as a source of great leadership insight even today.[5] However, its cultural context tends to be overlooked. In this chapter, we will be examining the cultural context that produced *The Prince* as a great Western source of insight about leadership. While we can certainly argue that Machiavelli's insights may have universal applicability, we are interested in connecting his leadership worldview to specific Western values that resonate with Western societies and organizations today.

Case study: Niccolò Machiavelli's *The Prince*

Leaders or followers rarely stop to ponder how their behavior reflects centuries of experiences that shape their outlook on life today. In reality, we are all products of these historical developments. When Machiavelli wrote *The Prince*, he reflected the values associated with Florence under the Renaissance, but his approach to leadership also reflected a long history of the study of leadership by Western philosophers and leaders alike. Before we present a synopsis of *The Prince* and an analysis of the case study and its connection to a Western perspective on leadership, we need to explore this history as the backdrop to a deeper understanding of leadership from a Western context.

Origins of the Western worldview

The term "West" encapsulates more than a geographical area (Figure 6.1). It also provides a unique cultural perspective that can be traced to five historical periods spanning almost three millennia—the Ancient Greek city-states; the Roman republic and empire; the Renaissance; the Enlightenment; and the Industrial Revolution. Machiavelli's leadership thought, while technically part of the Renaissance, is a product of historical processes that converged in Florence under the House of Medici.

Using the leadership continuum developed in Part I, we can analyze the Western worldview as a pendulum, oscillating between centralization of power under a monarchy ("I") and decentralization of power under a republic ("WE"). In other words, there is no single leadership model of the West. Rather, the Western worldview is part of a continuous struggle (or, perhaps a conversation) between opposing forces—each trying to become the dominant perspective.

The powerful city-states (*polis*) that appeared around 750 BCE in what is today Greece served as the birthplace for Western civilization.[6] Two city-states, in particular, excelled in different ways—Athens with its focus on the arts; and Sparta with military might. The impressive Athenian architecture signaled the advancement of a civilization that nurtured the self-confidence of a society with radical ideas—representative government, individual liberty, and the

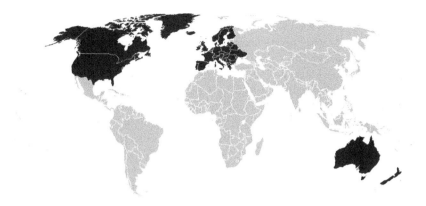

Figure 6.1 The "Western world"

cultivation of the mind.[7] Philosophers, such as Plato and Aristotle, shaped ideas about a republican form of leadership under which leaders were accountable to their followers. For Sparta, in contrast, the security of the city was viewed as paramount. Duty to the *polis* was to be prized—as a virtue to be emulated.[8]

Parallel to the rise of city-states in the Greek peninsula, a quiet village in central Italy by the Tiber River grew to become a powerful contender on the world stage.[9] Rome experienced both forms of political organizations—monarchy and republic. It first organized itself as a monarchy (753 BCE), but eventually collapsed and re-emerged in 509 BCE as a republic, the same general period when Athens dominated the Greek peninsula. The republic consisted of a powerful representative body (the senate) that collectively made decisions on behalf of its citizens.[10] While we may quibble with the true nature of this democratic representation—only the aristocracy (*patricians*) held power to the exclusion of the low-income citizens (*plebeians*)—the republic offered a competing framework for organizing the leader–follower relationship. This is a distinction that Machiavelli would make later about the principalities ruled by a monarch and a republic.

By contrast, the Roman Empire (27 BCE–393 AD) adopted a more centralized leadership model.[11] The senate continued to operate, but the emperor—beginning with Gaius Julius Caesar Octavianus—exerted considerable power and control over the known world. Although the period was filled with tales of brutality and intrigue, the Roman Empire's legal framework and institutions dramatically influenced the Western worldview.[12] Building a vast empire required not only military and economic might, but also the bureaucratic sophistication to sustain the flow of goods and services across diverse territories. This required a unifying force, which the empire eventually found in Christianity.

The adoption of Christianity as the dominant religion in the Roman Empire under Constantine I in 312 AD also helped unify the vast territory under a common set of values and norms. Historians debate the true nature of Constantine's "conversion"—whether genuine or a pragmatic (shall we say "Machiavellian"?) strategy to expand his power and control over the empire's domains, but through the Council of Nicaea in 325 AD, the empire enforced a unified Christian doctrine.[13] Regardless of his true motives, Constantine's actions had the monumental impact of linking Christianity to the West. The rise of a powerful Roman Catholic Church was able to carry that centralized leadership system beyond the fall of the Roman Empire by the hands of the "barbarians" in 476 AD. The true impact of this linkage is that much of the Western leadership ethics today is associated with Judeo-Christian principles (e.g., the Ten Commandments).

This centralization of power did not last forever. The rise of the Renaissance in the fourteenth century provided another pivotal historical point in the development of a Western worldview.[14] By the late Middle Ages in the late 1400s, the centralized leadership system by the Roman Catholic Church was showing signs of decline. The pendulum began to swing back toward decentralization. Attention was paid once again to the Greco-Roman contributions to the Western worldview—individualism, emphasis on observation as the foundation of scientific discovery, humanism, and secularism as the basis of law and organizational life. The Renaissance first flowered in Florence under the powerful Medici family and later throughout Europe.

This was the prelude to the context in which Niccolò di Bernardo dei Machiavelli (1469–1527) wrote his famous book. Machiavelli lived in Florence at a time when city-states rivaled for power in what is modern Italy.[15] The House of Medici had risen to prominence through banking and commerce and become a major force behind Florence's Renaissance in the arts, culture, and politics.[16] Machiavelli had a comfortable upbringing and eventually joined the republican government in Florence during a period when the Medici family was in exile (Figure 6.2). Machiavelli served as a diplomat for the republic. Through his travels, he came to observe firsthand how leaders handled power and vied for control over territories and populations. These insights provided the basis for his extensive knowledge of power politics.[17]

When the republic fell in 1513 and the Medici family was restored to power, Machiavelli not only lost his coveted job, but he was also briefly imprisoned and tortured for suspected conspiracy. After his release, he retreated to his family estate outside of Florence, and that is where he wrote *The Prince* (*Il Principe*) as a gift to the Medicis. In fact, he dedicated the manuscript to Lorenzo de' Medici, "The Magnificent" (1449–1492), probably the most brilliant of the Medicis who had ruled Florence.[18] This turned out to be a fruitless attempt to garner power, since the Medici family rejected the book and never gave him a government position.

The Florentine republic was restored in 1527, and Machiavelli saw this as an opportunity to get his job back. However, he could no longer be trusted by the supporters of the republic since he had attempted to ingratiate himself into the Medici government with *The Prince*. He died the same year, dis-

Figure 6.2 Rosso Fiorentino (1494–1540), "Portrait of Niccolò Machiavelli"
Casa del Machiavelli, Sant'Andrea, Percussina, Italy
Photo credit: Scala/Art Resource, New York

illusioned and heartbroken. *The Prince* did not gain wide acceptance until the late 1500s when absolute monarchs adopted the book as a useful manual on how to gain and maintain power; thus the pejorative term *Machiavellian* (for a liar and schemer) was born. However, a manual on how to lie and scheme was not the intent of its author. Rather, the book was meant to serve as a guide for the leader wishing to survive in an uncertain environment—the reality of sixteenth century Italy.

The European environment around the sixteenth century was experiencing a great deal of change. The Protestant Reformation challenged the monopoly of the Catholic Church.[19] Just four years after Machiavelli had written *The Prince*, Martin Luther's Reformation, beginning in 1517, fragmented the City of Man and connected the individual worshiper directly to the City of God without the Church's mediation. As city-states contended for power in the Italian peninsula, Machiavelli was simply reflecting the critical import-ance of power in a world undergoing dramatic changes. Once again, the absence of a unifying center of power opened up societies to the uncertainty of decentralization.

The Renaissance and the Reformation set the stage for the advent of the Enlightenment in the eighteenth century, an intellectual movement that dramatically reshaped societies around the world.[20] The American and the French revolutions highlighted in Part I were a direct result of ideas developed during this period. Rejecting the authority of the Church as the sole domain of knowledge, this period focused on logic as the process by which knowledge is acquired.

The Enlightenment—also called the Age of Reason—freed the individual from dogma and allowed society once again to organize itself around the republican and democratic ideals from the classical Greco-Roman periods. The Age of Reason, while associated with the eighteenth century, had a lasting impact on the world for the next two centuries. Combining the Protestant Reformation with the commercial rebirth under the Renaissance and the technological revolution under the Enlightenment, capitalism flourished and led to the Industrial Revolution of the nineteenth century in both Europe and the United States.[21]

The Industrial Revolution, although a Western event, had global implications. While Constantine I helped connect Christianity to the Western worldview, the Industrial Revolution connected capitalism to this same worldview. As a major merchant world power of the nineteenth century, the English "conversion" to classical liberalism (e.g., free trade, free mobility of capital)—inspired by Adam Smith's *Wealth of Nations* (1776)—helped spread the gospel of capitalism worldwide as a Western value.[22] By the beginning of the twentieth century, as the West dominated the world both politically and economically, non-Western societies also had to contend with the increasing expansion of Western culture through colonialism and commerce. The emergence of a truly global marketplace served as the platform from which Western values and norms came to be disseminated, including Machiavelli's perspectives on power politics and leadership.

Much of the debate today about Western leadership draws from the themes articulated during the historical periods presented in this section. *The Prince*, therefore, is part of this ongoing Western narrative about the proper balance between the primacy of the individual and the primacy of the community. In keeping with the format introduced in Part I, before we analyze *The Prince* and its contribution to our perspective on Western leadership, we first need to provide a synopsis of the book.

Synopsis of the book

The Prince is a short book, but its insights are profound and require careful examination.[23] The book is divided into 26 chapters—the shortest of which is only about a page long, while the longest is still only roughly 11 pages. In each chapter, Machiavelli provides specific examples from ancient and current leaders. For the purpose of this synopsis, we will relate only the book's main themes. A reader wishing for a more detailed illustration of the argument should read Machiavelli's work in its entirety.

The first 11 chapters deal with the qualities of states, as well as the causes of their prosperity or failure. These chapters also discuss the methods by which princes seek to obtain such states—what Machiavelli referred to as "principalities." Machiavelli begins *The Prince* by making a distinction between two forms of government—republics and monarchies. Consistent with the purpose of the work to give advice to the House of Medici rulers, he focuses only on monarchies—those passed down through heredity and those newly founded.[24] He is particularly interested in discussing the leadership challenges that a new monarch faces when establishing his legitimacy. He probes these challenges using a healthcare analogy. Suppose you are a doctor, and you are asked to treat an illness. It is easier to treat it earlier rather than later; however, it is more difficult to make an accurate diagnosis of the disease in its early stages. The challenge for a doctor then is to accurately diagnose an illness early—before the disease is fully recognizable—since the treatment will be much more likely to succeed. Conversely, if the doctor waits too long to fully diagnose the disease, it may be too late.

Likewise, a leader is better off treating a problem early as opposed to letting it fester: "For knowing afar off (which it is only given to a prudent man to do) the evils that are brewing, they are easily cured. But when, for want of such knowledge, they are allowed to grow so that everyone can recognize them, there is no longer any remedy to be found."[25] Leaders are supposed to identify the problems before the symptoms are fully recognizable; and that requires insight, which the book is designed to provide its readers.

A government can be organized in one of two ways—one under which the monarch is the only unquestioned ruler (which Machiavelli describes as "a prince and his servants") and one under which he is surrounded by an elite (which Machiavelli describes as "a prince and his barons"). When planning to conquer these types of government, Machiavelli argues that the first case is difficult because the servants express their allegiance to only one ruler, while the second is easier because the invader can always rely on a baron to defect. However, once conquered, the first case is actually easier to rule over because there are no other sources of power, while the second proves to be the most difficult to govern because of the presence of other potential challengers—the barons.

Alternatively, in cases of free states—those "accustomed to live at liberty under their own laws," Machiavelli suggests three ways to deal with them: 1) to destroy them; 2) to go and live there in person; or 3) to allow them to live under their own laws. There is no right or wrong way to govern under these situations. The prince must determine which approach will best help him maintain his power under the circumstances.

Machiavelli offers counsel to princes on how to expand their power and how to acquire new domains in various ways. Certainly some can obtain their realm through their own military might, or force. Others may be obtained by the power of others, or by fortune. There is yet a third way to achieve power (besides ability and fortune)—through what Machiavelli calls "villainy." In such cases, Machiavelli recommends that the new prince "must arrange to commit all his cruelties at once, so as not to have to recur to them every day."[26] Afterward, the new prince can dole out benefits little by little, "so that they may be better enjoyed."[27] Machiavelli introduces a fourth means of achieving power—by the "favor of his fellow-citizens." He calls these states "civic principalities" and argues that they are achieved through cunning and assisted by fortune. There are two ways to achieve this position—through popular acclamation or through the support of the aristocracy. In the former case, the population is seeking protection from the aristocracy, while the latter is based on the wish of the nobility to oppress the population. Machiavelli suggests that it is actually easier to maintain power if a prince is brought to power through the support of the populace. After all, the aim of the populace is "more honest than that of the nobility, the latter desiring to oppress, while the former merely to avoid oppression."[28] The religious principalities are the last type of rule that Machiavelli discusses—e.g., the Church-controlled territories. Once acquired (either by ability or by fortune), ancient religious customs help maintain the leader in power—"secure and happy."[29] Machiavelli argues that these customs are so powerful that the leader can essentially rely on them without the need of a strong army to defend the principality. Regardless of the way in which a leader comes to power, Machiavelli argues that the biggest challenge for the leader is not to conquer a domain, but to keep it.[30]

Having discussed the different types of government and principality, Machiavelli turns in the next 12 chapters of the book to the topic of a prince's power and leadership skills. This section is probably the best known of *The Prince* because Machiavelli provides direct leadership lessons, which have been applied to different leadership challenges through the centuries. A Western leader in the twenty-first century may find many recommendations provided in this section of the book useful.

Machiavelli begins by first defining different kinds of militia and mercenary soldier. Military capability is viewed as the prince's main source of power. Machiavelli argues that the chief foundations of all states are "good laws and good arms."[31] For the purpose of this section of the book, he chooses to focus on the latter. Machiavelli is particularly interested in the prince's use of auxiliary forces (a powerful neighbor's military) versus using native troops. He counsels a prince to avoid the use of auxiliary forces for fear of being beholden to a more powerful foreign leader and focus instead building one's own military— "no prince is secure without his own troops."[32]

The military is of particular importance to Machiavelli, and he cautions that the effective prince should be able to relate to his troops. In particular, he should have an understanding of military matters, otherwise he cannot hope to gain their respect. Further, he should study military affairs all the time "never remain idle in peaceful times."[33] Machiavelli also recommends that the prince should exercise his mind by reading history and studying the actions of great leaders. This is of particular importance to building the prince's own power.

Machiavelli's approach to power is pragmatic. He claims the prince's most important task is to ensure security and wellbeing for himself and his domain. Machiavelli believes the leader must not leave anything to chance. Leadership qualities must be nurtured and pruned. He argues that when looking at virtues and vices, the leader must make sure that they will not bring him ruin, but also realize that his virtues may be detrimental to his realm's security. Likewise, his vices may at times prove beneficial. Being too virtuous might become "problematic." Some of the Prince's qualities may win him praise, others may win him blame. He takes a pragmatic approach regarding generosity and frugality, as well as cruelty and clemency. Is it better to be loved or feared? Ideally, the prince should be both, but "as it is difficult for the two to go together, it is much safer to be feared than loved."[34]

Love and fear are reoccurring themes in *The Prince*. Machiavelli explores the importance of "keeping faith" as a leadership quality. He presumes that there are two methods for the leader to advance his interests—one by law, and the other by force. He says that the first method is associated with human beings (rule of law), and the latter is better associated with beasts (the use of force). The prince should be prepared to use both—law and force—depending on the circumstance.[35] However, the leader must be cautious of how and when these approaches are used. Appearances are of utmost importance.

As the prince seeks to promote his virtues as a leader, Machiavelli stresses the importance of *appearing* to possess good leadership qualities. He observes, "Everybody sees what you appear to be, few see what you are, and those few will not dare to oppose themselves to the many, who have the majesty of the state to defend them."[36] Here Machiavelli develops the argument that public opinion is critical for a leader. He famously asserts that "the end justifies the means."[37] If the leader succeeds in his task, the means will be declared honorable by the general population. The prince should also avoid those actions that will bring about his being despised and hated. By developing a great reputation, the leader can avoid being challenged. In particular, he cautions that the leader should not make himself hated by the populace. It is not important *to be good*, or moral and ethical; indeed, true virtuousness might challenge the prince's power, but the prince should always *appear* to be good.

Ultimately, the best fortress that a leader could use to preserve his power is the love of the people. Reputation, therefore, is central to leadership. Machiavelli recommends that the leader should pay attention to the population—"mingle with them from time to time and give them an example of his humanity and munificence, always upholding, however, the majesty of his dignity, which he must never be allowed to fail in anything whatever."[38]

While the prince may be wise by mingling with his subjects, he also shows great leadership qualities by selecting able people with whom to surround himself: "The first impression that one gets of a ruler and of his brains is from seeing the men that he has about him."[39] Machiavelli recommends that the prince should avoid selecting ministers who mainly think of themselves first. In today's parlance, a leader should select lieutenants who are watching out for your welfare more than their own.

Quite often, leaders are tempted to surround themselves with those who are only inclined to use flattery. Machiavelli counseled the Medici rulers against that. The prince should give his ministers full liberty to speak the truth to him. He should be a "great asker." By asking, the prince also determines when others should speak—as opposed to the other way around. However, once the prince has heard all sides of the argument, he should make his decision and stick to it.

Machiavelli closes the treatise with specific recommendations for the Italian context. He warns that the Italian princes from recent history have lost their states by ignoring the issues that he brings up in his book. He observes that although fortune may be the ruler of half of our lot in life, "she allows the other half or thereabouts to be governed by us."[40] In other words, human agency does matter in shaping one's own future. The prince must remain flexible and not fall victim to fatalism—"the prince who bases himself on fortune is ruined when fortune changes." Indeed, Machiavelli's attempt to ingratiate himself to the Medici family by writing *The Prince* was his own attempt to control his fate.

Machiavelli concludes the book with a call to action—an exhortation to liberate Italy from "the barbarians." Ironically, while he counsels princes in previous chapters to shun flattery, he himself engages in it as he makes his concluding remarks: "There is nothing now she [Italy] can hope for but that your illustrious house may place itself at the head of this redemption."[41] He describes Lorenzo, The Magnificent, as playing the role of the liberator: "May your illustrious house therefore assume this task with that courage and those hopes which are inspired by a just cause, so that under its banner our fatherland may be raised up."[42]

Analysis: Leadership as a prize

The Prince serves as a catalog of leadership insights drawn from a Westerner's diplomatic experiences. As such, his work suggests different themes that we still today consider part of the Western approach to leadership. However, Machiavelli also struggles to reconcile divergent perspectives—the notion of individual freedom in a world in transition, at his time the Renaissance. Since he is focused on monarchies as opposed to republics, he makes the argument that, in the absence of overarching institutions, the leader is the focus of leadership. In this analysis, we extract some of the Western leadership themes present in Machiavelli's work, but we also move the argument beyond the Renaissance. The current Western perspective on leadership attempts to balance the primacy of the individual with the social exigencies of a complex civilization, or the primacy of the collective.

Western leadership themes

We can see both sides of the leadership continuum reflected in a Western tradition (Figure 6.3): 1) leader-centric individualism juxtaposed with transactional leadership based on the rule of law; 2) pragmatic/utilitarian individual morality balanced by a secular code of ethics; and 3) freedom of expression contrasted with a democratic community.

"**I**" (Individualism)   (Collectivism) "**WE**"

Leader-centric   *Social contract (transactional leadership)*
Individualism   *Rule of law*
Pragmatism/utilitarianism   *Strong democratic institutions*
Freedom of expression   *"Ethical community"*

Figure 6.3 The Western worldview on the leadership continuum

The historical background as just discussed is critical to helping us understand the leadership themes associated with the Western worldview. As Figure 6.3 shows, the Western worldview encompasses both sides (I/WE), but through unique cultural lenses. On the "I" side, it tends to emphasize the individualist perspective, as expressed in Ayn Rand's *Anthem* in Part I. The individual is praised over the collective. This theme carries into the Western notion of leadership—with its focus on the leader.

Inevitably, notions about "the leader" and "leadership" become intertwined. Unsurprisingly, if a Westerner is asked to define leadership, he or she is likely to identify positive characteristics of a leader—courage, honesty, integrity. This individualist (leader-centric) perspective of leadership also carries a connotation of value—leaders are better than followers. After all, if followers were smart, they would be leaders, not followers. It is common to hear the admonition, "Be a leader, not a follower," as if to be the latter connotes inferiority. Despite the emergence of the study of "followership," the idea still draws skepticism from the mainstream.

In Part I, we discussed the Great Man Theory as the first major focus of the scientific study of leadership in the late 1800s and early 1900s. That was consistent with the Western perspective of "leadership as a prize." Individuals compete for power. Whoever "wins" is called the leader. Followers, therefore, are relegated into the role of subordinates—the ones who did not have the ability or the "gift" to be promoted and given a title on a business card. Much of the business leadership literature in the West, particularly from the twentieth century, tends to reflect this perspective. Being a leader in the West is associated with ambition and seeking ways to move to the top. This makes sense given the cultural context of the early study of leadership.

The theme of "leadership as a prize" is consistent with the Industrial Revolution and capitalism. Companies compete for markets and customers.

The most successful company then is declared the "leader" in the industry. This leader-centric perspective has also been used in the Western system of nation-states. The most powerful countries are viewed as the leaders in the international system. Following the end of the Cold War, for instance, the United States was perceived as the leader because it was the sole remaining superpower. Power, therefore, is seen as granting one the legitimacy to lead, whether that is an individual, companies, or countries.

Machiavelli's *The Prince* reflects this Western perspective of the relationship between power and leadership. The prince, as the leader, has to find ways to gain power in order to get to the top. Once in power, the leader also has to use strategies to keep himself or herself in power. This insight reflects pragmatism—another theme in the Western perspective. Leaders develop strategies based on logic and rational calculations. From that standpoint, *The Prince* can be viewed as a "how-to" text, not necessarily different from the business leadership literature in the West today.[43] As Machiavelli warned, obtaining a domain is not the hard part; the hard part is keeping it.

Machiavelli paints a more extreme image of the leader–follower relationship because that was the environment in sixteenth-century Florence. City-states competed for power under a decentralized environmental context. In the absence of a strong central authority (e.g., the Roman Empire, the Roman Catholic Church), rulers were left to their own devices to establish order within their principalities. As the "father" of modern political realism, Machiavelli envisioned an environmental context that encouraged meritocracy—leaders were given power because they had won it.

The Renaissance as a cultural movement also reinforced the theme that human beings were in control of their destiny. Humans were not victims of nature. Rather, they were given freedom to subdue it. In leadership, that means that the prize is up for grabs. Anyone can have it, as long as they work hard for it. In other words, human agency matters. Machiavelli in the *The Prince* provides an analogy that reflects a Western leadership theme: life is like an "impetuous river" casting down everything in its path—"everything yields to its fury without being able to oppose it." Yet, when the river is quiet, "men can make provision against it by dykes and banks, so that when it rises it will either go into a canal or its rush will not be so wild and dangerous."[44] Leaders are expected to anticipate adversity and turn challenges into opportunities for success. They should be in control of their own fate.

This analogy also stresses the utilitarian perspective in a Western worldview. There is always the potential that leaders will be unable to subdue the river. However, they can plan ahead and find ways to control it. The very writing of *The Prince* carried the assumption that Machiavelli, through his many experiences as a diplomat, had uncovered the "secrets" of statecraft. As he says in *The Prince,* his intention was "to write something of use to those who understand."[45] Once revealed in a manual, leaders would know how to gain and maintain power.

While the "I" side of Western leadership is clearly defined in terms of individualism, we cannot leave out the "WE" side. The Greek and Roman influence certainly shaped the communitarian side of Western societies—the republican spirit of a self-governing *polis* under the rule of law. Individuals, while striving to assert their freedom and advance their individual interests, are also social beings. The Enlightenment stressed the notion of a "social contract" under which free citizens come together and bind themselves as a community under rules and laws that govern the collective. The same community offers political equality and justice for all. Individuals, therefore, use institutions and law to protect their own freedom.[46]

On the "WE" side, the republican experience also nurtured a deep distrust in the consequences of a leader having too much power. Institutions and law, therefore, also protect citizens from one individual abusing power. There is an implicit association between too much power and abuse of power.[47] The European experience under absolute monarchs certainly demonstrated the arbitrary and capricious behavior of leaders who were not accountable to their fellow citizens.

While this has helped to temper abuses of power, this distrust has created a paradox in the Western perspective of leadership. The very system that encourages leaders to pursue power in order to lead effectively also seeks to diffuse power in order to protect the freedom of its individuals from possible abuse of power.[48] If leaders try to centralize power around themselves, they are labeled "autocratic." The outcome of this paradox is a frustrating give-and-take game, which for a non-Western may seem perplexing and inefficient. Why encourage individuals to seek power to lead, while at the same time undermining their ability to gain more power in order to lead effectively?

This approach is not without moral implications. At the outset, we must accept that in *The Prince* there is an attempt to separate morality from leadership. The leader is presented as an amoral player in the world of power politics. This perspective has contributed to the negative stereotype of Machiavelli in the leadership literature.[49] To be Machiavellian is to suspend the moral dimension of leadership and use all means at a leader's disposal in order to accomplish the goals.

While Machiavelli is often portrayed as the founder of modern political realism, the moral dimension of Western leadership is more complex than *The Prince* suggests. Machiavelli was writing at a time when the central authority of the Roman Catholic Church had been challenged and secularism was on the rise. The Enlightenment morphed Christianity into a "code of ethics," which established the general rules of conduct for both leaders and followers.

Ethics calls for leaders and followers to do "what is right." However, the definition of right depends on the society's value system. For the West, this system is grounded in the Judeo-Christian worldview, which includes concepts of equity (e.g., equality before the law), justice (e.g., impartiality when considering rules), and fairness (e.g., do unto others as you would like done to you). Leaders should show all these qualities toward their followers. Just because they have "won the prize," it does not mean that they do not have certain obligations toward the collective.

Machiavelli is controversial because he challenges leaders to take pragmatism to an extreme. He draws a dichotomy between man (the rule of law) and beast (the use of force). The wise leader should abandon the "man side" at times and resort to the "beast side" in order to survive. This perspective seems to suggest that the leader should hold on to the "prize" even to the point of abandoning society's "code of ethics." Virtue is admirable, but results are what matter.

By the same token, the transactional nature of the leader–follower relationship is derived from Western principles of justice. Just leaders seek to do what is best for society. In return, followers reward leaders with their support. Once leaders violate those principles, they are deemed unworthy of the "prize" and replaced through rational-legal means such as due process. Ideally, we see these principles at work in for-profit organizations under which the CEO delivers value to employees and shareholders, as well as in politics under which the democratically elected official delivers on promises issued during a campaign. Unfortunately, this is not always the case.

The "code of ethics" operates both at the individual level, as in how leaders and followers conduct themselves personally, and the collective, as in how democratic institutions treat their citizens. Leaders and followers are held accountable based on a commonly accepted set of values. The practice of those values by both leaders and followers makes the collective an "ethical community."

Summary and concluding remarks

We began Part II with an evaluation of the Western perspective on leadership because it is the familiar worldview advanced under globalization. However, subsequent chapters should challenge this worldview with other perspectives that are based on non-Western norms and values. This chapter, therefore, will serve as the launching point for a deeper exploration of the diversity of views on leadership. Those comparisons will challenge our definition of "normal" when studying and practicing leadership.

Table 6.1 offers a summary of the main insights derived from our exploration of leadership in a Western context. Leadership is viewed as a prize to be earned by the leader as a product of a competitive process. Followers are equated with subordinates and relegated to an inferior role in the relationship. Leaders are ultimately responsible for the goals of their organizations, although they may seek input from their followers. Success is measured by the leaders' ability to mobilize resources and people in order to achieve those goals. Competition defines the environmental context. Goal attainment can make the difference

Table 6.1 Characteristics of Western leadership

	Western worldview
Leadership viewed as a . . .	Prize (meritocracy)
Leader-follower relationship	Transactional (rules based; social contract)
How decisions are made?	Through rationality, logic, pragmatism
Responsibilities of the leader	Motivate followers, results orientation
Responsibilities of the follower	Dependable, committed, motivated
Moral dimension of leadership	Secular "code of ethics" (derived from Judeo-Christian Values)

in its ability to create the "leader" (associated with success) or a "follower" (negative connotation).

The leader–follower relationship is primarily transactional. Leaders know that they must earn their prize by meeting the expectations of their followers. They are accountable to their followers insofar as the goals are met. They make decisions through rational means and are tasked with motivating the followers to gather resources and meet the organizational goals. Assessment is a powerful word in the West because it conveys the Western need to pragmatically measure success and know precisely whether the goals are being met. This mindset reflects the logic and utilitarian view that leaders need to validate their position through results.

Followers also have a role to play in leadership. They must be dependable, committed, and motivated, otherwise, leaders are not able to successfully achieve results. In Western leadership literature, as we saw in Part I, attention is paid to the ways leaders can motivate their followers. Once motivated, followers contribute to the overall attainment of goals.

As we explore new perspectives on leadership, we will compare their worldview to the Western themes. Our main goal in this comparison is to generate discussion about the different ways to view leadership. Beyond an intellectual exercise, this comparison can also help you understand why leaders and followers are behaving in certain ways. This awareness has a practical application—by understanding their leadership perspective, you can better communicate with leaders and followers from different cultures.

Cultures, however, are dynamic, so we should also keep in mind that the worldview is ever shifting. As Part I indicated, the late twentieth century has seen a growing interest in the contribution that followers are making to leadership. Our very definition of leadership as a process separated "leadership" from the behavior of leaders. In defining leadership as a process, we moved our analysis toward a realm that would seem foreign to Machiavelli. Globalization is empowering followers to become much more active participants in leadership. This dynamic is still consistent with the Western worldview. Rather than leaders and followers morphing into communitarian ideals, followers are competing with leaders for power.

In the West, we have seen a stronger emphasis on the follower and the importance of collaboration. While we applaud the recent movement toward more collaboration between leaders and followers, we are not ready to discount the continuing relevance of the Western perspective that leadership is taken as a "prize." In other words, Machiavelli continues to be relevant today.

Questions for discussion

*   Based on this chapter's description of the Western perspective, are you a "Westerner?" Why, or why not?
*   Machiavelli talks about the importance of being feared rather than being loved. Do you agree? Why or why not?
*   Do you think it is ever ethical to use the power of the beast (force) to lead followers? Under what circumstances would you advocate for this? Is a leader really "leading" if force is used?
*   How do you define "successful leadership?" Do you think your definition might be influenced by your culture? How so?
*   What are the practical implications of trying to balance individualism and collectivism when working in a position of leadership in the West?

Additional resources

H. Liebert, G.L. McDowell and T.L. Price, eds., *Executive Power in Theory and Practice*, New York: Palgrave Macmillan, 2012.

T. Phillips, *Niccolò Machiavelli's* The Prince: *A 52 Brilliant Ideas Interpretation*, Oxford: Infinite Ideas, 2008.

J.T. Wren, *Inventing Leadership: The Challenge of Democracy*, Northampton, MA: Edward Elgar, 2007.

Notes

1   N. Machiavelli, *The Prince*, New York: The Modern Library, 1950, pp.19–20. Available at http://www.gutenberg.org/files/1232/1232-h/1232-h.htm. Accessed August 15, 2014.
2   For a discussion regarding this phenomenon, see L. Crothers *Globalization and American Popular Culture*, Lanham, MD: Rowman & Littlefield Publishers, 2013.
3   For sources that give readers an introduction to Western civilization, see J.J. Spielvogel, *Western Civilization*, Boston, MA: Wadsworth, Cengage Learning, 2012; J.G. Coffin and R.C. Stacey, *Western Civilizations: Their History & Their Culture*, New York: W.W. Norton & Co., 2012.
4   M. Rejai and K. Phillips, *Concepts of Leadership in Western Political Thought*, Westport, CT: Praeger, 2002.
5   M.A. Ledeen, *Machiavelli on Modern Leadership: Why Machiavelli's Iron Rules Are as Timely and Important Today as Five Centuries Ago*, New York: Truman Talley Books, 2000; M. Jinkins and D.B. Jinkins, *The Character of Leadership: Political Realism and Public Virtue in Nonprofit Organizations*, San Francisco: Jossey-Bass, 1998.
6   R.W. Mathisen, *Ancient Mediterranean Civilizations: From Prehistory to 640 CE*, New York: Oxford University Press, 2012; M.H. Hansen, *Polis: An Introduction to the Ancient Greek City-State*, New York: Oxford University Press, 2006.

7 J.P. Arnason, K.A. Raaflaub, and P. Wagner, eds., *The Greek Polis and the Invention of Democracy: A Politico-Cultural Transformation and its Interpretations*, Malden, MA: Wiley-Blackwell, 2013.

8 Sparta and Athens remained allies as they battled a common enemy in the Persian Wars, with Athens as the dominant player politically and economically. Eventually, as the Athenian economic might declined, rivalry between the two sides came to blows through the long Peloponnesian War (431–404 BCE)—famously chronicled by Thucydides. While Sparta emerged victorious, Athenian ideas did not disappear. Since the purpose of this chapter is not to provide a complete survey of European history, we have purposefully skipped the Macedonian invasions of Greece, which gave rise to Alexander the Great and marked the end of the classical period in Ancient Greek history.

9 A. Everitt, *The Rise of Rome: The Making of the World's Greatest Empire*, New York: Random House, 2012.

10 K. Bringmann, *A History of the Roman Republic*, W. J. Smyth trans., Malden, MA: Polity, 2007; P. Matyszak, *Chronicle of the Roman Republic: The Rulers of Ancient Rome from Romulus to Augustus*, New York: Thames & Hudson, 2003; T.R. Glover, *Democracy in the Ancient World*, New York: Macmillan, 1927.

11 M. Sommer, *The Complete Roman Emperor: Imperial Life at Court and on Campaign*, London: Thames & Hudson, 2010.

12 D.G. Cracknell and C.H. Wilson, *Roman Law: Origins and Influence*, London: HLT, 1990; H.F. Jolowicz, *Roman Foundations of Modern Law*, Westport, CT: Greenwood Press, 1978.

13 J.D. Roth, ed., *Constantine Revisited: Leithart, Yoder, and the Constantinian Debate*, Eugene, OR: Pickwick Publications, 2013; T. Barnes, *Constantine: Dynasty, Religion and Power in the Later Roman Empire*, Malden, MA: Wiley-Blackwell, 2011; C.M. Odahl, *Constantine and the Christian Empire*, London: Routledge, 2004.

14 We purposefully omitted a millennium in our discussion of the West (from 476 AD to the 1400s—the so-called "Middle Ages") because the collapse of the Roman Empire in Western Europe did not necessarily mean the end of centralization. The Roman Catholic Church continued to flourish in the West and became the most powerful institution during the Middle Ages. Kings and queens swore allegiance to the Pope and in turn were declared legitimate leaders of their domains. See J. Hitchcock, *History of the Catholic Church: From the Apostolic Age to the Third Millennium*, San Francisco: Ignatius Press, 2012; R.I. Moore, *The War on Heresy*, Cambridge, MA: Belknap Press of Harvard University Press, 2012.

15 R.A. Goldthwaite, *The Economy of Renaissance Florence,* Baltimore MD: Johns Hopkins University Press, 2009; R.J. Crum and J.T. Paoletti, eds., *Renaissance Florence: A Social History*, New York: Cambridge University Press, 2008; D.E. Muir, *Machiavelli and His Times*, Westport, CT: Greenwood Press, 1976; J.R. Hale, *Machiavelli and Renaissance Italy*, New York: Collier Books, 1963.

16 P. Strathern, *The Medici: Godfathers of the Renaissance*, London: Jonathan Cape, 2003; C. Hibbert, *The House of Medici: Its Rise and Fall*, New York: Perennial, 2003; J.R. Hale, *Florence and the Medici*, London: Phoenix, 2001; J. Cleugh, *The Medici: A Tale of Fifteen Generations*, New York: Dorset Press, 1990.

17 G.R. Berridge, M. Keens-Soper, and T.G. Otte, eds., *Diplomatic Theory from Machiavelli to Kissinger*, New York: Palgrave, 2001. For a general introduction to Machiavelli's political thought, see M. Viroli, *Machiavelli*, New York: Oxford University Press, 1998.

18 K. Paparchontis, *100 World Leaders Who Shaped World History*, San Mateo, CA: Bluewood Books, 2001; M. Mallett and N. Mann, eds., *Lorenzo the Magnificent: Culture and Politics*, London: Warburg Institute, University of London, 1996.

19 L.W. Spitz, *The Protestant Reformation, 1517—1559*, Saint Louis, IL: CPH, 2001.

20 D. Outram, *The Enlightenment*, New York: Cambridge University Press, 2013; S.D. Jordan, *The Enlightenment Vision: Science, Reason, and the Promise of a Better Future*, Amherst, NY: Prometheus Books, 2012.

21 P.N. Stearns, *The Industrial Revolution in World History*, Boulder, CO: Westview Press, 2013; L.T. Wyatt III, *The Industrial Revolution*, Westport, CT: Greenwood Press, 2009.

22 A. Smith, *An Inquiry into the Nature and Causes of the Wealth of Nations*, London: W. Strahan and T. Cadell, 1776. Scholars have drawn parallels between the British Empire in the nineteenth century and the Roman Empire's ability to project their cultural values through their political and economic hegemony. See S.J. Butler, *Britain and its Empire in the Shadow of Rome: The Reception of Rome in Socio-Political Debate from the 1850s to the 1920s*, New York: Bloomsbury, 2012; N. Vance, *The Victorians and Ancient Rome*, Cambridge, MA: Blackwell Publishers, 1997. When Max Weber provided his perspectives on the concept of legitimate authority, as discussed in Chapter 1, he reflected the impact that the Industrial Revolution and liberal democracy had brought about in the West—to the point of expressing a unique worldview. The Western worldview was rational and based on the legitimate authority derived from the law. Weber celebrated the Protestant work ethic as a foundation for the success of capitalism and liberal democratic regimes in the West. See M. Weber, *The Protestant Ethic and the Spirit of Capitalism*, S. Kalberg trans., New York: Oxford University Press, 2011.

23 For the purpose of this synopsis, we have used N. Machiavelli, *The Prince*, New York: Modern Library, 1950.

24 He cites two forms of newly founded monarchies—an entirely new monarchy, and one acquired through the annexation of another state. In annexed dominions, he further makes a distinction between those that were already accustomed to another prince and those that were previously free states.

25 Machiavelli, *The Prince*, p. 11.

26 Ibid, p. 35.

27 Ibid.

28 Ibid, p. 36.

29 Ibid, p. 42.

30 Machiavelli also encourages the Prince to think about the steps that need to be taken in case he does not have the power to stand alone. In such cases, he is obliged to take refuge within the city walls and stand on the defensive. As a leader, it becomes his responsibility to make the preparations to be prepared for a state of siege. He will also have to reassure his subjects that the siege will not last long. Machiavelli argues that the leader's subjects will be more disposed to fight for the leader if they see that he has planned ahead and is well provided to defend himself.

31 Ibid, p. 44.

32 Ibid, p. 52.

33 Ibid, p. 54.

34 The justification for this position is found in the argument that "men have less scruple in offending one who makes himself loved than one who makes himself feared; for love is held by a chain of obligation which, men being selfish, is broken whenever it serves their purpose; but fear is maintained by a dread of punishment which never fails."

35 Regarding the beasts, Machiavelli brings up two types of animal that leaders should aspire to emulate—a fox (recognizing traps) and a lion (frightening the wolves). Ibid, p. 61.

36 Ibid, p. 66.

37 Ibid.

38 Ibid, p. 85.

39 Ibid.
40 Ibid, p. 91.
41 Ibid, p. 95.
42 Ibid, p. 98.
43 For instance, S.L. Tubbs, *Keys to Leadership: 101 Steps to Success*, Boston, MA: McGraw-Hill Custom Publishing, 2005; D. Cottrell and E. Harvey, *Leadership Courage: Leadership Strategies for Individual and Organizational Success*, Dallas, TX: Walk the Talk, 2004.
44 Machiavelli, *The Prince*, p. 91.
45 Ibid, p. 56.
46 E. Putterman, *Rousseau, Law and the Sovereignty of the People*, New York: Cambridge University Press, 2010; J. Rousseau, *The Social Contract*, G.D.H. Cole trans., Buffalo, NY: Prometheus Books, 1988.
47 A.R. Pratkanis and E. Aronson, *Age of Propaganda: The Everyday Use and Abuse of Persuasion*, New York: W.H. Freeman/Holt and Co., 2002; D.E. Zand, *The Leadership Triad: Knowledge, Trust, and Power*, New York: Oxford University Press, 1997.
48 T.E. Cronin and M.A. Genovese, *The Paradoxes of the American Presidency*, New York: Oxford University Press, 1998.
49 L.F. Gunlicks, *The Machiavellian Manager's Handbook for Success*, Lanham, MD: National Book Network, 1993.

7 Leadership in a Latin American cultural context

Whether you're guilty or innocent is irrelevant, General; what matters is whether you're in favor or not with the President.[1]

Miguel Ángel Asturias, *The President*

In the previous chapter, we presented the Western worldview as dominated by a secular individualistic perspective, tempered by rules and institutions that see leader–follower relations as a social contract (transactional leadership). While the Western perspective came to be associated with northern European values, the Latin American worldview drew its inspiration from southern Europe, including the Iberian Peninsula. Some scholars, in fact, consider Latin America a "Mediterranean variation of Western civilization."[2]

For Latin America, deep spiritual beliefs have created a worldview that reflects an acceptance of a natural order that for a Westerner may seem fatalistic. The natural order guides the leader–follower relationship the same way that a river defines the flow of objects floating in the river. The river as a metaphor may bring about images of harmony and stability. However, the Latin American worldview conceptualizes nature not as a lazy river, but rather as a whitewater experience, full of rocks and dangers along the way.[3]

The leaders and followers' challenge, therefore, is to "play their part," and the natural order will sort out who should be on top and who should be on the bottom. As they move through the whitewater rapids, some will be thrown off the boat, while others will conquer the waters. The strongest ones—defined in terms not only of physical prowess, but also in mental ability and resilience—will always come out on top.

In this chapter, we introduce a novel by the Nobel-Prize winner Miguel Ángel Asturias (1899–1974). His novel *The President* will help us highlight some basic Latin American leadership themes. Both Western and Latin American perspectives see leadership as a process that brings out the competitive side of human relations. The West "regulates" this competition through rules and institutions that are designed to control nature. Latin American culture does not presume that nature can be controlled. Rather, leadership is in itself

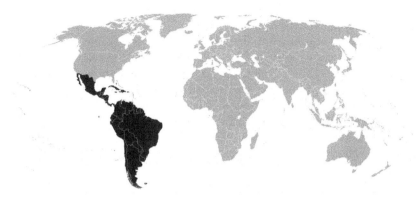

Figure 7.1 Latin America

a byproduct of nature. In the natural world, leaders lead because they possess the natural abilities to be leaders, while followers are expected to accept this order and show loyalty and devotion to their leaders. This division of labor generates a hierarchical view of the leader–follower relationship. In Latin America, this perspective may be seen through socioeconomic stratification and the importance of status in demonstrating one's position in the social hierarchy.

Contrariwise, the leader–follower relationship in Latin America is also dynamic. The leaders must constantly demonstrate their "worthiness" to be at the top. They must attend to the leader–follower relationship through referent power—the ability to persuade others to follow them through desirable particular attributes and personal relationships. In Latin America, this ability is called *personalismo*. While in the West, we focused on transactional leadership, the Latin American worldview puts more stock in charismatic leadership, to use Max Weber's taxonomy discussed in Part I, as the source of legitimate power in the leader–follower relationship. *Personalismo* ascribes different roles to leaders and followers. Leaders are expected to hold the organization/society together, thus providing order, while exhibiting a bold leadership style marked by charisma that inspires followers to show loyalty and devotion. Under this worldview, rules and institutions are designed to reflect the personal power of those on top.[4] However, when leaders change, so may the rules and institutional norms.

In the last section of the chapter, we highlight the moral dimension of leadership in the Latin American worldview. While the Western perspective tends to reflect the Protestant-secular experience of northern Europe, the Latin American worldview draws inspiration from southern Europe, long under the influence of the Roman Catholic Church and its values. This influence divides the world into distinct camps—good and evil.[5] In the natural order, these two sides are in constant battle and competition. Leaders present themselves as representatives of good, while their opponents are portrayed as enemies, allied with evil. The stark contrast between the two camps makes compromise a difficult task.

Leadership in Latin America, therefore, is intense and deeply personal. This is the picture Asturias paints in his novel *The President*. Asturias was a poet, journalist, diplomat, and novelist. His novel *The President* provides a fictional portrayal of a Latin American leader fending off challenges from potential competitors. While Machiavelli wrote *The Prince* as a guide to help a leader stay in power through the pragmatic use of the "beast," Asturias wrote *The President* to denounce the excesses of a system that elevates the importance of the beast to the point that humanity is ultimately controlled by it. Although in his novel, Asturias presents a highly critical view of this approach to leadership, the novel does provide a concise artifact to conceptualize some key notions associated with a traditional view of leadership in Latin America.

Case study: Miguel Ángel Asturias' *El Señor Presidente*

Asturias' novel constitutes a snapshot of the whitewater nature of life in a Latin American context. The novel was written in Paris in 1933, and Asturias—fearing for his life—did not bring it with him when he moved back to Guatemala because the country was ruled by the dictator Jorge Ubico, presumably the archetype used in the novel. *The President* was eventually published in 1946 in Mexico after Ubico's fall and it received wide acclaim. When presenting the Nobel Prize to Asturias in 1967, the Permanent Secretary of the Swedish Academy, praised the novel: "This magnificent and tragic satire criticizes the prototype of the Latin American dictator who appeared in several places at the beginning of the [twentieth] century and has since reappeared, his existence being fostered by the mechanism of tyranny which, for the common man, makes every day a hell on earth."[6]

This prototype represented the traditional view of the Latin American leader as a *caudillo*, a strong dictator on horseback. Following the independence movements in the early 1800s, many Latin American countries fell under the control of *caudillos* who provided order and stability amid competing factions.[7] *Caudillismo* came to be viewed as the way Latin American leaders gained control of societies and organizations, demanded complete loyalty from their followers, shaped the future of their institutions, and made their mark in history.

Asturias was born in Guatemala at a time in Latin American history when the military represented the face of the *caudillo* in politics. His own family had a run-in with a military dictator (Estrada Cabrera) when his father—a supreme court justice—disagreed with the ruling *caudillo*. The family was forced to leave Guatemala City and take refuge at home of his grandfather, a respected colonel in the Army.[8]

After completing his law degree, Asturias went to Europe where he pursued his graduate studies in anthropology at the Sorbonne. While in France, he showed interest in Mayan culture and the plight of the Indian peasants in Central America.[9] He wrote *El Señor Presidente* while in Paris (1923–1933), although he had started writing it 10 years earlier as a short story while still a law student in Guatemala.

Asturias had a prolific writing career, while spending much of his life either as a Guatemalan diplomat in other countries or in exile during periods of military directorship. While serving as an ambassador to France in 1967, he received the Nobel Prize in literature "for his vivid literary achievement, deep-rooted in the national traits and traditions of Indian peoples of Latin America."[10]

When he died in 1974, he left a trove of literary accomplishments that helped shape the style and substance of Latin American literature into the twenty-first century. Today, he is viewed as a powerful voice that offers a critique of a region deeply divided between those with power and privilege and those who suffer under oppression. What is important for our analysis is that Asturias' novel *The President* serves as a representation of the main themes that encapsulate how leadership is perceived in a Latin American cultural context.

Power is at the center of everything that takes place in *The President*. The ones who have it seek to protect it, while the others who do not have it seek ways to gain more of it. It is a struggle for survival, and a worldview that paints a picture of a society steeped in intrigue, uncertainty, and a search for power, the ultimate leadership currency. Before presenting a synopsis of the novel, we need to provide some historical background and the environment that propelled the writing of the book.

Origins of a Latin American worldview

The reference in the beginning of the chapter to Latin America as a "Mediterranean variation of Western civilization" should provide clues as to some of the basic characteristics of the Latin American worldview. While it has some elements of the Western perspective on leadership, it also followed its own path, separate from that of northern Europe. Latin America is the product of European colonization, but it also experienced the mixing of cultures, including local civilizations such as the Mayans, Aztecs, Incas as well as groups from Africa.[11] The first Europeans who reached the Latin American shores were *conquistadores* of Iberian origin (e.g., Portuguese and Spanish), and they carried different cultural experiences than the northern Europeans who arrived in North America.

The *conquistadores* arrived in the Americas charged with bravado having just expelled the Moors from the Iberian Peninsula.[12] This contributed two symbols that would carry them through the initial exploration of the new world—the sword and the cross. They applied both with vigor against the indigenous populations, dedicating the new land to the Crown and the Church.[13] The absolute monarchies in the Iberian Peninsula propagated the view that God—through his Divine plan—had placed rulers over societies, and those arrangements were not to be questioned. The Church represented the link between heaven and earth and served as the official interpreter of the Judeo-Christian values through its dogma. Together, the cross and the sword became a powerful defender of the natural order. While in the previous chapter we discussed the Protestant Reformation in northern Europe championing the rise of capitalism, secularism, and democratic values, Latin Americans had to contend with the Spanish Inquisition and the fear of the spread of "heresy" into the New World.[14]

This fear of heretical ideas also fueled the drive toward independence from Europe as the Iberian Peninsula came under Napoleonic control in the early 1800s. Therefore, right from the beginning, Latin America rejected the values that shaped the Western worldview (e.g., constitutional monarchy) and attempted to uphold the continuation of its own traditional values (e.g., absolute monarchy). In Brazil, the Portuguese crown prince broke away from the motherland once the Portuguese parliament sought his allegiance to a new constitutional monarchy in 1820. In Spanish America, the rejection of the Iberian rule left the region without a crown. Legendary *caudillos,* such as Santa Anna in Mexico and Rosas in Argentina, provided much needed stability and presented themselves as virtually absolute monarchs, without the crown.

Ironically, the paths of the Western and Latin American countries crossed in the nineteenth century. In the previous chapter, we stressed the rise of capitalism and the Industrial Revolution influencing the Western worldview marked by competition, individualism, and a strong work ethic. Northern Europe's economic expansion directly impacted Latin America. As the West sought new trade routes into Latin America, it encouraged the rise of *caudillismo* and oligarchies in the region, because they provided the stability for foreign investment in critical commercial ventures, such as coffee, sugar, mineral extraction, and railroads to bring the goods to ports for export.

By the end of the nineteenth century, another European export had an impact on Latin America—positivism, a philosophy that praised the achievements of science and sought to apply the insights on the natural world to the social order as expressed in social Darwinism.[15] While England incorporated classical liberalism into its economic policies under the Enlightenment, such as that represented in Adam Smith's *Wealth of Nations*, most of Latin America came under the influence of the French positivist philosopher Auguste Comte (1789–1857). Considered the founder of sociology and the precursor of the social sciences, Comte argued that the same laws used to describe natural phenomena could be used to understand social life.[16] The idea of order, social hierarchy, and human progress resonated with Latin Americans, eager to reconcile the cultural legacy of a centralizing Church with the region's lack of economic development.[17]

The rise of a Western economic power in North America (e.g., the United States) provided continuity in this interlocking of two models (classical liberalism and *caudillismo*) benefitting from each other.[18] Pro-West *caudillos* guaranteed order, which facilitated foreign investors bringing progress—measured in terms of new technologies being introduced for the extraction of resources and to the benefit of a small elite. This cycle of asymmetrical interdependence throughout the twentieth century reinforced the Latin American worldview—centralization around a powerful caudillo, social stratification, and a focus on the natural order of life.

Asturias wrote his novel as a critique of the Latin American worldview when taken to an extreme—a cruel *caudillo* paranoid of potential challengers, the dehumanizing nature of social stratification, and the oppressive consequence of powerlessness among those at the bottom of the social hierarchy. It is symbolic that he finished his novel while in Europe—as if looking at Latin America from the outside—and chose not to publish the book after moving back to Guatemala for fear of challenging *caudillismo*. When Ubico fell from power in 1944, the new regime, under Professor Juan José Arévalo, appointed Asturias cultural attaché to the Guatemalan Embassy in Mexico where the novel eventually was published (1946). Asturias got a second chance, where Machiavelli, as the previous chapter presented, did not.

Synopsis of the novel

The story in *The President* takes place in an unnamed country of Latin America during an unspecified year, although there are strong parallels between the main leader's ruthless dictatorship and the Guatemalan government under dictator Jorge Ubico.[19] The novel is divided into three parts.[20] The first takes place in a three-day period, while the second covers the following four days. After this week-long period, the third part recounts the outcome of the plot through a more extensive time horizon—weeks, months, and years. In typical Latin American fictional style, the characters are interlocked in an intricate web of relationships, chance encounters, and trivial actions with tragic unanticipated consequences. For the purpose of this synopsis, we will recount the main events associated with the general plot of the novel. There are several subplots, which are mentioned only through footnotes in this section.

The main character in the novel is the President, who is never named. He has two close advisers—the Judge Advocate General (the Judge) and Miguel Angel Face, also called "the favorite" because of his close association with the President as his confidante.[21] The two were once fierce rivals, and the President uses this rivalry to his advantage (see Table 7.1).

The President is getting ready to face re-elections. Although the outcome of the ballot seems to be a foregone conclusion, he is concerned that there may be a revolution in the offing, led by General Eusebio Canales. The General's chief "sin" against the President was to make the public statement that the "The Generals are the Princes of the Army."[22] This statement directly challenged the power of the President because princes aim to become kings, and in a Latin American cultural context, we can only have one king. The President was looking for an opportunity to eliminate this potential rival.

The novel opens on the cathedral porch with a group of beggars in the middle of the night. We are introduced to one of them, the Zany, also called "the idiot," who is known to become frantic whenever he hears the word

Table 7.1 Characters in *The President*

Miguel Angel Face	The President's confidential adviser ("The favorite; he was as beautiful and as wicked as Satan")
Gen. Eusebio Canales	One of the President's rivals (accused of killing Colonel José Parrales Sonriente)
Camila	Gen. Eusebio Canales' daughter
Judge Advocate General	The President's close ally; Angel Face's rival; investigates Colonel Parrales Sonriente's death
Zany	Homeless man who kills Colonel Parrales Sonriente
Lucio Vasquez	Policeman assigned to keep an eye on Gen. Canales' house
Genaro Rodas	Vasquez' close friend
Fedina	Genaro Rodas' wife; Camilla is supposed to be the godmother to their child

"mother" addressed to him. On the opening night of the novel, Colonel José Parrales Sonriente, on his way to see his friend, the President, approached the sleeping "idiot" and with a smile shouted, "Mother!" Zany sprang to life, attacked the colonel, and ran away screaming, leaving the officer's motionless body on the cathedral porch. What began as a mischievous prank became a major news event of national importance. Who killed Colonel Parrales Sonriente? And, furthermore, why?

The President used this event as his opportunity to destroy General Canales. The Judge Advocate General was given the task of investigating the murder. The only eye witnesses were the homeless beggars near the cathedral. The police rounded them up and coercively extracted "confessions" that General Canales was behind the assassination.[23] Given the "evidence" against General Canales, the President asked the Judge to arrest the general. The Judge arranged for round the clock surveillance of the general's house, in preparation for his arrest.

In the meantime, the President secretly ordered Angel Face to alert General Canales about the imminent arrest and counsel him to flee the night before his arrest. The President hoped that through this plan General Canales would be killed in the process of fleeing. The fact that General Canales was trying to flee would also serve as evidence that he was indeed guilty. Unbeknownst to the President, Angel Face was in love with General Canales' daughter, Camila, and developed a competing plan to kidnap her on the night before the general's arrest.[24]

The first part of the book ends with Angel Face's abduction plan being put into action. He brought with him a "party of roughs" who made it look like they were there to rob the General's house. As part of Angel Face's plan, Camila screamed that there were robbers in the house. The police keeping an eye on the house moved in. Instead of killing the fleeing general, as the President expected, the corrupt police—as predicted in Angel Face's plan—began looting the house, which gave the General and his daughter the opportunity to flee unharmed.

The second part of the novel begins with the commotion of the fake robbery and Angel Face secretly taking Camila to a bar across the street as a temporary safe house. In the morning, the Judge arrived at the General's house to execute the arrest order and found that he had escaped. As expected, he was furious and wanted answers. Who had warned the General about the imminent arrest?[25]

Angel Face reached out to Camila's uncle, who also lived in town, in hopes that her uncle's family would take her in. Nervous about the murder charges against the General, the family declined Angel Face's request. Camila then heard the difficult news that the Canales family had disowned her and her father. Deeply saddened, Camila became gravely ill with a fever.[26] The second part of the book ends with General Canales on the road to exile plotting a revolution against the President.

The final part of the novel begins with a lawyer (Carvajal)—one of General Canales' supporters—in jail. The Judge had arrested him on the same day the General was to be arrested. The lawyer was brought before a tribunal to face his indictment. Despite all of the formalities, it was clear what fate awaited him: death.

In the meantime, Camila was getting worse, and her doctor said that only a miracle would save her. In desperation, Angel Face married Camila on her deathbed, but eventually the new bride recovered. On learning about the marriage, the President turned this new development to his advantage. He hosted a party for the newlyweds, and the newspapers reported that the President himself had been a witness at the wedding. The news reached General Canales who died of shock. In the end, the revolution was called off because of the General's death.

The President was not done. He asked Angel Face to go to Washington to argue his case for the United States to support his re-election.[27] On his way to board the boat for the long journey, Angel Face was arrested by order of the President. An imposter took his place and boarded the boat to Washington. The real Angel Face was imprisoned and tortured and accused of not carrying out the President's orders against General Canales. While in jail, he received a false report that Camila was now the President's mistress. He lost all hope. In reality, Camila was pregnant with Angel Face's baby and thought that her husband was still in Washington. However, he never answered her letters. She was refused a passport, so she was unable to leave the country in search of her husband. Camila had a son (Little Miguel) and moved to the countryside, leaving the national stage and was no longer a threat to the President. Eventually, over the course of years, Angel Face died in prison.

In the end, the novel had a "happy ending," for the President. He managed to eliminate the main threats against his rule.

Analysis: The natural order of leadership

Asturias' novel provides an excellent artifact from which to extract some general themes related to leadership in a Latin American cultural context. While a work of fiction, it actually draws inspiration from the reality that Asturias faced when growing up in Latin America. The discussion of the Latin American worldview presented in the previous section provides the backdrop from which to highlight these themes.

Latin American leadership themes

We can discern from this artifact five general themes (see Figure 7.2): 1) duality between the public and the private spheres; 2) centralization of power (*caudillismo*); 3) preeminence of personality over institutions (*personalismo*); 4) importance of loyalty in the leader–follower relationship; and 5) the balcony moment (leader stands out, separate from the follower).

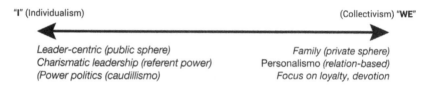

Figure 7.2 The Latin American worldview on the leadership continuum

Latin American scholar Paul Goodwin characterizes the Latin American worldview as "dualistic."[28] The family constitutes the basic unit of social organization ("WE"). Within the family, one finds all the positive attributes of social relations—generosity, warmth, welcoming spirit. By contrast, the "real world" is corrupt, evil, and ruthless. In the real world, the individual is supreme ("I"). In order to face the outside world, we need to garner as much power as possible in order to be ready for combat (power politics). This worldview fits closely with the leadership continuum discussed in Part I. This duality provides the leaders and the followers with a way to reconcile the competing forces of the extreme sides of the continuum. In the Western perspective, these competing forces are reconciled through transactional leadership (the social contract). In Latin America, the image of the family becomes the operating metaphor that charismatic leaders use to extract loyalty and devotion from their followers.

We see this dualism when Camila seeks out protection from her extended family after escaping arrest from the President's forces. The rejection from her uncle is particularly painful because it denies the safety associated with the home ("WE"). As Asturias says in the novel:

> A house makes it possible to eat one's bread in privacy—and bread eaten in privacy is sweet, it teaches one wisdom—a house enjoys the safety of

permanence and of being socially approved. It is like a family portrait with the father wearing his best tie, the mother displaying her finest jewels and the children's hair brushed with real eau de Cologne. The street, on the other hand, is an unstable, dangerous, adventurous world, false as a looking-glass—the public laundry of all the dirty linen in the neighborhood.[29]

This dualism constitutes the "natural order" that guides the behavior of leaders and followers in Latin America—both in private (with the family) and in public (in business organizations and political institutions). Under this worldview, we can see the critical importance of power and a sense of place in the social hierarchy. In the street, the stakes are high—life and death. Once Camila loses the safety of her family connections, she is left alone in the street and becomes a pawn in the ruthless world of leadership.

The dualistic worldview also helps us understand how the leadership continuum is applied to the Latin American cultural context (Figure 7.2). The public sphere tends to favor the "I" side (command and control, hierarchical leadership style), while the private sphere leans toward the "WE" side (the image of the family as a cohesive organizational unit). To say that the "WE" side represents a communal perspective, however, is not completely accurate. Even within a family unit, there are specific roles and clear delineation of placement in the social order. As a patriarchic order, there is an expectation that the father figure is supreme. To challenge this traditional view is to subvert what is perceived as the natural order.

In this context, the Latin American "WE" is entirely different from the Western "WE." While the latter promotes the perspective of a social contract (a community that comes together through transactional leadership), the Latin American "WE" assumes a much deeper level of commitment on the part of the community members (the family as the organizational metaphor). In the Western "WE," loyalty does not run as deep as in Latin America. Through utilitarianism and pragmatism, followers may switch sides at will. In Latin America, switching sides represents a betrayal in the leader–follower relationship, as Angel Face discovered at the end of the novel.

The main survival strategy in this natural order is to acquire power either by attaching oneself to the powerful *caudillo* or challenging the existing power structure. It is obvious from the beginning of the novel that the President sits at the top of his society. General Canales is introduced as a challenger to the existing order. In this scenario, the other players must choose sides. Angel Face tries to defy this natural order and he pays dearly. The Judge Advocate, however, survives by playing the game astutely and remaining loyal to the President. While Angel Face is first introduced as the "favorite," he falls from grace by trying to do things his way—outside the priorities of the leader.

As we noted in the synopsis, General Canales' chief sin against the President was to make the public statement that "The Generals are the Princes of the Army."[30] This statement challenged the power of the President because princes hope to become kings, and we can only have one king. This message is made clear when we are told of the President's "fear of able leaders" in reference to rumors of a brewing revolution.[31] This statement draws attention to the hierarchical nature of leadership in Latin America's worldview. Being a leader means not only to hold positional legitimacy at the top position in an organizational chart, but also to possess enough power to ward off potential challengers.

Those who are not members of the elite can attain positions of leadership, but that is usually attained through force, which paradoxically challenges the existing natural order, while at the same time reinforcing the idea of natural selection. Latin American history is filled with *caudillos* who lost their positions once overthrown by more powerful *caudillos*. The natural order presumes the existence of a balance of power, which changes over time. The President in the novel is shown to be from humble beginnings, but through superior skills, he is able to challenge the ruling elite and replace it with his own pecking order. In the process, he becomes the new elite.

The President's fear of "able leaders" makes it difficult to institutionalize an organizational culture that promotes leadership from the bottom up. As leaders emerge from the bottom, they become a challenge to those on top. It is not surprising that leadership development programs have not been fully embraced in Latin America as they have in the United States and Europe. While there is an emphasis in the West on leadership dispersion, or fragmentation of power at all levels, in Latin America, the tendency has been the opposite, centralization of power around a few leaders at the top. In *The President*, there is a clear hierarchy, and when Angel Face goes against it by disobeying the wishes of the supreme leader, he is severely punished. Likewise, when General Canales even hints that someone may vie for the President's power, as when he suggests that "the Generals are the Princes of the Army," he becomes the target of the President's fury.

The preeminent role that the leader plays at the top also has a detrimental effect on the institutionalization of rules and norms. In the previous chapter, we highlighted the importance of rules and norms in the Western context. Asturias' novel, however, presents leadership in Latin America as deeply personal, as we see throughout the story. There are moments when rules and laws are mentioned, but they are primarily tools for individual gain. When the formal indictments against Canales and Carvajal were announced, 14 witnesses came forth under oath and said that they had seen them kill the colonel on the cathedral porch. One witness even mentioned overhearing Carvajal say to Canales, "Now that we have killed 'the man with the little mule' the military leaders will have to hand over their weapons and recognize you, General, as the Supreme Head of the Army."[32] When Angel Face alerts General Canales of the imminent arrest, the latter is first determined to stand his ground because he knows he did not kill the colonel. Angel Face, however, counsels the General against foolishly sticking around: "Whether you're guilty or innocent is irrelevant, General; what matters is whether you're in favor or not with the President."[33]

When Carvajal's wife pleads mercy to the Judge Advocate, the latter is quick to point out that "The law comes before individuals."[34] However, we all know that Carvajal's fate has already been settled. After all, as the Judge Advocate adds in the same conversation, "The political situation of our country does not permit the Government showing any pity whatsoever to its enemies, Señora."[35] To show pity is to exhibit weakness, which in the natural order, can mean the end of one's position of power and leadership.

The *caudillo* leader sits at the top, dispensing favors to followers based on loyalty. This relationship is also reciprocal in the sense that the followers come to expect a leader who is worthy of admiration. While being cunning is certainly an effective way to stay on top, the leader must also demonstrate charisma and super-human qualities. In the novel, the fictional country was celebrating a national holiday to honor a day when the President escaped an assassination attempt. The President made an appearance on the balcony and addressed "his people." In return, the crowd screamed "Long live the President!" He was praised as "the illustrious protector of the poorer classes." For many Latin Americans, the image of past charismatic leaders draws historical parallels. Leaders have to earn their place in the pantheon of great leaders by displaying traits associated with those past legends, such as Simon Bolivar, also known as the "Liberator."[36] This charisma gives the leader a kind of power to garner a following (Figure 7.3).

Figure 7.3 Castillo Cervantes Jose Ignacio, "Triumphal Entry of Simon Bolivar and His Army," nineteenth century

Bogota, Quinta's Bolivar, Colombia
Photo credit: Album/Art Resource, New York

The image of the balcony—that high up place from which the leader addresses his or her adoring followers below—is a powerful metaphor for leadership in Latin America. It not only exemplifies the place charisma holds in a Latin American context, but also the role of referent power (see Chapter 2).[37] The leader stands as the center of attention—likely delivering an inspirational speech—while the followers look up and cheer. To illustrate this, Asturias gives his President a balcony in the novel, and he basks in the glory, being introduced as the "son of the people" to which the crowd screams— "Long live the President!"

The extreme dualism between leader and follower that is metaphorically seen in the distance between the leader on the balcony and the followers in the crowd below finds its counterpart in the moral dimension of leadership in Latin America. The Judeo-Christian worldview divides the celestial realm between good (heaven) and evil (hell). This perspective resonates with the Latin American conception of the two spheres—private (the family image of heavenly harmony) and public (the corrupt environment where fierce battles take place).

This dualism is once again seen in the division between *machismo* and *marianismo*. Both *machismo* and *marianismo* represent the heavenly domain. The male leader, ready for combat against evil, reflects the image of the all-powerful God the Father, while the female leader represents *marianismo*—the image of the Virgin Mary, seen as calm, loving, compassionate, and self-sacrificing.[38] For the macho leader, compromising is a sign of weakness. The leader does not give in to evil. That would undermine the leader's authority and invite further defeats. While the *marianista* leader is expected to take on a motherly role and heal the organization, particularly following periods of crisis.[39]

In this struggle between good and evil, leaders are ready to demonize their opponents and present themselves as redeemers.[40] When leaders announce their cause to the world, the struggle takes on epic proportions. Charisma tends to be the tool used to garner followers. Charismatic leaders present a transformational vision of the future. Members of an organization or society must choose sides. There is no room to sit on the fence, as the beggars in Asturias' novel found out once interrogated. They are either on one side or the other. Power becomes the arbiter in the negotiation. Followers have strong survival instincts, and they choose sides based on the balance of power. They choose to follow whoever seems to have the most power. In the beggars' case, they chose to lie in order to protect themselves. When another bystander chose to stand by the truth, he was quickly dispatched.

Epic battles also invite extreme measures that are done in the name of defeating evil. Latin American dictatorships during the Cold War engaged in all types of human rights violation in the name of protecting the natural order.[41] Marxism was declared evil; therefore, the leaders saw it as within their right to use all possible means to achieve their goal. For that matter, the United States supported the messianic rhetoric in Latin America and looked the other way as pro-West dictators tortured and made suspects disappear without due process.[42] The epic nature of the Cold War confrontation between capitalism against communism played right into the Latin American dictators' hands and reinforced their leadership worldview. General Canales attempts to go against the order. As he laments:

> It is a more despicable and therefore a sadder thing to be a soldier simply in order to keep a gang of ruffians, exploiters and self-important betrayers of their country in power, than it is to die of hunger in exile. By what right are soldiers forced to be loyal to régimes which are themselves disloyal to ideas, to the world and to their nation?[43]

The General had high ideals—leadership that truly served the interests of the people—but the novel left us with the unfortunate conclusion that this is an idealistic dream. Asturias gives the impression that leadership in the "real world" of Latin America belongs to an uncompromising elite that rules in the name of the natural order.

Summary and concluding remarks

In the previous chapter, we applied six statements related to our Five Components of Leadership Model to the Western worldview. Based on the analysis of the Asturias' novel, we can now compare the different world-views based on these statements (Table 7.2). While the Western perspective views leadership as a prize, the Latin American side sees it as an entitlement based on the natural order. In a way, the Latin American perspective serves

Table 7.2 Western and Latin American comparative views of leadership

	Western worldview	*Latin American worldview*
Leadership viewed as a . . .	Prize (meritocracy)	Entitlement (Natural Order)
Leader-follower relationship	Transactional (rules based; social contract)	Charismatic leadership (referent power)
How decisions are made	Through rationality, logic, pragmatism	Through personalismo (relationship orientation), power politics
Responsibilities of the leader	Motivate followers, results orientation	Order, patronage (relationship building), progress (boldness)
Responsibilities of the follower	Dependable, committed, motivated	Loyal, deeply devoted, passionately committed
Moral dimension of leadership	Secular "code of ethics" (derived from Judeo-Christian values)	Good vs. evil (derived from Judeo-Christian values)

as a truism—the powerful are entitled to be leaders because they have proved themselves to be the most powerful; therefore, deserving of the leader mantle.

Both sides—Western and Latin American—take into consideration the competitive nature of the environmental context. A Western leader thrives on competition. However, rules and institutional norms curb the excesses of power politics. In the Latin American case, competition becomes the main method through which the natural process of leadership selection takes place. Machiavelli, reflecting the Western perspective, proposed a rational and calculated use of the beast. Asturias' novel shows the "natural use" of the beast. Machiavelli's pragmatism creates a transactional relationship between leaders and followers. Asturias' President, however, uses *personalismo* to paint the leader as a savior figure, ready to use the beast in the epic struggle between good and evil.

What are the followers to do in this epic struggle? They are to show loyalty, devotion, and passion toward their savior (charismatic leadership under referent power). Through charisma, leaders motivate followers to demonstrate this high level of devotion. In Asturias' novel, however, we also see the element of coercion in a leader's strategy to build followership. Followers may choose a leader out of fear; again, another element of Machiavelli's admonitions. However, the Machiavellian leader calibrates love and fear through pragmatism. In the Latin American case, loyalty is taken to an extreme where betrayal can result in little mercy—as Angel Face painfully discovered at the end of the novel.

Machiavelli and Asturias certainly show contrasting perspectives on leadership. However, we can only take this contrast to a point. Much of what we discussed in this chapter can be viewed as the traditional perspective on Latin American culture. Howard J. Wiarda, a highly regarded Latin Americanist, calls these values the "old ethos."[44] Under globalization, he argues, "the old values are fading but have not yet disappeared, while the new ideas are coming in but have not yet become institutionalized. The result is both excitement *and* possibilities for conflict."[45] The outcome of this clash of ideas is yet to be determined, but for leaders and followers, as well as those from other cultural frameworks trying to understand Latin American perspective on leadership, it can have a dizzying effect.

One of the clashing areas deals with the dynamic between *personalismo* and the rule of law or an institutional view of leadership. Asturias wrote his novel during a time when the norm was the *caudillo* who molded the rule of law according to his wishes as is seen in the quote in the beginning of the chapter. As Latin American organizations have embraced democratization and decentralization of power, leaders have had to operate within the bounds of the rule of law. Powerful leaders, however, can still change the rules.

The role of the followers also has been affected by these changes under globalization. The "old ethos" assumes a relatively passive, loyal, and devoted follower who easily submits to the will of the leader—until another powerful leader mobilizes other followers to challenge the existing order. Under the evolving shift toward democracy, particularly through social media and rapid means of communication—individuals are not necessarily connected to any leader; yet, they are voicing their own interests in the street.

Even with the increasing influence of the Western worldview in Latin America, we are not ready to discard the "old ethos." The region is still dominated by *personalismo*, preference for the centralization of power under a charismatic leader, distrust of emerging leaders, potentially manipulated followers, and reliance on rigid hierarchies. The twenty-first century may be bringing about deep changes on a global scale, but the Latin American worldview may remain entrenched in the "old ethos" for decades to come.

Questions for discussion

*   What parts of the Latin American view of leadership do you find appealing? Why?
*   How does the concept of "followership" discussed in Chapter 3 fit with the Latin American worldview?
*   Discuss the metaphor of an organization as a family. How does the Latin American worldview incorporate this metaphor into its definition of leadership?
*   What is the role of loyalty and devotion to a leader in the Latin American worldview? How is this different from the Western worldview?

Additional resources

M. Carmagnani, *The Other West: Latin America from Invasion to Globalization*, R.M. Giammanco Frongia trans., Berkeley: University of California Press, 2011.

J. Haar and J. Price, eds., *Can Latin America Compete? Confronting the Challenges of Globalization*, New York: Palgrave Macmillan, 2009.

Notes

1 M.Á. Asturias, *The President*, Frances Partridge trans., Prospect Heights, IL: Waveland Press, 1997, p. 63.
2 P. Goodman, Jr., *Latin America*, 8th edn., Guilford, CN: Dushkin/McGraw-Hill, 1998, p. 6.
3 In the previous chapter, Machiavelli—reflecting the Western perspective—used the river metaphor to suggest the ability of humans to control their environment to actually shape their destiny.
4 This stands in contrast to the Western perspective, which sees rules and institutions as designed to control personal power.
5 This good vs. evil perspective is similar to the Puritan worldview that has influenced the American mindset. See K.D. Wald and A. Calhoun-Brown, *Religion and Politics in the United States*, Lanham, MD: Rowman & Littlefield Publishers, 2011; D. Larson, *The Puritan Ethic in United States Foreign Policy*, Princeton NJ: Van Nostrand, 1966.
6 A. Österling, "The Nobel Prize in Literature 1967." Available at http://www. nobelprize.org/nobel_prizes/literature/ laureates/1967. Accessed August 15, 2014.

7 For representative cases, see W. Fowler, *Santa Anna of Mexico*, Lincoln: University of Nebraska Press, 2007; J. Lynch, *Argentine Caudillo: Juan Manuel de Rosas*, Wilmington, DE: SR Books, 2001; N.S. Perea, *The Caudillo of the Andes: Andrés de Santa Cruz*, New York: Cambridge University Press, 2011.

8 There are obvious similarities between Asturias' childhood experience and the plot in *The President*.

9 M.Á. Asturias, *Legends of Guatemala*, K. Washbourne trans., Pittsburgh: Latin American Literary Review Press, 2011; S. Henighan, *Assuming the Light: The Parisian Literary Apprenticeship of Miguel A'ngel Asturias*, Oxford: Legenda, 1999.

10 "The Nobel Prize in Literature 1967." Available at http://www.nobelprize.org/ nobel_prizes/literature/ laureates/1967. Accessed August 15, 2014.

11 J.C. Chasteen, ed., *Born in Blood and Fire: Latin American Voices*, New York: W.W. Norton & Company, 2011; B. Keen, ed., *Latin American Civilization: History and Society, 1492 to the Present*, Boulder, CO: Westview Press, 2000.

12 C. Lowney, *A Vanished World: Muslims, Christians, and Jews in Medieval Spain*, New York: Oxford University Press, 2006.

13 J. Pohl and C. M. Robinson, *Aztecs and Conquistadores: The Spanish Invasion and the Collapse of the Aztec Empire*, New York: Osprey Publishing, 2005; M. Meltzer, *Francisco Pizarro: The Conquest of Peru*, New York: Benchmark Books, 2003; C.H. Lippy, R. Choquette and S. Poole, *Christianity Comes to the Americas, 1492–1776*, New York: Paragon House, 1992.

14 H. Rawlings, *The Spanish Inquisition*, Malden, MA: Blackwell Publishing, 2006; J. Lynch, *New Worlds: A Religious History of Latin America*, New Haven, NJ: Yale University Press, 2012.

15 R.L. Woodward, Jr., ed., *Positivism in Latin America, 1850–1900: Are Order and Progress Reconcilable?* Lexington, MS: Heath, 1971.

16 M. Gane, *Auguste Comte*, New York: Routledge, 2006; K. Thompson, *Auguste Comte: The Foundation of Sociology*, New York: Wiley, 1975.

17 S. Nuccetelli, O. Schutte, and O. Bueno, eds., *A Companion to Latin American Philosophy*, Malden, MA: Wiley-Blackwell, 2010; S. Nuccetelli, *Latin American Thought: Philosophical Problems and Arguments*, Boulder, CO: Westview Press, 2002.

18 For a review of U.S. foreign policy toward Latin America during the twentieth century, see R. Pastor, *U.S. Foreign Policy Toward Latin America and the Caribbean*, Princeton NJ: Princeton University Press, 1992; L. Schoultz, *National Security and United States Policy Toward Latin America*, Princeton NJ: Princeton University Press, 1987. For a representative example, see P.J. Dosal, *Doing Business with the Dictators: A Political History of United Fruit in Guatemala, 1899–1944*, Wilmington, DE: SR Books, 1993.

19 K. Grieb, *Guatemalan Caudillo, The Regime of Jorge Ubico: Guatemala, 1931–1944*, Athens: Ohio University Press, 1979.

20 For the purpose of this synopsis, we use Miguel Ángel Asturias, *The President*, Frances Partridge trans., Prospect Heights, IL: Waveland Press, 1997. The Orion Publishing Group was contacted for reprint rights, however attempts at tracing the copyright holder of *The President* by Miguel Ángel Asturias were unsuccessful.

21 Angel Face is also described in the novel several times as being "as beautiful and wicked as Satan."

22 Asturias, *The President*, p. 62.

23 One of the beggars, the Mosquito, who stuck to the truth, was quickly eliminated. Later in the novel, the Zany returned to the cathedral, and a policeman (Lucio Vasquez), accompanied by a close friend (Genaro Rodas), killed the Zany by the porch steps.

24 Angel Face developed this plan with the help of Vasquez (the policeman) and a bar owner (La Masacuata) whose bar was located across the street from the General's

home. Vasquez privately shared the arrest order with Rodas (a close friend), who shared the plot with his wife (Niña Fedina); Camila was supposed to become the godmother for the couple's baby.

25 Fedina went to the house looking for Camila to warn her of the arrest order. She is arrested and tortured. Using her baby as leverage, the judge interrogated Fedina. Eventually, the baby was left to die without her mother's care. Through this interrogation, the judge learned of Angel Face's complicity in the General and Camila's escape.

26 The judge went to the President with an indictment against the four who contributed to the General's escape—Angel Face, Vasquez, Fedina, and Genaro. The President rejected the indictment request and ordered Fedina to be released. The judge complied with the order but sold her to a brothel. She arrived at the establishment while still holding her dead baby wrapped in a blanket. Once the prostitutes found the dead baby, they were upset and took her to the hospital. The owner of the brothel was furious with the judge and complained to Angel Face, who recommended that she go to the President and tell him the whole story. The judge arrested Vasquez and interrogated him. Vasquez said that the President himself ordered him to kill the Zany, but Vasquez had no proof of the order.

27 During the same conversation, the President shared that the Judge Advocate also had the plan to kidnap Camila during the General's arrest. We are left with the realization that the judge had planned to sell Camila to the brothel. When that plan was foiled, he sold Fedina instead.

28 Goodman, *Latin America*, p. 6.

29 Asturias, *The President*, pp. 125–126.

30 Ibid, p. 62.

31 Ibid, p. 157.

32 Asturias, *The President*, p. 203.

33 Asturias, *The President*, p. 63. This observation is consistent with more quantitative sources that examine Latin American leadership, for example see the cultural model developed by Geert Hofstede and introduced in Part I. If we take Mexico, for instance, as representative of the Latin American worldview, we can see how Hofstede's dimensions describe the region's approach to leadership. Mexico's score for power distance ("the extent to which the less powerful members of institutions and organisations within a country expect and accept that power is distributed unequally") is 81, compared to the United Kingdom (35)—a representative of the Western worldview. As Hofstede indicates, "At a score of 81, Mexico is a hierarchical society. This means that people accept a hierarchical order in which everybody has a place and which needs no further justification. Hierarchy in an organization is seen as reflecting inherent inequalities, centralization is popular, subordinates expect to be told what to do and the ideal boss is a benevolent autocrat." Another particularly telling indicator from Hofstede's model is uncertainty avoidance—defined as "The extent to which the members of a culture feel threatened by ambiguous or unknown situations and have created beliefs and institutions that try to avoid these." Mexico has a "very high preference for avoiding uncertainty," compared to the United Kingdom's 35. Likewise, for the individualism dimension, the two countries' scores are reversed—Mexico's 30, compared to the United Kingdom's 89. As Hofstede points out, "Mexico, with a score of 30 is considered a collectivistic society. This is manifest in a close long-term commitment to the member 'group,' be that a family, extended family, or extended relationships. Loyalty in a collectivist culture is paramount, and over-rides most other societal rules and regulations. The society fosters strong relationships where everyone takes responsibility for fellow members of their group." The Hofstede Centre. Available at http://geert-hofstede. com/mexico.html. Accessed April 26, 2014.

34 Ibid, 215.
35 Ibid.
36 R. Harvey, *Bolivar: The Liberator of Latin America*, New York: Skyhorse, 2011; D. Bushnell and L.D. Langley, eds., *Simón Bolívar: Essays on the Life and Legacy of the Liberator*, Lanham, MD: Rowman & Littlefield Publishing, 2008.
37 According to Goodwin, José Velasco Ibarra from Ecuador once boasted: "Give me a balcony and I will be president!" Goodman, *Latin America*, 6.
38 E.P. Stevens, "Marianismo: The Other Face of Machismo in Latin America," in A. Minas, ed., *Gender Basics: Feminist Perspectives on Women and Men*, Belmont, CA: Wadsworth/Thomson Learning, 2000, pp. 456–462.
39 Juan and Evita Perón played this dual role in the 1940s quite effectively as they ruled Argentina on behalf of *los descaminados* (the shirtless ones or, the poor and working class). See L.B. Hall, "Evita Peron: Beauty, Resonance, and Heroism," in S. Brunk and B. Fallaw, eds., *Heroes and Hero Cults in Latin America*, Austin: University of Texas Press, 2006: 229–263.
40 E. Krauze, *Redeemers: Ideas and Power in Latin America*, H. Heifetz and N. Wimmer trans., New York: Harper Perennial, 2012.
41 Many military dictatorships in Latin America viewed the Cold War as a battle between good versus evil and brought the power of the state to bear against anyone deemed pro-communism. The interrogation tactics mentioned in the novel *The President* were not unlike the ones eventually denounced in the real Latin America. See P. Kornbluh, *The Pinochet File: A Declassified Dossier on Atrocity and Accountability*, New York: New Press, 2004; P.H. Lewis, *Guerillas and Generals: The "Dirty War" in Argentina*, Westport, CT: Praeger, 2002.
42 M.J. Kryzanek, *Leaders, Leadership, and U.S. Policy in Latin America*, Boulder, CO: Westview Press, 1992.
43 Asturias, *The President*, p.187.
44 H.J. Wiarda, *Latin American Politics*, New York: Wadsworth Publishing Company, 1995, p. 66.
45 Ibid. Italics in original.

8   Leadership in an Islamic cultural context

> On a journey, the leader of the people is their servant.
>
> Mohammad

We turn now to examine leadership from an Islamic perspective. Islam is currently the fastest growing religion in the world. A recent study estimates that Muslims will make up more than 26% of the world's population by 2030.[1] Although adherents to the religion can be found around the globe, there are countries, such as Indonesia and Malaysia, and regions, such as the Middle East and North Africa, where the majority of the population is Muslim. Likewise, some of these countries officially recognize Islam as the core of their political system (see Figure 8.1).

Despite the large number of adherents, many in the West are unaware of the basic teachings of Islam and the history of its founder, Mohammad. This is unfortunate. Islamic scholar Akbar S. Ahmed notes, "Without an understanding of history, it is difficult to explain Muslim behavior and impossible to understand Muslim politics."[2] In this chapter, we seek to tell the story of Islam and explain the religion's core teachings while drawing out the implications this worldview may have on an understanding of leadership.

It is impossible to succinctly summarize 1400 years of history in a single chapter. So we have chosen an artifact to help illustrate the early founding of Islam. The epic film *The Message* (1977) directed by Moustapha Akkad and starring Anthony Quinn as Mohammad's uncle, Hamza, tells the story of the birth of Islam and in so doing highlights the religion's key teachings.[3] The film also presents Mohammad as the prime example of an Islamic leader to which other Islamic leaders should aspire. Islamic scholars and historians from the University of Al-Azhar in Cairo and the High Islamic Congress of the Shia in Lebanon approved the accuracy and fidelity of the film before it was made.[4] Undoubtedly, there are some Muslims who would not sympathize with the film. There are significant differences between Sunni and Shia Muslims who hold different accounts of the early history of Islam, as well as major doctrinal differences. In keeping with Sunni Islamic tradition, *the person of Mohammad is*

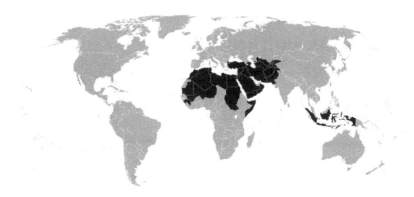

Figure 8.1 The "Islamic world"

never shown in the film, neither does Mohammad speak. Rather, the director, Akkad, used a variety of cinematographic and narrative devices to creatively and respectfully tell the story. Akkad remarked, "Being a Muslim myself who lived in the West, I felt that it was my obligation, my duty, to tell the truth about Islam."[5] The film does indeed provide a concise and compelling account of the early history of Islam and its founder, and is especially helpful to those who have never been introduced to the religion.

The film's producer and director, Akkad, ran into multiple difficulties during the production of the film, including a loss of backing from Saudi Arabia and a hurricane that destroyed a major set.[6] He finally completed the film in Libya with the blessing of the dictator Muammar Gaddafi.[7] When the film was released in 1977, originally titled *Mohammad, Messenger of God*, a small group of American Hanafi Muslims, led by Hamaas Abdul Khaalis, held siege to three buildings in Washington, D.C. One of the group's demands was that the film be pulled from theaters. (Although, it is doubtful that anyone in the group had even *seen* the film because it had only just been released in theaters at the time of the siege.) Over the course of 39 hours in the Hanafi Siege, two people were killed. In response to the crisis, the director, Akkad—who was, himself, Muslim—vowed to burn the film if it contained anything disrespectful to Islam.[8] Nevertheless, the film was, indeed, frozen until the crisis was resolved.

Film critics also found fault in the film and one even described it as "so reverential toward its subject as to seem mechanical."[9] Nevertheless, the film was nominated for an Academy Award for its musical score and remains the only film of its kind with the high-production values that can be offered by a Hollywood film. Throughout this chapter, then, we will reference the film as an accessible artifact to understand some of the key teachings of Islam and an Islamic approach to leadership.

Case study: Moustapha Akkad's *The Message*

Before we launch into the film, we need to provide a bit of context on the historical narrative that sets the stage for the founding of Islam. The heart of Islam is Allah—the Arabic term for God—"The One who is to be worshipped." The term holds unyielding implications as a reference to monotheism—or the worship of one god. Correspondingly, the Arabic word "Islam" can be translated to mean "submission" or "surrender." Moreover, the Arabic root word for "Islam" is "*salam*" meaning "peace." Thus, the term "Islam" may be best understood as "peace through surrender to Allah." A Muslim, then, is a follower of Islam, or "one who surrenders to Allah."

To find the original source of Islam, we have to go back to circa 2130 BCE to the story of Abraham[10] found in the Jewish Torah, the book of Genesis in the Old Testament, and Islam's Holy Book, the Quran. Jews, Christians, and Muslims all trace their origins to Abraham. Muslims even refer to Jews and Christians as "fellow people of the Book," and the three religions all worship the same god. There are many similarities between the accounts of Abraham's life found in these texts, but there are some significant differences. Since we are telling the story of Islam, we will relay the account found in the Quran.

It is said that God, Allah, told Abraham that he would have a son, and that God would establish a great nation through him. However, for many years Abraham and his wife Sarah did not conceive a child, so Abraham took a second wife, Hagar.[11] This was a common practice in the culture at the time. Hagar did indeed bear Abraham a son, Ishmael.[12] Meanwhile, Sarah also gave birth to a son, Isaac. In a test of Abraham's faith, God told Abraham to abandon Hagar and Ishmael in the desert.[13] Hagar desperately searched for water to provide for her child and cried out to God to help her. Allah heard her prayer and sent his archangel Gabriel who caused a spring to bubble up in the desert, sparing Hagar and Ishmael. They then settled in what is now modern-day Mecca in Saudi Arabia.

This is where the three religions more substantially diverge in their accounts. All the religions agree that Abraham had a vision, or a dream, in which he believed Allah told him to sacrifice his son as an offering to God, but they disagree on which son was to be offered to God, Isaac or Ishmael. Jewish and Christian traditions claim that the son who was to be sacrificed was Isaac, whereas the Islamic tradition claims that the son to be sacrificed was Ishmael. Muslims believe that when Abraham told Ishmael about his dream, his son willingly submitted to God's will and surrendered himself to Allah and Abraham to be sacrificed. Just as Abraham was about to plunge the knife into his son, God stopped him. Abraham had passed another test. God knew that Abraham loved him more than he loved his son. Rather than demanding that Abraham sacrifice Ishmael, God provided Abraham with a lamb to be sacrificed in place of his son. (This event is still re-enacted and celebrated in Islam as *Eid-al-Adha*, the Celebration of the Sacrifice.) Abraham and Ishmael sacrificed the lamb and built a temple "to the one true God." That temple, known as the Kaaba, still stands today in modern-day Mecca in Saudi Arabia, and has become Islam's most holy site.

Synopsis of the film

After setting this scene, we are now ready to better understand the context of the film. We fast forward to circa 570 AD, more than two and a half millennia after Abraham and Ishmael built the Kabba. The shrine still stands in the center of Mecca, but the original purpose of the Ancient House has lapsed. Over the centuries, Mecca had become a crossroads of trade, and local tribes had begun using the Kaaba to worship their own gods in the form of idols, rather than the God of Abraham, Allah. Once a year, the local tribes would make a pilgrimage to Mecca for a great fair, and the Kaaba would play host to their idols.

Into this culture, a child named Mohammad was born. He was orphaned when he was a child and was raised by his grandfather, and later by his uncle, Abu Talib. Mohammad grew up as a shepherd and eventually became a well-respected merchant and caravan leader. When he was 25, he met and married his first wife, Khadija, an affluent widow and businesswoman who was 15 years his senior. Mohammad was known to often retire alone to the hills surrounding Mecca to meditate. When he was 40 years old, he was given the first in a series of revelations that were to last for 23 years in which the Archangel Gabriel— the same angel who saved Hagar and Ishmael—dictated Islam's Holy Book, the Quran, to Mohammad. Gabriel told Mohammad that the people of Mecca were to worship only one God, Allah. After his vision, Mohammad called on the people of Mecca to stop worshiping the idols of their local tribes, and embrace the one true God, Allah.

The people of Mecca did not take kindly to Mohammad's message. Mecca's culture and economy were tied to the Kaaba and the celebration of local deities. Families divided and the people of Mecca became embroiled in a bitter feud. Over time, Mohammad's followers began to grow in number, and the leaders of Mecca began persecuting them. This led these early followers to declare openly the first precept of Islam, "There is no God but God, and Mohammad is his prophet." The persecution became more intense. Some of Mohammad's followers sought and received refuge in Abyssinia where there was a Christian emperor. Mohammad and his remaining followers were driven from Mecca into the desert where they lived for three years. It was here that Mohammad's beloved wife, Khadija, died, as did his uncle, Abu Talib. Muslims call this time the Year of Grief.

At long last, the leaders of the neighboring city of Yathrib asked Mohammad to come to their city to serve as its leader and still the civil unrest that plagued them. (The name of the city was later changed to Medina.) Mohammad agreed to serve as the leader of the city under the condition that the inhabitants would accept and embrace the teaching of the Oneness of God. (Consequently, Jewish clans were also allowed to remain in the city.) Mohammad sent his followers to Medina and stayed in the desert until they were safe. The leaders of Mecca plotted to kill the Prophet, but they failed. Under threat of death, Mohammad journeyed to Medina and joined his followers where together they built Islam's first mosque. (This migration, known as Hijra, in 622 AD marks the first year of the Islamic lunar calendar, demarked by the abbreviation AH— After Hijra.)

However, the leaders of Mecca were not content to leave Mohammad and his followers in peace. They confiscated all of his and his followers' remaining land and possessions in Mecca. Although Mohammad did not immediately respond to the persecution, the Prophet eventually did call his followers to arms against the leaders of Mecca. The two sides engaged in a battle in which Mohammad's followers were victorious. The people of Mecca returned in vengeance a year later, and this time the Muslims were not as fortunate. The Muslims believed that Allah sent them a defeat to try their faith. Rather than returning to battle, the Muslims regrouped and returned to Mecca as unarmed pilgrims and reaffirmed their faith in Allah.

The leaders of Mecca gave the Prophet the conditions of truce, and Mohammad agreed to make a pilgrimage to Mecca the following year in exchange for 10 years of peace between the Muslims and the people of Mecca. The truce was broken a few years later, however, and Mohammad returned to Mecca with 10,000 troops. This time the leaders and people of Mecca surrendered peacefully, and Mohammad became the ruler of Mecca. At Mohammad's orders, the people of Mecca were left unharmed—even its leader and his wife, who later became Muslims. On his return, the Prophet cleansed the Kaaba of its idols destroying them, and reestablished the Ancient House as a temple to the one true God as Abraham had intended.

Origins of an Islamic worldview

Over the course of 23 years, Mohammad received many revelations from God and these became the Quran. Mohammad was illiterate and could not read or write. Thus, Allah's revelation of the Quran to Mohammad is considered to be the first of only two miracles claimed by Islam. (The other is an account in which Mohammad received a beatific vision of the past and future of humankind and met the former prophets of Judaism and Christianity.) The Quran became the basis for the Islamic faith and is considered by Muslims to be the immutable word of God by which all of life's thoughts and actions should be measured. A second text, the *Hadith*, a collection of the deeds and sayings of the Prophet Mohammad, is also an important source of inspiration and the basis of *Shariah* or Islamic law and Islamic leadership.

Mohammad died in 632 AD, but not before he had united the Arabian peninsula under the teachings of Islam. After his death, Mohammad's succession was contested and this schism ultimately divided Islam into two major groups, Shia Muslims and Sunni Muslims, although, today, there are many other sects of Islam as well. Sunnis make up approximately 80% of practicing Muslims and can be found in China, Southeast Asia, Africa, and the Middle East, whereas Shia Muslims make up about 10 per cent of all of Muslims and are more heavily concentrated in the Middle East in countries such as Iraq and Iran, although there is also a very large population in Pakistan.

The five pillars of Islam

Although there are a wide variety of approaches to Islam and interpretations of passages in the Quran, all Muslims everywhere hold a common set of core practices—what is referred to as Islam's "five pillars": the *shahada*—the pledge of commitment to God and the teachings of His Prophet, Mohammad; prayer (*salat*); charity (*zakat*); fasting (*sawm*); and a pilgrimage to Mecca (*hajj*). We can see each of these pillars established in our case study, *The Message*.

The first pillar, the *shahada*, is a Muslim's declaration of faith and commitment to the teachings of Mohammad. The direct translation is "I bear witness that there is no god but the God and Mohammad is the messenger of God." This pledge is the *key* teaching of Islam, and there is a reason it is first among its pillars. As we see in our case study, this was the primary contention between the leaders of Mecca and Mohammad. Muslims believe that any person who speaks this pledge and sincerely commits to it even once in his or her lifetime is considered to be a Muslim in the eyes of Allah. When this oath is repeated by Muslims today, it harkens back to this first declaration by Mohammad's early followers.

The second pillar of Islam is prayer. All Muslims are to pray five times each day—before sunrise, noon, late afternoon, before sunset, and before retiring for the evening. The consistent schedule is meant to remind Muslims of their devotion to God. Before praying, the person praying is to ceremonially wash. The person praying then recites prescribed pieces from the Quran while facing Mecca. In fact, the term "Quran" means "recitation" in Arabic. While praying, the person performs a set of prostrations, usually on a small rug, to indicate submission to Allah and His will.

We see a beautiful illustration of this practice in the film in the scene in which Mohammad and his followers build their first mosque in Medina. Bilal, a former slave and one of the first converts to Islam, was a close companion of Mohammad. When the mosque was finished, Bilal was chosen to be the first *muezzin*, the person who calls Muslims to prayer. In the film, Bilal climbs the mosque's minaret and sings: "God is greatest. I bear witness that there is no deity but God. I bear witness that Mohammad is the messenger of God." This same call to worship can be heard today in thousands of mosques throughout the world.

Charity is the third pillar of Islam. Each year, every financially stable Muslim is to give at least 2½ per cent of his wealth and assets to the poor and to advance the cause of Islam. Islam's concept of charity goes beyond a simple good deed. Charity, or *zakat* as it is called in Arabic, is also a means of purifying oneself for wrongdoings. The practice is intimately tied to the Islamic teaching of social justice and equality, which we will discuss in more detail in the next section of our chapter.

Fasting is the fourth pillar of Islam, and is specifically linked to the holy month of Ramadan, the ninth month in the Islamic calendar. During this time, Muslims are to fast from sunrise to sunset. (There are exceptions for children, the elderly, and others for whom fasting would present a physical hardship.) This is a spiritual time for Muslims in which they are to pray, read the Quran, and focus on the teachings of their faith. At the end of the month, the fast is broken with a celebration—*Eid al-Fitr*—and a three-day feast. This is one of the two major holidays in the Sunni Muslim tradition.

Finally, there is the pilgrimage to Mecca (*hajj*)—the fifth and final pillar of Islam. Every Muslim who is financially and physically able is to make a journey to Mecca at some point in his or her lifetime. To this day, Muslims all over the world make a pilgrimage to Mecca during the Islamic month of *dhu al-hijjah*. (Although Muslims may go to Mecca at other times of the year in what is referred to as the lesser pilgrimage.) During *dhu al-hijjah*, Muslims en masse circle the Kaaba while wearing special garments made of two simple pieces of white cloth. This month culminates in the major Islamic holiday, *Eid al-Adha*. At this time, sheep are slaughtered to symbolize Abraham's willingness to sacrifice his son Ishmael to God, and any excess meat is given to the needy in keeping with the practice of charity. Again, our film provides a cinematic reenactment of this event in its portrayal of Mohammad and his followers' first pilgrimage to Mecca. The film provides a helpful visual representation of all of these major aspects of Islam.

An ideal society

The early history and five pillars of Islam discussed here do not simply provide background to understanding the Islamic faith. More profoundly, this is a living history with deep implications for Muslim societal values and norms. One leading Islamic scholar notes, "History [for Muslims] is not a random series of unconnected acts; there is a clear pattern of cause and effect as Muslims attempt to line up to a notion of an ideal society inspired by their vision of God."[14] This concept of an ideal society is fundamental to understanding an Islamic approach to leadership.

One author who most succinctly summarizes Islam's social teachings of an ideal society is Huston Smith in his highly acclaimed book, *The World's Religions*. Smith observes: "Westerners who define religion in terms of personal experience would never be understood by Muslims, whose religion calls them to establish a specific kind of social order. Islam joins faith to politics, religion to society inseparably."[15] Smith summarizes four of the major social teachings of Islam, all of which can be seen in our case study: the importance of fair economic systems, the raising of the status of women, racial equality, and the just and proper use of force.[16]

The first of Smith's observations concerns itself with economics. Islam believes financial systems must operate fairly to allow all participants an equal chance to compete and obtain economic independence. This is, in part, related to the importance of the *zakat*, or the 2½ per cent of a Muslim's income that is to be given directly to the poor. But this is not the only practice of economic fairness that Islam addresses. Muslims also believe that everyone should have an equal chance to pursue his own economic independence. This denial was partly what early Muslims found so egregious about the leaders of Mecca confiscating their land and possessions. Islam also commands that inheritances are to be distributed to all heirs and not just the firstborn son, and that daughters are also to be included in inheritance rights.

This admonition is in keeping with Islam's theme of social justice and women. Islam elevated the status of women who, before Mohammad's teaching, were considered mere objects to be traded and disposed of at will. Female children were often buried alive, and we see a reference to this practice in the film. Islam demanded that this practice be forbidden and that women be given an inheritance, the freedom to choose their spouse, and the right to divorce. Islam also granted women the right to vote 1300 years before the West. Although these rights seem self-evident to us today, this was radical thinking in Mohammad's time and culture.

This theme of social justice continues in Islam's insistence of racial equality. As we mentioned earlier and as seen in our film, Bilal—one of the first converts to Islam and its first *muezzin*—was an Ethiopian. He was one of Mohammad's companions and held a great deal of influence in the early history of Islam. Moreover, Mohammad spoke to racial equality in his farewell sermon:

> All mankind is from Adam and Eve, an Arab has no superiority over a non-Arab nor a non-Arab has any superiority over an Arab; also a white has no superiority over a black, nor a black has any superiority over a white except by piety and good action.

This concept is further illustrated in our case study when Hamza refers to the *Hadith* and Mohammad's saying that all people are as equal before God as "the teeth of a comb."[17] Islam established a theme of racial equality that remains an emphasis of the faith today (Figure 8.2).

Finally, Islam lays forth the conditions for the use of force. Islam does allow for the use of force, but force is only to be applied in response to an aggressor or to right an injustice. Likewise, the force used to reply to such actions should be equal to, and not greater than, the force originally used. This leads to the concept of *jihad*, the Islamic concept of a just war. A just war, a *jihad*, must either be defensive or used to right a wrong. The Quran states "Defend yourself against your enemies, but do not attack them first: God hates the aggressor" (2:190). But there is another meaning to *jihad* that goes much deeper, what Muslims refer to as the "greater *jihad*." This is the internal and sacred struggle

Figure 8.2 Film still from *The Message* (1977): Anthony Quinn as Hamza and Johnny
Sekka as Bilal

Photo credit: *The Message*, Anthony Quinn/Sid Avery & Associates. DBA mptv (mptvimages.com)

all Muslims are called to fight in order to overcome their baser instincts. The
greater *jihad* calls Muslims to righteousness and piety as they seek to live by
the teachings of the Quran and seek Allah's will. Again, this concept is reflected
in our case study by Mohammad's hesitancy to go to war with the leaders of
Mecca. Now that we have a basic understanding of the history of Islam, its
basic tenets, and its social values, we can more deeply discuss an Islamic view
of leadership.

Analysis: Leadership as a trust

The Message introduces the viewer to the early history of Islam and its teachings
(see Figure 8.3). The film also introduces the viewer to an Islamic view of
leadership as established by Mohammad. Some of the key themes as related to
leadership are: 1) the importance for leaders to follow the teachings of Islam;
2) the idea that leaders are given a trust to care for their followers; 3) the
significance of justice; 4) the importance of community; and 5) the reciprocal
relationship between leader and followers.

The first lesson we can discern from our artifact is the idea that a good
leader should ultimately be a good Muslim. As we mentioned earlier, Islamic

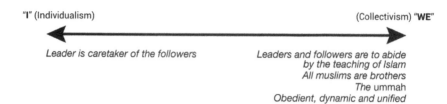

"**I**" (Individualism)   (Collectivism) "**WE**"

Leader is caretaker of the followers   *Leaders and followers are to abide*
                                                                            by the teaching of Islam
                                                                            All muslims are brothers
                                                                            The ummah
                                                                Obedient, dynamic and unified

Figure 8.3 The Islamic worldview on the leadership continuum

leadership scholars agree that leadership in the Islamic tradition is based on Islam's holy book, the Quran, and the *Hadith*, the reports of the words and deeds of Mohammad.[18] This is most clearly expressed in the expectation of Islamic leaders to be virtuous and hold to the teachings and practices of Islam. This may best be summarized as the importance that leaders be righteous.[19] This is the expectation in both spiritual and worldly affairs.[20] Islamic leadership scholars Rafik I. Beekun and Jamal Badawi make a case for this central role of religion in Islamic leadership in their leadership model, which positions Allah and the teaching of Islam at its core.[21] This emphasis on religion as the source of leadership instruction can be difficult for those in the West to understand. In the West, religion is considered primarily regulated to the private sphere, but religion is key to an understanding of the ideal form of Islamic leadership.

However, an Islamic approach to leadership does implicate many theories of leadership to which Westerners can relate. Not the least of these is the idea that leaders should possess certain traits and behaviors that were so influential in the early history of the contemporary study of leadership and referred to in Chapter 1. Ideal Muslim leaders are expected to possess traits as emulated by the Prophet Mohammad. Indeed, the very name "Mohammad" means "praiseworthy" and his followers—in leadership positions or not—are to follow his example. The Prophet Mohammad is explicitly referred to as "the perfect human" and an "excellent model of conduct."[22] Some of these traits include mercy, goodness, kindness, and justice. This expectation has some weighty implications for those Muslims who find themselves in positions of leadership.

There is a reason for these high expectations. Unlike the West where leadership is viewed as a prize for leaders to win, Islam views leadership as a trust bestowed on the leader by the followers to help them reach their common goal. It is a leader's duty to care for the followers, and there are eternal implications in the process. Islamic leadership studies scholar Abbas J. Ali makes this point:

> The community entrusts a leader with the authority to conduct affairs on behalf of and for the benefit of the people. The Prophet Mohammad[23] stated: 'A ruler who has been entrusted with the affairs of the Muslims but makes no endeavor [for their material and moral uplift] and is not sincerely

concerned [for their welfare] will not enter paradise along with them' and 'authority is a trust; one must be qualified for it and execute it duly otherwise, in the day of judgment, it is a shame and regret.'[24]

The eternal religious implications of leadership may strike the Westerner as strange. As some observers note, "What distinguishes Islamic leadership most from traditional western notions of leadership is the close attachment of leadership to religion, especially its moral and human roots."[25] But again, this intermingling of the secular and the sacred is the quintessential hallmark of Islamic leadership.

There is another contemporary theory of leadership that is implied through this process of leaders carrying out this trust. Muslim leaders are to be servants of their followers. This is not unlike the idea of servant leadership proposed by Robert Greenleaf in which the leader's primary purpose is to enable his or her followers to be their best and reach their goal.[26] In fact, Mohammad himself said, "On a journey, the leader of the people is their servant." Indeed, several scholars have noted the root of servant leadership in Islam.[27] Mohammad was careful to note that he was only a man, a human being just like all of his followers, and did not claim any special treatment because of his position as God's messenger. This point is clearly emphasized in a key verse in the Quran:

> Say, O [Muhammad], "I am only a man like you to whom it has been revealed that your god is but one God; so take a straight course to Him and seek His forgiveness." And woe to those who associate others with Allah.[28]

This humility and placing the good of the followers and the goal above one's self-interests is undoubtedly in keeping with Greenleaf's idea of servant leadership, but there is another level to Islamic leadership that is uniquely joined to this idea; that is, the leader as "guardian" or "caretaker" to the followers.

In emphasizing this idea of leader as guardian, Beekun and Badawi cite the words of Mohammad to make their point:

> All of you are guardians and are responsible for your wards. The ruler is a guardian and man is a guardian of his family; the lady is a guardian and is responsible for her husband's house and his offspring; and so all of you are guardians and are responsible for your wards.[29]

Further, it is reported from Abu Hurairah:

> The Prophet of Allah (peace be upon him) said, 'A commander (of the Muslims) is a shield for them. They fight behind him and they are protected by him (from tyrants and aggressors). If he enjoins fear of Allah, the Exalted and Glorious, and dispenses justice, there will be a (great) reward for him; and if enjoins otherwise, it rebounds on him.'[30]

Other scholars note, "According to the Quran, each individual has been appointed on this earth as the vice-regent of the Almighty to discharge a set of defined responsibilities and obligations."[31] This idea of guardianship has been noted by other scholars sometimes employing the metaphor of "leader as shepherd" or "leader as caretaker" to illustrate this concept.[32] Again, this idea means that the leader places the good of the followers as his or her primary concern. One scholar notes, "This commitment to serving aligns Islamic teaching with the relational-based practices of communitarian cultures."[33]

This view of leadership can also be seen at various points in the film. The first is Mohammad's care for his people in the desert when they were first exiled from Mecca. Even when the people of Medina called Mohammad to be their leader and rule their city, Mohammad stayed near Mecca until all of his followers were safely in the city of Medina before leaving for Medina himself, even though this placed him in danger from the leaders of Mecca who tried to have him killed. In other places in the film, Mohammad also leads his army into battle and fights alongside them to defend them from their enemies. But this idea of leader as caretaker is true on a much deeper level as well, that is, the purpose of creating the ideal Islamic society.

The Islamic notion of a leader's responsibility goes far beyond the immediate task at hand and extends to the purpose of creating a just society based on the teachings of Islam.[34] This is the core purpose of Islamic leadership. As we see in our case study, when the people of Mecca had committed a great injustice against the early Muslims by robbing them of their land and possessions, Mohammad sought to right the wrong by leading his followers into battle. One scholar argues, "So intense is this idea of economic justice of the common [person] that its importance is not less than that of monotheism or One God and His worship" and "in the absence of seeking the general welfare of men, worship of God—even of one God—is not only meaningless but sheer hypocrisy."[35] Islamic leadership scholar Ali Mohammad Mir articulates the importance of this vision in a more contemporary context:

> From an Islamic viewpoint, leadership must be seen from the perspective of the worldly mission a Muslim has to fulfill. In its simplicity, it is to work for the collective well-being of society through the propagation of all that is good (*Amr Bil Maroof*) and defeating all that is evil (*Nahi-Al-Munkar*).[36] In the Islamic leadership model, leaders pursue a vision of creating a society that is just, welfare-oriented, egalitarian, and free from discrimination, exploitation, and oppression.[37]

The purpose of Islamic leadership, as Mir notes here, underscores the significance of the social teachings of Islam. As servants and guardians of the community, Islamic leaders are duty bound to work for and seek a just community prescribed by Islam for their fellow Muslims far and wide.

It is important for Westerners to understand that this community is *not* exclusively restricted to a leader's immediate followers, but that this community extends to *all Muslims everywhere*—the *ummah* in Arabic. This is encapsulated by the belief that all Muslims are brothers as stated in the Quran: "The believers are but brothers, so make settlement between your brothers. And fear Allah that you may receive mercy." [38] This concept is also echoed in Mohammad's farewell sermon in which he preached, "Learn that every Muslim is a brother to every Muslim and that the Muslims constitute one brotherhood." This was radical thinking at the time of Mohammad in which cultural bonds were based on familial kinship. The *ummah*, by the same token, bases kinship on the foundation of a shared faith in Allah and the teachings of Islam. With this in mind, it is important to note that a perceived injustice done to a Muslim in one situation is interpreted as an injustice done to all Muslims everywhere.[39] The servant–guardian leader's care is expected to extend to this larger community.

However, within this community, the leader–follower relationship is not exclusively one way—leaders are also answerable to their followers. Traditional Islam contends that leaders and followers mutually influence each other in a reciprocal relationship.[40] One researcher notes:

> The traditional view of leadership in Islam is that leadership is a shared influence process. Leaders are not expected to lead or maintain their roles without the agreement of those who are led, and at the same time, decision made by these leaders were expected to be influenced by input from their followers. The process is dynamic and open-ended and the ultimate aim is to sustain cohesiveness and effectiveness.[41]

This is very much like transformational leadership covered in the previous section of the book. Recall that in transformational leadership, the leader and follower influence each other in a mutual relationship that elevates *both* parties to "higher levels of motivation and morality."[42] In further evidence of this expectation for mutual consideration in Islamic leadership we look to the Islamic idea of *shura*, the method of making decisions through consultation with the community as a praised form of decision making in the Quran and as practiced by the Prophet Mohammad.[43]

This leads us to more deeply consider the follower's responsibility in the leadership process. If, indeed, the leader is following the teachings and practices of Islam, the followers are called to be obedient to the leader and unified in the process of achieving the common goal. Islamic scholars Beekun and Badawi identify these behaviors expected of followers and tie their reasoning to passages in the Quran. The authors say, "Islam considers obedience to the leader so important that it views any kind of insubordination to be abhorrent except in very specific circumstances."[44] The researchers use the following verses from the Quran and the *Hadith* to emphasize their point:

> O you who believe! Obey Allah, and obey the Messenger, and those charged with authority among you. If you differ in anything among

yourselves refer it to Allah and His Messenger if you do believe in Allah and the Last Day: that is best and most suitable for final determination.[45]

And:

> The best of your rulers are those whom you love and who love you, who invoke Allah's blessings upon you and you invoke His blessings upon them. And the worst of your rulers are those whom you hate and who hate you and whom you curse and who curse you. It was asked (by those present): Shouldn't we overthrow them with the help of the sword? He said: No, as long as they establish prayer among you. If you then find anything detestable in them, you should hate their administration, but do not withhold yourselves from their obedience.[46]

Likewise, Faris and Parry state, "Followers have a religious obligation to obey their leaders so long as there is no disobedience of God and the Prophet. Because God and the Prophet have placed expectations upon all Muslims to be morally righteous, this requirement might arguably place an onus on leaders to be ethical and trustworthy."[47] If a leader is not upholding the teachings and practices of Islam, however, their followers are under no compulsion to follow their leader. As Abu Bakr, Mohammad's successor said, "Obey me so long as I obey Allah and His Messenger. If I disobey them, then you have no obligation to follow me."[48]

Summary and concluding remarks

Examining Table 8.1, we can begin to see the gulf that separates Western and Islamic understandings of leadership. Whereas the West views leadership as a temporal prize, the Islamic world views leadership as a trust with eternal consequences. The West views leadership as something to be pursued and attained to benefit one's own self, while Muslims believe leadership should be used to benefit the entire community, and certainly not to be *pursued*, but rather to be *bestowed* on the leader by the group.

Likewise, there is a vast division between the transactional expectations of the West's social contract and the moral transformational expectations of the Islamic world. Even the "secularization" of transformational leadership championed by those in the West would be foreign to the religious interpretation of the concept in the Islamic world. To be a transformational leader in the West has little or nothing to do with religion. Rather, the West champions a secular code of ethics that specifically attempts to separate "church and state" and even "religion and leadership." This interpretation of transformational leadership is completely foreign to the Islamic mind, where the idea of motivating each other to "higher levels of morality" is specifically equated with encouraging each other to be a better Muslim. This division is especially evident in the Western "secular code of ethics" that is independent

Table 8.1 Western and Islamic comparative views of leadership

	Western worldview	Islamic worldview
Leadership viewed as a . . .	Prize (meritocracy)	A trust (The leader is the servant and the caretaker of the followers)
Leader-follower relationship	Transactional (rules based; social contract)	Transformational (The leader and followers should motivate each other to a higher morality as defined by Islam)
How decisions are made	Through rationality, logic, pragmatism	Through consultation while seeking Allah's will
Responsibilities of the leader	Motivate followers, results orientation	Work for justice
Responsibilities of the follower	Dependable, committed, motivated	Obedient, dynamic, and unified
Moral dimension of leadership	Secular "code of ethics" (derived from Judeo-Christian values)	The teachings of the Quran and the Hadith

from religion, as opposed to the Islamic code of ethics, which is based on the Quran and the words and teachings of the Prophet Mohammad.

Even the impetus behind decisions is different between the two cultures. While the West seeks measurable, tangible, and immediate results, Muslims seek Allah's will while they establish a just society that has resounding implications throughout eternity. This quest can seem mystical to those in the West. In contrast, Muslims believe that Allah has given them all they need to know in "all walks of life ranging from economics, jurisprudence, diplomacy and governance, to aspects focusing on individual well-being, such as social values and etiquettes, family relationship, and lifestyle."[49] In testimony to this, those familiar with the Muslim and Arabic-speaking world will notice the constant use of the phrase "*Insha'Allah*," which literally translated means "God willing."[50]

Seeing these differences, those in the West and the Islamic world might be able to better understand some of the reasons for the division between them. However, there are similarities as well. Some of the most ideal forms of leadership discussed in the contemporary literature on leadership—such as servant leadership, transformational leadership, and consultative decision making—have their roots in the early history of the Islamic world. Under the greater umbrella of globalization, these worlds, likewise, continue to influence each other in many ways.

An important point that readers should keep in mind is that what we have presented here is an *ideal* of Islamic leadership. Certainly, just as in the West and other cultures, there are those leaders who do not follow the best of the ideals valued by the civilization and may differ in their interpretation of the teachings of Islam. Others have also pointed out, because of the strong cultural values of the group and long-term understanding of history, Muslims may be inclined to follow a leader who is part of their culture rather than supporting a leader who is a part of another group that has historically been hostile to Muslims.[51] Likewise, just as there are many styles and approaches to leadership in the West, the observer may find many styles and approaches to leadership in Islam. One author identifies several such styles ranging from autocratic, sheikocratic, traditional (group oriented), and spiritually enlightened as just a few of the other types of leadership one may find in an Islamic society. [52] These other styles are likely to be the result of the multiple cultures found in many Islamic countries.[53]

Islam itself is not a monolithic religion and expands national and cultural boundaries; thus, some approaches to leadership in Islamic cultures may reflect as much a part of the local or national culture as they do greater Islam. Regardless of these other factors, the Islamic approach to leadership we have described here emphasizes the main point of the Five Elements of Leadership model that we have been developing throughout the course of this book, that is, leadership is greatly affected by the values and norms in which it is enacted.

Questions for discussion

*   What role do you believe religion should play in a person's approach to leadership?
    Do you think your culture influences your response? How so?
*   What aspects of an Islamic approach to leadership do you find compelling?
*   How have the teachings and values of Islam been viewed in your culture?
*   What is your higher purpose of studying and practicing leadership?
*   What is your vision of an "ideal society" or a "better world"?
*   What do you believe is the greatest division between a Western and an Islamic approach to leadership? What might be done to help bridge this gap?

Additional resources

J. Adair, *The Leadership of Muhammad*, Philadelphia, PA: Kogan Page, 2010.
B.D. Metcalfe and F. Mimouni, *Leadership Development in the Middle East*, Cheltenham: Edward Elgar, 2011.
M.H. Morgan, *Lost History: The Enduring Legacy of Muslim Scientists, Thinkers, and Artists*, Washington, DC: National Geographic Society, 2007.

Notes

1   Pew Research Religion and Public Life Project, "The Future of the Global Muslim Population." Available at http://www.pewforum.org/2011/01/27/the-future-of-the-global-muslim-population/. Accessed August 17, 2014.
2   A.S. Ahmed, "Foreword," in T. Sonn, *A Brief History of Islam*, Malden, MA: Blackwell, 2004, p. xiv.

3 *The Message*, motion picture, Filmco International Productions, Los Angeles, 1976.
4 The director, Akkad, placed a slide in the first few minutes of the film verifying this. He also speaks about the approval sought from these groups in the documentary portion of the DVD, which discusses the making of the film. *The Making of an Epic: Mohammad the Messenger of God*, documentary, Filmco International Productions, Los Angeles, 1976.
5 Ibid.
6 Akkad shot the film in both English and Arabic with two different casts in the leading roles.
7 Later Akkad worked once again with the Gaddafi government to film *The Lion in the Desert*, also with Quinn.
8 M. Burnley, "*The Message*: The Movie about Islam that Sparked a Hostage Crisis in D.C.," *The Atlantic*, November 20, 2012. Available at http://www.theatlantic.com/international/archive/2012/11/the-message-the-movie-about-islam-that-sparked-a-hostage-crisis-in-dc/264939/. Accessed August 17, 2014.
9 Ibid.
10 "Ibrahim" in Arabic.
11 The Torah refers to Hagar as Abraham's "handmaiden," while the Quran refers to her as another of Abraham's wives. There is substantial theological division on this point, but for our purpose of relating the basic story of Islam's founding, we have chosen not to develop this idea.
12 "Ismail" in Arabic.
13 The Old Testament account says that Sarah was jealous of Hagar and Ishmael, while the Quran says that God told Abraham to leave Hagar and Ishmael.
14 Ahmed, "Foreword," in T. Sonn, *A Brief History of Islam*, p. xii.
15 H. Smith, *The World's Religions*, San Francisco: HarperCollins, 1958/1991, p. 249.
16 Ibid, pp. 248–257.
17 This is from the *Hadith*: "All people are equal, as equal as the tooth of a comb. There is no claim of merit of an Arab over a non-Arab, or a white over a black person, or a male over a female. Only God-fearing people merit a preference with God."
18 For example, see R.I. Beekun and J. Badawi *Leadership: An Islamic Perspective*, Beltsville, MD: Amana Publications, 1999.
19 See N. Faris and K. Parry, "Islamic Organizational Leadership within a Western Society: The Problematic Role of External Context," *Leadership Quarterly*, 22 (2011): 135.
20 M. Kriger and Y. Seng "Leadership with Inner Meaning: A Contingency Theory of Leadership Based on the Worldviews of Five Religions," *Leadership Quarterly*, 16 (2005): 771–806. We have kept our spelling of Quran rather than Kriger and Seng's alternative spelling "Qur'an" in order to remain consistent throughout our text. We have also italicized the spelling of *al-Rajal al-Kamil* in keeping with our practice of italicizing all non-English words.
21 Beekun and Badawi, *Leadership: An Islamic Perspective*, pp. 17–22.
22 This is detailed in the Islamic Doctrine of the Perfect Man (*Al-Insan al Kamil*).
23 The author uses a different spelling of the Prophet's name in this paragraph, but we have kept the "Mohammad" spelling to remain consistent for our readers.
24 A.J. Ali "Leadership and Islam," in B.D. Metcalfe and F. Mimouni, eds., *Leadership Development in the Middle East*, Cheltenham: Edward Elgar, 2012, p. 89. Ali here is citing E. Abu Dawod, *The Directory of Inquirers*, Jeddah, Saudi Arabia, 1996. Beekun and Badawi echo the idea that leadership is a trust. See Beekun and Badawi, *Leadership: An Islamic Perspective*, p. 39.
25 Faris and Parry, "Islamic Organizational Leadership," p. 136.
26 See Chapter 2.

27 See Kriger and Seng, "Leadership with Inner Meaning," p. 778; Beekun and Bedawi, *Leadership: An Islamic Perspective*, p. 15; and J. Adair, *The Leadership of Muhammad*, Philadelphia, PA: Kogan Page, 2010.

28 Sahih International 41.6.

29 Beekun and Badawi are citing the Hadith. Ibn Umar, *Sahih Bukhari*, 7:128.

30 Here Beekun and Badawi are citing Abu Hurairah, in *Sahih Muslim*, Hadith no. 4542. See Beekun and Badawi, *Leadership: An Islamic Perspective*, p. 15.

31 A.M. Mir "Leadership in Islam," *Journal of Leadership Studies*, 4, 3 (2010): 69.

32 In other translations of the *Hadith*, "guardian" is translated as "shepherd." See *Sahih al-Bukhari*. See also Kriger and Seng, "Leadership with Inner Meaning," p. 778.

33 Denny Roberts, "Book chapter." Email, June 11, 2014.

34 Kriger and Seng say "Justice (*'adl*) is perceived as the primary link between the community and the leader." See Kriger and Seng, "Leadership with Inner Meaning," p. 778.

35 This is stated by Islamic scholar Fazlur Rahman. Ibid. See also T. Sonn, "Islam and Economics" in J. Neusner, ed., *Religious Belief and Economic Behavior*, Atlanta, GA: Scholars Press Issues, 1999, pp. 165–189.

36 The author cites S.M.M. Lari's *Imamate and Leadership* to make his argument.

37 A.M. Mir "Leadership in Islam," p. 69.

38 The Quran 49:10 *Sahia International*.

39 This provides somewhat of a context for understanding the Islamic world's response to the conflicts between Palestine and Israel and between Pakistan and India.

40 See Kriger and Seng, "Leadership with Inner Meaning," p. 778.

41 A. Ali, *Islamic Perspectives on Management and Organization*, Cheltenham: Edward Elgar, 2005.

42 J.M. Burns, *Leadership*, New York: Harper & Row, 1978, p. 20. Faris and Parry also cite Bass and Avolio's conceptualization of transformational leadership. See Faris and Parry, "Islamic Organizational Leadership," p. 135. Also see R. Beekun "Effective Leadership Steps for Strategy Implementation in Islamic Organizations." Available at http://makkah.wordpress.com/leadership-and-islam. Accessed August 17, 2014.

43 Also see R. Campbell, "Leadership Succession in Early Islam: Exploring the Nature and Role of Historical Precedents," *Leadership Quarterly*, 19 (2008): 428; Kriger and Seng, "Leadership with Inner Meaning," p. 777; and Mir, "Leadership in Islam," p. 71 for the importance of mutual consultation in Islamic leadership.

44 Beekun and Badawi, *Leadership: An Islamic Perspective*, p. 49.

45 Beekun and Badawi here cite *Al Nis*, 4:59.

46 Beekun and Badawi here cite Awf ibn Malik in *Sahih Muslim*.

47 Faris and Parry, "Islamic Organizational Leadership," p. 136.

48 K. Armstrong, *Muhammad: A Biography of the Prophet*, New York: HarperCollins, 1992, p. 258.

49 Mir, "Leadership in Islam," p. 69.

50 Denny Roberts, "Book chapter." Email, June 11, 2014.

51 *Inside Islam*, DVD, Burbank, CA: MPH Entertainment Productions and History Channel, 2002.

52 See Ali, "Leadership and Islam," pp. 99–100.

53 Denny Roberts, "Book chapter." Email, June 11, 2014.

9 Leadership in a traditional African cultural context

A person is a person because of other people.
African proverb

Africa is a massive continent that contains more than one billion people and 55 nation-states. It is home to thousands of ethnic groups with their own customs, traditions, and languages. The continent plays host to indigenous cultures as well as Islamic and Western cultures, such as the predominantly Muslim countries found in the north and the highly westernized country of South Africa located at the southern tip of the continent (see Figure 9.1). Thus, to attempt to speak of a singularly "African" approach to leadership is to invite criticism. Nevertheless, there are some common leadership themes found in many cultures throughout Africa that can be helpful for the student of leadership in attempting to better understand this part of the world—particularly sub-Saharan Africa.

In order to better understand a uniquely African approach to leadership, we are going to examine a custom that is intimately tied to African identity—dance.[1] In this chapter, we will be examining a form of African dance called the circle dance. Circle dances are found in many cultures throughout the world, but they hold particular significance in an African context. The shape of a circle holds a great deal of meaning and importance to African identity. It represents wholeness, interconnectedness, unity, and eternity. We will investigate the way these values are represented in the circle dance and mirrored in an ideal African approach to leadership.

Case study: The African circle dance

Anthropologists have long observed how dance is intimately tied to African life.[2] Famed African anthropologist, choreographer, and dancer Pearl Primus declared, "Dance is the soul of Africa. It is the foundation of all the arts and it weaves a tale about the daily lives of the people."[3] There are dances to celebrate births, passages into adulthood, marriages, and myriad other life events,

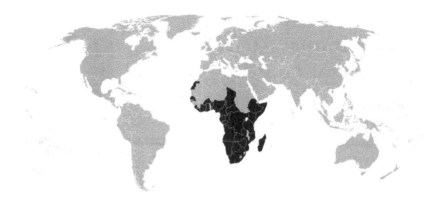

Figure 9.1 Sub-Saharan Africa

and these dances reinforce cultural beliefs and ideologies.[4] One author notes that dance and music in Africa serves "to codify and preserve the living community and its history."[5] Thus, dance is used to celebrate and reinforce cultural values and norms and so it provides us with a particular lens through which to better understand what the society has to say about leadership. Not only is dance in Africa used to celebrate life's passages, but it is also used to promote social unity, to make political statements, and to perform religious rituals and ceremony. Dance author Kariamu Walsh observes:

> The pervasive quality of dance in African societies is indicative of its importance in the daily lives of Africans . . . The information that one can receive about the various societies can be useful in studying and appreciating African cultures.[6]

We will describe the circle dance and the implications it has for leadership in an African context in more detail later in this chapter, but now we turn to the historical context out of which this dance developed.

Origins of an African worldview

Africa's earliest "recorded" history dates back as early as 3000 BCE with the building of the pyramids in ancient Egypt.[7] In later times, cities, kingdoms, and empires such as Timbuktu and Ancient Carthage, the Kingdoms of Sahelian and the Akan, and the Ashanti Empire and the Ajuran Sultanate were just a few of the great centers of commerce, education, and culture in the African world.

Africa's glory was dimmed, however, with the birth of the slave trade that blighted Africa between the 1500s and 1800s. New World and European markets demanded slaves and found an ample supply on Africa's Atlantic coast. Warring groups within Africa sold their prisoners to slave traders to be sent to Europe and North and South America. It is impossible to calculate the toll on human lives the slave trade exacted from Africa. Many Africans died during capture, and many of the people sold into slavery did not survive the journey to the New World. It is estimated that between 10 and 20 million people died during this period.[8] Of course, there were many others who did survive the journey only to die in slavery thousands of miles from their home. The African diaspora brought about by the slave trade bled the region of many of its current and future leaders.

But the slave trade was not to be the last injury inflicted on Africa and its future leadership. Africa was rich in natural resources and land. Western European countries seeking the raw materials needed to fuel the Industrial Revolution carved Africa up with capricious borders with no thought for indigenous groups and without input from African leaders. In what became known as the "Scramble for Africa," countries such as Great Britain, France, Belgium, Germany, Italy and Portugal all grabbed a piece of the continent.[9] The colonization resulted in a wide chasm between the indigenous Africans and the European colonizers—the Europeans holding the vast majority of the wealth and power. This continued through the early part of the twentieth century.

After World War II, and throughout the 1950s and 1960s, many African countries fought for and received their independence from colonial rule. In the 1990s, Africa continued its movement towards democracy as seen in places such as South Africa with the end of apartheid.[10] Thus, much of Africa still continues to reestablish itself after centuries of conflict. Out of this struggle, there were some noble leaders who rose to power, such as South Africa's Nelson Mandela; however, this period also witnessed the rise of several dictators such as Uganda's Idi Amin. Currently, Africa is experiencing what some refer to as a "renaissance" in which Africans seek to reclaim their cultural heritage and pride.[11] This includes developing distinctively African approaches to leadership. However, Africa's political history is only a part of its story. To understand leadership in an African context, one also needs to acknowledge the importance of Africa's tribal and religious cultural legacies.

The first people living in Africa lived in closely tied tribal ethnic groups, and this structure still exists today even within the context of a nation-state system.[12] This tribal legacy is of particular importance to Africa. In the West, a person's identify is linked to the individual, whereas in Africa, a person's identity is linked to the group.[13] This is also the case in other collectivist societies. (See Chapters 10 and 11.) In this case, the "group" is the person's family, village, and tribe, which are based on ethnicity and kinship. These tribes are the primary way most Africans still identify themselves. For example, it is common for Africans to identify themselves by their last name, village, and tribe rather than distinguishing themselves by their first name.

Living kinsmen are not the only members of the tribe. Although Christianity and Islam are major religions in Africa, many Africans simultaneously practice traditional African religions. Many African cultures venerate their ancestors who are seen as inhabiting the spirit world between heaven and earth. Ancestors are believed to continue to watch over the tribe after their death, and are considered to serve as intermediaries between the living members of the tribe and God. They are perceived as playing an active role in village life and their favor is courted with reverence and their wrath is feared. Their wisdom is valued by the living and their counsel is sought on contemporary issues that affect the tribe.[14]

This very brief description of African history and culture gives us a starting point to link together some values and norms found in African leadership that are also exhibited in the circle dance.

Description of the dance

The circle dance is the dominant dance format found in Africa.[15] The dance is performed in a circle—of course—and is performed in collaboration with musicians, dancers, and spectators. The music for the dance is polyrhythmic, meaning that there are usually at least two simultaneous rhythms occurring at any one time. Drumming is particularly important because it establishes and maintains the various beats. Those dancing may move in synchronization with any of the various rhythms being played. This creates a scene in which a variety of dancers and participants may simultaneously move to any of the cross-rhythms while still creating a unified whole. At times, the dance may feature a circle solo in which the other dancers and participants temporarily give a single performer the focus and prominence. Picture three concentric circles in which a solo performer dances in the center while surrounded by the other dancers and musicians, who in turn are surrounded by the larger community of observers.

Figure 9.2 pictures a fresco found in the northern part of Africa depicting an ancient ritual dance that is not unlike the circle dance in form. One can imagine the dancers, the musicians, the village, the tribe, and even the tribal ancestors encircling the scene. The fresco gives us a picture of the place the circle dance has had throughout Africa's long history. The dance symbolically encapsulates a traditional African approach to leadership.

Analysis: Leadership through *ubuntu*

The circle dance provides us with some major themes found in traditional African leadership. These themes include: (1) the significance of collaboration, active participation, and consensus; (2) identity founded on one's relationship with others; (3) the expectation that leaders be authentic; and (4) the significance of shared cultural beliefs.

The first aspect of African leadership we can see highlighted in the circle dance is the importance of collaboration. Dancers, musicians, and spectators all work together to create the dance. In Africa, this collective creation is expressed though the concept of *ubuntu*. A literal translation of the word reads, "I am because you are and you are because I am."[16] The concept conveys the essential

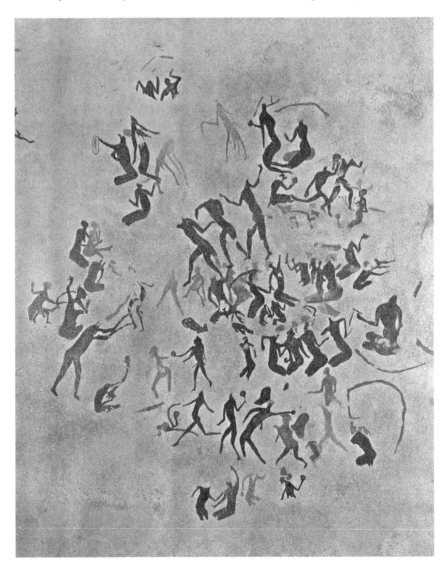

Figure 9.2 Ritual dance. Prehistoric fresco from Tissili n'Ajjar, Algeria, second millennium BCE

Henri Lhote Collection. Musée de l'Homme, Paris
Photo credit: Erich Lessing/Art Resource, New York

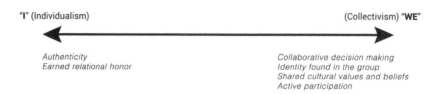

"I" (Individualism)   (Collectivism) "WE"

Authenticity   Collaborative decision making
Earned relational honor   Identity found in the group
                                                      Shared cultural values and beliefs
                                                      Active participation

Figure 9.3 The African worldview on the leadership continuum

idea that the community is primary to understanding African identity. The African concept of *ubuntu* is placed at the far "WE" end of the leadership continuum (see Figure 9.3). This is not to say that the individual has no import-ance in an African worldview, but rather the individual is created though his/her relationship with others.[17] One author defines *ubuntu* as "humaneness—a pervasive spirit of caring and community, harmony and hospitality, respect and responsiveness—that individuals and groups display for one another."[18]

On another level, this focus on relationships can also be witnessed in the family, village, and tribal structure that is so much a part of traditional African society. One's identity is created through belonging. "This holistic approach is supported by an ideology that reveres the concentric linkages of individual to family, to extended family, to clan, to village, and ultimately to the entire community. The individual is a member not of just the nuclear family, but also the extended family or clan."[19]

The philosophy of *ubuntu* has dramatic implications for leadership. Some of these implications include the importance of interconnected relationships, the expectation of developing consensus in decision making, a generous understanding of time when completing tasks, the value of social harmony, and the sharing of resources.[20] These values may pose a challenge for Westerners encountering African culture. The command and control style of leadership that is often favored by Western leaders is likely to be unproductive in an African context. A Western style of leadership may strike the African as lacking sophistication and as ignoring the role community and consensus play when making decisions. In the African way of thinking, the "best" decision may not be the fastest or even the most productive decision; rather, the "best" decision may be one that promotes social harmony and honors the voices of everyone in the group. The consensus approach may also take more time than does a traditional Western "top-down" approach to decision making, but again, for the African, this approach to time is an important part of the process. Everyone must be given the chance to express his or her own voice.[21]

We can see the concept of *ubuntu* modeled in the circle dance. The dance itself is created through interdependence and collaboration with others—dancers, musicians, and observers. Again, Kariamu Welsh describes the scene:

> The fluidity of audiences in African dance is symbolic of a particular stance toward participation. Participation is anticipatory and responsive. In order

for an event to be successful, everyone must be fully involved. Silence and stillness are not valued in the African performance arena. In fact, to be silent is to be critical in a negative way, and to be still shows disdain and contempt for the performance. The music and dance should move the observers so that it is manifested in movements that include bobbing heads, shoulders shifting, hips rolling, and feet stomping or some variation of the theme.[22]

This collaboration creates a whole that is larger than the sum of its parts. Everyone has the chance to contribute to the dance, and this diversity is expressed through the polyrhythmic nature of the music. Many beats may be simultaneously expressed and followed, just as many voices may be heard while developing consensus. The goal is not to complete the dance in as little time as possible; rather the goal of the dance is to have the full participation of everyone present and create harmony between the many rhythms expressed. Only when all rhythms are expressed and harmony is achieved is the dance complete. Everyone is expected to participate, in both the dance and the leadership process.

The concept of *ubuntu* also helps the outsider understand the traditional African process of selecting leaders. African leadership researcher Jacob U. Gordon identifies the five foundations of African leadership as: family, ageism, kinship, religion, and tribalism.[23] Leadership in much of Africa is based on kinship and age. The emphasis placed on old age and maturity is particularly important in traditional African culture. Older people are considered more worthy of leadership positions because it is believed that wisdom comes with age. It is also believed that older leaders are able to build harmony in the group, even if they are not as technically equipped to address the task.[24] In many cases, younger people would not be comfortable leading older people, neither would they be respected if they were to try to do so. In Africa, it is expected that leadership be an earned relational honor.

Again, we can see this value mirrored in the circle dance, specifically in the circle solo in which a particular dancer is singled out and given the focus. One author notes that the Nguni people refer to this as "*Zisina zidedelana*" meaning that every dancer will have a chance to take center stage.[25] Younger people should not covet leadership positions because they will have their chance to lead after they have proved themselves and matured, at which point they too can lead the dance.

The importance placed on age is also observed in the respect given to the tribal ancestors and their continued place as leaders in the tribe. Certain dances are designed to help the dancer enter a trance state to communicate with the tribal ancestors to ask them for advice and counsel on current problems.[26] Ancestors are considered a valuable source of wisdom even after they have passed.

However, just as there are limitations on who can be considered a leader, there are limitations, however, on who can be considered an ancestor.

Leadership scholar David N. Abdulai notes that to be an ancestor the deceased must have been an adult who has died a natural death as evidence of the person having lived an ethical life, and—importantly—the ancestor must have been a praiseworthy member of the tribe when the person was alive.[27] The focus traditional African culture places on interconnection and ethical conduct demands that leaders be authentic.

As we will discuss in Chapter 12, authentic leadership is defined in several ways, but most definitions contain the common themes that if one is to be a good leader, he or she must possess self-understanding and behave ethically.[28] Leadership scholars Fred O. Walumbwa and George O. Nedeg argue that authentic leadership is particularly helpful in understanding an ideal of African leadership. When examining the past tribal structure for leadership in Kenya, the authors observe:

> Leaders were chosen on the basis of their ability to provide good and moral leadership. Leadership outside of the family at the clan and community level invariably went to those who had proved themselves as reliable, confident, brave and impartial. Effective leaders were creative and imaginative people. They knew that leadership is a responsibility and a service . . . Trust and truth were cherished. Leaders were bound to keep their word. Power stemmed from people who gave it royal sanction through their rituals, symbolisms, and most important of all respect for the office.[29]

Thus, in traditional African culture, a leader was expected to uphold the values of the tribe and be a moral and upright person. Although tribes often did have a system of royal succession, leadership based on kinship was not guaranteed. If the leader did not uphold the values of the tribe, he could be removed.[30]

The assumption that leaders must be authentic and morally good in order to lead effectively is also expressed in the African philosophy of *seriti* (Sotho) or *isithunzi* (Nguni).[31] *Seriti/isithunzi* is a physical energy that creates the individual self, but it rises out of the individuals' interactions with others.[32] It is an individual attribute, but its legacy can also be passed on to later generations of the family and tribe. African leadership scholar Mike Boon explains:

> One's *seriti* or *isithunzi* reflects one's moral weight, influence and prestige. It is what identifies us as good, or indeed, what will identify us as depleted of goodness. The more good deeds one does in life, the more one shares humanity, and the greater one's *seriti* grows. If we do bad or evil, our *seriti* is reduced.[33]

From a leadership perspective, one is expected to have a strong *seriti* if one is leading the group. If the leader does not possess a strong *seriti*, not only does the leader diminish himself or herself, but the leader also diminishes the whole tribe's *seriti*.

Again, we can see the importance of authentic leadership and *seriti* mirrored in African dance. One author observes:

> In many parts of Africa, one must be of good character to participate in dance. The dancer and the drummer are evaluated within the context of the society. Any person recognized as immoral or bad could not possibly uphold, display, or demonstrate the community's most treasured dances, regardless of his or her natural abilities. An outstanding performance is a reflection of a person's high moral character. This connection between character and skill is an important one and is indicative of the holistic way in which many Africans see each other. Behavior is not isolated from other spheres in one's life, such as performance. It is incongruous to the traditional African worldview that one can be evil and dance well.[34]

In the same vein of thought, one could not be evil and lead well.

There is a particular story about the *Asantehene*, the ruler of the Ashanti people in Africa that illustrates this connection between dance and leadership well. In Ghana, the *Asantehene* is not allowed to ascend to his leadership position until he dances before the people. It is assumed that if the new leader can dance well, then he will be committed to the people and respect their culture.[35] Thus, a good dancer will be a good leader because the dance is an outward display of the leader's authenticity and high ethical values.

Summary and concluding remarks

When examined as a whole, a traditional African perspective of leadership begins to emerge. Leadership in traditional African culture is an earned relational honor based on kinship and age. Like the West, leadership is a "prize" but the way the prize is earned is based not on being able to accomplish the task as quickly and efficiently as possible, but rather on the leader's ability to create harmony in the group. Likewise, the African prize of leadership can only be earned after one has lived a long life and obtained wisdom and experience (see Table 9.1).

In the West, leadership is considered a transaction between leaders and followers. Whether or not a leader is "morally good" is somewhat beside the point; leaders in the West are considered "good" if they are effective at the task to be accomplished. True, leaders are expected to be ethical in accomplishing their goals, but one's personal life and ethics are secondary. In contrast, traditional African leaders are expected to be authentic and behave ethically in relationship to their followers in all aspects of their life. They are expected to exemplify the values of the community.

This moral dimension of leadership is based on the African concept of *ubuntu*, a humanistic value in which one finds identity in relationship with others in the community. Traditional African followers expect to actively participate in the leadership process rather than simply being directed from the "top." Decisions are to be made collectively and in collaboration while building

Table 9.1 Western and African comparative views of leadership

	Western worldview	*African worldview*
Leadership viewed as a . . .	Prize (meritocracy)	Earned honor (relational)
Leader-follower relationship	Transactional (rules based; social contract)	Authentic
How decisions are made	Through rationality, logic, pragmatism	Collectively
Responsibilities of the leader	Motivate followers, results orientation	Empower, relate to community, respect tradition
Responsibilities of the follower	Dependable, committed, motivated	Active participation
Moral dimension of leadership	Secular "code of ethics" (derived from Judeo-Christian values)	Humanistic value of the community

consensus. This is very different from the Western value placed on rationality, logic, and pragmatism, often marked by a command and control style of leadership. The "best" decision from a Western standpoint is the one that most effectively accomplishes the task and achieves the goal. The "best" decision from an African standpoint is the decision that takes into account all perspectives and provides relational harmony. This can pose a challenge when leaders and followers from Western and traditional African cultures mix because the expectations of leaders is very different for the two cultures. Traditional African leaders are expected to empower their followers and relate to the community and respect the traditions of the group rather than simply motivating them to obtain results. Likewise, followers can experience "culture shock" when working in the opposite culture. In a Western culture, followers expect to "pay their dues" to obtain a position of leadership as quickly as possible. This can prove frustrating in a culture that values age and relational status. One's "turn to lead" may come late in life and not until one has become an ancestor after death.

As a continent, Africa has experienced centuries of culture shock and is now at a crossroads. How does one embrace the future and thrive in the pluralistic world brought on by globalization while still remaining distinctly African? This is a particularly difficult question to ask after the devastation experienced in the first two waves of globalization that reached Africa's shores. Africa is now beginning to reclaim its identity and re-embrace its traditional forms of leadership.

One may wonder why Africa—with such rich cultural traditions that emphasize the importance of collaboration and ethics—seems to be experiencing such crises. Africa has myriad and complex problems including poverty, violence, corruption, military dictators, ethno-religious conflict, HIV/AIDS, human rights abuses, and environmental insecurity. Indeed, many authors trace many of these crises directly to a failure of leadership throughout Africa.[36] Many would say that the crisis of leadership Africa is experiencing is simply a mirror of the kind of leadership Africa experienced under colonial rule. One author identifies the new breed of African leader that arose out of this context as "the takers."[37] These hybrid leaders took the worst values of their immediate predecessors and applied them to an African context. There is no doubt that this was likely the case.

However, Africa is now experiencing a renaissance. Leaders such as Bishop Desmond Tutu, Nelson Mandela, and Wangari Maathai have worked to move Africa back towards a traditionally African humanistic ethic that benefits the community. Likewise, leadership researchers are seeking ways that Africa can claim its cultural heritage in the context of leadership.[38] Only time will tell how Africa will ultimately solve Africa's problems. However, the way forward may very well point to the ancient past.

Questions for discussion

- How does Africa's embracing of its traditional approach to leadership affect its relationship with the rest of the world? How does globalization affect this process?
- Consider the idea of *ubuntu*. Are you also a product of your interaction with others in your community? How is *your* identity created?
- What implications does the concept of *ubuntu* have on the Western value of individualism?
- What might be potential negative aspects of *ubuntu*?
- What might be your biggest challenge working in a traditionally African cultural context?

Additional resources

W. Bokelmann, O. Akinwumi, U.M. Nwankwo, A.O. Agwuele, *African Leadership Challenges and Other Issues*, Berlin: Mediateam Educational Publishers, 2012.

M. Boon, *The African Way, The Power of Interactive Leadership*, 3rd edn., Cape Town: Zebra Press, 2007.

E. van Zyl, C. Dalglish, M. du Plessis, L. Lues, E. Pietersen, *Leadership in the African Context*, Cape Town: Juta and Co. Ltd, 2009.

Notes

1 This chapter was inspired by a report of a session at the 2010 Skoll World Forum on Social Entrepreneurship. "Collaborative Leadership: Play it Like an African Circle Dance." Available http://skollworldforum.org/2010/04/26/collaborative-leadership-play-it-like-in-an-african-circle-dance/. Accessed August 20, 2014.

2 See G. Gorer, *Africa Dances*, New York: Penguin, 1945.

3 Quoted in K. Welsh, *African Dance*, 2nd edn., New York: Chelsea House Publishers, 2010 p. 20.

4 K. Welsh, *African Dance*, p. 21

5 F.Y. Caulker-Bronson, "African Dance: Divine Motion" in M.H. Nadel and M.R. Strauss, *The Dance Experience*, 3rd edn., Hightstown, NJ: Princeton Book Company Publishers, 2014.

6 K. Welsh, *African Dance*, p. 21.

7 See C.A. Diop, *The African Origin of Civilization: Myth or Reality*, M. Cook, ed./trans., Chicago: Lawrence Hill, 1974; K. Shillington, *History of Africa*, 3rd edn., Basingstoke: Palgrave Macmillan, 2012.

8 P.D. Curtin, *The Atlantic Slave Trade: A Census*, Madison, WI: University of Wisconsin Press, 1969; P. Manning, "The Enslavement of Africans: A Demographic Model," *Canadian Journal of African Studies*, 15, 3 (1981): 499–526; P. Manning, *Slavery and African Life: Occidental, Oriental, and African Slave Trades*, Cambridge: Cambridge University Press, 1990; J.E. Inikori and Stanley L. Engerman, eds., *The Atlantic Slave Trade: Effects on Economies, Societies, and Peoples in Africa, the Americas, and Europe*, Durham, NC: Duke University Press, 1992.

9 R.J. Reid, *A History of Modern Africa: 1800 to the Present*, 2nd edn., Hoboken, NJ: Wiley Blackwell, 2012; A.A. Boahen, *African Perspectives on Colonialism*, Baltimore, MD: Johns Hopkins University Press, 1989.

10 M. Meredith, *The Fate of Africa: A History of the Continent Since Independence*, rev. edn., New York: Public Affairs, 2011.

11 C.A. Diop, *Towards the African Renaissance: Essays in African Culture and Development, 1946–1960*, Trenton, NJ: Red Sea Press, 2000.

12 The term "tribe" is fraught with political implications. The term has sometimes been used pejoratively to distinguish between "progressive" and "primitive" ethnic groups. While we acknowledge the term has been use this way in the past, we use the term here simply to distinguish the importance of localized ethic groups and cultures to an African worldview.

13 See J.S. Mbiti, *African Religions and Philosophy*, London: Heinemann, 1969.

14 D.A. Abdulai, "Cultural Mythology and Global Leadership in South Africa," in E.H. Kessler and D.J. Wong-Mingji, *Cultural Mythology and Global Leadership*, Cheltenham: Edward Elgar, 2009, pp. 209–224. Abdulai makes a helpful distinction between the practice of ancestral veneration and ancestral worship in his work.

15 K. Welsh, *African Dance*, p. 36.

16 M. Mapadimeng, "*Ubunto/Botho*, the Work Place and the Two Economies," *Journal of Development Studies*, 37, 2 2007: 258.

17 N.M. Kamwangamalu, "*Ubuntu* in South Africa: A Sociolinguistic Perspective to Pan-African Concept," *Critical Arts*, 13, 2 1999: 1–7.

18 M.P. Mangaliso, "Building Competitive Advantage from *Ubuntu*: Management Lessons from South Africa," *Academy of Management Executive*, 15, 3 (2001): 24.

19 Ibid, p. 25.

20 Ibid. Also see C. Malunga, *Understanding Organizational Leadership Through Ubuntu*, London: Adonis & Abbey, 2009,

21 See D.M. Tutu, *No Future Without Forgiveness*, New York: Image/Doubleday, 1999.

22 K. Welsh, *African Dance*, p. 36–37.

23 J.U. Gordon, *African Leadership in the Twentieth Century*, Lantham, MD: University Press of America, 2002, p. 169.

24 Abdulai, "South Africa," p. 214; Mangaliso, "Building Competitive Advantage," p. 30.

25 Mangaliso, "Building Competitive Advantage," p. 30.

26 K. Welsh, *African Dance*, p. 16.

27 Abdulai, "South Africa," pp. 210–211. Abdulai cites P. Sarpong *Ghana in Retrospect: Some Aspects of Ghanaian Culture*, Accra-Tema: Ghana Publishing Corporation, 1974; J. Pobee, "Aspects of African Traditional Religion," *Sociological Analysis*, 37, 1 (1976): 1–18.

28 F.O. Walumbwa, B.J. Avolio, W.L. Gardner, T.S. Wernsing, and S.J. Peterson, "Authentic Leadership: Development and Validation of a Theory-based Measure", *Journal of Management*, 34 (2008): 89–126.

29 F.O. Walumbwa and George O. Ndege, "Cultural Mythology and Global Leadership in Kenya," in E.H. Kessler and D.J. Wong-Mingji, *Cultural Mythology and Global Leadership*, Cheltenham: Edward Elgar, 2009, p. 231.

30 D. de Vries, "The Role of Culture and History in the Applicability of Western Leadership Theories in Africa," in J.D. Barbour, G.J. Burgess, L.L. Falkman, and R.M. McManus, eds., *Leading in Complex Worlds*, San Francisco, Jossey-Bass, 2012.

31 A. Schutte, *Philosophy for Africa*, Cape Town: University of Cape Town Press, 1993.

32 Ibid.

33 M. Boon, *The African Way: The Power of Interactive Leadership*, 3rd edn., Cape Town, South Africa: Zebra Press, 2007, p. 31.

34 K. Welsh, *African Dance*, p. 24.

35 Ibid, p. 26.

36 W. Bokelmann, O. Akinwumi, U.M. Nwankwo, and A.O. Agwuele, *African Leadership Challenges and Other Issues*, Berlin, Mediateam IT Educational Publishers, 2012.

37 Boon, *The African Way*, p. 48.

38 T. Jackson, *Management and Change in Africa: A Cross-Culture Perspective*, London: Routledge, 2004.

10 Leadership in a Buddhist cultural context

It is better to conquer yourself than to win a thousand battles.

The Buddha

The ancient philosophy of Buddhism has much to offer the contemporary student of leadership. Recently, scholars and practitioners have embraced this confluence and have investigated the way they might apply some of the fundamental aspects of Buddhism to the study and practice of leadership.[1] In seeking to make these connections, however, Buddhism can be a difficult worldview to summarize. This confusion is compounded because of the existence of so many forms of Buddhism. (See Figure 10.1.)

Regardless of this diversity, however, there are a few common tenets that all Buddhists believe, specifically the importance of the Buddha and his teachings about the four noble truths, the Eightfold Path, and the unity of all things. We will develop each of these a little further in this chapter.

As modeled in previous chapters, we will present a case study illustrating the basic concepts of Buddhism and their implications for leadership. In this chapter, we will analyze Hermann Hesse's classic novella *Siddhartha: An Indian Tale*. Hesse had a lifelong preoccupation with the East, and this is not the first time his work has inspired thoughts about leadership. His book *A Journey to the East* formed the basis of Robert K. Greenleaf's idea of servant leadership referred to in Chapter 2. Although written in 1922 and originally published in Germany, Hesse's work serves as an artful way to present some of the major themes found in Buddhism that are relevant to a Buddhist perspective of leadership.[2]

Hesse's story is about the son of an Indian brahmin and his quest for enlightenment. Hesse sets the novel in the sixth century BCE in the time in which the Buddha lived, and even casts the Buddha in a pivotal role in the story to illustrate one of the book's major themes. Many writers have noted the similarity between the life of the Buddha and the life of Hesse's character, Siddhartha.[3] Hesse's protagonist even bears one of the same names as the Buddha—Siddhartha—a detail that can cause some confusion for first time

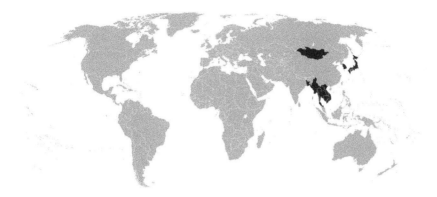

Figure 10.1 Primarily found in the Far East and Southeast Asia, sects of Buddhism can be found in Japan (Zen), Thailand, Myanmar, Cambodia, Laos, and Sri Lanka (Theravada), China, North and South Korea, Vietnam, and Taiwan (Mahayana), and Tibet (Tibetan).

readers of the story. Others have pointed out that Hesse's metaphysical position in his book "agrees essentially, if not with the 'genuine' teaching of the Buddha, at least with a major school of interpretation."[4] Although *not intended* to be a primer on Buddhism or its founder, in many ways the book does act as a *useful bridge* from Western to Buddhist—or more broadly Eastern—thought.[5] For our purposes, Hesse's novella also provides a succinct vehicle for understanding leadership in a Buddhist cultural context.

Case study: Hermann Hesse's *Siddhartha: An Indian Tale*

Origins of a Buddhist worldview

Before beginning our synopsis and analysis of Siddhartha, a brief lesson on Buddhism and its founder is in order. The story of Buddhism begins with a prince, Siddhartha Gautama (c.563–483 BCE). His father was a great king, Suddhodana, living in the region we now refer to as Nepal. Legend says that Gautama's mother, Queen Maya, had a dream before the child was conceived and knew he would be very special. However, she died a few days after the child was born. A holy man paid a visit to King Suddhodana and examined his son, Siddhartha Gautama. The holy man was awestruck. He told King Suddhodana the child was destined to be either a great emperor or a great teacher. In hopes for the former, Gautama's father tried to keep the child sheltered from all pain and sorrow and provided him with every possible luxury in an effort to sway his boy to choose the life of an emperor. The tale says that when Gautama was a young man he went for a series of rides in the country and was introduced to what have come to be known as the four sights—an old man, a man riddled with disease, a corpse, and a monk quietly meditating.

Having been protected from such suffering in his life, Gautama was overwhelmed by the sight of age, disease, death, and contentment in the midst of such strife. In seeking to make sense of what he saw, he forsook his palace luxuries, even his wife and child, and began living the life of a wandering ascetic in hopes of achieving enlightenment.

During this time, Gautama joined a religious sect—the Shakya. He became famous for his extreme asceticism and self-mortification. He excelled in his religious devotion and took the name Shakyamuni, or Sage of the Shakyas. However, it was also in this period that he came to realize his life had been one attached to the extremes of indulgence and self-mortification, and neither extreme provided him the enlightenment he desired. This is where Gautama discovered what he called "the Middle Way" in which he renounced his attachment to both extreme luxury and extreme asceticism. As the story would have it, this understanding led Gautama to his life-defining moment when he meditated under the Bodhi tree in his quest for enlightenment. In an effort to break Gautama's meditation and keep him from discovering the eternal truths

Figure 10.2 Seated Buddha, Thailand, thirteenth century CE
Bronze
Musée des Arts Asiantiques-Guimet, Paris
Photo credit: © RMN-Grand Palais/Art Resource, New York

of the universe, the tale says that Mara—the Hindu god of death and pain—marshalled his forces of fear and sensual delights to divert Gautama from his quest. Mara failed. The god demanded to know who would stand witness to Gautama's enlightenment, at which point Gautama touched the earth and said, "The earth is my witness" and the earth shook in testimony to Gautama's achievement (see Figure 10.2). It was at this moment that Siddhartha Gautama achieved enlightenment. Today we refer to Siddhartha Gautama, or Shakyamuni, as "the Buddha" meaning "one who is fully awake."

The four noble truths

During his period of meditation under the Bodhi tree, it is said Siddhartha Gautama realized the true nature of existence, what Buddhists refer to as the four noble truths:

> Life is suffering.
> Suffering is caused by attachment.
> There is a way out of suffering.
> The way out of suffering is the Eightfold Path.

The idea of "suffering," as expressed in the first noble truth, might be best understood as "anxiety" or "fear of loss." Certainly physical suffering—such as pain, sickness, and death—is included here. It is important to note that these were the first three of Buddha's four sights. These forms of suffering are common to all humankind. However, also included in this idea of suffering is our desire to constantly recreate our fleeting moments of happiness; as is a more insidious suffering derived from our constant desire to satisfy our own material self-interests. The first noble truth does not deny that happiness exists, but rather it forces us to reconcile that we suffer because we seek to attach ourselves to those things that bring us happiness only to be disappointed by them when they go away. Buddhism does not claim that there is no joy in life, but rather, that the joy and happiness we experience is ephemeral, or fleeting.

This leads us to the second noble truth, "suffering is caused by attachment." If the first noble truth is difficult for Westerners to comprehend, the second noble truth is even more so. The reasonable response is to ask, "How could an attachment to our loved ones or the things that bring us happiness cause suffering?" To understand this, we must reconcile ourselves with the ephemeral nature of all things. With love comes attachment, and when we lose that which we love, we suffer. How many times have any of us been disappointed and saddened by the end of a friendship or a romantic relationship? And yet many times these relationships once brought us great joy. More seriously, we may become emotionally devastated by the death of someone we love. We suffer because we do not accept the transitory nature of life. This is not to say that Buddhism proposes that we not love others; indeed, just the opposite is true. But rather Buddhism suggests that we cultivate a spirit of loving kindness, or compassion, to all beings, not just towards those to which we are attached. This is the only way one can find lasting happiness. If the first two noble truths present the illness, the next two present the cure.

The Eightfold Path

The Buddha says there is a way out of suffering, and that way is what is called the Eightfold Path. The image of the Eightfold Path as a wheel depicted in Figure 10.3 is important and helpful to understanding the concept that one needs all parts of the wheel working together simultaneously in order to function properly. There is no one place to start on the wheel; rather, the practitioner of Buddhism must engage in all of these practices simultaneously.

Nevertheless, the practice of the right view provides a transition from the four noble truths to the Eightfold Path.[6] If suffering is the beginning of the problem, the right view is the beginning of the solution. The idea behind the right view is that one must seek to understand the deep reality of the four noble truths in order to achieve enlightenment and remove oneself from attachment and the suffering it causes. It reminds the practitioner to see things the way things really are, as opposed the way he or she wishes them to be. This leads us to right intent.

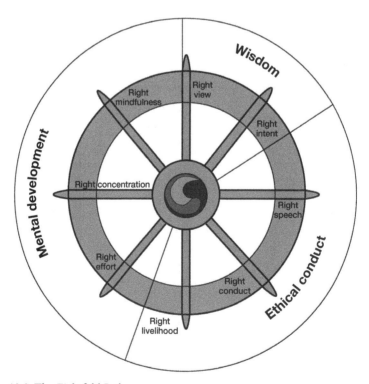

Figure 10.3 The Eightfold Path

The idea of right intent focuses on a person's determination to achieve enlightenment. Right intent might be best understood as willpower and self-discipline. The Buddhist path to enlightenment is not an easy one to follow. The successful practitioner must develop the resolve to see the process through. These first two practices compose what Buddhists refer to as the "way of wisdom." The next three practices are concerned with ethical living or the "way of morality."

Right speech certainly entails refraining from lying or coarse language, but it also includes the idea that one should avoid gossip or being hurtful to others. More importantly, it encourages the practitioner to only speak when necessary and to *value listening and silence*. This can be particularly difficult for Westerners. Buddhists monks have been known to sit in silence for days. For the Buddhist, right speech is not only what you *do* say; what you *don't* say is equally important.

Historically, right conduct was more specifically prescribed and included prohibitions against killing, causing harm, stealing, sexual misconduct, and even abstaining from alcohol and drugs. Buddhists still acknowledge these elements of right conduct today, but would add that *any form of unethical behavior* that may bring harm to one's self or to others should be avoided.

To pursue the right livelihood is to work in a profession that is of benefit to humankind and does not cause harm or violate the other precepts, such as right conduct and right speech. Again, historically Buddhism held proscriptions against specific professions, but modern Buddhism interprets this element to prohibit any profession that might bring about harm to others.

The last three elements of the Eightfold Path include right effort, right mindfulness, and right concentration. Collectively, these three practices are considered the way of meditation. These components of the Eightfold Path focus on personal mental development and emphasize the pursuit of understanding the full context of situations and one's responses to them.

Right effort is concerned with the practice of avoiding negative mental states and emotions, such as anger, desire, and aggression; however, it is equally concerned with developing positive mental states such as generosity, empathy, and kindness. Right effort places you in the state of mind to be able to practice the other elements of the way of meditation.

Mindfulness is the process of purposefully concentrating on the present moment as a means to develop awareness and clarity of thought. The focus on *awareness* here is crucial to understanding Buddhism. Indeed, the very meaning of the word "Buddha" is "one who is fully awake." The purpose of practicing mindfulness is to nurture the ability to clearly and accurately see the current moment as it presents itself. We will discuss mindfulness in more detail later in this chapter, but it is a key aspect of the way of meditation.

Finally, concentration is the process of focusing one's mind for the purpose of achieving tranquility or insight. It is central to the way of meditation and is practiced as one meditates in silence and focuses all one's mental faculties. Although there are many ways to practice concentration, some of the most common are fixing attention on a particular object, focusing on one or all of the five senses, or reciting a *mantra,* a word that is repeated again and again. Through the process of concentration, the meditator is able to achieve a peace or an insight that has previously eluded him.

The four noble truths are practiced in conjunction with the Eightfold Path as a way to acknowledge suffering and as a way to rid one's self of attachment that leads to this suffering in the quest for one's own enlightenment. These two teachings are fundamental to understanding Buddhism, but there is at least one more teaching that we must discuss to have a basic understanding of the way a Buddhist worldview affects one's view of leadership—the interconnected unity of all things.

The interconnected unity of all things

Buddhism does not have a concept of a deity as one would find in monotheistic religions such as Judaism, Christianity, and Islam. This fact has led some to refer to Buddhism as a philosophy or ethical system rather than a religion in the classic sense of the term. Although Buddhism does not claim a deity of its own, it is not uncommon to see representations of Hindu and brahmin deities in ancient Buddhist temples as well as in modern Buddhist homes. Buddhism emerged from these traditions. True, many Buddhist texts refer to a "heavenly" realm and heavenly beings; however, those Buddhists who believe in a heavenly realm also note that these inhabitants are subject to death and reincarnation just as those in the "earthly" realm. Many times, references and representations such as these may be best interpreted as personifications of human virtues and foibles. This can cause confusion for someone newly introduced to Buddhist cultures.

Regardless, rather than a transcendent deity, Buddhism proposes an underlying interconnected unity of all things that is independent of any supernatural being. This belief has direct implications on the concept of the self—the soul or ego. Buddhism does not adhere to the idea that people have an individual self, but rather we only *perceive* our senses, thoughts, and emotions as belonging exclusively to us as individuals. These senses and perceptions are available to everyone, so they cannot be linked to a single person. That does not mean that we do not try to attach ourselves to a particular idea of who we are, or a self; however, it is this attachment that leads to our suffering.

Picture a deep well filled with water. As you dip a cup in the well, the water fills the cup to the brim. When the cup is in the water, one may say that *my* cup is full, but in a very real sense, it is simply a part of the water in the well. The same is true of the Buddhist concept of the individual self. Likewise, if you take the cup out of the well you can drink the water in it, but you soon become thirsty once again, and long for the contents of the well. In short, you soon suffer. One Buddhist scholar explains it this way: "Life being one, all that tends to separate one aspect from another must cause suffering . . . Our duty to our fellows is to understand them as extensions, other aspects, of ourselves—fellow facets of the same Reality."[7] To the Buddhist mind, nothing is truly separate. One's self extends to all living things. What diminishes one diminishes all. Practicing compassion for everyone is practicing compassion for one's self. Or as the Buddha says *"Consider others as yourself."*[8] In an interconnected universe, it would only stand to reason that your actions would eventually have an effect on you. Thus, "enlightenment," in the Buddhist sense of the term, is that point at which a person experiences the full implications of this unity. This concept can be foreign and even disconcerting to Western thinking with its central placement of the individual, but it is probably the best example of the difference between individualism and collectivism. Now that we have a little better understanding of Buddhism, we can better understand Hesse's story and, ultimately, what it has to say about leadership.

Synopsis of the novella

Hesse's story begins with his protagonist, Siddhartha, as a young man living with his mother and father in a small village. His father is a noble brahmin—a spiritual leader and a member of a high caste. Siddhartha has grown up reading religious books and mastering the spiritual ways of his father. He is intelligent and handsome, and his mother and father dream of his becoming a great sage. Nevertheless, Siddhartha "had started nursing discontent within himself."[9] One day, he sees the Samanas—a wandering group of homeless ascetics who practice self-mortification as a way to reach peace and enlightenment. The pilgrims pass through his town and Siddhartha is captivated. In hopes the Samanas can lead him to the enlightenment he desires, he begs his father to allow him to leave his comfortable home and to join them. At first his father refuses to let him go, but Siddhartha tenaciously stands in silence until his father gives him his blessing to leave.

Siddhartha is joined on his journey by his boyhood friend, Govinda, and together they spend three years mastering the teaching and practices of their Samana leaders. During this time, Siddhartha continues to suffer in his discontent. Hesse writes that, to Siddhartha, "The world tasted bitter. Life was torture. A goal stood before Siddhartha, a single goal: to become empty, empty of thirst, empty of wishing, empty of dreams, empty of joy and sorrow."[10] In other words, Siddhartha longed to become enlightened. But even having mastered the teachings and techniques of the Samanas with precision, he was still not satisfied. So Siddhartha and his friend Govinda leave the Samanas to seek Gautama, the Buddha, in hopes he can show them the way to the enlightenment they seek (see Table 10.1).

They meet the Buddha, and they hear him preach the four noble truths and the Eightfold Path. Govinda is deeply moved by the Buddha and becomes one of his disciples. Siddhartha, however, rejects the Buddha's teachings in favor of his own path to enlightenment. He leaves his friend, Govinda, and the Buddha in search of "the secret that is Siddhartha."

In his quest, Siddhartha meets a ferryman who escorts him across a river from the life he once knew as an ascetic—*samana*—to his new life of discovering

Table 10.1 List of characters in *Siddhartha*

Siddhartha	Protagonist, a man in search of enlightenment
Govinda	Siddhartha's friend
Siddhartha's father	A brahmin priest
The Samanas	A group of travelling ascetics
Gautama	The Buddha
Vasudeva	A ferryman and Siddhartha's spiritual guide
Kamala	A courtesan and Siddhartha's lover, mother of young Siddhartha
Kamaswami	A merchant who teaches Siddhartha business
Young Siddhartha	Siddhartha and Kamala's son

the world of sensual pleasure—*samsara*. There, Siddhartha takes a lover, a courtesan named Kamala, who mentors him in the "ways of love." Another teacher, a businessman named Kamaswami, guides him in the ways of business and Siddhartha eventually becomes a very wealthy merchant. For years he indulges all his sensual appetites. His path to contentment remains elusive, however, until he, once again, seeks his answers from within himself rather than in the trappings of his "soft, well upholstered hell."[11] He leaves Kamala, Kamaswami, and his life of abundance. He becomes despondent and considers taking his own life, but as he is about to do so, he remembers an ancient Hindu mantra that he once chanted while meditating as a boy. The sacred mantra symbolizes the essence of the universe and the unity of all life.

After coming to his senses, Siddhartha meets Vasudeva, the ferryman who escorted him across the river to his new life 20 years earlier, and tells him his story. Vasudeva listens intently and offers his home to Siddhartha so that he may stay with him and "learn from the river." Siddhartha stays and does learn.

Twelve years pass, and word reaches the countryside that Gautama—the Buddha—is dying. Siddhartha's lover, Kamala, has long since given up her days as a courtesan and is now in search of her own enlightenment. She travels with her son to meet the Buddha and to hear his teaching before he passes away; however, along the way she is bitten by a poisonous snake. The ferryman, Vasudeva, hears Kamala's cries for help, rushes to her, and carries her into his hut where Siddhartha is tending the fire. As Kamala and her son enter the home, Siddhartha sees her and recognizes his love, Kamala, and also recognizes her son as his own. Kamala dies leaving the boy in Siddhartha's care.

Now an old man and once again seeking inner peace and enlightenment, Siddhartha has given up his wealth and privilege and is living the life of a humble ferryman with his friend and mentor, Vasudeva. Siddhartha deeply loves his child, but the boy rebels against his father and his simple life along the river and he runs away back to his comfortable life in the city. Siddhartha longs to find the boy, and shelter him from the world. Siddhartha is grieved by the loss of his son, but ultimately he realizes that his son must follow his own path, just as he had done so many years prior. Thus, the story ends much as it began, with a father breaking his attachment to a son to allow him to begin his own quest. Siddhartha finally finds the peace he has so long sought after. At the end of the story, Vasudeva dies, and Siddhartha becomes the ferryman. He once again meets his longtime friend Govinda and shares his peace and understanding with him. The cycle is complete.

Analysis: Leadership as a personal journey

We have detailed Buddhist teaching and Hesse's story to provide a context for understanding leadership from a Buddhist perspective. Hesse's novel presents several of Buddhism's major themes, specifically the four noble truths, the Eightfold Path, and the interconnected unity of all life. We can see each of these teachings in *Siddhartha*. We can also find some common leadership themes that can be placed on the leadership continuum: (1) leadership in a Buddhist culture is viewed as a personal journey towards obtaining wisdom and enlightenment; (2) the Buddhist teaching of the Four Noble Truths and the Eightfold Path guides this journey; (3) leaders are to be role models for their followers; (4) in turn, followers are to defer to the leader's wisdom, and; (5) leaders should make their decisions based on wisdom and compassion for the good of the community. These concepts will be investigated somewhat deeper as we progress into the case study (Figure 10.4).

Leadership in the Buddhist tradition is seen as a personal journey. Whether it is in the home of his wealthy father, living the life of a wandering aesthetic, in the arms of his beloved Kamala, or longing for his child's love, Siddhartha's suffering seems to know no end. Buddhism would argue that this unhappiness is not unique to Siddhartha, but is simply a part of the human condition. In each of these cases—and Buddhism would argue in every case—this suffering was caused by attachment. Siddhartha was attached to an idea of himself, an ego. Although he sought many paths away from this suffering, his suffering always returned as long as he held an idea of himself as separate from the world around him. This is a central idea of Buddhism. It was not until Siddhartha gave up his attachment to his own ego that he found the end to his suffering. He had to release his attachment to the vision of himself as a priestly scholar.

"I" (Individualism)   (Collectivism) "WE"

Leadership is a personal journey   *Life is interconnected – there is no "individual"*
Leaders are to be role models (Bodhisattva)   *Decisions should be made with wisdom and compassion*
Everyone must find his/her own way   *Defer to the wisdom of the leader*
                                    All should follow the Four Noble Truths and the Eightfold Path

Figure 10.4 The Buddhist worldview on the leadership continuum

He had to release his attachment to his friend. He had to release his attachment to his lover and his wealth. Finally, he had to release his attachment to his own son. It was not until Siddhartha gave up his attachment to an idea of himself and the way he thought the world should be that he was able to find a way out of his misery and reach the enlightenment he longed for.

Hesse's novel helps explain the Buddhist idea that one is not ready or fit to lead until he or she can lead one's own self. Buddhist writer Walpola Rahula describes this idea:

> Man's position, according to Buddhism, is supreme. Man is his own master, and there is no being or higher power that sits in judgment over his destiny. "One is one's own refuge. Who else could be the refuge?," said the Buddha. He admonished his disciples to be a refuge to themselves, and never to seek refuge in or help from anybody else. He taught, encouraged, and stimulated each person to develop himself and to work out his own emancipation, for man has the power to liberate himself from all bondage through his own personal effort and intelligence.[12]

Likewise, it is often reported that Buddha's last words to his disciples before he died were "Be a light unto yourself"—that is, everyone must find his or her own way through life rather than following the Buddha or anyone else.

The notion of a person being responsible for following his or her own path is seen throughout Hesse's story, and specifically seen in Siddhartha's refusal to allow anyone to define his life's trajectory for him. This is witnessed when he leaves his father's home to join the Samanas, as well as when he initially rejects the Buddha's teaching. Although Siddhartha's experience ultimately leads him to find that the Buddha's teachings are true, he must discover this for himself. He must seek to know the "secret of Siddhartha."[13] He tells the Buddha:

> But there is one thing which these so clear, these so venerable teachings do not contain: they do not contain the mystery of what the exalted one has experienced for himself, he alone among hundreds of thousands. This is what I have thought and realized, when I have heard the teachings. This is why I am continuing my travels—not to seek other, better teachings, for I know there are none, but to depart from all teachings and all teachers and to reach my goal by myself or to die.[14]

This idea comes full circle at the end of the novel and is further illustrated by the relationship between Siddhartha and his son. Although Siddhartha wants to protect his son from making the mistakes he has made, and teach him all he knows, the boy rejects his father's love and instruction. Siddhartha's mentor, the ferryman Vasudeva, admonishes him:

> Which father, which teacher had been able to protect him from living his life for himself, from soiling himself with life, from burdening himself

with guilt, from drinking the bitter drink for himself, from finding his path for himself? Would you think, my dear, anybody might perhaps be spared from taking this path. That perhaps your little son would be spared, because you love him, because you would like to keep him from suffering and pain and disappointment? But even if you would die ten times for him, you would not be able to take the slightest part of his destiny upon yourself.[15]

It is not until Siddhartha releases his son to pursue his own journey that Siddhartha can find peace himself. This is in keeping with a Buddhist understanding of leadership as a personal journey.

Although leadership is a personal journey, collectively, Buddhists believe the road they should follow on this journey is the Eightfold Path. There are hundreds of Buddhist texts that relate to the subject of ethics, but understanding Buddhism in the confines of a single ethical system is difficult.[16] As a starting point, then, this section examines an ethical view that all Buddhists would have in common; that is, the Eightfold Path referred to earlier in this chapter.

Buddhism's Eightfold Path (Figure 10.3) can be divided into three basic areas: wisdom, ethical conduct, and mental development. For our purposes here, we focus on those elements that pertain to ethical conduct: right speech, right action, and right livelihood.

The Buddhist concept of right speech is more encompassing than a set of proscriptions. Certainly, Buddhist texts—such as the Pāli canon the *Tripitaka*—warn against falsehoods, lies, rude language, backbiting, slander, abuse, and foolish or malicious gossip. However, it also encourages speaking truthfully and honestly, as well as speaking with kindness and gentleness to promote harmony. Most importantly, it encourages listening and noble silence, or only speaking when one has something helpful to say. An ideal example of someone practicing right speech is found in our text in the ferryman, Vasudeva. Hesse describes him:

> This was among the ferryman's virtues one of the greatest: like only a few, he knew how to listen. Without him having spoken a word, the speaker sensed how Vasudeva let his words enter his mind, quiet, open, waiting, how he did not lose a single one, awaited not a single one with impatience, did not add his praise or rebuke, was just listening.[17]

This short passage is an example of listening being a crucial element of right speech that we referenced earlier in this chapter. To Buddhist culture, silence is communication. It honors the speaker and displays the values of humility and mindfulness that are so important to the culture's values and norms. Equally important, however, is right action.

Right action is based on Buddhism's five precepts. They can be interpreted more as a guide for living rather than a list of specific commandments. Buddhist scholar Rupert Gethin notes, "Indeed, good conduct is ultimately understood in Buddhist thought not in terms of adherence to external rules, but as the expression of the perfected motivations of non-attachment, friendliness, and wisdom."[18] The five precepts forbid: killing or taking any life, taking what is not freely given, lying, engaging in sexual misconduct, and using alcohol or drugs that would cause heedlessness. Buddhists have various interpretations of these precepts. For instance, some Buddhists are vegetarians in honor of the first precept, while others are not. Regardless of the way in which the precepts are expressed, they provide a basis for ethical conduct that, at its heart, is intended to help its adherents act in wisdom and compassion while actively avoiding hurting others.

Siddhartha follows the five precepts throughout most of the novel. Even when he becomes a merchant, much of his success is due to his following the precepts and the sound relationships they help him establish with others. Gradually, however, he starts to ignore the precepts. Hesse writes:

> For a long time, Siddhartha had lived the life of the world and of lust, though without being a part of it. His senses which he had killed off in hot years as a Samana, had awoken again, he had tasted riches, had tasted lust, had tasted power; nevertheless he had still remained in his heart for a long time a Samana.[19]

Eventually, however, Hesse says:

> That high, bright state of being awake, which he had experienced that one time at the height of his youth . . . that supple willingness to listen to the divine voice in his own heart, had slowly become a memory.[20]

When Siddhartha strayed from right action his life seemed to follow a downward spiral. Siddhartha's descent corresponds with his failure to pursue a right livelihood. As we mentioned earlier, Buddhist scriptures provide a list of professions that Buddhists are to specifically avoid, but a more modern interpretation of the Buddha's thoughts include any occupation that would involve violating the elements of right speech and right action or that would bring suffering to others. The well-known contemporary Vietnamese Buddhist monk and author, Thich Nhat Hanh, describes right livelihood as "a way to earn your living without transgressing your ideals of love and compassion."[21] In our story, Siddhartha's profession and success as a merchant was in no way a violation of right livelihood until he allows his vocation to be placed above love and compassion for others:

> He had been captured by the world, by lust, covetousness, sloth, and finally by that vice which he had used to despise and mock the most as the most foolish one of all vices: greed. Property, possessions, and riches also had finally captured him; they were no longer a game and trifles to him, had become a shackle and a burden. On [sic] a strange and devious way, Siddhartha had gotten into this final and most base of all dependencies, by means of the game of dice.[22]

Thus, right livelihood is intimately linked to right speech and right action regardless of the profession one pursues. Author Walpola Sri Rahula reminds us, "This moral conduct is considered as the indispensable foundation for all higher spiritual attainment. No spiritual development is possible without this moral basis."[23] The importance Buddhism places on ethical conduct is seen throughout the teachings of the Buddha as well as in Hesse's novel. Siddhartha cannot attain the peace and enlightenment he seeks until he follows the Eightfold Path.

Buddhist cultures value wisdom as a basis for decision making. But how does one define "wisdom"? One may readily point to someone he or she considers "wise," but that person may hold a quality that seems mysterious or difficult to articulate. This is not uncommon. One author observes, "Wisdom is about as elusive as psychological constructs get."[24] Leadership scholar Shih-ying Yang argues:

> Depending on how it is defined, wisdom can be important to leadership in three ways. First, *wisdom*, when defined as a personal quality, *is an essential component of outstanding leadership*, because when applied to leading others, such a quality allows a person to demonstrate characteristics of outstanding leaders. Second, *wisdom*, defined either as ego strength, or higher level of reasoning, or a collective system of practical knowledge, *is an outcome of learning acquired from leadership experiences*. Third, *wisdom*, when defined as a positive real-life process, can *be displayed through leadership*.[25]

Likewise, a person's concept of wisdom may be dramatically influenced by his or her culture. Studies asking participants to define wisdom indicate a sharp divide between Western and Eastern conceptualizations. A Western understanding of wisdom often associates the concept with cognitive, knowledge, and skill abilities almost exclusively; whereas an Eastern view of wisdom is much more intuitive, encompassing and emphasizing the experiential, the personal, and interpersonal transformative aspects of wisdom *as well as* the cognitive aspects of wisdom valued in the West.[26] This Eastern inclusive view of wisdom as "a reflective understanding that emerges through experience and gives equal weight to cognitive, affective, intuitive, and interpersonal domains of consciousness."[27]

This idea of wisdom matches what we see in *Siddhartha*. In the beginning of the story, Siddhartha had the ability to master concentration and mindfulness as a boy in the house of his priestly father, and early in his life as a Samana, but his practice lacked the wisdom of *experience* that is so necessary to an Eastern understanding of the term. Cognitive ability was not enough. He had to mature and experience life before he was able to grasp the deeper wisdom his effort was able to offer him. Once Siddhartha gained his experience and "tasted all the world had to offer," he was able to find a "magical insight" and intuitively grasp the truth and wisdom of the universe.[28]

Likewise, this wisdom cannot be expressed in words. At the end of the tale, when Siddhartha reunites with his friend Govinda, he attempts to share his wisdom and insight with him. Siddhartha tells his friend:

> Knowledge can be conveyed, but not wisdom. It can be found, it can be lived, it is possible to be carried by it, miracles can be performed with it, but it cannot be expressed in words and taught.[29]

This passage summarizes an Eastern view of wisdom with its emotive and affective elements that refuse verbal expression and embrace paradox. One author observes, "Siddhartha's ultimate message, however, that wisdom is not communicable, remains both the key and the obstacle to penetrating those mysteries."[30] We see this paradox reflected in Hesse's story. As the philosopher says, "Life must be understood backwards, but can only be lived forwards."[31] Wisdom must be experienced. It cannot be taught.

Although there is one way to train the leader's mind to be receptive to this wisdom, and that is through the *practice of mindfulness*. Although there are many definitions of this term, most of them focus on concentrating on the present moment as a means to develop clarity of thought. For the purpose of presenting this concept as it applies to leadership, mindfulness is defined here as: Being fully aware of the present moment, and one's own response to it, clearly and without judgment.

It is worth taking a moment to unpack this definition. Certainly *learning* from one's past is an aspect of wisdom that is developed through mindfulness, but the past cannot be changed, so dwelling on it is considered a waste of time at best and potentially harmful at worst. Likewise, practicing mindfulness reminds us that the future is unclear and certainly not guaranteed. This does not mean that one should not make plans for the future, but rather, one should focus on and act in the present moment.

The definition of mindfulness presented here also draws attention to one's own emotional and physical response to the present situation. This is akin to the concept of emotional intelligence offered by Daniel Goleman, which he defines, *in part*, as the capacity for recognizing one's own feelings.[32] Knowing how one is feeling in a situation allows one to respond to it more thoughtfully. Rather than allowing your feelings to control your response to circumstances, mindfulness encourages you to observe your emotional and physical state to enable you to rationally respond to the state of affairs presented.

The phrase in the definition that refers to seeing the present moment "clearly and without judgment" warns those practicing mindfulness not to project past experiences on a current situation, or to participate in wishful thinking. Those who practice mindfulness are to focus on the way things really are, rather than the way they would like them to be. Additionally, it means to refrain from placing a value judgment of "good" or "bad" on the situation, but rather to simply see the present moment as neutrally and factually as possible.[33]

Those in the field of leadership studies have linked the practice of mindfulness to effective leadership. In their book *Resonate Leadership*, authors Richard

Boyatzis and Annie McKee argue that cultivating the capacity for mindfulness is "essential for sustaining good leadership."[34] Even His Holiness, the Dalai Lama, has made the explicit connection between mindfulness and effective and ethical leadership, he says, "A leader with a well-trained mind becomes the one to emulate." [35]

Practicing mindfulness leads to wisdom and compassion. A Buddhist perspective of decision making holds that the leader's decisions should be motivated by a sense of compassion for others. The goal of Buddhism is to end suffering. When one realizes the deep interconnected nature of all life, someone else's suffering becomes one's own suffering. Practicing compassion for another is to practice compassion for one's self. The leader's actions are to be motivated out of this sense of compassion, which can only be realized by seeking wisdom and practicing mindfulness. Once a leader has comprehended these truths, he or she is ready to be a leader and a role model to others.

The emphasis Buddhism places on leaders being role models to their followers cannot be understated. Once again, the Dalai Lama crystalizes this point:

> In Buddhism, we consider it very important that people teaching Buddhist principles apply those principles to their own conduct. In India at the time of Buddha, teachers and philosophers were taken seriously only if they lived as they preached . . .The same principle applies to true leaders as to these early philosophers. A leader will be respected only when he acts according to the principles in which he says he believes.[36]

Additionally, teaching and coaching are a part of the responsibilities of leaders in the Buddhist tradition. The Buddhist idea of a *bodhisattva* is an enlightened mentor, if you will, who out of compassion for others refrains from entering nirvana in order to train and serve others.

The importance of role modeling is seen throughout Hesse's story. Siddhartha's father is a role model for his son when he refuses to speak in anger when Siddhartha tells him he wants to leave and join the Samanas. Siddhartha carefully learns and masters the ways of the Samanas, and looks to his leaders to learn how one should behave. Buddha acts as Siddhartha's role model in seeking enlightenment through one's self. As a courtesan, Kamala is Siddhartha's role model and teaches him how to give and receive sexual pleasure as expressed in the *Kama Sutra*. And as a successful businessman, Kamaswami is Siddhartha's role model and teaches him the ways of business. But perhaps the clearest example of a role model in Hesse's story is the ferryman, Vasudeva, and the example he sets for Siddhartha and all those around him.

The first appearance of Vasudeva in the novel is short lived, but not insignificant. Vasudeva has found the enlightenment that Siddhartha longs for, but he also knows Siddhartha is not ready to grasp it. He does not force his knowledge on Siddhartha, rather he suggests to Siddhartha that he will return one day to learn from the river. It is not until 20 years later in the story that Siddhartha is able to understand the wisdom of Vasudeva's words. Once

Siddhartha fails to find rest in the world of *samsara*, and leaves his lover Kamala and his riches, he is finally ready to see what Vasudeva has to offer, and returns to learn from his unlikely role model. Vasudeva speaks little and listens much. He does not need to speak. He provides a living example of the way to find the enlightenment Siddhartha seeks. Siddhartha becomes wise in deferring to Vasudeva's wisdom.

Likewise, Govinda is the perfect Buddhist follower. He defers to the wisdom of his leaders, whether that leader be Siddhartha, the Samanas, or the Buddha. Throughout the book, Govinda follows Siddhartha from the time the two of them were children. He continues to follow his friend even when Siddhartha leaves his home and family and joins the Samanas. But Hesse makes it clear that, in order for Govinda to reach the enlightenment he also seeks, he must leave his friend and begin his own journey. This is hard for Govinda to accept. After Govinda and Siddhartha meet the Buddha, Govinda asks Siddhartha:

> We have both heard the exalted one, we have both perceived the teachings. Govinda has heard the teachings, he has taken refuge in it. But you, my honored friend, don't you also want to walk the path of salvation?[37]

Siddhartha replies:

> Govinda, my friend, now you have taken this step, now you have chosen this path. Always, oh, Govinda, you've been my friend, you've always walked one step behind me. Often I have thought: Won't Govinda for once also take a step by himself, without me, out of his own soul? Behold, now you've turned into a man and are choosing your path for yourself. I wish that you would go it up to its end [sic], oh my friend, that you shall find salvation![38]

Govinda must travel his own path if he is to find the enlightenment that he seeks. Not unlike Buddhist philosophy, the Buddhist prescription for followers is paradoxical. Yes, one should defer to the wisdom of teachers, yet one must also test all that is said to see if it is true and lead one's self.

Buddhist followers are not required or expected to blindly follow or mindlessly defer to their leaders. Just the opposite is true. However, if the leader possesses and shows evidence of wisdom, that follower should defer to the leader's direction. Legend has it that the ancient Zen master Lin Chi reportedly said, "If you meet the Buddha on the road, kill him." The meaning of Lin Chi's words are obviously symbolic, but they emphasize the Buddhist ideal that followers must listen and heed the teachings of their leaders, but ultimately, they must critically and actively pursue their goal to seek truth and lead themselves.

Summary and concluding remarks

A Buddhist approach to leadership attempts to synthesize Buddhist teachings, specifically the interconnected unity of all things, the four noble truths, and the Eightfold Path. Such an understanding envisions leadership as a personal journey one must make to self-discovery. Decisions are to be made with wisdom and compassion. The portion of the Eightfold Path that specifically focuses on ethical conduct provides a moral compass for leaders, but all elements of the Eightfold Path must be practiced simultaneously if one is to lead effectively. Leaders are to be role models who follow this path, and who themselves are seeking to become more enlightened. Followers are to defer to the wisdom of their leaders if their leaders show evidence of wisdom and mindfulness; nevertheless, followers are responsible for their own critical thought and active participation in achieving their goals. These elements of leadership can be seen in Hermann Hesse's *Siddhartha* and the symbols, characters, and prose found in the novel. Although not a primer on Buddhism, Hesse's novel provides an accessible way for Westerners to better understand some of the key themes found in Buddhist leadership (see Table 10.2).

The basics of Buddhist thought detailed here have vast implications to one's understanding of and prescriptions for leadership. As some note, the Buddhist teaching of the absence of divisions between ourselves and others leads to "the radical idea that there are no essential inherent distinctions between leaders and followers."[39] Buddhist concepts such as the recognition of life's suffering found in the Four Noble Truths encourages leaders to develop a spirit of empathy and compassion; while the acknowledgment of the impermanence of all things forces leaders and followers to seek a higher purpose for their goals rather than focusing on their own self interests.[40] Similarly, when leaders and followers see the interconnected nature of their actions they are motivated to behave in a moral and ethically responsible way. All leaders, regardless of their culture, would be wise to follow this path.

Table 10.2 Western and Buddhist comparative views of leadership

	Western worldview	*Buddhist worldview*
Leadership viewed as a . . .	Prize	Personal journey
Leader–follower relationship	Transactional	Teacher/student
How decisions are made	Through rationality, logic, pragmatism	With wisdom and compassion
Responsibilities of the leader	Motivate followers, results orientation	Role model
Responsibilities of the the follower	Dependable, committed, motivated	Defer to the wisdom of the leader
Moral dimension of leadership	Secular "code of ethics"	The Eightfold Path

Questions for discussion

• To what extent must one know one's own self before one is ready to lead others?

• Does the Eightfold Path resonate with your approach to ethics? Why or why not?

• Who do you identify as a role model? How does this person set an example of leadership?

• How do you define wisdom? Does your definition of wisdom resonate more with a Western or an Eastern definition of the term?

• How do you reconcile the Buddhist ideal of leadership as a personal journey with the importance placed on followers deferring to the wisdom of their leaders?

• What elements of a Buddhist approach to leadership do you find compelling? Why?

Additional resources

M. Carroll, *The Mindful Leader: Awakening Your Natural Management Skills Through Mindfulness Meditation*, Boston, MA: Trumpeter, 2011.

M.H. Dickmann and N. Stanford-Blair's *Mindful Leadership: A Brain Based Framework*, 2nd edn., Thousand Oaks, CA: Corwin Press, 2009.

Notes

1 For example, R. Boyatzis and A. McKee, *Resonate Leadership: Renewing Yourself and Connecting with Others Through Mindfulness, Hope, and Compassion*, Boston, MA: Harvard Business School Press, 2005.

2 There is a long-standing disagreement among scholars as to what extent Hesse's *Siddhartha* follows Buddhist, Hindu, or even Christian thought. Our purpose is to simply introduce the new student of Eastern worldviews to some of the basic concepts found in Buddhist thought as opposed to argue for a particular reading of Hesse's novel. Although scholars disagree to what extent Hesse's novel can be faithfully read as exclusively Buddhist in form and structure, the book does provide Western readers with an artful and accessible introduction to Eastern thought. For more regarding this discussion see: L. Shaw, "Time and Structure of Hermann Hesse's 'Siddhartha'," *Symposium*, XI (1957): 202–224; H. Kassim "Toward a Mahayana Buddhist Interpretation of Hermann Hesse's 'Siddhartha'," *Literature East and West*, 18 (1974): 233–243; B. Schludermann and R. Finlay "Mythical Reflections of the East in Hermann Hesse," *Mosaic*, 2 (1969): 97–111; and K.D. Verma "The Nature of Perception of Reality in Hermann Hesse's "Siddhartha'," *South Asian Review*, 11–12 (1988): 1–10. Two noteworthy scholars who argue in opposition to a Buddhist reading of *Siddhartha* are T. Zilokowski, *The Novels of Hermann Hesse: A Study in Theme and Structure*, Princeton, NJ: Princeton University Press, 1965, pp. 146–177; and M. Boulby, *Hermann Hesse: His Mind and Art*, Ithaca, NY: Cornell University Press, 1967, pp. 121–157.

3 Literary author S. Narasimbaial notes "A study of the life of the Buddha reveals various points of similarity with that of Siddhartha; one could almost see them moving on parallel lines although there is variation in the sequence of events." See "Hermann

Hesse's 'Siddhartha': Between Rebellion and Regeneration," *Literary Criterion*, 16 (1981): 64–65.

4 R.H. Paslick, "Dialectic and Non-Attachment: The Structure of Hermann Hesse's Siddhartha," *Symposium*, XXVII (1973): 66.

5 T. Ziolkowski warns "it would be naïve to read the book as an embodiment of exegesis of Indian philosophy." T. Ziolkowski *The Novels of Hermann Hesse*, Princeton: Princeton University Press, 1965, p. 150. For example, E.L. Stelzig notes *Siddhartha* "takes the concept of individuality much more seriously than any Asiatic teaching." Quoted in *Herman Hesse's Fictions of the Self: Autobiography and the Confessional Imagination*, Princeton, NJ: Princeton University Press, 1988, p. 177.

6 Sometimes referred to as "right knowledge" or "right understanding".

7 C. Humphrey's, *Buddhism*, Harmondsworth: Pelican Books, 1951, p. 91.

8 *The Dhammapada* 10:1

9 Hermann Hesse *Siddhartha*, iTunes: Public Domain, p. 5. Available at www.apple.com/itunes/. We have used the iTunes Public Domain version of the book to provide page numbers for quotes. Also Available at http://www.gutenberg.org/files/2500/2500-h/2500-h.htm. Accessed August 16, 2014.

10 Ibid, pp. 15–16.

11 Ibid, p. 104.

12 W. Rahula, *What the Buddha Taught*, New York: Grove Press, 1959/1974, p. 1. Rahula's words are a reflection of the time in which they were written. The term "humanity," as opposed to "man," may be more reflective of the meaning of Rahula's intent.

13 Hesse, *Siddhartha*, p. 44.

14 Ibid, p. 39.

15 Ibid, p. 130.

16 Buddhist ethics do not fall into a strict division of virtue ethics, deontology, or consequentialism as do some ethical systems in the West. This does not mean that some have not tried to do just that. Damien Keown is probably the most well-known Buddhist ethical scholar. In his book, *The Nature of Buddhist Ethics*, he argues that Buddhist ethics are best understood as analogous with Aristotelian virtue ethics. See D. Keown, *The Nature of Buddhist Ethics*, London: Macmillan, 1992. Ethicists Morgan and Lawton echo this approach when they identify the traits of leaders prescribed in the Pāli canon. Among these traits are: generosity, practicing high moral character, personal sacrifice, honesty, kindness and gentleness, leading a simple life, being free from hatred, promoting peace, patience, tolerance, and understanding, and leading in harmony with followers desires. P. Morgan and C.A. Lawton, *Ethical Issues in Six Religious Traditions*, Edinburgh: Edinburgh University Press, 1996, p. 66. Other ethicists argue that at least Mahayana Buddhist ethics should be seen as ideal utilitarianism—that is, that one should act to maximize happiness and minimize suffering for the largest number of people, regardless of a person's personal investment in a matter. C. Goodman, "Consequentialism, Agent-Neutrality, and Mahayana Ethics," *Philosophy East and West*, 58, 1 (2008): 17–35. Others may find "some resemblances between deontological approaches and Buddhism," although such approaches are usually found to be based more in psychology than in normative ethics. M.G. Barnhart makes this observation in "Theory and Comparison in the Discussion of Buddhist Ethics," *Philosophy East and West*, 62, 1 (2012): 16–23.

17 Hesse, *Siddhartha*, p. 112.

18 R. Gethin, *The Foundations of Buddhism*, Oxford: Oxford University Press, 1998, p. 172.

19 Hesse, *Siddhartha*, p. 80.

20 Ibid.

21 Thich Nhat Hanh, *The Heart of the Buddha's Teaching*, Berkeley, CA: Parallax Press, 1998, p. 104.

22 Hesse, *Siddhartha*, pp. 83–84.

23 Rahula, *What the Buddha Taught*, p. 47.

24 R.J. Sternberg, ed., *Wisdom: It's Nature, Origins, and Development*, New York: Cambridge University Press, 1990, p. ix.

25 Shih-ying Yang "Wisdom Displayed through Leadership: Exploring Leadership-Related Wisdom," *Leadership Quarterly*, 22 (2011): 616–32. (Emphasis in original.)

26 For a review of the literature articulating different cultural conceptualizations of wisdom, see M. Takahashi and W.F. Overton "Cultural Foundations of Wisdom: An Integrated Development Approach," in R.J. Sternberg and J. Jordan, eds., *A Handbook of Wisdom: Psychological Perspectives*, New York: Cambridge University Press, 2005, pp. 32–60.

27 Ibid, 37–38.

28 G.W. Field identifies this term in his book *Hermann Hesse*, New York: Twayne Publishers, Inc., 1970, pp. 7, 81.

29 Hesse, *Siddhartha*, p. 152.

30 T.R. Whissen, "Siddhartha," in *Classic Cult Fiction*, New York: Greenwood Press, 1992, p. 211.

31 This quote is attributed to Danish philosopher, Søren Kierkegaard.

32 D. Goleman, *Working with Emotional Intelligence*, New York: Bantam Books, 1998, p. 317. It is not a coincidence that other authors have seen the connections between emotional intelligence and mindfulness and have sought to merge the leading voice in emotional intelligence, Daniel Goleman, and the leading voice in mindfulness, Jon Kabat-Zinn. See Chade-Meng Tan, *Search Inside Yourself*, New York: HarperOne, 2012; A. Fraser, *The Healing Power of Meditation*, Boston, MA: Shambhala Publications, 2013; D. Goleman and J. Kabat-Zinn, *Mindfulness at Work*, New York: Macmillan Audio, 2007.

33 In the past decade, research on mindfulness has grown in fields as diverse as education, medicine, and psychology. This research appears to indicate manifold benefits. Scientists have found that practicing mindfulness through meditation decreases stress, depression, and anxiety, as well as increasing concentration. For an example of this type of research see V. Bostanov, P.M. Keune, B. Kotchoubey, and M. Hautzinger, "Event-related Brain Potentials Reflect Increased Concentration Ability after Mindfulness-based Cognitive Therapy for Depression: A Randomized Clinical Trial," *Psychiatry Research*, 199, 3 (2012): 174–180.

34 R. Boyatzis and A. McKee, *Resonate Leadership: Renewing Yourself and Connecting with Others Through Mindfulness, Hope, and Compassion*, Boston, MA: Harvard Business School Press, 2005, p. 114.

35 See His Holiness, the Dalai Lama, and L. Van Den Muyzenberg, *The Leader's Way: The Art of Making the Right Decisions in Our Careers, Our Companies, and the World at Large*, New York: Broadway Books, 2009.

36 His Holiness, the Dalai Lama, and Van Den Muyzenberg, *The Leader's Way*, p. 30.

37 Hesse, *Siddhartha*, p. 34.

38 Ibid.

39 M. Kriger and Y. Seng, "Leadership with Inner Meaning: A Contingency Theory of Leadership based on the Worldviews of Five Religions," *The Leadership Quarterly*, 16 (2005); 771–806. Here, the authors are referencing B. Gray and M. P. Kriger, "Leadership Lessons and Indications from the Buddhist Tradition for Creating Adaptive Organizations." Symposium Paper presented at the 2005 Annual Meetings of the National Academy of Management, Honolulu, Hawaii.

40 S. Parameshwar, "Inventing Higher Purpose through Suffering: The Transformation of the Transformational Leader," *Leadership Quarterly*, 17 (2006): 454–474.

11 Leadership in an East Asian cultural context

The best leaders are those the people hardly know exist. When she has accomplished her task, the people say, "Amazing: we did it, all by ourselves!"[1]

Tao Te Ching

We travel now to East Asia to consider how the cultural values and norms in Confucian and Taoist cultures may affect one's perspectives on leadership. For the last 30 years, East Asia—and specifically China—has seen an unprecedented rate of economic growth and increasing world influence. To some in the West, this may seem like a fairly recent phenomenon. However, when looking through the long lens of history, this trend seems almost constant. In fact, China has always considered herself the "Middle Kingdom," poised between heaven and earth, and its influence for the greater part of human history has reached far and wide. Other countries in East Asia have also been dramatic actors on the world's stage. Major world wars in the twentieth century were fought with Japan, but the country later rose to become a global leader in manufacturing and technology. Likewise, South Korea and Taiwan have proved themselves to be remarkably adaptable and have risen to become leaders in international politics and economics (see Figure 11.1).

Although there are vast cultural and political differences between countries in East Asia, they do have some commonalities; specifically, they have all been influenced by three of the world's great wisdom traditions, Buddhism, Taoism, and Confucianism. In this chapter, we seek to examine the implications these roots have on an East Asian approach to leadership. Since we have already devoted a single chapter to Buddhism's implications on leadership, in this chapter we will focus on these other two philosophical traditions, Confucianism and Taoism, with a particular emphasis on the latter (see Figure 11.2).

Confucius, originally K'ung Fu-zue or "Master Kung," was a teacher who lived in the northeast part of China between 551 and 479 BCE. He was a minor governmental figure in a small province during the Chou Dynasty in an era known for its moral laxity and internal conflicts. Confucius was disappointed with his provincial ruler's corrupt behavior, so he left his position in the court

Figure 11.1 Parts of East Asia with Confucian and Taoist influences

Figure 11.2 Portrait of Shuo Kuo (Confucius), Qing Dynasty (1644–1911)

Ink on paper rubbing; mounted on cloth and hanging scroll, 141 × 108 cm
Gift of Horace H.F. Jayne, 1924
Philadelphia Museum of Art, Philadelphia
Photo credit: Philadelphia Museum of Art/Art Resource, New York

and became a traveling sage. As he traveled the region, he taught his disciples and attempted to persuade other rulers to follow his ethical system for governmental and personal relations. Although he did not find a political patron to take up his system in his lifetime, ultimately all of China came to embrace his teachings. His precepts were incorporated into Chinese law in 210 BCE and his impact on East Asian thought can still be seen today.[2]

Confucius's teachings are usually considered to be broadly ethical rather than explicitly religious, although there are some later incarnations of Confucian thought that are more religious in tone.[3] Rather than looking to a supernatural source to find redemption, Confucius believed in the inherent goodness of human beings, similar to the Western philosophy of humanism. Confucius argued human perfectibility could be obtained by developing specific virtues (*jen*) and following a prescribed code of conduct (*li*), which he systematized in his teachings. After his death, his sayings were compiled in the *Analects of Confucius*, and the book still inspires thoughts about leadership in contemporary times.[4]

Another influential teacher who lived at the time of Confucius was the philosopher and poet Lao Tzu (see Figure 11.3).[5] There is significant scholarly disagreement on whether Lao Tzu was an actual historical figure or whether he exists merely in legend. Although it is generally agreed that, at least as a legend, Lao Tzu was an older contemporary of Confucius and also lived in China circa sixth century BCE. Tradition holds that he was the keeper of the archives in the imperial court in LuoYang, the ancient capital of China. Lao Tzu's poetic book the *Tao Te Ching* (*The Way and Its Power*) is considered by many as the founding work of Taoism, and this masterpiece also holds powerful insights about leadership as we will see later in our case study.

The origins of the *Tao Te Ching* are as legendary as its author. The story is that Lao Tzu, saddened by his people's warring and turmoil, decided to remove himself from society and seek solitude at the end of his life. He rode his water buffalo across the desert towards the western boarders of China. When he came to the Hankao Pass, the gatekeeper at the pass recognized Lao Tzu as a great sage and pled with him to halt his journey and return to China. When Lao Tzu refused, the gatekeeper begged him to at least leave behind a record of his teachings so that his wisdom would not be lost to future generations. Lao Tzu agreed, and in three days he returned to the pass and left the gatekeeper a slender book of poetry of 5000 words, the *Tao Te Ching*. He continued his journey never to return, but his little book forever changed the culture he left behind.

We begin our discussion of an East Asian approach to leadership with these two teachers and their philosophies because they may be best understood in relationship to each other. Just as the ancient Chinese symbol of the *t'ai chi t'u* pictured at the beginning of this chapter represents complementary opposites—the yin and the yang—these philosophical systems fit together as complementary opposites in the East Asian approach to leadership. Throughout this chapter, we will delve further into these two philosophies and specifically examine the *Tao Te Ching* as an artifact from Taoist culture to better understand a particularly

太
上
老
君

Figure 11.3 Anonymous, Lao Tse (Lao Tzu) astride a bull, accompanied by a servant,
　　　　seventeenth century

Chinese scroll painting
Bibliothèque National de France (BnF), Paris
Photo credit: Snark/Art Resource, New York

Taoist approach to leadership. Although Taoism is practiced in many forms,
we will focus our attention specifically on classical Taoism, which is expressed
more philosophically than religiously.[6]

Case study: Lao Tzu's *Tao Te Ching*

Legend has it that Confucius and Lao Tzu met at one point in their lives when
Confucius paid a visit to "the Old Master," Lao Tzu. Knowing that he was
going to visit the great sage, Confucius dressed in his finest robes. As Confucius
sat reading the ancient classics, Lao Tzu unassumingly appeared and stood before

him. Confucius rose and ceremoniously bowed to the Old Master. Lao Tzu was not impressed with Confucius's fine robes and manners. He said to Confucius, "Put away your polite airs and your vain display of fine robes. The wise man does not display his treasures to those he does not know. And he cannot learn from the Ancients." Confucius replied, "Why not." Lau Tzu said, "The swan does not need to bathe daily to remain white." Later, Confucius reflected on the meeting. He said, "I know a bird can fly; I know a fish can swim; I know animals can run. Creatures that run can be caught in nets; those that swim can be caught in wicker traps; those that fly can be hit by arrows. But the dragon is beyond my knowledge; it ascends into heaven on the clouds and wind. Today I have seen Lao Tzu, and he is like the dragon!"[7]

The story provides a representative anecdote that illustrates the opposing systems of Confucianism and Taoism. Compared to Confucianism's elaborate code of conduct, Taoism can seem mystical. Whereas Confucius attempted to perfect the human being and society through a prescribed code of conduct and virtues, Lao Tzu saw life as already perfect if it be embraced in its natural state. Their goal was the same, but their prescribed means for obtaining this goal were profoundly different. Nevertheless, these two approaches remain para-doxically engrained in the East Asian conscious even today.[8]

Origins of a Confucian worldview

Confucius believed that humanity could be perfected and group harmony achieved through a carefully prescribed tradition of societal order. Humans were inherently good; they only needed to be taught how to behave in order to find this goodness.

Jen (the supreme virtue)

Confucius believed that: "To put the world in order, we must first put the nation in order; to put the nation in order, we must put the family in order; to put the family in order, we must cultivate our personal life; and to cultivate our personal life, we must first set our hearts right." The first step in achieving this goodness and putting our hearts right is through the cultivation of the "supreme virtue," *jen*—translated as benevolence, empathy, human heartedness, or even a universal love for others. The model practitioner of this ultimate virtue is the *chun tzu*. The *chun tzu* is a truly mature person and represents humanity at its best, and being such a model should be everyone's ultimate goal. The person with a carefully cultivated *jen* simultaneously embraces dignity and respect for one's self while extending dignity and respect to others. *Jen* might be best summarized by Confucius's famous "Silver Rule"—"Do not do to others what you would not want others to do to you" the inverse of Jesus of Nazareth's "Golden Rule"—"Do for others what you would have them do for you." However, both these aphorisms encapsulate Confucius's concept of *jen* well.

Li (code of conduct)

Jen is foundational for understanding the basics of Confucian thought, but equally important is the Confucian concept of *li*. *Li* might be best thought of as a "code of conduct," a social order that extends to all human relationships. By practicing the proper *li*, society is able to establish harmony. It is the external means for expressing one's inner *jen*. This code is quite elaborate, but there are a few key concepts that serve as its foundation.

The first vital concept of this code is that every person in society has a specific role to play and a precise way of performing his or her role.[9] With this role comes a rank and position that carries specific prescribed duties and obligations. This principle has crucial implications for a Confucian approach to leadership. For each term, such as "ruler" and "subject"—or for our purposes, "leader" and "follower"—there is a prescribed meaning and, hence, a prescribed way of acting. Or, as Confucius says, "Let the ruler be ruler, the subject subject; let the father be father, the son son."[10]

The Five Great Relationships

Confucius was not content to simply state this overarching principle; he also categorized the particular types of relationship that constituted social life. The Five Great Relationships, as he termed them, were: parent and child, husband and wife, elder sibling and younger sibling, elder friend and junior friend, and ruler and subject.[11] Each of these relationship pairs, in turn, has a prescribed way of relating to each other. Parents are to be loving towards their children and, in turn, children are to be reverential towards their parents. Elder siblings are to be gentle to their younger siblings, and, in turn, younger siblings are to be respectful of their elder siblings. Husbands are to be good to their wives, and, in turn, wives are to listen to their husbands. Elder friends are to be considerate of their younger friends, and, in turn, the younger friend should defer to their elder friends. Rulers are to be benevolent to their subjects, or followers, and, in turn, subjects should be loyal to their rulers.[12] Although these prescribed social relationships and their hierarchical implications conflict with the egalitarian values and norms of the West, it must be said that social equality is not Confucius's goal; his goal is social order.

Examining the Five Great Relationships, the reader notices two themes: the importance of the family and the respect for age. These are fundamental aspects of Confucian order. Three of the Five Great Relationships refer specifically to order in families. Confucius saw the family as the basic unit of society and key to greater social harmony. Confucianism has even been described as an ethic that models the community on the family.[13] Confucius believed that: "The strength of the nation derives from the integrity of the home." In the family, how one treats one's elders is of particular importance. Children are to care for their elders and revere them for their wisdom. In Confucian teaching, old age is considered something that a person should look forward to with anticipation and value it for the sagacity and maturity it brings. This veneration of age is central to understanding Confucius's concept of *li*.

These are just a *few* of the basic teachings of Confucius's code of conduct, the sum of which compose his concept of *li* and which provides a sense of filial and communal propriety that is still honored in East Asia today.[14] We present these concepts in particular because they serve to capture Confucianism's most basic teachings and provide a stark contrast to Taoism's natural order.

Origins of a Taoist worldview

In contrast to Confucianism's emphasis on social order, we now turn to the teachings of Lao Tzu and Taoism. Both philosophical systems seek human perfection and social harmony; but whereas Confucianism attempts to reach these goals through an elaborate code of social conduct, Taoism attempts to reach these goals through acting with the natural order of the universe, what Taoists call the "Tao."[15]

The Tao

Before we can explore these implications, we must understand what Lao Tzu means by "Tao." The *Tao Te Ching* begins with the declaration: "The Tao that can be spoken is not the eternal Tao. The name that can be named is not the eternal name."[16] Thus, when someone attempts to explain the term "Tao" they defy Taoism's first fundamental principle. The literal translation of the word is "the path," or "the way," and it may be best conceived as the ultimate reality, a way of living, or a system of guidance that is in keeping with the natural state of the universe. Thus the word "Tao" may imply any of these meanings depending on the context, but the meanings are still interrelated.[17] For Lao Tzu and other Taoists, the Tao is perfect and can be readily found in nature. Earth is simply a reflection of heaven. If we embrace nature on its own terms and live in accordance with Tao, we can live in harmony with the world and those around us. It is easier and more productive to work with nature than trying to fight against it. It is only when we try to control nature and impose elaborate arbitrary laws on people that we upset this natural harmony.

Wu wei

Taoists express the idea of living with this natural harmony of the Tao as *wu wei*. A literal translation of the term is "without action" or "not doing," but a more meaningful way of expressing this idea might be "acting without forcing or controlling." This concept may seem counterintuitive, especially in terms of a Western approach to leadership. However, we must be careful to remember that the concept of *wu wei* does not mean a leader fails to act; rather, the leader acts in accordance with the natural order—the Tao—as it presents itself in the situation.

When we refer to the natural order in this sense, the picture is *not* of a swimmer struggling to *fight against* a river's whitewater rapids such as we described when speaking of leadership in Latin America. Rather, the picture of the natural order the Taoist draws is of a swimmer flowing with the currents of the river and *working with* them to stay afloat.

There is a story from Taoist literature that illustrates this point. One day Confucius saw an old man tumble into a waterfall. He was sure that the old man had drowned, but suddenly, the old man rose up from the water and strolled away from the riverbank unharmed by his experience. Confucius rushed to the old man and inquired, "Aren't you hurt? How could you survive the power of the waterfall? What mystical power do you possess?" The old man replied, "Nothing special. I learned when I was a boy to sink and rise with the natural currents of the water. I survive because I don't fight the water's superior power."[18] The story illustrates the concept of *wu wei*. Taoists believe actions taken in accordance with the Tao are easier and more productive than trying to force or control situations ourselves.[19]

Water is a reoccurring metaphor throughout Taoist literature and specifically in the *Tao Te Ching*. It serves to illustrate the concept of *wu wei* and acting with nature rather than against it. Lao Tzu writes:

> Water is the softest and most yielding substance.
> Yet nothing is better than water
> for overcoming the hard and rigid,
> because nothing can compete with it.[20]

Consider the way a river slowly carves a deep canyon over millions of years. The image provides a tangible picture of the concept of *wu wei*—doing without forcing. It is a helpful illustration of the Taoist belief:

> Everyone knows that the soft and yielding
> overcomes the rigid and hard,
> but few can put this knowledge into practice.[21]

This principle is continually referred to throughout the *Tao Te Ching*. Taoism encourages flexibility and adaptability when encountering obstacles. Those who live in accordance with the Tao are able to adapt to the difficulties they face while exerting the least effort possible; they bend so as not to break; they practice *wu wei*. Another passage from the *Tao Te Ching* illustrates this point:

> The living are soft and yielding;
> the dead are rigid and stiff.
> Living plants are flexible and tender;
> the dead are brittle and dry.
>
> Those who are stiff and rigid are the disciples of death.
> Those who are soft and yielding are the disciples of life.

The rigid and stiff will be broken.
The soft and yielding will overcome.[22]

The notion of *wu wei* is so foundational to Taoist thought that a famous Taoist scholar argues that "the concept of 'complying with nature through non-action' must be taken as the very essence of the *Tao Te Ching*, and the other tenets are developed to support it."[23] The idea is based on the principle that life in its pure state is simple. If we could regain that simplicity of the natural order of the world, the world would be a better place.

The uncarved block

Remember, Taoists believe the human being is naturally good. The *Tao Te Ching*'s use of the metaphor of an uncarved block of wood (*p'u*) also illustrates the importance Taoism places on following the natural order. The secret to virtuousness is returning to our natural state—the uncarved block. Taoism encourages its adherents to see life as it is, without judgment, rather than viewing people and circumstances in terms of dualities, such as right and wrong, good and bad, or beautiful and ugly. The *Tao Te Ching* records:

If you embrace the world with compassion,
then your virtue will return you to the uncarved block.
The block of wood is carved into utensils
by carving void into the wood.

The Master uses the utensils,
yet prefers to keep to the block
because of its limitless possibilities.
Great works do not involve discarding substance.[24]

There is a traditional Taoist story that illustrates this concept well: One day a farmer was plowing his fields and his one and only horse ran away. Hearing the news, the farmer's neighbor paid him a visit and expressed his sympathy: "I'm so sorry for your bad fortune," said the neighbor. The farmer replied, "Who knows what is good or bad. We will wait and see." The next day, the horse came home and brought three other wild horses with him. The farmer's neighbor exclaimed: "Congratulations! What good fortune for you!" The farmer said, "Who knows what is good or bad. We will wait and see." The next day the farmer's son broke his leg while trying to tame one of the wild horses. The neighbor once again expressed his sympathy: "I'm so sorry for your bad fortune." And the farmer one again replied, "Who knows what is good or bad. We will wait and see." The next day an army marched through the farmer's town and rounded up all the healthy young men to go to war, but the farmer's son was left behind because he had a broken leg.[25] The Taoist story reminds the reader to see life as it is *rather than how we would wish it to be*.

To the Taoist's mind, good and bad, right and wrong, ugly and beautiful are more a matter of one's perception than objective reality.

Yin and yang

In an apparent paradox, a central element of Taoism embraces dualities, but not as opposites; rather, dualities are considered complements to each other.[26] As we noted earlier, this Taoist concept—symbolized by the *t'ai chi t'u*—is referred to as the yin and the yang. Once again, examine the line drawing pictured at the beginning of this chapter. Notice the way the contrasting black and white elements of the symbol interrelate to one another to form a unified whole. Taoists believe light and dark, male and female, life and death, good and evil, day and night; dualities work together to create the whole—one rises out of the other. To the Taoist, each duality is interconnected and interdependent upon the other. The *Tao Te Ching* explains:

> Know the masculine,
> but keep to the feminine:
> and become a watershed to the world.
>
> If you embrace the world,
> the Tao will never leave you
> and you become as a little child.
>
> Know the white,
> yet keep to the black:
> be a model for the world.
> If you are a model for the world,
> the Tao inside you will strengthen
> and you will return whole to your eternal beginning.
>
> Know the honorable,
> but do not shun the disgraced:
> embracing the world as it is.[27]

Each element of a duality only exists because of the other. Likewise, the small circles found inside the separate portions of the *t'ai chi t'u* remind the viewer that there are no absolutes; each duality contains a part of the other. To the Taoist, polarities are not dichotomies. All of life is relative. Or as Lao Tzu says:

> All things carry Yin
> yet embrace Yang.
> They blend their life breaths
> in order to produce harmony.[28]

A pair of complementary opposites that is particularly important to understanding this concept is masculine and feminine. Where the yin is considered the masculine and active element of the dyad, the yang is considered the feminine and passive. Although Taoism acknowledges the need for both of these elements, the feminine yang is considered the superior. Indeed, Taoism may be considered as the feminine counterpart, or the yang, to Confucianism's masculine yin. The value Taoism places on receptivity mirrors the fundamental Taoist concept of *wu wei*. As opposed to forcing one's own will on others and the situation, Taoism advocates "being" rather than "doing" by being open and adaptable to ever changing people and contexts.

Now that we have a basic understanding of a few of the major concepts of classical Taoism, we can more fully understand the implications Taoist values and norms have on leadership.

Analysis: Leadership as service

The *Tao Te Ching* poetically encapsulates the teachings of classical Taoism. Its natural imagery and romantic tone is in stark contrast to Confucianism's prosaic code of conduct. When one first begins to explore this little lyrical text, it becomes easy to see why Confucius referred to Lao Tzu as "the dragon beyond his knowledge ascending into heaven on the clouds and wind." Taoist concepts are often expressed in poetic paradoxes. Yet studying the *Tao Te Ching* offers some deep truths about leadership. Some of the key themes that relate to leadership are: 1) leaders should practice an adaptable style of leadership; 2) leaders should be servants to their followers; 3) leaders should act with moderation, humility, and compassion; 4) leaders should rely on intuition, and; 5) the follower's responsibility for his or her own self-development (see Figure 11.4).

Probably the most difficult aspect of Taoism for Westerners to understand, specifically as it applies to leadership, is the Taoist concept of *wu wei*. When first introduced to the concept, many mistakenly think that Lao Tzu is advocating for a completely hands-off approach to leadership. Critics argue that such a leadership style would be ineffective and invite anarchy and frustration among followers. But this interpretation fails to understand Lao Tzu's point; Lao Tzu is not advocating for "no action" as much as he is advocating for "right action." A Taoist approach to leadership maintains that leaders should be adaptive and work with the character of the followers, the goal, and the environmental context—in other words, leaders should adapt to the nature of the situation. One author explains, "Lao Tzu is not recommending a laissez-faire approach. He is suggesting that good leadership involves doing what needs to be done as opposed to acting in accordance with a preconceived plan for purely personal reasons."[29]

A passage from the *Tao Te Ching* illustrates this concept. Lao Tzu writes:

> It is easier to carry an empty cup
> than one that is filled to the brim.

"I" (Individualism)   (Collectivism) "WE"

The leader's use of intuition   The leader should adapt to the
Self-development   followers and the context
                                                 The leader should serve the group with
                                                 moderation, humility, and compassion

Figure 11.4 The Taoist worldview on the leadership continuum

> The sharper the knife
> the easier it is to dull.
> The more wealth you possess
> the harder it is to protect.
>
> Pride brings its own trouble.
> When you have accomplished your goal
> simply walk away.
> This is the pathway to Heaven.[30]

This passage from the *Tao Te Ching* and the overall concept of *wu wei* cautions leaders to only do what is *necessary* in a particular situation and no more. The leadership implication of this concept is that leaders should refrain from using coercive power. Any type of coercive power is thought to be a last resort, and then only to be practiced with the utmost moderation. Lao Tzu writes:

> Those who lead people by following the Tao
> don't use weapons to enforce their will.
> Using force always leads to unseen troubles.[31]

Another passage that illustrates this concept reads:

> Weapons are meant for destruction,
> and thus are avoided by the wise.
> Only as a last resort
> will a wise person use a deadly weapon.
> If peace is her true objective
> how can she rejoice in the victory of war?
> Those who rejoice in victory
> delight in the slaughter of humanity.
> Those who resort to violence
> will never bring peace to the world.[32]

The focus Taoism places on *wu wei* encourages leaders to use moderation in their actions, which is one of Taoism's "three treasures" or values—the other two being humility and compassion. The concept of *wu wei* may seem counterintuitive for the Westerner whose cultural values and norms may prize overcoming—or even destroying—obstacles blocking the path rather than working with or around such obstacles. But such an approach may provide a more effective and efficient way to deal with problems and may ultimately benefits leaders and followers to help them to reach their common goal.

Another related reoccurring leadership theme throughout the *Tao Te Ching* is the importance of leaders humbly aiding their followers without imposing their own will upon them.[33] The reoccurring metaphor of water found throughout Taoism and the *Tao Te Ching* serves to illustrate this importance:

> The supreme good is like water,
> which benefits all of creation
> without trying to compete with it.
> It gathers in unpopular places.
> Thus it is like the Tao.[34]

The importance Lao Tzu places on humility comports well with Robert Greenleaf's idea of servant leadership. Recall that servant leadership is Greenleaf's term for the approach to leadership that places followers and the common goal above the personal aspirations of the leader. (See Chapter 2.) Lao Tzu further develops his water metaphor to illustrate this point:

> Rivers and seas are rulers
> of the streams of hundreds of valleys
> because of the power of their low position.
>
> If you want to be the ruler of people,
> you must speak to them like you are their servant.
> If you want to lead other people,
> you must put their interest ahead of your own.
>
> The people will not feel burdened,
> if a wise person is in a position of power.
> The people will not feel like they are being manipulated,
> if a wise person is in front as their leader.
> The whole world will ask for her guidance,
> and will never get tired of her.
> Because she does not like to compete,
> no one can compete with the things she accomplishes.[35]

As in servant leadership, the Taoist tradition values leaders who seek to benefit their followers rather than benefiting themselves. Both Taoist leadership and servant leadership demand a great deal of humility on the part of the leader. A Western approach to leadership often fails to identify humility as a character trait associated with great leaders.[36] However, the role humility plays in successful and principled leadership is increasingly becoming more apparent.[37] Lao Tzu identified the importance of humility millennia ago:

> Those who stand on tiptoes
> do not stand firmly.
> Those who rush ahead
> don't get very far.
> Those who try to outshine others
> dim their own light.
> Those who call themselves righteous
> can't know how wrong they are.
> Those who boast of their accomplishments
> diminish the things they have done.
> Compared to the Tao,
> these actions are unworthy.
> If we are to follow the Tao,
> we must not do these things.[38]

Again, this focus on humility mirrors Greenleaf's contemporary theory of servant leadership. Greenleaf writes:

> Ego focuses on one's own survival, pleasure, and enhancement to the exclusion of others; ego is selfishly ambitious. It sees relationships in terms of threat or no threat, like little children who classify all people as "nice" or "mean." Conscience, on the other hand, both democratizes and elevates ego to a larger sense of the group, the whole, the community, the greater good. It sees life in terms of service and contribution, in terms of others' security and fulfillment.[39]

This Greenleaf quote provides a thoughtful segue into the last of Taoism's three treasures: compassion. Throughout the *Tao Te Ching*, Lao Tzu expresses the idea that leaders must have compassion for their followers. This is often conveyed in his admonition for leaders to treat all followers equally and without negative judgment. For example, Lao Tzu writes:

> The Master has no mind of her own.
> She understands the mind of the people.
>
> Those who are good she treats as good.
> Those who aren't good she also treats as good.
> This is how she attains true goodness.
>
> She trusts people who are trustworthy.
> She also trusts people who aren't trustworthy.
> This is how she gains true trust.

The Master's mind is shut off from the world.
Only for the sake of the people does she muddle her mind.
They look to her in anticipation.
Yet she treats them all as her children.[40]

Notice the similarity in themes between this passage and Greenleaf's quote. In both cases, the authors encourage leaders to compassionately work with followers and refrain from placing them in categories such as "good" or "bad." Categories and classifications invite prescriptions for interaction, thus limiting a follower's potential or preventing leaders from objectively interpreting a follower's behaviors.[41] When the leader extends compassion, the leader acts as "a valley" or "an empty space in a vessel" to receive and value all followers equally. When grouped together, the three treasures of moderation, humility, and compassion provide a Taoist prescription for leader–follower relations:

There are three jewels that I cherish:
compassion, moderation, and humility.
With compassion, you will be able to be brave,
with moderation, you will be able to give to others,
with humility, you will be able to become a great leader.
To abandon compassion while seeking to be brave,
or abandoning moderation while being benevolent,
or abandoning humility while seeking to lead
will only lead to greater trouble.[42]

But servant leadership is not the only contemporary leadership theory that finds a parallel in a Taoist approach to leadership.

Taoism's emphasis on balance that is encapsulated in the complements of yin and yang also finds a counterpart in twenty-first century leadership studies. A behavioral approach to leadership that proposes leaders find a balance between task orientation and relationship orientation is one such example. (See Chapter 2.) Likewise, theories of organizational culture and motivation, such as "Theory X" and "Theory Y" that we discussed in Chapter 5 also mirror these complementary opposites.[43] But this is not to say that the leader should nurture each of these polarities equally. Although later Taoists attempted to find a balance between yin and yang, Lao Tzu and the early Taoists argued that the yin—the female qualities—were the qualities to be cultivated.[44] Taoist scholar Ch'en Ku-ying notes, "Lao Tzu believes that those who preserve femininity will ultimately overcome those who make a display of strength, and that those who seek the last place will overcome those who contend for the first place."[45] The *Tao Te Ching* illustrates this:

Know the masculine,
but keep to the feminine:
and become a watershed to the world.[46]

Many scholars consider Taoism as the most feminine of all the world's great wisdom traditions.[47] Certainly the preference the *Tao Te Ching* shows for cultivating "feminine" qualities is a chief explanation for this interpretation. Likewise, the Tao is often referred to as the "Great Mother of all things."[48] As seen in the previous passage, the *Tao Te Ching* also uses the feminine metaphor of "the void," the "valley," and the "empty space within the vessel" to communicate the importance of nurturing the passive qualities prized by Taoism. Again the *Tao Te Ching* declares:

> Thirty spokes are joined together in a wheel,
> but it is the center hole
> that allows the wheel to function.
>
> We mold clay into a pot,
> but it is the emptiness inside
> that makes the vessel useful.
>
> We fashion wood for a house,
> but it is the emptiness inside
> that makes it livable.
>
> We work with the substantial,
> but the emptiness is what we use.[49]

Although Western culture has more recently become more appreciative of a passive or "yang" style of leadership, there is still an obvious preference for active, or "yin," styles of leadership. Taoism's insistence on values such as the innate goodness of humanity and the preference for passivity over aggression represent major differences between Eastern and Western leadership styles.

Although much of what we have discussed thus far falls on the "we" side of our continuum, there are at least two principles of Taoist leadership that are more in keeping with the individualist side of the spectrum: its focus on the leader's intuition and the importance of follower self-development.

Intuition is particularly important to a Taoist approach to leadership. Taoists believe a leader can only know how to respond to a unique situation by being able to correctly read the followers, context, and environment. Although various types of "data" can certainly help the leader understand the leadership moment, they are not always sufficient. Lao Tzu writes:

> Five colors blind the eye.
> Five notes deafen the ear.
> Five flavors make the palate go stale.
> Too much activity deranges the mind.
> Too much wealth causes crime.
> The Master acts on what she feels and not what she sees.
> She shuns the latter, and prefers to seek the former.[50]

Much of the wisdom arising from intuition comes from experience, which is a continual theme in the *Tao Te Ching*. Just as the Tao defies explanation but invites experience, so must the leader immerse in the full context of the situation in order to respond with thoughtful intuition. But more important than experience is the leader's ability to patiently wait until the answer to the problem becomes clear. Lao Tzu writes:

> Who can be still
> until their mud settles
> and the water is cleared by itself?
> Can you remain tranquil until right action occurs by itself?[51]

Rather than forcing a conclusion, and thus going against Taoism's basic principle of *wu wei*, Lao Tzu encourages patience and thoughtfulness to allow the solution to a problem to arise on its own.

The other more individualist aspect of Taoist leadership is the importance it places on self-development. Followers are also to be *students* of the Tao. For example, Lao Tzu writes:

> Those who know others are intelligent;
> those who know themselves are truly wise.
>
> Those who master others are strong;
> those who master themselves have true power.[52]

Taoism, in general, and Lao Tzu, in particular, prescribe the absolute minimal amount of intervention on the part of the leader to allow followers ample room to develop themselves. The leader should not try to control the followers. Again, Lao Tzu writes:

> Thus the Master makes things change
> without interfering.
> She is probing yet causes no harm.
> Straightforward, yet does not impose her will.[53]

A commentator observes, "By acting according to 'non-action', the ruler acts, but does nothing other than assist the natural processes. From this we can see that Lao Tzu is not opposed to human endeavor—he acknowledges the necessity for man to 'act' in expressing his natural potential."[54] A general theme in the *Tao Te Ching* that illustrates this principle is the metaphor of the uncarved block described earlier. Rather than thinking of followers as something to be carved and shaped into what the leader desires, leaders should allow followers to craft themselves into their own ideal. Lao Tzu's insistence that the leader refrain from excessive intervention is designed to allow followers to develop their natural capability. One author notes, "Lao Tzu encourages all things to develop their subjective potential; his remonstrance against unnatural activity is to protect the natural potential of things from external interference and distortion."[55] This emphasis on self-determination places a great deal of responsibility on the followers to develop themselves. In so doing, they must also seek to emulate all of the traits prescribed for leaders such as flexibility, openness and humility.

Taken together, we see a pattern of Taoist leadership emerge. (See Table 11.1.)

Table 11.1 Western and Taoist comparative views of leadership

	Western worldview	Taoist worldview
Leadership viewed as . . .	Prize (meritocracy)	Service
Leader/Follower relationship	Transactional (rules-based; social contract)	The Three Treasures: moderation, humility, and compassion
How decisions are made	Through rationality, logic, pragmatism	*wu wei* (doing without forcing)
Responsibilities of the Leader	Motivate followers, results orientation	Serve followers; enabling orientation
Responsibilities of the Follower	Dependable, committed, motivated	Student
Moral dimension of Leadership	Secular "code of ethics" (derived from Judeo-Christian Values)	The *Tao*

Summary and concluding remarks

The *Tao Te Ching* contains myriad leadership insights. The notion of servant leadership that has recently experienced increased popularity in the West has its roots in this ancient text. Nonetheless, servant leadership in the West is still simply considered one among many theories and models of leadership available to the Western leader. It is still viewed with skepticism regarding its ability to translate into "real world" results. In general, leadership in the West is a prize to be earned, and power is something to be wielded. This thinking is in stark contrast to Taoism's notion that service is the foundation on which leadership is built.

Taoism's notion of leadership as service has profound implications for the leader–follower relationship. The transactional nature of leadership in the West is built on a system of rewards and punishments that encourages leaders and followers to fulfill their mutual obligations. This use of coercive power is a common tool to be used to obtain follower compliance in the West. A Taoist perspective, contrariwise, views coercive power as a last resort. Rather a

Taoist's leader's *modus operandi* when dealing with followers should be marked by moderation, humility, and compassion.

The notion of *wu wei* probably represents the greatest difference between Western and Taoist perspectives on leadership. The idea of "doing by not doing," or doing without forcing or controlling, can be difficult for the Western mind to conceive. For the Western leader, the goal is of primary importance and should be reached in as little time as possible. If this requires forcing a square peg into a round hole, so be it. Contrarily, the practice of *wu wei* requires patience and a long-term time orientation. This runs counter to typical Western ideals. A Taoist approach to leadership not only values reaching the ultimate goal, but also values the means used to achieve the goal, which Taoists insist should be as gentle and noninvasive as possible.

A leader is not to be judged merely on whether or not the goal is reached, but the way the leader enables followers to reach the goal themselves. In the West, followers are often conceived of as merely a means to an end, e.g. Machiavelli. (See Chapter 6.) Contrarily, Taoist leadership conceives of *followers as the end*; they are the goal. "Lao Tzu sees aggressiveness, competitiveness, and deception as the basic cause of social disorder, and because of this he makes every effort to induce man to return to his natural mentality. Thus he takes 'simplicity' as the highest level of personal cultivation."[56] Thus, leaders should employ the least intrusive means possible in order to allow followers the freedom to reach their utmost potential on their own.

Taoists believe followers should ultimately be in the position to lead themselves. This places a great deal of responsibility on the follower for his or her own self-development. Followers must also practice *wu wei* and moderation while treating others with humility and compassion. Thus, the ideal Taoist follower should be a student of the Tao, seeking the way to achieve a natural harmony with others and their own situation.

This brings us back to the Tao, the moral guide of Taoist leadership. We do not expect this chapter to say all there is to say about the Tao. After all, the only way to truly understand the Tao is to experience it. As Lao Tzu warns, words cannot contain the Tao's complexity. However, the Tao does ask us to consider if we are living in harmony with others and honoring the natural order of our situation, those around us, and ourselves. Perhaps the best way to explain the Tao is simply to invite the reader to ask himself or herself this question. Lao Tzu suggests that we already know the answer, if we are willing to face the truth.

The *Tao Te Ching* is not the only ancient Taoist text that inspires contemporary thoughts about leadership. Other Taoist texts such as the writings of Chuang Tzu, Sun Tzu's *The Art of War*, and the *I Ching* (*The Book of Changes*) still inspire leadership scholars and practitioners today.[57] These ancient masters thought a great deal about leadership, and we would be wise to learn from them. On being introduced to a Taoist approach to leadership for the first time, many Westerners resonate with Confucius's estimation of Lao Tzu as "a dragon beyond their knowledge." This is understandable given the way many

Taoist concepts are presented in riddles, aphorisms, and metaphors. The difference in form speaks to the divide between East and West. However, students of leadership who are willing to take the time to investigate a Taoist approach to leadership might find a wealth of insight waiting for them. For those who overlook these insights or consider them beyond their grasp, we leave a final word from Lao Tzu and the *Tao Te Ching*:

> When a superior person hears of the Tao,
> She diligently puts it into practice.
> When an average person hears of the Tao,
> he believes half of it, and doubts the other half.
> When a foolish person hears of the Tao,
> he laughs out loud at the very idea.
> If he didn't laugh,
> it wouldn't be the Tao.[58]

Questions for discussion

- What insight might the story of the man who fell into the waterfall provide to leaders dealing with a difficult situation?
- Consider the concept of *wu wei*. How might you explain this idea in your own words?
- What other leadership insights might you glean from considering the metaphors of water, the empty vessel, or the uncarved block?
- What aspects of a Taoist approach to leadership might you apply to your own leadership style?
- Consider the symbol for the yin and the yang. What insights about leaders and followers might the meaning of the symbol hold?
- Read the quote from the *Tao Te Ching* that is found at the end of the chapter once again. How do you interpret the quote? What does it mean?

Additional resources

Chao-Chuan Cheng and Yueh-Ting Lee, eds., *Leadership and Management in China*, Cambridge, Cambridge University Press, 2008.

T. Cleary, *The Book of Leadership and Strategy: Lessons of the Chinese Masters. Translations from the Taoist Classic Huainanzi*, Boston, MA: Shambhala, 1992.

J. Heider, *The Tao of Leadership: Lao Tzu's Tao Te Ching Adapted for a New Age*, Atlanta, GA: Humanics New Age, 1985.

Notes

1 For our analysis, we have chosen to use J.H. McDonald's "Paraphrase of the *Tao Te Ching*", Public Domain, 1996. Available at http://www.wright-house.com/religions/taoism/tao-te-ching.html. The quote at the beginning of this chapter is from McDonald, *Tao Te Ching*, Chapter 17.

2 See L.D. Rainey, *Confucius and Confucianism: The Essentials*, Hoboken, NY: Wiley-Blackwell, 2010; T.R. Reid, *Confucius Lives Next Door: What Living in the East Teaches Us About Living in the West*, New York: Vintage Books, 1999; and D.A. Bell, *China's New Confucianism: Politics and Everyday Life in a Changing Society*, Princeton, NJ: Princeton University Press, 2008; Also see W.W. Smith, Jr., *Confucianism in Modern Japan: A Study of Conservatives in Japanese Intellectual History*, 2nd edn., Tokyo: Hokuseido Press, 1973.

3 There is a later branch of Confucianism that is more religious in character; however, in this chapter we will only be addressing the philosophical implications of the tradition.

4 For example, see W.T. de Bary *Nobility and Civility, Asian Ideas of Leadership and the Common Good*, Boston, MA: Harvard University Press, 2004.

5 We have chosen to use the Wade-Giles English versions of Chinese pronunciations rather than the newer pinyin system. We have done this to retain consistency throughout this chapter. The pinyin system refers to Lao Tzu as Laozi and the *Tao Te Ching* as the *Dao de jing*.

6 H.G. Creel, remarks, "The more one studies Taoism, the clearer it becomes that this term does not denote a school, but a whole congeries of doctrines." Although this is certainly the case with Taoism, we have chosen to focus exclusively on classical Taoism to avoid confusing readers with Taoism's varied manifestations. See H.G. Creel, *What is Taoism? And Other Studies in Chinese Cultural History*, Chicago, IL: University of Chicago Press, 1970, p. 1.

7 This is a variation on common legend regarding the meeting between Lao Tzu and Confucius. The original story appears in Ssu-ma Ch'ien's the *Records of the Grand Historian*.

8 For more on the way Confucianism is expressed in East Asian leadership today see Chao-Chuan Cheng and Yueh-Ting Lee, eds., *Leadership and Management in China*, Cambridge: Cambridge University Press, 2008.

9 Confucius refers to this concept as the rectification of names, which is the idea that society must agree on the meaning of the terms it uses and then follow the order that is established by the understanding of those terms. Although we might be inclined to take this concept for granted, there are deep implications embedded in Confucius's idea. Confucius explains, "If names be not correct, language is not in accordance with the truth of things. If language be not in accordance with the truth of things, affairs cannot be carried on to success." Confucius, *The Analects*, J. Legge, trans. Available at http://www.gutenberg.org/cache/epub/3330/pg3330.html. Accessed August 17, 2014.

10 Ibid.

11 Confucius originally used the terms "father and son" and "younger brother to older brother" to describe these terms, but modern scholarship generally agrees to use the gender neutral terms of "parent," "child," and "sibling."

12 See H. Smith, *The World's Religions*, San Francisco: HarperCollins, 1958/1991, pp. 175–176.

13 See J. Ching, *Confucianism and Taoism*, Ashland, OR: Blackstone Audio, 2006.

14 The scope of this chapter limits this explanation of Confucianism. But there is another aspect of *li*—what Confucius referred to as the "Doctrine of the Mean." The Doctrine of the Mean cautions us to avoid extremes to embrace moderation in all things in an attempt to reach equilibrium and harmony. Its closest Western counterpart is Aristotle's "Golden Mean," which also consists of the admonition to avoid extremes. For primary sources, see *The Sacred Books of Confucius and Other Confucian Classics*, Ch'u Chai and Winberg Chai, eds. and trans., New York: Bantam Books, 1965. Also see B.W. Van Norden, *Introduction to Classical Chinese Philosophy*, Indianapolis,

IN: Hackett Publishing Company, 2011; P.R. Goldin, *Confucianism*, Berkeley: University of California Press, 2011.

15 Although we acknowledge the debate on whether or not Lao Tzu is the actual author of the *Tao Te Ching*, we will be expressing the leadership lessons contained in the text as written by a single author. Again, we will be using the McDonald text produced for the Public Domain.

16 Lao Tzu/McDonald, *Tao Te Ching*, Ch. 1.

17 See Ch'en Ku-ying, *Lao Tzu Text, Notes, and Comments*, R.Y.W. Young and R.T. Ames, trans. and adapts., San Francisco: Chinese Materials Center, Inc., 1977, p. 2.

18 See B. Watson, *Chuang Tzu: Basic Writings*, 3rd edn., New York: Columbia University Press 2003; *The Complete Works of Chuang Tzu*, New York: Columbia University Press, 1968.

19 This story also encapsulates the Taoist's major contention with Confucian thought.

20 Lao Tzu/McDonald, *Tao Te Ching*, Ch. 78.

21 Ibid.

22 Ibid, Ch. 76.

23 Ch'en Ku-ying, *Lao Tzu Text*, p. 15.

24 Lao Tzu/McDonald, *Tao Te Ching*, Ch. 28.

25 This story can be found in the *Huai Nan Tzu* (The Masters/Philosophers of Huainan).

26 The yin and yang's complementary positions also relate to Taoism's "Five Elements" theory, but a discussion of this concept is beyond the scope of this chapter. See C. Fu and R. Bergeon, "A Tao Complexity Tool: Leading from Being," in J. Danelo Barbour, G.J. Burgess, L. Lid Falkman, and R.M. McManus, eds., *Leading in Complex Worlds*, San Francisco: Jossey-Bass, 2012, pp. 227–251; also see C. Fu and R. Bergeon, "A Tao Model: Rethinking Modern Leadership for Transformation," in J. Danelo Barbour and G. Robinson Hickman, eds., *Leadership for Transformation*, San Francisco: Jossey-Bass, 2011, pp. 15–31.

27 Lao Tzu/McDonald, *Tao Te Ching*, Ch. 28.

28 Lao Tzu/McDonald, *Tao Te Ching*, Ch. 42.

29 Daniel Heller, *Taoist Lessons for Educational Leaders, Gentle Pathways for Resolving Conflict*, Lanham, MD: Rowman & Littlefield Publishers, 2012, p. 19.

30 Lao Tzu/McDonald, *Tao Te Ching*, Ch. 9. Heller also uses this passage from the *Tao Te Ching* to explain this concept.

31 Lao Tzu/McDonald, *Tao Te Ching*, Ch. 30.

32 Lao Tzu/McDonald, *Tao Te Ching*, Ch. 31.

33 Ch'en Ku-ying, *Lao Tzu Text*, p. 19.

34 Lao Tzu/McDonald, *Tao Te Ching*, Ch. 8.

35 Lao Tzu/McDonald, *Tao Te Ching*, Ch. 66.

36 See P. Northouse's chapter on trait leadership in *Leadership: Theory and Practice*, 6th edn., Los Angeles: Sage Publications, 2012, pp. 19–42. None of the major studies referenced in this chapter identifies humility as a trait associated with leadership traits or characteristics.

37 See R. Nielson, H.S. Ferraro, and J.A. Marrone, *Leading With Humility*, London: Routledge, 2013.

38 Lao Tzu/McDonald, *Tao Te Ching*, Ch. 24.

39 R.K. Greenleaf and L.C. Spears, eds., *Servant Leadership, 25th Anniversary Edition: A Journey into the Nature of Legitimate Power and Greatness*, Mahwah, NJ: Paulist Press, 2002, p. 4.

40 Lao Tzu/McDonald, *Tao Te Ching*, Ch. 49.

41 Heller, *Taoist Lessons*, p. 58.

42 Lao Tzu/McDonald, *Tao Te Ching*, Ch. 67.

43 See S. Durlabhji "The Tao of Organization Behavior," *Journal of Business Ethics*, 53, 4 (2004): 401–409.

44 M. LaFargue, *The Tao of the Tao Te Ching*, Albany, NY: State University of New York Press, 1992, pp. 37, 253.
45 Ch'en Ku-ying, *Lao Tzu Text*, pp. 10–11.
46 Lao Tzu/McDonald, *Tao Te Ching*, Ch. 28.
47 Max Kaltenmark observes, "The Tao is frequently referred to as the Mother, the progenetrix and foster-mother of all creatures." *Lao Tzu and Taoism*, Roger Greaves, trans., Stanford, CA: Stanford University Press, 1969, p. 37.
48 Lao Tzu/McDonald, *Tao Te Ching*, Chs 1, 20, 25, 52, 59.
49 Ibid, Ch. 11.
50 Ibid, Ch. 12.
51 Ibid, Ch. 15.
52 Ibid, Ch. 33.
53 Ibid, Ch. 58.
54 Ch'en Ku-ying, *Lao Tzu Text*, p. 24.
55 Ibid, p. 35.
56 Ibid, pp. 37–38.
57 There are numerous popular texts that draw lessons from these ancient writings. Popular sources include D. Dreher, *The Tao of Personal Leadership*, New York: HarperCollins, 1996; S.M. Herman, *The Tao at Work: On Leading and Following*, San Francisco: Jossey-Bass, 1994; R.L. Wing, *The Tao of Power: Lao Tzu's Classic Guide to Leadership, Influence, and Excellence*, Garden City, NY: Doubleday, 1986.
58 Lao Tzu/McDonald, *Tao Te Ching*, Ch. 41.

Part III

Leadership for what?

We began this book with John Gardner's admonition to understand leadership before proceeding to action. The first two parts of this book presented the Five Components of Leadership Model, exploring our working definition of leadership as a process. Now that we have probed the different facets of leadership, we can weave the connection between knowledge and practice. We are now ready to explore the praxis of leadership by offering a question: "Leadership for what?"

While we find leadership to be a fascinating topic in itself—the way a political scientist might view the study of politics as an end in itself; that is, because it is interesting—we also recognize that many aspiring leaders are drawn to this field because they seek practical knowledge of how to lead.

The field of leadership does not provide a "how to" manual that can be tucked away on a bookshelf. Instead, the practice of leadership requires constant introspection and examination of lessons learned under many different contexts. Leadership involves so many variables that it is impossible to distill the process into a precise formula, e.g., given situation X, apply leadership style Y. The Five Components of Leadership Model helps us organize the main elements of leadership in a way that will give the student and practitioner a general guide of "how to think" about leadership; but this is only a starting point in what should be a lifelong developmental process.

While Parts I and II explored the five components of leadership at a more theoretical level, Part III is designed to be more personal. We want you to evaluate how you will apply the concepts covered in these chapters to yourself. We will use the language developed in previous chapters to ask some tough questions about your approach to leadership.

In Chapter 12, our focus is on the leader. The question (Leadership for what?) is applied to the way we seek to develop ourselves as leaders—leadership for personal development. In particular, we explore the concept of authentic leadership. How does your behavior as a leader align with your personal values? Do your actions reflect your personal convictions? How have your life experiences shaped you as a leader? Leadership development at the personal level requires in depth introspection about the way the environmental context and society's values and norms shape you every day of your life. This self-awareness can be a powerful tool in your effort to lead more effectively.

In Chapter 13, we change the focus to the followers. Rather than leadership for developing oneself, we explore the leader's responsibility to develop others. Consistent with Burns' idea of transformational leadership examined earlier, both the leader and the follower should be mutually enhanced by the leadership process. This chapter asks you to consider the leader's role in attending to the followers' needs.

In Chapter 14, we close the book by focusing on the common goal. Leadership for what? To contribute to the greater good. Ultimately, leadership is not about the leader or the follower. Rather, leadership deals with the way leaders and followers work together towards a goal that is bigger than either the leader or the follower. We invite you to think about leadership as a process that enhances organizations, communities, and societies, moving us beyond individual interests. We have long conceptualized leadership as an individual enterprise, when, in reality, leadership by its very nature is a collective undertaking, designed to benefit everyone. To that end, leadership is value driven and has at its core the belief that leaders and followers, when working together for the greater good, will add value to their institutions and to the world.

12 Leadership to develop oneself

These beautiful and varied themes are the products of the soil.[1]
Antonín Leopold Dvořák

Leadership for what? To develop oneself. We begin Part III with an exploration of leadership as a personal endeavor. Many of the leadership books found in the popular press seek to develop a specific set of behaviors.[2] They tend to focus on the desirable competencies of leaders as if separate from the environmental and cultural contexts that we introduced in the Five Components of Leadership Model. When equipped with desirable competencies, leaders can be effective contributors to organizations and society if they have an awareness of how contexts influence their behavior. This level of awareness about contexts requires *personal* leadership development.

The artifact that we examine in this chapter is a symphony by Antonín Leopold Dvořák. This chapter focuses on leaders developing their own voice; and that resonates with the way composers develop their own musical style. Their own compositions do not appear out of a vacuum. Rather, they experiment and borrow elements from other styles while building their own sound. They draw from their environmental context in order to create their unique musical voice. We argue in this chapter that leaders follow a similar creative path. While they have personal characteristics unique to themselves, they also draw from their environmental experiences, such as their families, the historical periods in which they live, their socioeconomic conditions, and their education.

While many of these factors fall outside the leader's control, the individual has some degree of agency in the process of their own development. Likewise, one's personality, biology, and cognitive ability are unique. Our purpose in this chapter is to explore the combination of these forces derived from a person's individual characteristics and their environmental context to create their authentic and unique leadership voice.[3]

In this chapter, we explore the concept of authentic leadership. Leaders may be products of their environment, but they provide a unique interpretation of those experiences. In composing their own symphony, leaders develop a way of leading that sets them apart from others—for the better, or not. These leadership styles are grounded in certain values that are derived from the cultural context of their societies, including the people around them such as their family and friends. Those values, in turn, help shape their behavior as leaders.

Case study: Antonín Leopold Dvořák's *New World Symphony*

The artifact we have chosen to analyze in this chapter is Symphony No. 9 in E Minor, Opus 95, *From the New World*, composed by Antonín Leopold Dvořák (1841–1904). The piece is commonly referred to as Dvořák's *New World Symphony*. Although it may seem unusual to analyze a musical text to provide an understanding of leadership, more and more scholars outside the field of music are beginning to acknowledge the insight musical sources may provide for other disciplines, including leadership.[4]

Background on the symphony

A native of Bohemia—now the Czech Republic—Dvořák composed the *New World Symphony* in New York while he was serving as the director of the National Conservatory of Music of America between 1892 and 1895. A benefactor of the Conservatory, Jeanette Thurber, persuaded Dvořák to come to the United States to serve as the director of the newly founded conservatory with the goal of creating a uniquely American style of music. Dvořák's *New World Symphony* is a testament to the achievement of that goal.[5]

During his time in the United States, Dvořák was inspired by African American and Native American folk music. The National Conservatory opened its doors to all talented students, regardless of race or gender—an extremely progressive policy for that time in the United States. His friend at the Conservatory, Harry T. Burleigh, an African American musician, introduced Dvořák to Negro spirituals, and he embraced them wholeheartedly. Given the prevalence of racist attitudes and beliefs at that time in American history, Dvořák's enthusiastic acceptance of African Americans and African American music shocked his critics. He raised the ire of many when he told the *New York Herald*:

> I am now satisfied that the future music of this country must be founded upon what are called the Negro melodies. This must be the real foundation of any serious and original school of composition to be developed in the United States. When I first came here last year I was impressed with this idea, and it has developed into a settled conviction. These beautiful and varied themes are the products of the soil. They are American . . . These are the folk songs of America, and your composers must turn to them . . . In the Negro melodies of America I discover all that is needed for a great and noble school of music.[6]

These influences can be heard in the *New World Symphony* through its use of African American and Native American rhythms and scales that testify to the "sound of the soil" of which Dvořák spoke. Although Dvořák paid homage to these musical styles more "in spirit" rather than quoting any of these melodies in full, black and Amerindian music saturate the *New World Symphony*.

Indigenous folk music and stories were a constant source of inspiration to Dvořák, both in the New World and his native Bohemia. He was specifically stirred by Henry Wadsworth Longfellow's poem *The Song of Hiawatha*. Dvořák said the third movement in his *New World Symphony* was inspired by the wedding dance featured in the poem.[7] When premiering his *New World Symphony*, Dvořák said, "I have not actually used any of the [Native American] melodies. I have simply written original themes embodying the peculiarities of the Indian music, and, using these themes as subjects, have developed them with all the resources of modern rhythms, counterpoint, and orchestral color."[8] Thus, both African American and Native American influences can be heard throughout Dvořák's composition.

What is particularly special about the symphony for our discussion in this chapter is that the composition represents an amalgamation of Dvořák's Bohemian, continental, and classical influences combined with indigenous Native American folk music and African American spirituals that created a uniquely authentic American musical voice. The famous conductor and composer Leonard Bernstein described the work as "multinational" and identified French, Scottish, German, Chinese, and Czech influences throughout the work.[9] Nothing could be more uniquely American—in the broadest sense of the word, meaning from the Americas (the New World)—than a "melting pot" of cultures coming together to creating something entirely new.[10]

This "melting pot" metaphor is generally applicable to Dvořák as a musician. His father was a butcher, and Dvořák did not come from a privileged background, as did many esteemed composers at the time. He paid homage to this heritage by publishing his *Moravian Duets* and *Slavic Dances* early in his career. Throughout his life, Dvořák continued to call on the folk music found in his native Bohemia and incorporated these early influences with the new musical forms he encountered. It was this willingness to combine the old with the new, the working class with the elite, the folk with the cosmopolitan that created the composer's unique musical style. It also earned him the admiration and friendship of other famous composers at the time, such as Brahms and Tchaikovsky, and assured him a seat in the pantheon of great composers.

Although Dvořák's visit to the United Stated only lasted for a few years, the impact of this time lives on. His *New World Symphony* is still very much a part of the American psyche, and most would recognize its major themes even if they were unable to identify their original composer (see Figure 12.1). It is still beloved by conductors and audiences around the world. Dvořák's prophesy of the importance of African American music to the creation of a distinctive

Figure 12.1 New World Symphony manuscript, with Dvořák's signature. Public domain.

American musical voice has also proved to be true, as seen by the rise of jazz, blues, and rock 'n' roll, more than 50 years after Dvořák's prediction. In the end, Dvořák's homeland beckoned and he returned, but he forever changed the voice of American music.

Description of the symphony

Now that we have a bit more understanding of Dvořák and his influences, let us examine our artifact, the *New World Symphony*. A handwritten copy of the score is featured in Figure 12.1. We suggest you consider listening to the master-piece while reading this section to help you better appreciate the symphony. In addition, you will be able to follow what we mean by the solos and melodies highlighted in the piece.

As a traditional European symphony, the piece is divided into four movements—each with its own themes and individual expressions. In musical terminology, each movement has a *tempo* (traditionally expressed in Italian), which tells the performer the intended speed of the movement. If designated as *Allegro*, for instance, the orchestra is to play the movement in a brisk and cheerful tempo. The tempo, therefore, declares to the orchestra, and subsequently the listener, the composer's intensions.

The introduction to the first movement (*Adagio-Allegro molto*; meaning, slow tempo, combined with very lively sections) unfolds with an almost tumultuous posture. You can imagine Dvořák standing on the deck of the ship as he departs from his beloved Bohemia for the New World.[11] The music moves between quiet passages for strings and woodwinds to explosions of brass, perhaps expressing Dvořák's simultaneous excitement and anxiety about his new life. Within the turmoil, the composer hints at the main theme of the movement with only fragments of the melody. The introduction climaxes with two full orchestral hits and diminishes to quiet string trills.

The trills set the stage for the first movement's first main theme: the two French horns sing the melody together, and the low woodwinds respond. The theme appears in several other sections of the movement before Dvořák turns to the second theme utilizing French horns. Some say the instrumentation is reminiscent of bagpipes. The flutes state the second main theme against the backdrop of soft strings. Many commentators have noted this theme's similarity to the spiritual "Swing Low Sweet Chariot." The composer then develops both themes, playing them against one another. In the process, a new American musical voice—influenced by Dvořák's classical European experience coupled with an indigenous American sound—begins to fully manifest itself. The first movement concludes in a near verbatim restatement of the two themes.

The second movement (*Largo*; meaning, slow and dignified to the point of being stately) begins slow and brooding with an ominous feel. It quickly moves to the famous English horn solo that plays the symphony's most well-known melody—smooth and flowing with a spiritual quality. William Arms Fisher later added lyrics to the melody creating the song "Going Home," and listeners may recognize this tune. Although the lyrics were not a part of the original symphony, of course, the title of the song and the melancholy feel of this movement does express Dvořák's own homesickness at the time he composed his symphony. The tune is reminiscent of an African American spiritual, and links Dvořák to his love of folk music, in both his native Bohemia and the New World.

After the "Going Home" theme, a flute introduces a new theme—playful and more hopeful than the first. The excitement and anticipation introduced in the first movement returns, this time accompanied by a romantic expression. A brief hush is followed by a playful counterpoint between the two themes. The English horn is back singing the "Going Home" theme once again. Violins softly complete the second movement and soothe the listener with a peaceful lullaby.

The third movement (*Molto vivace*; meaning, very vivacious) begins with a sudden flourish and quickly builds into a frantic dance, which Dvořák claimed was inspired by the feast and dance described in Longfellow's poem, *The Song of Hiawatha*. A flute establishes a theme and is soon repeated and expanded on by strings and horns. The exuberant dance quickly turns into a playful melody. One can imagine the handsome Pau-Puk-Keewis dancing the Beggars Dance for the merriment of Hiawatha's wedding guests as described in the poem. Dvořák doffs his hat in spirit if not in actual form to the Native American folk melodies and stories that inspired him. The melody moves from section to section of the orchestra that seem to playfully respond to one another. After restating both themes, the orchestra turns to the coda, or the dramatic ending of the movement. Tremolo strings build suspense and grow louder while the horns and woodwinds hint at the two main themes. Soon the orchestra decrescendos to silence, only to punctuate the end of the movement with an explosive strike of sound.

The fourth—and final—movement (*allegro con fuoco*; meaning, faster than *allegro* and played with animation and enthusiasm) also begins with an introduction. The main theme in this instance is a march commanded by the horn section. The opening phrase of the introduction is now firmly embedded in popular consciousness, inspiring a sense of dread. (Consider the theme from the movie *Jaws* when listening to this portion of the symphony.) The music swells and then, once again, eases into quiet anticipation. Dvořák then introduces a new tune that is reminiscent of the folksong "Three Blind Mice." The mice scamper and run between the symphony's previously established themes, appearing and disappearing. The overall spirit is filled with intense expectation.

The symphony's themes coalesce into a dramatic finale, which seems to embody the hopeful expectation of the New World. The symphony's drama climaxes as woodwinds, brass, strings, and percussion join to overwhelm the listener in an emotionally climactic finish in which a single haunting horn signals that there are still parts of this story yet to be told. The ending, therefore, leaves us hoping for more to be revealed. As the following section will discuss, this artifact resonates with the idea that leaders are always an "unfinished story."

Analysis: Leadership to develop oneself

Leadership development is the product of experiences unique to each individual. It requires a creative process that gives rise to personal interpretations of their surroundings. The opening quote in this chapter reflects this spirit. Dvořák's *New World Symphony* gives us beautiful and varied themes drawn from the "soil"—meaning the life experiences that were unique to the New World— the mixing of customs and traditions, fused with the excitement of possibilities yet to be realized.

A vast ocean lay between the two worlds. The Old World, while rich in cultural expressions in its own right, came to be viewed in the New World as belonging to the past. The pioneering spirit of the New World was grounded in the belief that the present was full of possibilities—a bright future yet to be written. Leadership development at the personal level reflects that belief, as well. Leaders are always in the process of "becoming"—being dynamically shaped and reshaped as they strive to reach their fullest potential.

This analysis is divided into two sections. The first one focuses on the relationship between leaders' personal attributes and the environmental context, which harkens to Dvořák's reference to the "soil." The two influence each other giving rise to what the literature today calls "authentic leadership." The *New World Symphony* is truly the product of a variety of influences that came together to form a unique sound. The second section explores how authentic leadership is connected to a leader's personal values. What principles guide a leader's behavior? Can followers discern a leader's principles and values through the leader's actions? When facing challenging situations, should the leader compromise those values? If so, why? How do these principles and values evolve over time? We will explore these questions as we move forward through this chapter.

The authentic leader

In a way, all leaders are unique products of their environment, mixed with their own individual attributes. In the leadership literature, however, "authentic leadership" has a specific connotation, which we will explore here. Bill George, in his celebrated book, *Authentic Leadership: Rediscovering the Secrets to Creating Lasting Value*, defines authentic leaders in terms of five characteristics.[12] First, authentic leaders pursue their purpose with passion. They are not only deeply committed to the goals that they set out to accomplish, but they are also willing to work hard to accomplish them. They are willing to go the extra mile in order to bring their vision to reality. This high level of passion is contagious. Followers feel motivated when working with a passionate leader.

Second, authentic leaders practice solid values. While the next section will discuss in greater detail this connection between values and authentic leadership, it is important to emphasize right away that authentic leaders are grounded in certain norms that guide their behavior. Through introspection and careful consideration, they nurture values that will demonstrate their true character. Their actions, in turn, will match those values.

Third, authentic leaders lead with their hearts as well as their heads. Leadership should not be a mechanical process grounded solely in logic and rationality. While the head offers sensible paths toward achieving reasonable goals, leaders should also lead from the heart. They need to be emotionally invested in the process. Leadership as a process is complex, involving multiple variables and interconnections that are often beyond our ability to fully grasp. Leading is an art. It calls on individuals to exercise creativity and the art of improvisation through feelings and emotions that transcend formulas. There is no leadership manual. Rather, leaders learn from experience every day, and, in the process, they grow and mature.

Fourth, authentic leaders establish connected relationships. Leadership is not a one-person phenomenon. It is the product of connections among complex human beings who bring to the relationship myriad particularities. Through these relationships, leaders motivate followers to move toward common goals. Authentic leaders are connective agents. Our societies, economic and political systems, as well as our organizations, thrive on connectivity. We value diversity —even if bringing about conflict—because different perspectives feed the creative process.

Fifth, authentic leaders demonstrate self-discipline. While we earlier extolled the importance of the heart, that is not to be equated with unfettered impulse.

Authentic leaders demonstrate an ability to regulate their behavior in a way that promotes a healthy balance between the head and the heart. Achieving this balance requires thoughtfulness, self-awareness, and knowing one's limits. Authentic leadership is not solely an intellectual exercise.

These are common themes on which we can focus in order to answer the "Leadership for what?" question. By identifying these dimensions, leaders can seek certain experiences in order to learn, grow, and create their own unique style. Leadership development is dynamic, and leaders are constantly creating their voice. The level of learning and growing, however, varies, depending on their ability to reflect on their experiences.

As in any human endeavor, we all have certain personal attributes—through inherited characteristics and environmental conditions. What we make of these experiences, however, is up to each individual. Sometimes leaders fail to reach their full potential because they overlook certain characteristics that could have positive influences. Dvořák saw in the New World "beautiful and varied themes" that he turned into powerful melodies. It took courage and introspection to realize that the diversity of cultural influences in the New World was not a weakness—quite the opposite—it was a source of authenticity. Aspiring leaders often miss this connection when they try to imitate highly successful leaders as a "formula" for personal leadership development. We are wise to remember "No one can be authentic by trying to imitate someone else."[13]

Aspiring leaders also need to turn inward in order to assess the positive elements within themselves that need to be cultivated and brought forth. Consider the solo by the English horn in the beginning of the second movement. The English horn is rarely used in orchestrations of this kind. However, the English horn creates a unique mood at a specific moment in the symphony that no other instrument could hope to replicate. A trumpet could not have achieved the same mood. A trumpet should never try to be an English horn. Likewise, we should strive to develop our own individual voice, fully embracing that it is a product of both individual characteristics and the environment (the "soil").

When placed in the leadership continuum (Figure 12.2), we see how each side contributes to the development of an authentic leader. From the "I" side comes the recognition that leaders have individual characteristics that are unique to them. They need to foster their strengths while addressing their limitations. Through this introspective process, they can uncover areas for celebration and areas for improvement. From the "WE" side comes the understanding that leaders are the product of collective processes, such as cultural traditions, family values, and their environmental context, that give rise to a certain way of thinking that influences their leadership behavior. Leaders need to embrace and understand those roots.

The challenge of leadership development at the personal level is being able to discern the *assets* and *liabilities* from the "I" and "WE" sides in different contexts. There is no perfect list of assets and liabilities. As we mentioned in Chapter 1, scholars in the early part of the twentieth century attempted to

Figure 12.2 The leadership continuum and personal leadership development

make such a list and failed in the process. The inclusion of contingency and situational variables to leadership models in the middle of the century helped us understand that certain attributes can be an asset in certain situations and a liability in others. Leadership development, therefore, also includes the acquisition of *wisdom*—the ability to know the best combination of the "I/WE" sides under different circumstances. That high level of discernment does not come in a bottle or a manual. It is the product of many years of trial, failure, and growth.

The *New World Symphony* is a perfect metaphor for helping us understand the challenges of personal development. The symphony helps us capture those sentiments. In the first movement, we see Dvořák's classical European style, coupled with an indigenous American sound. We are the product of many different influences. The spiritual quality of the English horn solo in the second movement reminds us that, deep inside, we have a voice that is unique and that, given the right circumstances, it can make a powerful statement to the world. Likewise, the exuberant dance and North American folk melodies in the third movement give us the perspective that once the "I" side is in harmony with the "WE" side, we experience joy and fulfillment. The symphony ends with a sense of anticipation, and that is also a defining characteristic of authentic leadership. In the *New World Symphony*, we also see a dynamic process of continuous transformation. Leaders, in this sense, are also continuously developing.

Contrarily, there are aspects of the leader that may remain unchanging over time, such as a leader's values. Values provide a set of principles that guide the leader's behavior. They establish what is considered *right* and what is rejected as *wrong*. These values serve as a "moral compass," which provides constant feedback, telling leaders if they are on the right track.[14] These inner values guide our behavior in any situation.

Leaders develop their personal moral compass through a combination of the "I"—such as their individual cognitive processes, personality traits—and the "WE"—such as their socialization, cultural cues, family history—sides of the continuum. These moral compasses may vary from leader to leader, reflecting differences in the "I" side. However, they tend to conform to the cultural patterns in the collective, as discussed in Part II. Leaders and followers constantly negotiate the balance between their personal moral compass and the collective moral compass of their society's values.

Globalization affects this dynamic by bringing a variety of moral compasses into close proximity. One of the biggest leadership challenges of the twenty-first century is for leaders and followers to come to a consensus in terms of the collective moral compass. What happens to organizations and societies when their members use different personal moral compasses while trying to achieve a common goal?

In Part II, we introduced individual cultural perspectives as discrete units in a continuum. In reality, the twenty-first century has given us a complicated landscape, filled with individuals mixing and mingling different values. The metaphor of the "melting pot," which Dvořák used in his symphony as representative of the New World, can also be applied to the whole world under globalization.

Authentic leadership scholars Bill George and Peter Sims argue that authentic leaders do not compromise their values, particularly during difficult situations. Rather, authentic leaders use adversity to strengthen their values. This statement makes sense, but only up to a point. If the personal moral compass says "do not cheat," and you are faced with a situation that can be easily addressed by cheating, what do you do? Do you compromise your values, or do you stick to your convictions? George and Sims are clear in their message to leaders—take the more difficult road and do not compromise your values. The more difficult road will help you learn and grow.

However, we also need to take into consideration how our behavior affects someone else's moral compass. How are their personal and cultural moral compasses different from our own? What do we do if our moral compass seems to be diametrically opposed to someone else's moral compass? The issue is more complicated than George and Sims seem to suggest. Do some moral issues rise above individuals and cultures, and fall under the category of *universal* human rights? If so, how do we arrive at those universal values and norms? By the same token, are all values simply *culturally relative,* and all values equally deserving of acknowledgment and protection? We can take a Machiavellian perspective and simply connect power to norms and say that the most powerful dictates the "universal" moral compass—to be embraced by the collective. This can be construed as an amoral stand since the compass is not grounded in values, but simply the expression of the interests of the powerful individual. This can be particularly difficult when different cultures have very different views of what is right and wrong.

These are crucible types of question that you as a leader will confront in your organization and in your society. In order to face them, you will have to develop a deep sense of self-awareness in order to check those moments against your moral compass. Dvořák experienced this firsthand when he accepted the position as the director of the National Conservatory of Music of America. The conservatory admissions policy—open to all talented students, regardless of race or gender—was contrary to the values of many Americans in the late nineteenth century. The way he and the Conservatory embraced the equality of African Americans and women scandalized many in positions of power at the time. Today, this principle is considered mainstream in American society. This shift in the collective moral compass reminds us that values are dynamic and may change over time. However, the changes did not accidently take place. It required many leaders, such as Jeanette Thurber, the benefactor of the Conservatory, following her personal moral compass and advocating for racial and gender equality in the music field. Of course, Thurber also had the power to influence the moral compass of the Conservatory's Admissions Board.

The sáme dynamic is taking place at the global level, as leaders with strong personal moral compasses advocate for the collective embrace of certain values. Dvořák accepted the challenge and moved to the United States. In the process, his music greatly benefited from the African and Native American influences with which he came into contact. In embracing an ideal—racial and gender equality—he influenced the American collective moral compasses.

Globalization is intensifying this moral dimension of authentic leadership. Values are constantly being challenged and reshaped as more cultures come into contact and leaders face defining moments. What distinguishes differences in culture from moral imperatives? These moral questions are vitally important for leaders to ask as they seek to develop themselves. We are not going to give you the answers to these questions here—even if these answers were easy to give. Ultimately, you must make these decisions for yourself. The wise leader asks these questions long before being faced with an impending decision. The answers have lasting consequences.

Summary and concluding remarks

As the introduction to Part III indicated, we see the last three chapters of this book as an opportunity for you to explore how leadership applies to your own experiences at a personal level. The "Leadership for what?" question is designed to be personal. Therefore, it is no coincidence that we began the last section of this book with a chapter about personal leadership development. The artifact, Dvořák's *New World Symphony*, is designed to draw attention to the idea that leaders should have their unique "sound"—a personal leadership style that combines individual characteristics (the "I" side) with the environmental and cultural contexts (the "WE" side).

In this chapter, we have focused on the concept of authentic leadership because we want to challenge you to evaluate how your unique characteristics as a leader contribute to the leadership process. The trait approach of the early twentieth century attempted in vain to discover the best attributes of an effective leader. Personal leadership development is much more complex than developing specific traits. You also need to understand the way those individual attributes work in different environmental and cultural contexts.

Leaders must develop self-awareness in order to see how their strengths and weaknesses mesh within those different contexts. Whenever weaknesses are uncovered, leaders have options. They can work to try to eliminate them, or delegate the task to someone else better suited for it. This decision requires honesty, courage, and introspection.

We also introduced the moral dimension of authentic leadership in this chapter because we want you to explore what it means to lead with a personal moral compass and how it may affect the collective moral compass. While all human beings carry within themselves a moral compass, not everyone purposefully reflects on its content and continuously seeks to nurture it. This process of self-reflection is a key to personal leadership development.

Globalization in this century will accelerate cultural clashes in your everyday life. To be aware of cross-cultural challenges is not enough. Now, you must act on this awareness. As you interact with other leaders and followers with diverse moral compasses, you will have an opportunity to learn more about yourself, and, in the process, become more cognizant of how the "soil"—to use Dvořák's expression—has shaped you. Your life experiences will prepare you to help others grow. This is the topic of the next chapter.

Questions for discussion

- Consider a cultural practice that seems to challenge your moral compass. Under what circumstances do you think a leader should adapt to a moral compass that may be different from his or her own?
- Bill George calls defining moments in a person's life when their values are put the test "crucible moments." Describe one of the greatest "crucibles" in your life. How did it affect your approach to leadership principles?
- Should you uphold your values under all circumstances? Can you think of a situation where you would compromise your values in order to achieve your goals? Explain.
- Based on Bill George's five practices, do you consider yourself to be an authentic leader? Which of the five areas do you think you need to work on the most?
- A common theme in the literature surrounding authentic leadership is the positive impact that authentic leaders have on their organizations. Do a leader's actions have to be positive in order to be termed "authentic"?

Additional resources

B. George and D. Baker, *True North Groups: A Powerful Path to Personal and Leadership Development*, San Francisco: Berrett-Koehler Publishers, 2011.

W.L. Gardner, B.J. Avolio, and F.O. Walumbwa, eds., *Authentic Leadership Theory and Practice: Origins, Effects and Development*, Oxford: Elsevier JAI, 2005.

M. Morrison, *The Other Side of the Card: Where Your Authentic Leadership Story Begins*, New York: McGraw-Hill, 2007.

Notes

1 Quoted in J. Creelman, "Real Value of Negro Melodies," *New York Herald*, May 21, 1893.
2 See, for instance, K. Lawson, *The Trainer's Handbook of Leadership Development: Tools, Techniques, and Activities*, San Francisco: Pfeiffer, 2011; R. Barner, *Accelerating Your Development as a Leader: A Guide for Leaders and Their Managers*, San Francisco: Pfeiffer, 2011; B.D. Ruben, *What Leaders Need to Know: A Leadership Competencies Scorecard*, Washington, DC: National Association of College and University Business Officers, 2006.
3 There is a vast literature regarding the nature vs. nurture debate in child development. For examples, see D. Cohen, *How the Child's Mind Develops*, London: Routledge, 2013; D.P. Keating, ed., *Nature and Nurture in Early Child Development*, New York: Cambridge University Press, 2012; R.S. Feldman, *Child Development*, Boston, MA: Pearson, 2012.
4 For examples, see J.L. Hall, "The Sound of Leadership: Transformational Leadership in Music," *Journal of Leadership Education*, 7, 2 (2008): 47–68; E. Rodgers, C.R. Bradley, and S. Ward "Poetic Forms of Leadership Pedagogy: Rediscovering Creative Leadership through the Arts," *Journal of Leadership Studies*, 3, 4 (2010): 91–96. See M. Bonds, "Music as Language" and "Musical Grammar and Musical Rhetoric," in *Wordless Rhetoric: Musical Form as the Metaphor of the Oration*, Cambridge: Harvard University Press, 1991, 61–80; see also D. Sellnow and T. Sellnow, "John Corigliano's 'Symphony No. 1' as a Communicative Medium for the AIDS Crisis," *Communication Studies*, 44, 2 (1993): 87–101.
5 For more biographical information, see M.B. Beckerman, *New Worlds of Dvořák: Searching in America for the Composer's Inner Life*, New York: W.W. Norton and Company, 2003; D. Hurwitz, *Dvořák: Romantic Music's Most Versatile Genius*, Pompton Plains, NJ: Amadeus Press, 2005; K. Honolka, *Dvořák*, A. Wyburd, trans., London: Haus Publishing, 2004.
6 J. Creelman, "Real Value of Negro Melodies," *New York Herald*, May 21, 1893. There is debate as to what Dvořák actually said and what the reporter, James Creelman, inferred or paraphrased. However, he became closely associated with the quotes. See J. Horowitz, *Dvořák in America*, Chicago: Cricket Books, 2003, pp. 71–81.
7 "Dvořák on His New Work," *New York Herald*, December 15, 1893.
8 Ibid.
9 L. Bernstein, sound recording, *A Book-Of-The-Month Club Music Appreciation Record*, "Symphony Number 5 in E Minor, Opus 95, *From the New World*,". 1956. Available at https://www.youtube.com/watch?v=79D5sOD5duE. Accessed August 17, 2014.
10 E. Nellis, *Shaping the New World: African Slavery in the Americas, 1500–1888*, North York, Ontario, Canada: University of Toronto Press, 2013; G. Tomlinson, *The Singing of the New World: Indigenous Voice in the Era of European Contact*, New York: Cambridge University Press, 2009; N. Philbrick, *The Mayflower and the Pilgrims' New World*, New York: G.P. Putnam's Sons, 2008; T. Jacoby, ed., *Reinventing the Melting Pot: The New Immigrants and What It Means to be American*, New York: Basic Books, 2004.
11 Conductor Marin Alsop also notes this impression. See "Dvořák's Symphonic Journey to the New World," National Public Radio April 18, 2008. Available at http://www.npr.org/templates/story/story.php?storyId= 89758808. Accessed August 18, 2014.
12 B. George, *Authentic Leadership: Rediscovering the Secrets to Creating Lasting Value*, San Francisco: Jossey-Bass, 2014. For other approaches to authentic leadership, see

W.L. Gardner, B.J. Avolio, and F.O. Walumbwa, "Authentic Leadership Development: Emergent Trends and Future Directions," in W.L. Gardner, B.J. Avolio, and F.O. Walumbwa, eds., *Authentic Leadership Theory and Practice: Origins, Effects, and Development*, Oxford: Elsevier JAI, 2005, pp. 387–406; R.W. Terry, *Authentic Leadership: Courage in Action*, San Franciso, Jossey-Bass, 1993.

13 B. George, P. Sims, A.N. McLean, and D. Mayer, "Discovering your Authentic Leadership," *Harvard Business Review*, February 2007: 129.

14 Ibid.

13 Leadership to develop others

Hally: Every age, Sam, has got its social reformer. My history book is full of them.

Sam: So where's ours?[1]

Athol Fugard, from *"Master Harold"* . . .
and the Boys

Leadership for what? Leadership to develop others. Studying leadership to develop one's self is noble, but it is not enough. The true practitioner of leadership seeks to develop others. Author Max DePree encapsulates this thought best when he says, "The signs of outstanding leadership appear primarily among the followers. Are the followers reaching their potential?"[2] The theory behind DePree's observation is best expressed in James MacGregor Burns's concept of *transformational leadership*, which we introduced to you in Chapter 1. In this chapter, we will go deeper into Burns's concept of transformational leadership and flesh out its implications. As has been the model for our previous chapters, we will use a case study to illustrate these ideas, in this instance, South African playwright Athol Fugard's play *"Master Harold"* . . . *and the Boys*.

As we have seen in previous chapters, James MacGregor Burns provided the starting point for a host of leadership theories and concepts studied today. Not the least of these were his ideas of *transactional* and *transformational* leadership. Transactional leadership, Burns argued, was a simple exchange—a bargain between leaders and followers. A leader provides a follower with an incentive to motivate him or her to complete a task. The central criterion of transactional leadership is that "the bargainers have no enduring purpose that holds them together."[3] In reality, many theories and models of leadership embrace this idea, and they can be effective. Burns, however, thought leadership could be—and should be—more than a mere exchange. Rather, Burns thought leadership at its best was a transformational process in which leaders and followers engage each other in such a way as to raise one another to higher levels of motivation and morality.[4] (See Figure 13.1.)

For personal development	For developing others	For the greater good

"I" (Individualism)   (Collectivism) "WE"

Primacy of the leader   Primacy of the group

Transformational leadership

Figure 13.1 Transformational leadership on the leadership continuum

It is worth taking a moment here to discuss what Burns meant by "motivation" and "morality." By "motivation," Burns was suggesting that such leadership fuses the leader and the followers in a "mutual and continuing pursuit of a higher purpose"—that is, something that is transcendent to either the leader's or the follower's immediate goal.[5] By "morality," Burns was referring to the human and ethical conduct of both the leader and the led.[6] In short, Burns proposed transformational leadership helped both the leader and the follower reach their full potential and goals and to go beyond either of their immediate self-interests.[7]

Since the concept was first introduced, transformational leadership has been widely studied and theorized by scholars.[8] One of the most popular incarnations of Burns's idea was developed by James M. Kouzes and Berry Z. Posner in their book *The Leadership Challenge*. Although other scholars have researched and developed other ways of understanding transformational leadership, Kouzes and Posner's work provides a ready access point to understand transformational leadership because it defines transformational leadership *behaviorally* rather than *theoretically*. In their book, the authors identify five common practices of transformational leaders: inspiring a shared vision, modeling the way, challenging the process, enabling others to act, and encouraging the heart:[9]

- *Inspire a shared vision*: Leaders who pursue this practice envision a positive and ennobling future while enlisting followers to help achieve that vision and appealing to common aspirations.
- *Model the way*: This practice focuses on the way a leader sets a personal example and is careful to be certain his/her behavior matches the principles and values set for himself/herself and others.
- *Challenge the process*: This practice focuses on challenging the status quo, experimenting, and developing new ways of seeing and approaching issues. It also encourages leaders to take risks, learn from mistakes, and to grow.
- *Enabling others to act*: Enabling others means collaborating, building trust, listening to others, and empowering followers to grow and develop their own leadership.
- *Encouraging the heart*: Leaders who encourage the heart provide their followers with nurture and succor. They support them and show their appreciation while building an *esprit de corps*.

By defining transformational leadership behaviorally, researchers are better able to measure a leader's practice of transformational leadership and assist them to develop a more transformational style. In fact, Kouzes and Posner developed an instrument to do just that, the Leadership Practice Inventory, and it has become a standard for measuring transformational leadership behavior.

To better understand transformational leadership and the way it is practiced, we turn now to our case study, Athol Fugard's play *"Master Harold" . . . and the Boys*.

Case study: Athol Fugard's play *"Master Harold" . . . and the Boys*

The story centers on Hally, a 17-year-old white boy, and two black men, Sam and Willie—both in their 40s. The play is set in 1950 at the height of South African apartheid. Sam and Willie have been employees in Hally's mother's service since Hally was a little boy, and he has grown up with the two men.[10] Throughout the play, the characters reminisce about their life together and offer a running, although at times cloaked, commentary on the oppressive culture in which they live. The friendship between the characters transgresses racial lines, and one of the men, Sam, provides a loving father figure to Hally whose own biological father is a tragic alcoholic.

Background on the play

Fugard's play was met with rave reviews at its premier at the Yale Repertory Theater in the spring of 1982, and met with success once again in its subsequent Broadway run in 1987. At the time of its premier, one reviewer wrote, "If there is a more urgent and indispensable playwright in world theatre [today] than South Africa's Athol Fugard, I don't know who it could be."[11] Hailed by some as "the greatest evangelist of the century," Fugard was acknowledged by most critics, particularly concerning the rhetorical aspects of his play against the racially oppressive South African government.[12] The election of the National Party in 1948 officially instituted apartheid, or racial segregation between the ruling white minority and the oppressed black majority, in South Africa's political system.[13] The major thrust of apartheid was to classify people groups according to race, in efforts to segregate, and hence limit, people groups in regards to geography, occupation, and education. The segregation caused by apartheid eventually evolved into pass laws, which were restrictions on blacks' movements or employment; the Separate Amenities Act, which segregated facilities between blacks and whites; the Morality Act, which prohibited cross-racial sexual intercourse; and the Banning Order, which limited free association between blacks and whites.[14]

These racially motivated laws were met with protest from the black South African majority. The most notable of these protests was the Sharpeville Massacre in 1960 in which police killed 69 and wounded 180 black South

African protesters. The massacre was followed by protests and riots across South Africa, in many cases led by the African National Congress (ANC) headed by Nelson Mandela and its rival the Pan-Africanist Congress (PAC). The ANC and PAC were banned by the government and turned to armed conflict as they abandoned their more peaceful protests. Mandela was eventually tried by the white South African government, found guilty of treason, and sentenced to life in prison in 1964. It was at the infamous Rivonia Trial that Nelson Mandela delivered his famous "I Am Prepared to Die" speech.

At the time *"Master Harold" . . . and the Boys* was originally produced, Fugard was widely seen not only as a playwright, but also as a powerful voice in South African politics. Fugard even describes his own writing as "theater of defiance."[15] In fact, the play was originally banned in South Africa due to the political undertones of the text.[16] One critic notes, "[Fugard] remains enshrined as the radical opponent of apartheid, its most vociferous critic."[17] However, Fugard's plays, and specifically *"Master Harold" . . . and the Boys*, goes beyond the political to touch on the personal dynamics of racism, which, indeed, is Fugard's goal.[18] Although the characters in *"Master Harold" . . . and the Boys* are distinctly South African and its themes obviously engage the sociopolitical structure of South Africa, the play had—and continues to have— a special appeal for many audiences.[19] In addition, the unique texture of the play, such as the local setting and the familial characters, are constantly flattered by Fugard's metaphorical style, which also makes the play accessible to audiences from other cultures.[20]

Synopsis of the play

The play begins with Sam and Willie tidying up the St. George's Park Tea Room where they work as waiters. Willie begins to practice for an upcoming ballroom dance competition that Sam has encouraged him to enter. Willie dances as Sam provides instruction, but the duo's impromptu dance recital is interrupted by Hally's mocking applause. Hally has been watching from the doorway as the more accomplished Sam has launched into the quickstep in efforts to show Willie the proper form. Willie snaps to attention and salutes Hally. "At your service, Master Harold," says Willie, and Sam fetches Hally a towel to dry his hair that has become soaked in the rain. Hally flippantly places his order for lunch sending Sam to the kitchen, and establishing the pecking order. Sam informs Hally that he believes his mother has left to fetch his father from the hospital. Hally is ashamed of his father, an alcoholic amputee, and the possibility of his returning home fills him with dread. However, he quickly dismisses Sam's assumption and rationalizes that his father could not possibly be well enough to return home from the hospital.

Hally begins to recount his day in school. In response to Hally being punished for sketching an unflattering picture of his teacher, Sam tells Hally what happens to black South Africans when they are punished by the magistrate—a cruel caning on their bare backsides. Hally is repulsed by the image and tells Sam,

"Things will change, you wait and see. One day somebody is going to get up and give history a kick up the backside and get it going again," to which Sam replies, "Like who?"[21] This challenge inspires the two to a friendly debate over social reformers and "men of magnitude," in which both characters submit their candidates for approval.[22] This seemingly good-natured row sparks a reminiscence of earlier days when Sam, Willie, and Hally first began their "education" together. Hally relives his childhood playing checkers with Sam and Willie in their bedroom at his mother's former business, a boarding house. He vividly recalls hiding in their room in order to avoid his father and the disreputable tenants. Sam and Hally also reminisce about better times, specifically a time when Sam made a kite for Hally to fly when he was a child.

The trio's reminiscences are interrupted by a phone call from Hally's mother informing him that his father is insisting on coming home from the hospital. Hally panics at the thought of his father returning home and begs his mother to lie and bribe his father with alcohol to get him to stay in the hospital. When Hally replaces the receiver, Sam and Willie meet him with accusing eyes. Hally attempts to hide his shame, but the news of his father's return is too much for him. In a merciful effort to divert Hally's attention away from his guilt, Sam inquires him about his homework. Hally settles into his task while Sam and Willie return to their chores. Willie once again begins to practice his quickstep as he replaces the chairs around the tables on the freshly scrubbed floor. Sam and Willie's conversation is a second time directed at the upcoming ballroom championship introduced at the beginning of the play. Hally decides to write an essay about the competition and asks Sam to describe the event.

Sam's lesson is interrupted by a second phone call from Hally's mother informing him that his father is, indeed, home and waiting for Hally. The phone call ignites a spark of shame in Hally, and he unleashes a string of hateful comments about his father. When Sam tries to quiet the boy, Hally takes his vengeance out on Sam, climaxing in the moment Hally hurls a hurtful joke and racist epitaph, and Sam returns in kind. Hally then spits in Sam's face in an effort to teach him a "lesson in respect." The close relationship between the unlikely pair seems to have come to an end. In the final moments of the play, Sam seeks reconciliation with Hally, and asks him if he would like to fly another kite. However, Hally ultimately rejects Sam's plea and leaves to go home to his father, unable to accept the reconciliation and forgiveness Sam offers him. Willie attempts to comfort Sam as he deposits his last coin in the tearoom's jukebox and takes Sam into his arms and waltzes as the lights dim.

Analysis: Leadership to develop others

The primary way we see Fugard's play illustrate transformational leadership is simply the relationship Sam creates with Hally. As Burns declares, the emphasis of transformational leadership is the relationship created between leaders and followers. The special relationship between Sam and Hally defies the culture of apartheid and in itself is potentially transformational. Sam has engaged with

Hally throughout his life and his patience, kindness, and mentoring has challenged Hally's racist culture and upbringing. In a very real way, Sam is more of a father to Hally than is his biological father. It is only through this relationship that Sam is able to engage with Hally in such a way as to inspire both of them to higher levels of motivation and morality. The culture in South Africa at the time, however, is the biggest challenge to Sam as a leader and to Hally as a follower.

Consider this: From a transactional perspective, Sam is an employee in Hally's mother's tea room. He is rewarded with a wage to perform the services required of his employer. He has no immediate extrinsic motivation to further develop the relationship with his employer's son, Hally; yet he does so. But it is only in this relationship that Hally and Sam can hope to find something more than the immediate limitations their culture imposes on them. Although Hally seems to fall short of embracing the love and compassion Sam offers him, he is still challenged to move beyond his racist society and work for a better world—on a micro scale in his private life and on a macro scale in his country's future. Certainly Hally is affected by this relationship, but so is Sam. He, too, is challenged to move beyond the understandable hate and resentment caused by the way his country has treated him and other black South Africans.

This relationship sets the context for more specific ways Sam's leadership reflects a transformational style. As we move deeper into the analysis of the play, recall the five practices of transformational leadership identified by Kouzes and Posner: model the way, inspire a shared vision, challenge the process, enable others to act, encourage the heart. We can see each of these practices displayed by Sam throughout the play.

The first scene in the play contains a dialogue between Sam and Willie concerning ballroom dancing that serves to inspire a shared vision for social harmony throughout the remainder of the play. Willie rises from his position of scrubbing the floor and begins to practice his quickstep and asks Sam for direction. Sam is swift to give Willie multiple instructions telling him, "Make it smooth. And give it more style. It must look like you are enjoying yourself"; and, "Ballroom must look happy Willie, not like hard work. It must . . . Ja! . . . It must look like romance."[23] Willie straightaway becomes frustrated with Sam's instructions because he realizes that the dance championship for which he is practicing is soon approaching and he is not ready. These first few moments of dialogue in the play metaphorically confront the audience with the inability for people to live in harmony—that is, Willie's inability to master the quickstep. Thus, the metaphor of the impending dance competition contains several layers of meaning including a vision for social harmony, and the urgency to see justice served in efforts to create a more perfect world—specifically in South Africa at the time.

Fugard returns to the ballroom dancing metaphor later in the play when Sam attempts to convince Hally of its beauty and importance. At first Hally scoffs, but he eventually half-embraces the idea merely to fulfill a homework assignment and as a way to further provoke his racist teacher. This gives Sam the opportunity to fully articulate his vision. There is a particular passage that illustrates this well. Sam is describing the ballroom dancing championships for Hally's essay, and Hally inquires about the penalties for "stumbling into somebody."[24] Sam is aghast at Hally's question and collapses with laughter and then launches into Fugard's most polemic metaphor of the play:

> There's no collisions out there, Hally. Nobody trips or stumbles or bumps into anybody else. That's what that moment is all about. To be one of those finalists on that dance floor is like . . . like being in a dream about a world in which accidents don't happen . . . that's what I've been trying to say to you all afternoon. And it's beautiful because that is what we want life to be like. But instead, like you said, Hally, we're bumping into each other all the time. Look at the three of us just this afternoon: I've bumped into Willie, the two of us have bumped into you, you've bumped into your mother, she bumping into your dad . . . None of us knows the steps and there's no music playing. And it doesn't stop with us. The whole world is doing it all the time. Open a newspaper and what do you read? America has bumped into Russia, England is bumping into India, richman bumps into poorman. Those are big collisions, Hally. They make for a lot of bruises. People get hurt in all that bumping, and we're sick and tired of it now. It's been going on for too long. Are we never going to get it right? . . . learn to dance like champions instead of always being just a bunch of beginners at it?[25]

For a brief moment, Hally truly grasps Sam's vision. Hally exclaims, "You're right. We mustn't despair. Maybe there's some hope for mankind after all." As he refers back to his homework, he finds the title for his essay, "A World Without Collisions: . . . Ballroom Dancing as A Political Vision."[26] In these few pages, Sam inspires Hally with an ennobling vision of the future. But it is not just Sam's vision; Hally begins to own it for himself.

Sam's inspirational vision is further illustrated in his relationship with Willie. Throughout the play, we learn that Sam has taught Willie ballroom dancing. Willie is hooked and has entered a dance competition with his partner, Hilda. Tragically, Willie continually beats her when she struggles to learn the steps. (Even this situation is rife with metaphorical implications.) Sam challenges Willie to stop beating his girlfriend and at the end of the play, Willie, indeed, promises to do so and to ask Hilda for forgiveness. The ballroom dancing metaphor works on multiple levels. Ultimately, Sam inspires Willie to transfer his beautiful vision from ballroom dancing to his personal life. Willie is not simply motivated to win the dance completion, but he is motivated to behave more lovingly and kindly to another human being. This fits the very definition of Burns' "higher levels of motivation and morality." Before Sam can inspire his vision, however, he must challenge the very culture in which he and his followers operate.

Sam's relationship with Hally illustrates Kouzes and Posner's idea of "challenging the process" simply by providing a white South African boy with a black South African father figure. As we mentioned, such a relationship would have been held in contempt in the apartheid era. The special relationship between Sam and Hally in itself defies the culture. However, there is a particular moment in the play that more precisely provides evidence for this aspect of Sam's transformational leadership. Hally begins to recount his day in school in which he received a swat on his backside in response to his drawing an unflattering picture of his teacher. Sam then describes to Hally what happens to black South Africans when they are punished by the magistrate:

> *Sam*:   They make you lie down on a bench. One policeman pulls down
>   your trousers and holds your ankles, another pulls your shirt over
>   your head and holds your arms . . .
> *Hally*: Thank you! That's enough.
> *Sam*:   . . . and the one that gives you the strokes talks to you gently and
>   for a long time between each one.

Hally is repulsed by the image and tells Sam: "Things will change, you wait and see. One day somebody is going to get up and give history a kick up the backside and get it going again. They're called social reformers. Every age, Sam, has got its social reformer. My history book is full of them." To which Sam replies, "So where's ours?"[27] This seemingly innocent question is, perhaps, the very heart of the play: Sam challenges Hally to be that person.

There is also insight to be gleaned from the historical figures Sam and Hally submit for one another's consideration as social reformers who fit their definitions of "men of magnitude." (Unfortunately, given the time period and setting of the play, the idea of "women of magnitude" does not seem to cross anyone's mind.) Hally proposes historical figures such as Charles Darwin—although he has never even read Darwin's *Origin of the Species*. Darwin's submission insinuates the harsh "survival of the fittest" social implications of the cultural context in which Sam and Hally are living. Sam's proposal of Jesus, by way of contrast, relates to his position as a suffering servant to humankind. The juxtaposing of these two historical figures effectively represents the extremes of transactional and transformational leadership. In Darwin's survival of the fittest, one gives simply to receive—the crux of transactional leadership. (Hally's reference to the Darwin's example of the mistletoe and its parasites illustrates this idea nicely.) Contrarily, Sam's submission of Jesus is a quintessential representative of a transformational leader whose very purpose was to raise others to higher levels of motivation and morality. Critics have noted that many of Sam's actions throughout the play literally or metaphorically reflect much of the best of Jesus's teachings, including his admonition to forgive others for the injustices inflicted on them.[28]

This guides us to more deeply scrutinize the "men of magnitude" conversation. It was highly unusual for black South Africans to have access to quality education in the pre-apartheid and apartheid eras. In the play, we learn that Sam has been working with Hally on his homework assignments since Hally was in the fourth grade, and he is mostly self-educated. Hally claims that he has "educated" Sam, but it is plainly evident to anyone other than Hally that Sam is the teacher, and Hally is the student. Sam plays along with Hally's game because it gives him the opportunity to better himself with the formal education offered to Hally, while also providing him with an opportunity to positively influence Hally and teach him the importance of equality and social justice. If Hally is truly searching for a "man of magnitude," he need look no further than Sam. This mutuality between the leader and the follower is a hallmark of transformational leadership. Both Hally and Sam are the better for their relationship with each other. This leads us to examine the manner Sam illustrates the next practice of transformational leadership, "modeling the way."

Kouzes and Posner say it best when they state, "Modeling the way is essentially about earning the right and respect to lead through direct individual involvement and action. People first follow the person, then the plan."[29] Throughout the play, Sam provides Hally with a personal example of racial reconciliation. If Sam did not first establish a relationship with Hally, and then live up to the values and vision he proposes, he would have no chance to influence him. However, this relationship is threatened in the play's climax.

Late in the play, Hally receives a second telephone call from his mother and learns that she has retrieved his father from the hospital and that he is waiting for him at home. When Sam attempts to comfort Hally, the boy begins to wallow in his guilt and shame spewing his hate for his father:

> Do you know what is really wrong with your little dream, Sam? It's not just that we are all bad dancers. That does happen to be perfectly true, but there's more to it than just that. You left out the cripples . . . That's why we always end up on our backsides on the dance floor. They're also out there dancing, like a couple of broken spiders trying to do the quickstep.[30]

Sam forbids Hally from ridiculing his father because he knows it will only lead the boy to feel more guilt and shame, but he continues. When Sam attempts to comfort Hally, he finds Hally's contempt for his father turned to be unleashed on him. Hally heeds Sam to "mind his own business and shut up" and reminds him that he "is only a servant" to his father.[31] Sam protests:

> *Sam*:   I get paid by your mother.
> *Hally*:   Don't argue with me, Sam!
> *Sam*:   Then don't say he's my boss.
> *Hally*:   He's a white man and that's good enough for you.[32]

The insult is purposely provocative and hurtful. Sam turns to walk away, but Hally, in a desperate attempt to rid himself of his shame, demands that Sam shows him a sign of respect by referring to him as "Master Harold" rather than "Hally."[33] He then sides with his father:

> I can tell you now that [sic] somebody who will be glad to hear I've finally given it to you, will be my dad. Yes! He agrees with my mom. He's always going on about it as well, "You must teach the boys to show you more respect, my son" . . . You mustn't get the wrong idea about me and my dad, Sam. We also have our good times together. Some bloody good laughs. He's got a marvellous [sic] sense of humor. Want to know what our favorite joke is? He gives out this big groan, you see, and says, "It's not fair, is it, Hally?" Then I have to ask "What, Chum?" And then he says: "A nigger's [sic] arse" . . . and we both have a good laugh.[34]

Hally's abuse finally provokes Sam. Sam says, "It's me you're after. You should just have said, 'Sam's arse' . . . because that's the one you're trying to kick. Anyway, how do you know it's not fair? You've never seen it. Do you want to?" Sam drops his trousers and presents his naked backside for Hally's inspection as a response to his taunting insults.[35] In a final effort to rid himself of his humiliation, Hally spits into Sam's face. Sam responds:

> . . . you're a coward, Master Harold. The face you should be spitting in is your father's . . . but you used mine, because you think you're safe inside your fair skin . . . and this time I don't mean just or decent.
>
> Fugard, "*Master Harold*," p. 56

Sam lunges at Hally and threatens to hit him, but ultimately he walks away. Mark Cummings observes, "The joke and the response lessen the humanity of both characters; Hally degrades himself by the words he chooses to repeat, and Sam, degraded by the joke, degrades himself even further by striking back."[36]

No, Sam is not perfect. No leader is. He makes mistakes, as all leaders do. What is important for our analysis is that the relationship between them affects Sam as much as it does Hally; leader as much as follower. After the two have fought, Sam offers an olive branch to Hally. Sam says, "I've got no right to tell you what being a man means if I don't behave like one myself, and I'm not doing so well at that this afternoon. Should we try again, Hally?" (Fugard, "*Master Harold*," p. 59). He models the very idea of reconciliation he has proposed. Sam allows himself to be affected by Hally and thus they are both challenged to a higher level of motivation and morality: Hally to recognize Sam's love and acceptance he so desperately needs but cannot seem to accept due to his racist culture, and Sam to continue to seek reconciliation with Hally and to work for change—even if it is the personal change in himself, and in this case, one follower. Sam, and by extension Hally, are motivated to work toward reconciliation in their immediate relationship, but also on a greater scale in South Africa's racial divide. It is this kind of mutual engagement that Burns identifies as quintessentially transformational. Both characters touch one another on a deeply emotional level and encourage each other to aspire to higher levels of morality.

There is a particularly poignant moment in the play that illustrates this practice of transformational leadership well. One of Hally's fondest memories as a child was when Sam made a kite for him from paper and bits of string. Hally recalls his fear of embarrassment if they failed to fly the kite, and his joy the moment the "miracle happened" and it took flight. He remembers watching the kite for hours from a bench to which Sam had tied the string.

The kite story is a key moment in the play, but Fugard saves its full implications for the end of the play when Sam reveals to him why he made the kite for the child. Hally had received another telephone call years before, this time from a bar owner who had telephoned to report that Hally's father had passed out in a drunken stupor and soiled himself. In Hally's mother's absence, Sam and Hally were forced to rescue Hally's father. Sam recalls:

> Do you remember how we did it? You went in first, by yourself, to ask permission for me to go into the bar. Then I loaded him onto my back like a baby and carried him back to the boarding house with you following behind, carrying his crutches. A crowded Main Street with all the people watching a little white boy following his drunk father on a nigger's [sic] back . . . That's not the way a boy grows up to be a man! But the one person who should have been teaching you what that means was the cause of your shame. If you really want to know, that's why I made you that kite. I wanted you to look up, be proud of something, of yourself . . . and you certainly were that, when I left you with it up there on the hill. Oh ja . . . something else! . . . I couldn't sit down there and stay with you. It was a whites-only bench. You were too young to notice then. But not anymore. If you're not careful . . . Master Harold . . . you're going to be sitting up there all by yourself for a long time to come, and there won't be a kite in the sky.[37]

Sam's empathy and act of compassion illustrates the importance Kouzes and Posner place on encouraging the heart. One can only imagine the shame the little boy was feeling at the time, and Sam's kindness provided a much needed boost to Hally's low sense of worth and gave him a sense of pride once again. The final moment in Sam's monologue illustrates Kouzes and Posner's final practice of transformational behavior, "enabling others to act."

Sam gives Hally a choice. He can embrace Sam's vision and the love and acceptance he offers him, or he can continue to wallow in his shame and racist upbringing. As we mentioned in Chapter 3, followership is ultimately a choice. There is a scene that illustrates this point well. After the harsh words spoken between Hally and Sam, Hally starts to leave and make his way home to his father. Sam stops him:

Sam: Should we try again, Hally?
Hally: Try what?
Sam: Fly another kite, I suppose. It worked once, and this time I need it as much as you do.
Hally: It's still raining, Sam. You can't fly kites on rainy days, remember.
Sam: So, what do we do? Hope for better weather tomorrow?
Hally: I don't know. I don't know anything anymore.
Sam: You sure of that, Hally? Because it would be pretty hopeless if that was true. It would mean nothing has been learned in here this afternoon, and there was a hell of a lot of teaching going on . . . one way or the other. But anyway, I don't believe you. I reckon there's one thing you know. You don't have to sit up there by yourself. You know what that bench means now, and you can leave it any time you choose. All you've got to do is stand up and walk away from it.

Fugard, *"Master Harold,"* pp. 59–60

Sam shows that Hally has the power to choose how to respond to the world in which he lives. He need not be merely blown by the wind of his past. He has a choice. In Sam, he has the power to embrace that father he so desires. Although Hally seems to reject Sam's offer to try again, the play ends with Sam and Willie continuing to dance, which suggests that they, at least, will continue to work for a better world and hope that Hally will someday follow.

Summary and concluding remarks

In this chapter, we have more deeply explored James MacGregor Burns' concept of transformational leadership, specifically as delineated by Kouzes and Posner in their book *The Leadership Challenge*. We have applied each of the author's practices of transformational leadership to Athol Fugard's play *"Master Harold"* . . . *and the Boys*—inspiring a shared vision, modeling the way, challenging the process, encouraging the heart, and enabling others to act. We have seen how Sam's character demonstrates these practices with his followers, Hally and Willie. We have seen how transformational leadership affects the leader as well as the followers. And, finally, we have seen how transformational leadership can inspire both the leader and the led to higher levels of motivation and morality.

On another level, the playwright Athol Fugard is also a potentially transformational leader if we, his readers, also see ourselves as his followers. Fugard constructs a clear vision for the future, and he calls his audience to embrace it. Readers are left without a doubt as to the author's purpose. Sam becomes a voice for Fugard to call his audience, his followers, to a particular vision for the world. Likewise, as Sam tells Hally, what happens next is up to him, Fugard inspires his readers to take action. As one critic observes, Fugard seems to say, "What happens now is up to you, the public."[38] Most readers would find themselves irresistibly compelled to answer Sam's implied question, "Who will be our social reformer—our 'man of magnitude?'" with an enthusiastic and resounding "me!" Perhaps that is Fugard's intention. That, indeed, is the goal of any great playwright and any great leader. They issue their followers an irresistible call to the dance.

Questions for discussion

- In what contexts do you think transformational leadership works best? In what contexts might transactional leadership be appropriate?
- Burns implies that leadership has an ethical dimension; that is, leadership should motivate both the leader and the follower to "higher levels of morality." Do you agree or disagree? Why?
- Think of your own situation and the context in which you live. Who are the transformational leaders in your life or your time? Do they exemplify Kouzes and Posner's five practices of exemplary leadership? How so?
- How do you think you would "measure up" if you were to take Kouzes and Posner's Leadership Practice Inventory? In which of the five practices of exemplary leadership would you excel? Where would there be the most room for improvement? What could you do to improve this aspect of your own leadership?

Additional resources

B.J. Avolio, *Full Leadership Development: Building the Vital Forces in Organizations*, Thousand Oaks, CA: Sage, 1999.

B.M. Bass and B.J. Avolio, *Improving Organizational Effectiveness Through Transformational Leadership*, Thousand Oaks, CA: Sage, 1994.

B.M. Bass and R.E. Riggio, *Transformational Leadership*, 2nd edn., Mahwah, NJ: Lawrence Erlbaum, 2006.

Notes

1 A. Fugard's *"Master Harold" . . . and the Boys*, New York: Random House, 2009, p. 18.
2 M. DePree, *Leadership is an Art*, New York: Dell Trade, 1989, p.12.
3 J.M. Burns, *Leadership*, New York: Harper & Row, 1978, p. 20
4 Ibid.
5 Ibid.
6 Ibid, p. 4.
7 Burns later softened his position on the extreme dichotomy between transformational and transactional leadership and suggested that leaders operate on both sides of the spectrum and combine the two approaches. J.M. Burns, "Foreword," in R.A. Couto, ed., *Reflections on Leadership*, New York: University Press of America, 2007, p. viii.

8   For examples, see B.M. Bass, *Leadership and Performance Beyond Expectations*, New York: Free Press, 1985; B. Avolio, *Full Leadership Development: Building the Vital Forces in Organizations*, Thousand Oaks, CA: Sage, 1999; B.M. Bass and R.E. Riggio, *Transformational Leadership*, 2nd edn., Mahwah, NJ: Lawrence Erlbaum, 2006; B.M. Bass and B.J. Avolio, *Improving Organizational Effectiveness Through Transformational Leadership*, Thousand Oaks, CA: Sage, 1994; M. Sashkin, "Transformational Leadership Approaches: A Review and Synthesis," in J. Antonkis, A.T. Cianciolo, and R.J. Sternberg, eds., *The Nature of Leadership*, Thousand Oaks, CA: Sage, 2004, pp. 171–196.

9   See J.M. Kouzes and B.Z. Posner, *The Leadership Challenge*, 3rd edn., San Francisco: Jossey-Bass, 2002.

10 J.O. Jordan acknowledges, "Standard accounts of Fugard's life and career generally consider '*Master Harold*' . . . *and the Boys* to be the most autobiographical of all his plays, the one that reaches farthest back into the author's own past and that conforms most closely in the details of its central story to actual events and experiences in Fugard's life." See J.O. Jordan, "Life in the Theater: Autobiography, Politics, and Romance in '*Master Harold*' . . . *and the Boys*," *Twentieth Century Literature*, 39, 4 (1993): 461. Fugard specifically relates an incident when, as a boy, he spit in the face of his longtime friend, Sam Samela. See M. Gussow, "Athol Fugard looks at a Master–Servant Friendship," *New York Times*, March 21, 1982: D6. In reference to *"Master Harold"* . . . *and the Boys*, Weales notes "the glimpses of Fugard through his characters gave way to something very close to autobiography. He used real names (his childhood nickname Hally, Sam Semela, the St. George's Park Tea Room, and the Jubilee Boarding House) and real relationships—his with Sam, with his mother, with his father." See G. Weales, "Fugard Masters the Code," *Twentieth Century Literature*, 39, 4 (1993): 511. Also see Russell Vandenbroucke, *Truths The Hand Can Touch*, New York: Theater Communications Group, 1985; A. Fugard, *Notebooks 1960–1977*, New York: Theater Communications Group, 1990; D. Walder, *Athol Fugard*, Gordonville, VA: St. Martin's Press, 1990.

11 J. Kroll, "Masters and Servants," *Newsweek*, March 29, 1982: 52.

12 See A. Fugard, "Some Problems of a Playwright from South Africa," *Twentieth Century Literature*, 39, 4 (1993): 381–393.

13 R.M. Post notes, "Fugard places the events of '*Master Harold*' . . . *and the Boys* . . . in 1950s South Africa. Historically, this is about the time that the policy of apartheid, long in developing, began to be practiced." R.M. Post, "Racism in Althol Fugard's '*Master Harold*' . . . *and the Boys*," *World Literature Written in English*, 30, 1 (1990): 98.

14 F. Donahue specifically cites these acts as part of the sociopolitical climate of *"Master Harold"* . . . *and the Boys*. F. Donahue, "Apartheid's Dramatic Legacy," *Midwest Quarterly*, 36, 3 (1995): 323–324.

15 Ibid, 323. Although Fugard does acknowledge the political implications of his work, he reports that he finds the label "political playwright" to be extremely frustrating. Fugard says, "If anybody in an audience for one of my plays sits there expecting that I am going to make a political statement, or give a message, or lay out a blueprint for a better and juster [sic] South Africa, they are going to be disappointed. What is more, because of this expectation, and because they are looking in the wrong direction (this I think has happened to a lot of my critics in their reactions to my work), they will most probably miss what I have got to offer, which is a story . . . I don't want to be naïve about the business of storytelling. I'm not fighting shy of the fact that politics is in a sense a part of the substance of the stories I tell. The notion that there could be a South African story that doesn't have political resonance is laughable. When it comes down to it, any story from any time in history, from any society is political." See A. Fugard, "Some Problems of a Playwright," pp. 381–393.

We acknowledge Fugard's irritation at critics who only acknowledge the political implications of his work, and yet one cannot simply deny the fact that is how his works are sometimes "used" by audiences.

16 R.M. Post notes, " 'Master Harold' . . . and the Boys has been performed in Johannesburg before mixed audiences of blacks and whites. Performance and text come under different sections of the country's censorship laws." See R.M. Post, "Racism in Athol Fugard's 'Master Harold' . . . and the Boys," p. 102. The play was banned in South Africa for a time and was originally premiered in the United States. In fact, "Master Harold" . . . and the Boys is one of Fugard's few plays that has not had its world debut in South Africa.

17 J. Colleran, "Athol Fugard and the Problematics of the Liberal Critique," *Modern Drama*, 38, 3 (1995): 389–407.

18 Weales, "Fugard Masters the Code," pp. 503–516.

19 J. Colleran cites Fugard's plays are performed in the United States more than anywhere else in the world "rivaling both American and British dramas in popularity." See J. Colleran, "Athol Fugard and the Problematics of the Liberal Critique," p. 390.

20 For a specific discussion regarding Fugard's use of metaphor in its political context, see E. Sandoval, "The Metaphoric Style in Politically Censored Theater," Diss. Concordia University, Montreal, Quebec, Canada, 1986. See also E. Durbach " 'Master Harold' . . . and the Boys: Athol Fugard and the Psychopathology of Apartheid," *Modern Drama*, 30, 4 (1987): 505–513.

21 Fugard, *"Master Harold,"* p. 18.

22 Ibid, pp. 18–26.

23 Ibid, p. 7.

24 Ibid, p. 49.

25 Ibid, pp. 50–51.

26 Ibid, p. 51.

27 Ibid, p. 18. This seemingly innocent question is perhaps the very heart of the play. Interpreted through a sociopolitical lens, the play seems to be begging for just such a redeemer. F. Donahue remarks that Fugard's other plays "seem to say 'What happens now is up to you, the public.' Such a statement is in also in keeping with Fugard's existentialist philosophy, which values the primacy of choice in the human condition." See F. Donahue, "Apartheid's Dramatic Legacy," pp. 323–330; and R. Peck, "Condemned to Choose, but What? Existentialism in Selected Works by Fugard, Brink, and Gordimer," *Research in African Literatures*, 23, 3 (1992): 67–84.

28 See D.V. Urban's "Tolstoy's Presence in Fugard's 'Master Harold' . . . and the Boys: Sam's Pacifist Christian Perseverance and a 'Case of Illness'," *REN*, 62, 4 (2010): 311–326.

29 Kouzes and Posner, *Leadership Challenge*, p. 15.

30 Fugard, *"Master Harold,"* pp. 55–56.

31 Ibid, pp. 57–58.

32 Ibid, p. 58.

33 Ibid, p. 57.

34 Ibid, p. 60.

35 J.O. Jordan notes, "The plausibility of Sam's self-restraint following the spitting scene—and the viability of nonviolence generally as a response to apartheid, especially after 1976—has been questioned by Fugard's more militant critics, who see evidence in this crucial encounter of Fugard's classically liberal squeamishness about 'armed struggle' . . . the play endorses nonviolence and goes on to make its claim for black cultural autonomy in other terms, ones that inevitably will dissatisfy some audiences." J.O. Jordan, "Life in the Theater," p. 469.

36 M. Cummings, "A World without Collisions: 'Master Harold' . . . and the Boys in the classroom," *English Journal*, 78, 6 (1989): 72. R. Post, quoting Gerald Weales, states

240 Leadership for what?

that in this moment "Hally kills the father symbolically by attacking Sam. It is extremely ironic that the boy who wanted his father to stay in the hospital—to stay out of his life, in other words—and who speaks so unkindly of him would change so completely to side with his father against Sam and the black race. It is a blatant example of the effects of racism." R.M. Post, "Racism in Athol Fugard's 'Master Harold'," p. 100.

37 Fugard, *"Master Harold,"* p. 64.
38 F. Donahue, "Apartheid's Dramatic Legacy," pp. 323–330.

14 Leadership for the greater good

Love your neighbor as yourself.
Deuteronomy 6:5

Leadership for what? Leadership for the greater good. In the previous two chapters, we answered this question with a focus on the first two components of our working definition of leadership—leaders and followers. For our last chapter, we focus on the third component—the common goal—leadership development for the purpose of contributing to the greater good, beyond the leaders and the followers.[1]

For our last chapter, we invite you to think more broadly and consider how your actions—as a leader or as a follower—have an impact that goes beyond your personal interests. We will investigate how leadership takes on this macro level, the greater good, through the action of individuals and organizations at the micro level—small acts that ripple around the world.

The first section of the chapter introduces an artifact—François-Léon Sicard's "The Good Samaritan," a sculpture of two individuals brought together by special circumstances. However, Sicard's sculpture cannot be fully appreciated unless we understand the Parable of the Good Samaritan by Jesus of Nazareth. Further, the sculpture is placed in a setting—the Tuileries Gardens in Paris—that in itself also has symbolic power. Therefore, we explore in this chapter these three artifacts as a way to introduce the concept of leadership for the greater good.

For the analysis section, we explore the concept of leadership as social responsibility, as well as the moral dimension of the "Leadership for what?" question. The greater good is both aspirational and a target for purposeful action.[2] This chapter moves us beyond the Western utilitarian view of leadership as a prize and seeks to capture a more universal perspective of how leadership plays out at the level of humanity.

Case study: François-Léon Sicard's "The Good Samaritan"

The artifact in this chapter, while serving as an insightful message about the greater good, was created by a relatively unknown French artist.[3] As a student, Sicard showed great promise and so received a scholarship to study sculpture at the prestigious Fine Arts School in Paris.[4] One of Sicard's greatest achievements was his 1891 first-place finish in the Prix de Rome—a challenging scholarship competition for promising artists. This award allowed him to spend three years studying sculpture at the French Academy in Rome (1892–1895). On his return to Paris, he worked on the Good Samaritan sculpture (1896), which was placed in the Tuileries Gardens (see Figure 14.1).

Before introducing the sculpture, we will first recount the parable of the Good Samaritan in order to set the stage for a fuller analysis of the artifact. This powerful story has inspired a number of artistic expressions over the centuries. A famous 1633 etching by the Dutch painter, Rembrandt van Rijn, for instance, depicted the moment when the Samaritan delivered the wounded traveler to the inn. Eugene Delacroix, whose painting of "Liberty Leading the

Figure 14.1 François-Léon Sicard (1862–1934), "The Good Samaritan," 1896
Jardin des Tuileries, Paris
Photo credit: Archive Timothy McCarthy/Art Resource, New York

People" was featured in Chapter 4, also used the story of the Good Samaritan as the subject for a painting in 1849. Vincent van Gogh based his own painting of the Good Samaritan after Delacroix's in 1890. By the time Sicard created his marble version of the parable in 1896, the Good Samaritan had a distinguished lineage in the arts.

The parable of the Good Samaritan

Jesus of Nazareth narrates this parable as part of an exchange with an "expert in the law" who asks him how he may gain eternal life. He answers the question with another: "What does the law say about that?" The expert promptly cites the Law of Moses—drawing from Deuteronomy 6:5: "Love the Lord your God with all your heart and with all your soul and with all your strength and with all your mind"; and "Love your neighbor as yourself." Jesus agrees with the response, which prompts the expert to ask—who is my neighbor? The parable, therefore, is designed to explain how Jesus of Nazareth defines the concept of a neighbor.

This parable describes an event that took place on the road between Jerusalem and Jericho. The nation of ancient Israel was made up of 12 tribes, which did not always get along. Before Jesus' time, the nation split into two kingdoms—ten tribes to the north, Israel, with its capital in Samaria, and the other two tribes in the south, Judea, with its capital in Jerusalem. The northern kingdom came under heavy foreign influence, including control by the Assyrians at one point, which contributed to intermarrying and the worshiping of other gods and idols. Although both groups were Jews, the people in the southern kingdom of Judea treated the Samaritans with disdain as if they were outsiders and no longer true members of the nation of Israel. Jericho was in the northern kingdom. The road between Jerusalem and Jericho, therefore, connected two lands long associated with discord and animosity.

According to the parable, a Jewish man was traveling alone down that road when thieves ambushed him. They did not simply take away his possessions—including his clothes—but they also severely beat him and left him to die. This opening scene sets the stage on which subsequent characters (a priest, a Levite, and a Samaritan) encounter this half-dead victim and are faced with a moral dilemma—should I stop and help him?

The first individual to cross paths with the victim is a priest. Under the Mosaic tradition, temple priests came from the tribe of Levi. Therefore, technically all priests were Levites. However, not all Levites were priests. Some were placed in charge of tabernacle duties other than those performed by the priests.[5] All Levites were associated with the sacred rituals and traditions in the Jewish religion—one of which strictly forbade them from being in contact with a corpse.[6] The Levite mentioned in the parable was probably a non-priest member of the tribe of Levi. The Levites in general were well-respected religious leaders and would be recognized by Jesus' audience as role models in the community.

According to the parable, when the priest sees the victim, he moves to the other side of the road and continues without stopping to provide assistance. A Levite traveling down the same road later on comes across the same victim. Similar to the priests, the Levite does not stop. Instead, he too crosses to the other side of the road in order to avoid the victim.

The third traveler who encounters the victim is a Samaritan. In the parable, he is described as having pity on the half-dead man. He stops his journey, and instead of crossing to the other side, he provides immediate assistance by pouring oil and wine on the man's wounds and applying bandages.

The Samaritan goes even further by providing long-term care for the victim. He places the man on his donkey and takes him to an inn. According to the parable, the Samaritan stays overnight with the victim. The next day, he leaves extra money for the innkeeper and tells him he will come back later to check on the victim. The innkeeper is to keep track of any additional expenses incurred, and if they exceed the extra money given to the innkeeper, the Samaritan will settle the account when he returns.

The parable ends at that point. We do not know what happened to the victim. Did he survive? Did the innkeeper do a good job caring for him? Were there extra expenses incurred in caring for him? Did the Samaritan return as promised? Those answers are not included in the story. Rather, the focus of the parable is on the Samaritan's actions—in contrast to the priest and Levites' response.

Description of the sculpture

Sicard captured the parable of the Good Samaritan in stone. The picture of this sculpture (Figure 14.1) reveals the details of the artwork. However, we can expand on the picture by revealing some of the structural details. Unlike other artists who have used canvas to illustrate the general environment of the road between Jerusalem and Jericho, Sicard focused on the two main characters —the victim and the Samaritan. Both Delacroix and van Gogh captured the moment when the Good Samaritan is in the process of placing the half-dead traveler on his donkey for the journey to the inn. Sicard simplified the setting by simply depicting the moment when the Samaritan lifts up the wounded traveler to care for him and take him to the inn.

Many of the artistic renditions of the parable tend to show the victim lying down, and the Samaritan hovering over him as the dominant character[7] (see Figure 14.3). That is not the case in Sicard's sculpture. As Figure 14.1 shows, the two characters are intertwined, and the victim is actually at a slightly higher level compared to the Samaritan. An important detail of the sculpture is the wounded traveler's left hand, which purposefully touches the head of the Samaritan—as if to show a gesture of appreciation for the kindness shown to him. Another detail to highlight is the Samaritan's right leg, which supports the weight of the wounded traveler. The Samaritan uses his left arm to gently

Figure 14.2 Camille Pissarro (1830–1903), "The Garden of the Tuileries on a Spring Morning," 1899

Oil on canvas, 73.3 × 92.1 cm
Partial and Promised Gift of Mr. and Mrs. Douglas Dillon, 1992 (103.3) Metropolitan Museum of Art, New York
Photo credit: Image copyright © Metropolitan Museum of Art
Image source: Art Resource, New York

hold the wounded traveler's legs. The Samaritan in Sicard's work is not simply performing a good deed; he is intimately bound to the man's survival.

We chose this sculpture in part because of where it was placed after its completion—in the Tuileries Gardens, located between the Louvre Museum and the Place de la Concorde in Paris. Figure 14.2 shows an 1899 painting of the garden by the impressionist painter, Camille Pissarro (1830–1903).[8] He painted the garden as viewed from the window of his apartment.[9]

When Pissarro saw the garden from his window, he saw a public park. However, that had not always been the case. Queen Catherine de Medici first built the garden in 1563 as part of the Tuileries Palace.[10] It was then a private space, which allowed the royal family to host lavish, exclusive events with foreign visitors and the local nobility. The garden was opened to the public in 1667, but it remained royal property. The eastern part of the garden had a large square (the Grand Carré), depicted in Pissarro's painting, which served as the private garden for the royalty.

In Chapter 4, as we recounted the details of the French Revolution, we mentioned King Louis XVI and Queen Marie Antoinette being brought to Paris against their will. They actually stayed in the Tuileries Palace and had access to the garden. Following the royal couple's execution, the Tuileries garden became a national park (Jardin National) under the new republic. Throughout the nineteenth century, the Tuileries Palace and Garden became part of the national political intrigue—Napoleon's rise to power, King Charles X, and King Louis-Philippe, all discussed in Chapter 4. As each monarch rose to power, small sections of the garden were reserved for the royal family, but the general public continued to have access to the "National Garden."

Following the fall of Napoleon III's Second Empire (1852–1870), France became engulfed in a bloody conflict that divided the country between the Versailles-based national government and socialist rebels who envisioned the establishment of communes throughout the country.[11] The brief rise to power of the Paris Commune through municipal elections in 1871 eventually led to the storming of the city by national troops bent on suppressing the rebellious municipality. The Commune supporters, in a vain attempt to defend the city, burned down the Tuileries Palace, which was never rebuilt by the national government. Eventually the empty area where the palace once stood was incorporated into the garden space.

Symbolically, the conversion of the garden into a public park and the destruction of the palace came to represent a shift from the leader-centric model of the French royalty to the follower-centric model brought about in the nineteenth century through revolutionary transformation. Sicard's sculpture in the gardens serves as an excellent representation of the way the parable shows human beings working together for the greater good.

Analysis: Leadership for the greater good

The previous section introduced a sculpture within two contexts—a parable and a garden. The former serves as a narrative that is designed to draw attention to a big concept (loving your neighbor as you love yourself), while the latter (the garden, as depicted in Pissarro's painting) shows the creation of a space for everyone—not just the privileged few. The placement of the sculpture in the Grand Carré allows us to connect the parable to the vision of the greater good.

We begin this section by exploring the concept of leadership as social responsibility. Under this perspective, leaders and followers' actions go beyond individual interests and seek to serve society. They have a responsibility to promote the interests of the collective. The second part of this section, however, asks a deeper question: What happens when society's norms go against basic human values—e.g., liberty, equality? By defining the greater good at the "humanity level"—transcending local contexts—we can also explore the moral dimension of the "Leadership for what" question. Many of the leaders who have fought for the greater good have gone against society's norms. The Samaritan was no exception.

Leadership as social responsibility

Throughout this book, we have defined leadership as a process that brings leaders and followers together as they work toward a common goal. These artifacts (parable, sculpture, and garden) help us break down the traditional walls that separate these three components of leadership (leader, follower, and goal). In the parable, the Samaritan responded to the call, love your neighbor as you love yourself, without questioning motives and consequences; (Is this a ploy to deceive and hurt me? Is this situation going to disrupt my travel schedule? How much is this going to cost?). In the sculpture, we see two human beings—regardless of their status in society and organizations—coming together and sharing their humanity. Further, the sculpture is placed in a public space—a garden without walls separating the leaders from the followers (the royal family from the rest of society).

In the parable, the victim is not identified as a Jew, but we can safely assume that Jesus was addressing a Jewish crowd when telling this parable, so the audience would be thinking, "this person could have been me." Therefore, Jesus told a group of Jews that the Samaritan (the "outsider") was the one who showed compassion for a Jew, as opposed to the priest and Levite. While exploring the theological differences between the two groups falls outside the scope of this book, their deep animosity provides the shock value for the message and draws our attention to social responsibility.[12] The expert asked a pointed question of Jesus—"Who is my neighbor?" and Jesus provided an all-encompassing answer. In other words, your "neighbor" is whomever is in need of your help—the person next door or the person across the world.

This parable—and the way it is depicted in the sculpture—challenges us to consider how our actions impact a community's social capital, as articulated by Robert Putnam and Lewis Feldstein. They define social capital as "social networking, norms of reciprocity, mutual assistance, and trustworthiness."[13] Whenever we promote these values, social capital in a community increases; thus, making it stronger. Conversely, when these values are abandoned, social capital is depleted, with potential harmful effects to society.[14]

Putnam and Feldstein identify two types of social capital—bonding (linking people who are similar) and bridging (linking different types of people). The parable of the Good Samaritan focuses on bridging social capital, which Putnam and Feldstein argue is harder to create than bonding social capital. Bridging social capital requires us to broaden our concept of "neighbor," as illustrated in the parable. If we are able to transcend bonding social capital and build trustworthiness with people that we do not see as "our kind," we will be increasing a community's social capital.[15]

This depiction of the "neighbor" also challenges us to delve deeper into the servant leadership concept. We often think of service in terms of doing the community a favor by donating our time. We go into the community, perform the service, and then retreat to our home—separate from the community. This parable invites us to approach service as a "bridging social capital" experience in which you acknowledge your connection to the community. The Samaritan did not just drop the man at the inn. He changed his travel plans and spent the night at the inn. He promised to come back and attend to the victim's needs.

We sometimes tend to approach service as a "one-off" activity, such as serving a meal at a soup kitchen or a homeless shelter. There is nothing wrong with this certainly admirable donation of one's time. This parable, however, suggests further action. In the sculpture, we see the Samaritan literally and figuratively making the effort to lift the victim from his present condition. The notion of further action is a challenging proposition because it requires more time, and potentially, resources—just as the Samaritan pledged to the innkeeper. Leadership is a responsibility to the community.

Leadership as social responsibility has gained wider acceptance in recent decades, particularly through embracing concepts such as corporate social responsibility (CSR) and social entrepreneurship. CSR rejects the contention that the sole responsibility of a business organization is profit maximization. Instead, it adds social issues and sustainability to the priority list. For instance, organizations now talk about the "triple bottom line"—a reference to people (social issues), planet (sustainability), and profits (economic impact), as opposed to a single bottom line—profits.[16] This holistic view of social responsibility helps break down barriers that separate different sectors of society, much in the same way that Sicard's statue shows the victim and the Samaritan closely intertwined.[17]

In social entrepreneurship, leaders and followers focus on using innovative and creative approaches to solve social problems.[18] While the business sector includes profit making as one of the "triple bottom line" motivations, the social entrepreneur uses business development techniques in order to address social challenges.[19] Organizations engaged in social entrepreneurship are encouraged to look at challenges in new ways and take risks. Social entrepreneurs are defined in terms of activism. They respond to a specific call by acting on the challenge and developing the creative solutions that will address social needs.

This bottom-up approach to leadership does not usually involve individuals with positional power. In the parable, the Samaritan is not associated with any title or position of privilege, compared to the priest and Levite. Nevertheless, he responds to an idea ("Love your neighbor as yourself") that generates the energy that brings people together in powerful ways. Muhammad Yunus is widely used as a role model of social entrepreneurship using this type of follower-centric approach to leadership.[20] Through his bank, Grameen, the Bangladeshi social entrepreneur developed a pioneering micro-loan program that gave seemingly high-risk business entrepreneurs access to capital, otherwise unavailable from traditional banks.

Like the Samaritan, Yunus did not help aspiring entrepreneurs because he wanted the spotlight (Nobel Prize). Rather, he was motivated by an identified social need—access to capital by the poor. Nevertheless, the Norwegian Nobel

Committee, when announcing the 2006 Nobel Peace Prize to Yunus and his bank, noted, "Muhammad Yunus has shown himself to be a leader who has managed to translate visions into practical action for the benefit of millions of people, not only in Bangladesh, but also in many other countries."[21]

Both corporate social responsibility and social entrepreneurship are examples of collaboration among diverse players who contribute to the greater good. They bring together for-profit, nonprofit, higher education, and the public sector in creative ways to strengthen the "WE" side of the leadership continuum. While we may debate their motivations, our focus here is on innovation, risk taking, and bold thinking. Regardless of the Samaritan's motivation for stopping to help the wounded victim, in the end, the victim was better off. In the process, the Samaritan set the example for others to follow.

What happens when leaders and followers' actions move beyond the local cultural context and challenge us to see the greater good at the "human level"? In the parable, we can see the Samaritan serving a greater cause, beyond helping a wounded victim. He is serving humanity.[22]

The radical nature of the parable becomes even more evident when one considers Sicard's depiction of the two main characters. Notice the difference between Sicard's sculpture (Figure 14.1) and Baldassare Verazzi's depiction of the scene (Figure 14.3). Observe the presentation of the two in terms of their nakedness. Traditional paintings of the parable often show the Samaritan dressed in expensive clothes, while the victim is half-naked (and what clothes he does have are usually torn and dirty). This contrast illustrates a traditional view of the more fortunate helping the less fortunate. Sicard takes a different approach to the depiction of the two characters. They are both unclothed and their torso skin is touching, as if at that moment their fortunes are linked. This is not unlike the idea of transformational leadership that we discussed in Chapter 13.

In the previous chapter, we discussed James MacGregor Burns' definition of leadership in terms of transformation—leaders and followers working together to elevate one another toward a higher level of morality. Jesus' criticism of the religious leaders of his day focused on the way leaders can sometimes be caught in the role they are playing to such a confining extent that they miss out on opportunities to engage in radical action that can lift up humanity.

What happens when local values contradict those at the "humanity level"? Many of the historical figures associated with this moral dimension of leadership—Nelson Mandela, Mahatma Gandhi, Mother Teresa, and Martin Luther King, to name but a few—were not global icons when they first began their work. They were ordinary citizens who took on an extraordinary vision of society. What connects them is a deep commitment to addressing injustices that they observed around them and deciding to take action.

In a way, these icons reflected the Samaritan's mindset. They saw the greater good as more important than their own individual interest and local norms. In confronting the victim, the Samaritan could have conformed to the local

Figure 14.3 Baldassare Verazzi (1819–1886), "The Parable of the Samaritan," 1851

Oil on canvas, 176 × 276 cm
Accademia Di Bella Arti Di Brera Quadreria, Milan
Photo credit: © DeA Picture Library/Art Resource, New York

customs and avoided contact with someone outside of his group. However, there was a moral imperative ("Love your neighbor as yourself") that moved him into action, despite local norms.

Both the sculpture and the garden demonstrate this connection between moral imperatives and action. Sicard's sculpture symbolically shows Burns' conception of leadership in action (the process by which leaders and followers elevate themselves to a higher level of morality). The transformation of the garden from a private space for the privileged few to a public space for the enjoyment of the collective also has symbolic value. This transformation showed how leaders and followers can rebel against local customs and challenge the cultural context in the name of a higher moral imperative—liberty, equality, and fraternity (the motto of the French Revolution).

However, acting on a moral imperative often comes with a high price. Once leaders and followers decide to challenge the status quo and fight for a higher moral imperative, the stakes become much higher. Mandela defied the local authorities and spent 27 years in jail.[23] King and Gandhi had to contend with abuse and ultimately paid with their lives.[24] Mother Theresa gave up a great deal to help others.[25] By attending to the higher moral imperative of social justice, they all made themselves vulnerable.

Two thousand years ago, the road between Jerusalem and Jericho was a perilous journey with twists and turns and perfect for an ambush. Jesus picked an excellent place to illustrate a moment of vulnerability in anyone's journey.[26] The Samaritan, therefore, was a risk taker who sought to address the needs of others before his own. His actions seem to defy rationality and invite us to consider other opportunities to lead with vulnerability.

The relationship of the first three components of our leadership model (leaders and followers working together toward a common goal) provides the framework from which to further analyze this concept—leading with vulnerability. Vulnerability requires certain attributes from the leader. In particular, we can emphasize the importance of courage, risk taking, and humility. The Samaritan displayed tremendous courage when coming to the aid of the victim. As he decided to take the risk, the main focus of the parable became how his actions made a difference in the person's life. It was not about the Samaritan; and that is one of the reasons we chose Sicard's sculpture as the artifact. He is elevating the victim as if to say—my actions are about the victim, and that should be the focus of our attention.

Leaders are not the only ones who are vulnerable; followers must also be willing to take risks. Leadership by its very nature is a collective effort. The innkeeper had to trust the Samaritan to return to settle the account. Followers also invest themselves in leadership and take risks. Mandela, Gandhi, Mother Teresa, and King did not act alone in their movements. Thousands of their followers risked and lost their lives for the same aspirations. It is a huge disservice to our understanding of leadership to think that leaders single handedly bring about change.

Finally, in reference to the common goal, leading with vulnerability often involves a bold vision of the future. What compels leaders and followers to act courageously and take risks is a compelling cause that stirs their passion. While many charismatic leaders are able to sway the masses toward their dreams, the vision itself has to resonate with their followers at a deeper level. In this chapter, we have challenged you to see leadership not simply as the transaction between leaders and followers toward a common goal. Rather, as Sicard's sculpture aptly illustrates, leadership may also involve the ways individuals are brought together—at times, in unexpected ways—in order to serve humanity.

Summary and concluding remarks

In Part III, we highlighted three possible answers to the "Leadership for what?" question—to develop oneself, to develop others, and to contribute to the greater good. Each of these three perspectives has a place on the leadership continuum (Figure 14.4). Leadership for personal development falls under the leader-centric

For personal development	For developing others	For the greater good
"I" (Individualism)		(Collectivism) "**WE**"
Primacy of the leader		Primacy of the group
		Socially responsible leadership

Figure 14.4 Leadership for the greater good on the leadership continuum

side of the continuum. Leadership for developing others is placed in the middle—half-way between the two extremes. Both the leader and the followers are served in the process. Leadership for the greater good takes us beyond the individual interests of the leaders and followers.

These three approaches to leadership development are not mutually exclusive. Rather, they can complement one another. As you strive to develop yourself so you can become an authentic leader, as Chapter 12 discussed, the lessons you learn along the way can assist you in your role of developing others, as Chapter 13 explored. Before you help others, it is certainly helpful that you first know yourself. Leadership for the greater good, as this chapter showed, focuses on how leaders and followers attend to the interests of the collective.

By stopping to aid the victim, the Samaritan became an atypical character; and that made him an authentic leader. The Samaritan acted based on his values, even though it made him vulnerable in the process. This required courage and commitment to the needs of others. Through his unquestioned devotion to the needs of others, he also demonstrated how others should act. The parable serves as a powerful tool to educate others about leading with vulnerability. His actions have come to embody a much larger message about the greater good: "Love your neighbor as yourself."

In this chapter, we have invited you to move beyond the Western perspective of seeing leadership as a prize, and instead incorporate notions of leadership as a social trust and service to greater causes. Part II introduced you to a variety of cultural perspectives on leadership. We challenge you to assess your own cultural map and see how these different perspectives can assist you in developing the skills that will allow you to contribute to the greater good.

We do not want you to think that only larger-than-life leaders can make a difference in the world. Remember that we began this book drawing attention to our often idealized view of leadership through the rather grandiose image of George Washington crossing the Delaware. We are closing this book with a parallel image—Sicard's sculpture of an unnamed Samaritan helping a stranger and changing his travel plans in order to accommodate someone else's needs. This Samaritan has remained unnamed for 2000 years, but his actions continue to inspire societies to act boldly. The lesson should be clear—we do not need to be in a position of great authority and power to seek the greater good and have an impact.

A final thought that we challenge you to consider is that the parable's answer to the question (Who is my neighbor?) is only one example of how to contribute to the greater good. In this chapter, we also drew a connection between the sculpture and the place in which it is now located—the Tuileries Gardens in Paris. The garden, once the domain of royal families, is now a public park that allows the community to celebrate many aspects of the greater good, such as liberty, equality, and fraternity. As you become an authentic leader, you may inspire others to contribute their own passion to other causes that will benefit society in immeasurable ways.

Questions for discussion

- Assess social capital in your community. Is it high? It is low? Why? Consider the individuals and organizations that contribute to the social capital increase/decrease in your community.
- What is the role of community service in your society? How does community service contribute to the greater good?
- How is "success" defined from a greater good perspective?
- How do you personally contribute to the greater good as a leader/follower?

Additional resources

B.L. Koenig, *Going Global for the Greater Good: Succeeding as a Nonprofit in the International Community*, San Francisco: Jossey-Bass, 2004.

G. Levenson Keohane, *Social Entrepreneurship for the 21st Century: Innovation across the Nonprofit, Private, and Public Sectors*, New York: McGraw-Hill, 2013.

T.R. McFaul, *The Future of Peace and Justice in the Global Village: The Role of the World Religions in the Twenty-First Century*, Westport, CT: Praeger, 2006.

S. Waddock, *The Difference Makers: How Social and Institutional Entrepreneurs Created the Corporate Responsibility Movement*, Sheffield: Greenleaf Publishing, 2008.

Notes

1 Leadership, as a discipline, is not alone in pursuing this focus on the greater good. Other disciplines and professional tracks also have found a connection between their disciplinary/career aspirations and contributing to the greater good. See, for instance, J. Olson-Buchanan, L. Koppes Bryan, and L. Foster Thompson, eds., *Using Industrial Organizational Psychology for the Greater Good: Helping Those Who Help Others*, London: Routledge, 2013; J.A. Quelch and K.E. Jocz, *Greater Good: How Good Marketing Makes for Better Democracy*, Boston, MA: Harvard Business Press, 2007. Higher education also has advanced its aspirations within the context of the greater good. See W.W. McMahon, *Higher Learning, Greater Good: The Private and Social Benefits of Higher Education*, Baltimore, MD: Johns Hopkins University Press, 2009.

2 D.R. Forsyth and C.L. Hoyt, eds., *For the Greater Good of All: Perspectives on Individualism, Society, and Leadership*, New York: Palgrave Macmillan, 2011.

3 Sicard was born in the central city of Tours, France, where he studied at the Fine Arts School (L'école des Beaux-Arts) under Félix Laurent.

4   In Paris, Sicard studied under Louis-Ernest Barrias—a talented sculptor who had helped shape the Parisian art scene during the Franco-Prussian War (1870–1871). See H. Clayson, *Paris in Despair: Art and Everyday Life under Siege (1870–71)*, Chicago: University of Chicago Press, 2002.

5   Mark Leuchter and Jeremy M. Hutton, eds., *Levites and Priests in History and Tradition*, Boston, MA: Brill, 2011; Risto Nurmela, *The Levites: Their Emergence as a Second-Class Priesthood*, Atlanta, GA: Scholars Press, 1998.

6   T. Kazen, *Issues of Impurity in Early Judaism*, Winona Lake, IN: Eisenbrauns, 2010.

7   Delacroix painted another version of the parable in 1852, in which he provided this view of the Samaritan being a more dominant character on the canvas.

8   J. Pissarro and S. Rachum, *Camille Pissarro: Impressionist Innovator*, Jerusalem: Israel Museum, 1994; K. Adler, *Camille Pissarro: A Biography*, London: Batsford, 1978.

9   Pissarro himself helped shape impressionism as an artistic movement. His work was not allowed to be exhibited in the Salon in Paris because of its radical nature. In response, he organized a collective in 1873, which provided an alternative exhibition venue for artists who eventually developed the impressionist movement. In a way, Pissarro himself bucked conventional norms, just as the Good Samaritan did, and modeled the leadership needed to break new ground in the art world.

10 Queen Catherine de Medici was from Florence and used Renaissance-style tiles to decorate the garden—hence, the name of the garden (*tuileries* meaning "tilery" in French).

11 The conflict also traces its roots to the aftermath of the Franco-Prussian War (July 19, 1870–May 10, 1871), which left France under a National Assembly controlled by the conservative provinces' majority that did not share the same values as the working class in Paris. The national government sought to disarm the National Guard made up of workers who had fought in Paris during the German siege of the city. As the new national government sought to exert its authority over the whole country, the Paris Commune became a point of resistance against authoritarianism. See D. Gluckstein, *The Paris Commune: A Revolution in Democracy*, Chicago: Haymarket Books, 2011; R. Tombs, *The Paris Commune, 1871*, New York: Longman, 1999; A. Horne, *The Fall of Paris: The Siege and the Commune*, New York: St. Martin's Press, 1965.

12 Jesus used this type of shock value—Jews interacting with Samaritans in a positive way—to draw attention to his radical message. Also see when he addressed the Samaritan woman at the well (John 4) and the healing of a Samaritan man (Luke 17).

13 R.D. Putnam and L.M. Feldstein, *Better Together: Restoring the American Community*, New York: Simon & Schuster, 2003, p. 2.

14 Putnam and Feldstein worry that the United States, as a society, is moving too much to the "I" side of the leadership continuum and not attending to the "WE" collective side. They call for citizens to work more closely in their communities to increase social capital. Putnam famously sounded the alarm of a declining social capital in the United States in his *Bowling Alone: The Collapse and Revival of American Community*, New York: Simon & Schuster, 2000. See also his chapter, "Bowling Alone: America's Declining Social Capital," in Martin J. Gannon, ed., *Cultural Metaphors: Readings, Research Translations, and Commentary*, Thousand Oaks, CA: Sage, 2001, pp. 109–124.

15 This notion of increasing social capital has been applied to many different areas in a society. See, for instance, M. Calvert, M. Emery, and S. Kinsey, eds., *Youth Programs as Builders of Social Capital*, San Francisco: Jossey-Bass/Wiley, 2013; A.C. Costa and N. Anderson, eds., *Trust and Social Capital in Organizations*, Los Angeles: Sage, 2013; F. Masciarelli, *The Strategic Value of Social Capital: How Firms Capitalize on Social Assets*, Cheltenham: Edward Elgar, 2011.

16 A.W. Savitz and K. Weber, *The Triple Bottom Line: How Today's Best-Run Companies are Achieving Economic, Social, and Environmental Success—And How You Can Too*, San Francisco: Jossey-Bass, 2014.

17 The Harvard Kennedy School Corporate Social Responsibility Initiative—launched with support from corporations such as Chevron, Coca-Cola, and General Motors—claims that CSR "encompasses not only what companies do with their profits, but also how they make them. It goes beyond philanthropy and compliance and addresses how companies manage their economic, social, and environmental impacts, as well as their relationships in all key spheres of influence: the workplace, the marketplace, the supply chain, the community, and the public policy realm." Available at http://www.hks.harvard.edu/m-rcbg/CSRI/init_define.html. Accessed June 19, 2014.

18 B. Herchmer, *Leadership for Active Creative Engaged Communities*, Bloomington, IN: Universe Inc., 2012.

19 M. Clark, *The Social Entrepreneur Revolution: Doing Good by Making Money, Making Money by Doing Good*, London: Marshall Cavendish Business, 2009.

20 J.A. Harris, *Transformative Entrepreneurs: How Walt Disney, Steve Jobs, Muhammad Yunus, and Other Innovators Succeeded*, New York: Palgrave Macmillan, 2012.

21 "Nobel Peace Prize for 2006 to Muhammad Yunus and Grameen Bank—Press Release." Nobelprize.org. Available at http://www.nobelprize.org/nobel_prizes/peace/laureates/2006/press.html. Accessed June 21, 2014.

22 In some artistic interpretations of the parable, the Good Samaritan is identified as Jesus himself—a servant leader who chose as his mission to care for humanity. See R.A. Belliotti, *Jesus the Radical: The Parables of Modern Morality*, Lanham, MD: Lexington Books, 2013.

23 B. Denenberg, *Nelson Mandela: "No Easy Walk to Freedom,"* New York: Scholastic Inc., 2014; see also a profile of Mandela as a transformational leader in R.I. Rotberg, *Transformative Political Leadership: Making a Difference in the Developing World*, Chicago: University of Chicago Press, 2012, pp. 40–65.

24 D.J. Garrow, *Bearing the Cross: Martin Luther King, Jr., and the Southern Christian Leadership Conference*, New York: Perennial Classics, 2004. For insights about King's approach to leadership, see D.T. Phillips, *Martin Luther King, Jr., on Leadership: Inspiration and Wisdom for Challenging Times*, New York: Warner Books, 2001.

25 L.C. Slavicek, *Mother Theresa: Caring for the World's Poor*, New York: Chelsea House, 2007. E. Le Joly, *We Do it for Jesus: Mother Teresa and Her Missionaries of Charity*, New York: Oxford University Press, 1998.

26 For further insights on this topic, see D. A. Dorsey, *The Roads and Highways of Ancient Israel*, Baltimore, MD: Johns Hopkins University Press, 1991.

Bibliography

Abdulai, D.A. "Cultural Mythology and Global Leadership in South Africa," in E.H. Kessler and D.J. Wong-Mingji, *Cultural Mythology and Global Leadership*. Cheltenham: Edward Elgar, 2009.

Adair, J. *The Leadership of Muhammad*. Philadelphia, PA: Kogan Page, 2010.

Adler, K. *Camille Pissarro: A Biography*. London: Batsford, 1978.

Ahmed, A.S. "Foreword," in T. Sonn, *A Brief History of Islam*. Malden, MA: Blackwell, 2004.

Ali, A. *Islamic Perspectives on Management and Organization*. Cheltenham: Edward Elgar, 2005.

Ali, A.J. "Leadership and Islam," in B.D. Metcalfe and F. Mimouni, eds., *Leadership Development in the Middle East*. Cheltenham: Edward Elgar, 2012.

Alsop, M. "Dvořák's Symphonic Journey to the New World." *Weekend Edition Saturday*. National Public Radio, April 18, 2008. http://www.npr.org/templates/story/story.php?storyId=89758808.

Armstrong, K. *Muhammad: A Biography of the Prophet*. New York: HarperCollins, 1992.

Arnason, J.P., K.A. Raaflaub, and P. Wagner, eds. *The Greek Polis and the Invention of Democracy: A Politico-Cultural Transformation and its Interpretations*. Malden, MA: Wiley-Blackwell, 2013.

Asturias, M.Á. *The President*, translated by F. Partridge. Prospect Heights, IL: Waveland Press, 1997.

Asturias, M.Á. *Legends of Guatemala*, translated by K. Washbourne. Pittsburgh: Latin American Literary Review Press, 2011.

Avolio, B. *Full Leadership Development: Building the Vital Forces in Organizations*. Thousand Oaks, CA: Sage, 1999.

Barner, R. *Accelerating Your Development as a Leader: A Guide for Leaders and Their Managers*. San Francisco: Pfeiffer, 2011.

Barnes, T. *Constantine: Dynasty, Religion and Power in the Later Roman Empire*. Malden, MA: Wiley-Blackwell, 2011.

Barnhart, M.G. "Theory and Comparison in the Discussion of Buddhist Ethics." *Philosophy East and West*, 62, January (2012): 16–23.

Bass, B.M. *Leadership, Psychology, and Organizational Behavior*. New York: Harper & Brothers, 1960.

—— *Leadership and Performance Beyond Expectations*. New York: Free Press, 1985.

Bass, B.M., and B.J. Avolio. *Improving Organizational Effectiveness Through Transformational Leadership*. Thousand Oaks, CA: Sage, 1994.

Bass, B.M., and R. Bass. *The Bass Handbook of Leadership: Theory, Research and Managerial Applications*, 4th edn. New York: Free Press, 2008.

—— "Followers and Mutual Influence on Leadership," in *The Bass Handbook of Leadership: Theory, Research, and Managerial Applications*, 4th edn. New York: Free Press, 2008.

Bass, B.M., and R.E. Riggio. *Transformational Leadership*, 2nd edn. Mahwah, NJ: Lawrence Erlbaum, 2006.

Bass, B.M., and J.A. Vaughan. *Training in Industry: The Management of Learning*. Belmont, CA: Wadsworth, 1966.

Beach, V.W. *Charles X of France: His Life and Times*. Boulder, CO: Pruett, 1971.

Beckerman, M.B. *New Worlds of Dvořák: Searching in America for the Composer's Inner Life*. New York: W.W. Norton & Company, 2003.

Beekun R. "Effective Leadership Steps for Strategy Implementation in Islamic Organizations." http://makkah.wordpress.com/leadership-and-islam.

Beekun, R.I., and J. Badawi. *Leadership: An Islamic Perspective*. Beltsville, MD: Amana, 1999.

Bell, D.A. *China's New Confucianism: Politics and Everyday Life in a Changing Society*. Princeton, NJ: Princeton University Press, 2008.

Belliotti, R.A. *Jesus the Radical: The Parables of Modern Morality*. Lanham, MD: Lexington Books, 2013.

Bentham, J. *The Principles of Morals and Legislation*. Amherst, NY: Prometheus Books, 1988.

Berridge, G.R., M. Keens-Soper, and T.G. Otte, eds. *Diplomatic Theory from Machiavelli to Kissinger*. New York: Palgrave, 2001.

Berstein, L. *A Book-Of-The-Month Club Music Appreciation Record*. "Symphony Number 5 in E Minor, Opus 95, *From the New World* Sound recording. 1956. https://www.youtube.com/watch?v=79D5sOD5duE.

Bhagat, R.S., H.C. Triandis, and A.S. McDevitt. *Managing Global Organizations: A Cultural Perspective*. Northampton, MA: Edward Elgar, 2012.

Bligh, M.C. "Followership and Follower-Centered Approaches," in A. Bryman, D. Collinson, K. Grint, B. Jackson, and M. Uhl-Bien, eds. *The Sage Handbook of Leadership*. Los Angeles: Sage, 2011.

Boahen, A.A. *African Perspectives on Colonialism*. Baltimore, MD: Johns Hopkins University Press, 1989.

Bokelmann, W., O. Akinwumi, U.M. Nwankwo, and A.O. Agwuele. *African Leadership Challenges and Other Issues*. Berlin: Mediateam IT Educational Publishers, 2012.

Bonds, M. *Wordless Rhetoric: Musical Form as the Metaphor of the Oration*. Cambridge: Harvard University Press, 1991.

Boon, M. *The African Way: The Power of Interactive Leadership*, 3rd edn. Cape Town, South Africa: Zebra Press, 2007.

Bostanov, V., P.M. Keune, B. Kotchoubey, and M. Hautzinger. "Event-related Brain Potentials Reflect Increased Concentration Ability after Mindfulness-based Cognitive Therapy for Depression: A Randomized Clinical Trial." *Psychiatry Research*, 199, 3 (2012): 174–180.

Boulby, M. *Hermann Hesse: His Mind and Art*. Ithaca, NY: Cornell University Press, 1967.

Boyatzis, R., and A. McKee. *Resonate Leadership: Renewing Yourself and Connecting with Others Through Mindfulness, Hope, and Compassion*. Boston, MA: Harvard Business School Press, 2005.

Bringmann, K. *A History of the Roman Republic*, translated by W.J. Smyth. Malden, MA: Polity, 2007.

Brookhiser, R. *George Washington on Leadership*. New York: Basic Books, 2008. [Reprint, New York: Basic Books, 2009.]

Burke, K. *The Philosophy of Literary Form*, 3rd edn. Berkeley: University of California Press, 1973.

Burnley, M. "*The Message*: The Movie about Islam that Sparked a Hostage Crisis in D.C." *The Atlantic*, November 20, 2012. http://www.theatlantic.com/international/archive/2012/11/the-message-the-movie-about-islam-that-sparked-a-hostage-crisis-in-dc/264939.

Burns, J.M. *Leadership*. New York: Harper & Row, 1978.

—— "Foreword," in R.A. Couto, ed., *Reflections on Leadership*. New York: University Press of America, 2007.

Bushnell, D., and L. D. Langley, eds. *Simón Bolívar: Essays on the Life and Legacy of the Liberator*. Lanham MD: Rowman & Littlefield Publishing, 2008.

Butler, S.J. *Britain and its Empire in the Shadow of Rome: The Reception of Rome in Socio-Political Debate from the 1850s to the 1920s*. New York: Bloomsbury, 2012.

Caiani, A.A. *Louis XVI and the French Revolution, 1789–1792*. Cambridge: Cambridge University Press, 2012.

Calvert, M., M. Emery, and S. Kinsey, eds. *Youth Programs as Builders of Social Capital*. San Francisco: Jossey-Bass/Wiley, 2013.

Campbell, R.A. "Leadership Succession in Early Islam: Exploring the Nature and Role of Historical Precedents." *Leadership Quarterly*, 19 (2008): 426–428.

Canals, J., ed. *Leadership Development in a Global World: the Role of Companies and Business Schools*. New York: Palgrave Macmillan, 2012.

Carbone, G.M. *Washington: Lessons in Leadership*. New York: Palgrave Macmillan, 2010.

Carlyle, T. *On Heroes, Hero-Worship and the Heroic in History*. London: Oxford University Press, 1928.

Carmagnani, M. *The Other West: Latin America from Invasion to Globalization*, translated by R.M. Giammanco Frongia. Berkeley: University of California Press, 2011.

Carroll, M. *The Mindful Leader: Awakening Your Natural Management Skills Through Mindfulness Meditation*. Boston, MA: Trumpeter, 2011.

Cartron, M.B. *La Deuxième Révolution Française: Juillet 1830* [The Second French Revolution: July 1830]. Paris: Artena, 2005.

Caulker-Bronson, F.Y. "African Dance: Divine Motion," in M.H. Nadel and M.R. Strauss, *The Dance Experience*, 3rd edn. Hightstown, NJ: Princeton Book Company Publishers, 2014.

Cerra, A., K. Easterwood, and J. Power, *Transforming Business: Big Data, Mobility, and Globalization*. Hoboken, NJ: Wiley, 2013.

Chai, C., and W. Chai, eds. and trans. *The Sacred Books of Confucius and Other Confucian Classics*. New York: Bantam Books, 1965.

Chaleff, I. *The Courageous Follower: Standing Up To and For Our Leaders*, 3rd edn. San Francisco: Berrett-Koehler Publishers, 2009.

Chalier, C. *What Ought I to Do? Morality in Kant and Levinas*, translated by Jane Marie Todd. Ithaca, NY: Cornell University Press, 2002.

Chaplin, C. *My Autobiography*. London: Bodley Head, 1964.

Chasteen, J.C., ed. *Born in Blood and Fire: Latin American Voices*. New York: W.W. Norton & Company, 2011.

Cheng, C., and Y. Lee, eds. *Leadership and Management in China*. Cambridge: Cambridge University Press, 2008.

Ching, J. *Confucianism and Taoism*. Ashland, OR: Blackstone Audio, 2006.

Church, C.H. *Europe in 1830: Revolution and Political Change*. Boston, MA: Allen & Unwin, 1983.

Clark, M. *The Social Entrepreneur Revolution: Doing Good by Making Money, Making Money by Doing Good*. London: Marshall Cavendish Business, 2009.

Clayson, H. *Paris in Despair: Art and Everyday Life under Siege (1870–71)*. Chicago: University of Chicago Press, 2002.

Cleary, T. *The Book of Leadership and Strategy: Lessons of the Chinese Masters. Translations from the Taoist Classic Huainanzi*. Boston, MA: Shambhala, 1992.

Cleugh, J. *The Medici: A Tale of Fifteen Generations*. New York: Dorset Press, 1990.

Coffin, J.G., and R.C. Stacey. *Western Civilizations: Their History & Their Culture*. New York: W.W. Norton & Co., 2012.

Cohen, D. *How the Child's Mind Develops*. London: Routledge, 2013.

Coleman, W. and A. Sajed. *Fifty Key Thinkers on Globalization*. New York: Routledge, 2013.

"Collaborative Leadership: Play it Like in an African Circle Dance." Skoll World Forum on Social Entrepreneurship. http://skollworldforum.org/2010/04/26/collaborative-leadership-play-it-like-in-an-african-circle-dance/.

Colleran, J. "Athol Fugard and the Problematics of the Liberal Critique." *Modern Drama*, 38, 8 (1995): 389–407.

Cook, D.A. *A History of Narrative Film*, 2nd edn. New York: W.W. Norton, 1980.

Costa, A.C., and N. Anderson, eds. *Trust and Social Capital in Organizations*. Los Angeles: Sage, 2013.

Cottrell, D., and E. Harvey. *Leadership Courage: Leadership Strategies for Individual and Organizational Success*. Dallas, TX: Walk the Talk, 2004.

Cracknell, D.G., and C.H. Wilson. *Roman Law: Origins and Influence*. London: HLT, 1990.

Creel, H.G. *What is Taoism? And Other Studies in Chinese Cultural History*. Chicago IL: University of Chicago Press, 1970.

Creelman, J. "Real Value of Negro Melodies." *New York Herald*, May 21, 1893.

Cronin, T.E., and M.A. Genovese. *The Paradoxes of the American Presidency*. New York: Oxford University Press, 1998.

Crothers, L. *Globalization and American Popular Culture*. Lanham, MD: Rowman & Littlefield Publishers, 2013.

Crum, R.J., and J.T. Paoletti, eds. *Renaissance Florence: A Social History*. New York: Cambridge University Press, 2008.

Cummings, M. "A World without Collisions: 'Master Harold' . . . and the Boys in the Classroom." *English Journal*, 78, 6 (1989): 72.

Curtin, P.D. *The Atlantic Slave Trade: A Census*. Madison, WI: University of Wisconsin Press, 1969.

Dalai Lama, and L. Van Den Muyzenberg. *The Leader's Way: The Art of Making the Right Decisions in our Careers, Our Companies, and the World at Large*. New York: Broadway Books, 2009.

de Bary, W.T. *Nobility and Civility, Asian Ideas of Leadership and the Common Good*. Boston, MA: Harvard University Press, 2004.

de Vries, D. "The Role of Culture and History in the Applicability of Western Leadership Theories in Africa," in J.D. Barbour, G.J. Burgess, L.L. Falkman, and R. M. McManus, eds. *Leading in Complex Worlds*, San Francisco: Jossey-Bass, 2012.

Denenberg, B. *Nelson Mandela: "No Easy Walk to Freedom."* New York: Scholastic Inc., 2014.

DePree, M. *Leadership is an Art.* New York: Dell Trade, 1989.

Dickmann, M.H., and N. Stanford-Blair. *Mindful Leadership: A Brain Based Framework*, 2nd edn. Thousand Oaks, CA: Corwin Press, 2009.

Diop, C.A. *The African Origin of Civilization: Myth or Reality*, ed. and translated by M. Cook. Chicago: Lawrence Hill, 1974.

Diop, C.A. *Towards the African Renaissance: Essays in African Culture and Development, 1946–1960.* Trenton, NJ: Red Sea Press, 2000.

Donahue, F. "Apartheid's Dramatic Legacy." *Midwest Quarterly*, 36, 3 (1995): 323–330.

Dorsey, D.A. *The Roads and Highways of Ancient Israel.* Baltimore, MD: Johns Hopkins University Press, 1991.

Dosal, P.J. *Doing Business with the Dictators: A Political History of United Fruit in Guatemala, 1899–1944.* Wilmington, DE: SR Books, 1993.

Dreher, D. *The Tao of Personal Leadership.* New York: HarperCollins, 1996.

Durbach, E. "'Master Harold' . . . and the Boys: Athol Fugard and the Psychopathology of Apartheid." *Modern Drama*, 30, 4 (1987): 505–513.

Durlabhji, S. "The Tao of Organization Behavior." *Journal of Business Ethics*, 53, 4 (2004): 401–409.

Eagan, J.M. *Maximilian Robespierre: Nationalist Dictator.* New York: AMS Press, 1970.

Everitt, A. *The Rise of Rome: The Making of the World's Greatest Empire.* New York: Random House, 2012.

Faris, N., and K. Parry. "Islamic Organizational Leadership within a Western Society: The Problematic Role of External Context." *Leadership Quarterly*, 22 (2011): 132–151.

Feldman, R.S. *Child Development.* Boston, MA: Pearson, 2012.

Fiedler, F. *Leader Attitudes and Group Effectiveness.* Urbana: University of Illinois Press, 1958.

Field, G.W. *Hermann Hesse.* New York: Twayne Publishers, Inc., 1970.

Fischer, D.H. *Washington's Crossing.* Oxford: Oxford University Press, 2006.

Flynn, M.J., and S.E. Griffin. *Washington & Napoleon: Leadership in the Age of Revolution.* Dulles, VA: Potomac Books, 2012.

Follett, M.P. "The Essentials of Leadership," in P. Graham, ed. *Mary Parker Follett – Prophet of Management: A Celebration of Writings from the 1920s.* Boston, MA: Harvard Business School Press, 1995.

Forsyth, D.R., and C.L. Hoyt, eds. *For the Greater Good of All: Perspectives on Individualism, Society, and Leadership.* New York: Palgrave Macmillan, 2011.

Foss, S.K. *Rhetorical Criticism: Exploration and Practice*, 3rd edn. Long Grove, IL: Waveland Press, 2004.

Fowler, W. *Santa Anna of Mexico.* Lincoln: University of Nebraska Press, 2007.

Fraser, A. *The Healing Power of Meditation.* Boston, MA: Shambhala Publications, 2013.

Friedman, M. "The Friedman Doctrine: The Social Responsibility of Business is to Increase its Profits." *The New York Times Magazine*, September 13, 1970. http://query.nytimes.com/mem/archive-free/pdf?res=9E05E0DA153CE531A15750C1A96F9C946190D6CF.

Fu, C., and R. Bergeon. "A Tao Model: Rethinking Modern Leadership for Transformation," in J. Danelo Barbour and G. Robinson Hickman, eds. *Leadership for Transformation.* San Francisco: Jossey-Bass, 2011.

Fu, C., and R. Bergeon. "A Tao Complexity Tool: Leading from Being," in J. Danelo Barbour, G. J. Burgess, L. Lid Falkman, and R. M. McManus, eds. *Leading in Complex Worlds.* San Francisco: Jossey-Bass, 2012.

Fugard, A. *Notebooks 1960–1977*. New York: Theater Communications Group, 1990.
—— "Some Problems of a Playwright from South Africa." *Twentieth Century Literature*, 29, 4 (1993): 381–393.
—— *"Master Harold" . . . and the Boys*. New York: Random House, 2009.
Furneaux, R. *The Last Days of Marie Antoinette and Louis XVI*. New York: Dorset Press, 1990.
"The Future of the Global Muslim Population." Pew Research Religion and Public Life Project. Last modified January 27, 2011. http://www.pewforum.org/2011/01/27/the-future-of-the-global-muslim-population/.
Gane, M. *Auguste Comte*. New York: Routledge, 2006.
Gardner, J.W. *On Leadership*. New York: Free Press, 1990.
Gardner, W.L., B.J. Avolio, and F.O. Walumbwa, eds. *Authentic Leadership Theory and Practice: Origins, Effects and Development*. Oxford: Elsevier JAI, 2005.
Garrow, D.J. *Bearing the Cross: Martin Luther King, Jr., and the Southern Christian Leadership Conference*. New York: Perennial Classics, 2004.
George, B. Interview by N. Branton. *Leadership Coach Academy*. Online. January 17, 2008.
George, B. *Authentic Leadership: Rediscovering the Secrets to Creating Lasting Value*. San Francisco: Jossey-Bass, 2014.
George, B., and D. Baker. *True North Groups: A Powerful Path to Personal and Leadership Development*. San Francisco: Berrett-Koehler Publishers, 2011.
George, B., P. Sims, A.N. McLean, and D. Mayer. "Discovering your Authentic Leadership." *Harvard Business Review*, February 2007.
Gethin, R. *The Foundations of Buddhism*. Oxford: Oxford University Press, 1998.
Glover, T.R. *Democracy in the Ancient World*. New York: Macmillan, 1927.
Gluckstein, D. *The Paris Commune: A Revolution in Democracy*. Chicago: Haymarket Books, 2011.
Goldin, P.R. *Confucianism*. Berkeley: University of California Press, 2011.
Goldthwaite, R.A. *The Economy of Renaissance Florence*. Baltimore, MD: Johns Hopkins University Press, 2009.
Goleman, D. *Emotional Intelligence: Why It Can Matter More than IQ*. New York, Bantam, 1995.
Goleman, D. *Working with Emotional Intelligence*. New York: Bantam Books, 1998.
Goleman, D., and J.K. Zinn. *Mindfulness at Work*. New York: Macmillan Audio, 2007.
Goodman, C. "Consequentialism, Agent-Neutrality, and Mahayana Ethics." *Philosophy East and West*, 58, January (2008): 17–35.
Goodman Jr., P. *Latin America*, 8th edn. Guilford, CT: Dushkin/McGraw-Hill, 1998.
Gordon, J.U. *African Leadership in the Twentieth Century*. Lanham, MD: University Press of America, 2002.
Gorer, G. *Africa Dances*. New York: Penguin, 1945.
Gottfried, M. *Arthur Miller: His Life and Work*. Cambridge, MA: Da Capo Press, 2003.
Gough, H., and J. Horne, eds. *De Gaulle and Twentieth-Century France*. New York: Edward Arnold, 1994.
Gray, B., and M.P. Kriger. "Leadership Lessons and Indications from the Buddhist Tradition for Creating Adaptive Organizations." Symposium Paper Presentation from the Annual Meetings of the National Academy of Management, Honolulu, Hawaii, 2005.
Greenleaf, R.K. and L.C. Spears, eds. *Servant Leadership, 25th Anniversary Edition: A Journey into the Nature of Legitimate Power and Greatness*. Mahwah, NJ: Paulist Press, 2002.

Gregory, M.E. *Freedom in French Enlightenment Thought.* New York: Peter Lang, 2010.

Grieb, K. *Guatemalan Caudillo, the Regime of Jorge Ubico: Guatemala, 1931–1944.* Athens: Ohio University Press, 1979.

Griffin, E. *A First Look at Communication Theory,* 7th edn. Boston, MA: McGraw-Hill, 2009.

Grint, K. *Leadership: A Very Short Introduction.* Oxford: Oxford University Press, 2010.

Gronn, P. "Distributed Leadership as a Unit of Analysis." *Leadership Quarterly*, 13, 4 (2002): 423–451.

Gunlicks, L.F. *The Machiavellian Manager's Handbook for Success.* Lanham, MD: National Book Network, 1993.

Gussow, M. "Athol Fugard looks at a Master–Servant Friendship." *The New York Times*, March 21, 1982.

Haar, J., and J. Price, eds. *Can Latin America Compete? Confronting the Challenges of Globalization.* New York: Palgrave Macmillan, 2009.

Hale, J.R. *Machiavelli and Renaissance Italy.* New York: Collier Books, 1963.

Hale, J.R. *Florence and the Medici.* London: Phoenix, 2001.

Hall, J.L. "The Sound of Leadership: Transformational Leadership in Music." *Journal of Leadership Education*, 7, 2 (2008): 47–68.

Hall, L.B. "Evita Perón: Beauty, Resonance, and Heroism," in S. Brunk and B. Fallaw, eds. *Heroes and Hero Cults in Latin America.* Austin: University of Texas Press, 2006.

Hamerow, T.S. *Restoration, Revolution, Reaction: Economics and Politics in Germany, 1815–1871.* Princeton, NJ: Princeton University Press, 1958.

Hanh, T.N. *The Heart of the Buddha's Teaching.* Berkeley, CA: Parallax Press, 1998.

Hansen, M.H. *Polis: An Introduction to the Ancient Greek City-State.* New York: Oxford University Press, 2006.

Harness, K. *The Art of Charlie Chaplin: A Film-by-Film Analysis.* Jefferson, NC: McFarland & Company, 2008.

Harris, J.A. *Transformative Entrepreneurs: How Walt Disney, Steve Jobs, Muhammad Yunus, and Other Innovators Succeeded.* New York: Palgrave Macmillan, 2012.

Harvey, M., and R. Riggio, eds. *Leadership Studies: The Dialogue of Disciplines.* Cheltenham: Edward Elgar Publications, 2011.

Harvey, R. *Bolivar: The Liberator of Latin America.* New York: Skyhorse, 2011.

Heiberg, H. *Ibsen: A Portrait of the Artist,* translated by Joan Tate. Coral Gables, FL: University of Miami Press, 1969.

Heider, J. *The Tao of Leadership: Lao Tzu's Tao Te Ching Adapted for a New Age.* Atlanta, GA: Humanics New Age, 1985.

Heller, D. *Taoist Lessons for Educational Leaders, Gentle Pathways for Resolving Conflict.* Lanham, MD: Rowman & Littlefield Publishers, 2012.

Henighan, S. *Assuming the Light: The Parisian Literary Apprenticeship of Miguel Ángel Asturias.* Oxford: Legenda, 1999.

Herchmer, B. *Leadership for Active Creative Engaged Communities.* Bloomington, IN: Universe, 2012.

Herman, S.M. *The Tao at Work: On Leading and Following.* San Francisco: Jossey-Bass, 1994.

Hersey, P., and Blanchard K.H. *Management of Organizational Behavior.* Englewood Cliffs, NJ: Prentice Hall, 1969.

Hesse, H. *Siddhartha,* translated by Joachim Neugroschel. New York: Penguin Books, 1999.

Hibbert, C. *The House of the Medici: Its Rise and Fall.* New York: Perennial, 2003.

Higonnet, P. *Goodness Beyond Virtue: Jacobins during the French Revolution.* Cambridge: Harvard University Press, 1998.

Hitchcock, J. *History of the Catholic Church: From the Apostolic Age to the Third Millennium.* San Francisco: Ignatius Press, 2012.

Hofstede, G.H. *Culture's Consequences, International Differences in Work-Related Values.* Thousand Oaks, CA: Sage Publications, 1980.

Honolka, K. *Dvořák,* translated by A. Wyhurd. London: Haus Publishing, 2004.

Horne, A. *The Fall of Paris: The Siege and the Commune.* New York: St. Martin's Press, 1965.

Horowitz, J. *Dvořák in America.* Chicago: Cricket Books, 2003.

House, R.J., P.J. Hanges, M. Javidan, P.W. Dorfman, and V. Gupta. *Culture, Leadership, and Organizations: The GLOBE Study of 62 Societies.* Los Angeles: Sage Publications, 2004.

House, R.J., P.W. Dorfman, P.J. Hanges, M. Javidan, and M.S. de Luque. *Culture and Leadership across the World: The GLOBE Book of In-Depth Studies of 25 Societies.* Los Angeles: Sage Publications, 2014.

Humphrey, C. *Buddhism.* Harmondsworth: Pelican Books, 1951.

Huntington, S. *The Clash of Civilizations and the Remaking of World Order.* New York: Simon & Schuster, 2011.

Hurwitz, D. *Dvořák: Romantic Music's Most Versatile Genius.* Pompton Plains, NJ: Amadeus Press, 2005.

Inikori, J.E. and Stanley L. Engerman, eds. *The Atlantic Slave Trade: Effects on Economies, Societies, and Peoples in Africa, the Americas, and Europe.* Durham, NC: Duke University Press, 1992.

Inside Islam, directed by Mark Hufnail. Burbank, CA: MPH Entertainment Productions and History Channel, 2002. DVD.

Jackson, T. *Management and Change in Africa: A Cross-Culture Perspective.* London: Routledge, 2004.

Jacoby, T., ed. *Reinventing the Melting Pot: The New Immigrants and What It Means to be American.* New York: Basic Books, 2004.

Jarausch, K.H., and L.E. Jones, eds. *In Search of a Liberal Germany: Studies in the History of German Liberalism from 1789 to the Present.* New York: St. Martin's Press, 1990.

Jinkins M., and D.B. Jinkins. *The Character of Leadership: Political Realism and Public Virtue in Nonprofit Organizations.* San Francisco: Jossey-Bass, 1998.

Jolowicz, H.F. *Roman Foundations of Modern Law.* Westport, CT: Greenwood Press, 1978.

Jordan, J.O. "Life in the Theater: Autobiography, Politics, and Romance in 'Master Harold'. . . and the Boys." *Twentieth Century Literature,* 39, 4 (1993): 461.

Jordan, S.D. *The Enlightenment Vision: Science, Reason, and the Promise of a Better Future.* Amherst, NY: Prometheus Books, 2012.

Kaipa, P. and N. Radjou. *From Smart to Wise: Acting and Leading with Wisdom.* San Francisco: Jossey-Bass, 2013.

Kaltenmark, M. *Lao Tzu and Taoism,* translated by Roger Greaves. Stanford, CA: Stanford University Press, 1969.

Kamwangamalu, N.M. "*Ubuntu* in South Africa: A Sociolinguistic Perspective to Pan-African Concept." *Critical Arts,* 13, 2 1999: pp. 1–7.

Kant, E. *Foundations of the Metaphysics of Morals,* translated by Lewis White Beck. Upper Saddle River, NJ: Prentice Hall, 1997.

Kassim, H. "Toward a Mahayana Buddhist Interpretation of Hermann Hesse's 'Siddhartha'." *Literature East and West*, 18 (1974): 233–243.

Kazen, T. *Issues of Impurity in Early Judaism*. Winona Lake, IN: Eisenbrauns, 2010.

Keating, D.P., ed. *Nature and Nurture in Early Child Development*. New York: Cambridge University Press, 2012.

Keen, B., ed. *Latin American Civilization: History and Society, 1492 to the Present*. Boulder, CO: Westview Press, 2000.

Kellerman, B. *Bad Leadership: What it is, How it Happens, Why it Matters*. Boston, MA: Harvard Business Press, 2004.

—— *Followership: How Followers are Creating Change and Changing Leaders*. Boston, MA: Harvard Business Press, 2008.

—— *Leadership: Essential Selections on Authority, Power, and Influence*. New York: McGraw-Hill, 2010.

Kelly, R.E. "In Praise of Followers." *Harvard Business Review*, 66, 6 (1988): 142–148.

Kelly, R.E. "Rethinking Followership," in R.E. Riggio, I. Chaleff, and J. Lipman-Kelly, R.E., eds. *The Art of Followership: How Great Followers Create Great Leaders and Organizations*. New York: Doubleday, 1992.

Keohane, G.L. *Social Entrepreneurship for the 21st Century: Innovation across the Nonprofit, Private, and Public Sectors*. New York: McGraw-Hill, 2013.

Keown, D. *The Nature of Buddhist Ethics*. London: Macmillan, 1992.

Koenig, B.L. *Going Global for the Greater Good: Succeeding as a Nonprofit in the International Community*. San Francisco: Jossey-Bass, 2004.

Komives, S.R., S. Wagner, and Associates. *Leadership for a Better World: Understanding the Social Change Model of Leadership Development*. San Francisco, Jossey-Bass, 2009.

Kornbluh, P. *The Pinochet File: A Declassified Dossier on Atrocity and Accountability*. New York: New Press, 2004.

Kouzes, J.M., and B.Z. Posner. *The Leadership Challenge*, 3rd edn. San Francisco: Jossey-Bass, 2002.

Krauze, E. *Redeemers: Ideas and Power in Latin America*, translated by H. Heifetz and N.E. Wimmer. New York: Harper Perennial, 2012.

Kriger, M., and Y. Seng. "Leadership with Inner Meaning: A Contingency Theory of Leadership Based on the Worldviews of Five Religions." *Leadership Quarterly*, 16 (2005): 771–806.

Kroll, J. "Masters and Servants." *Newsweek*, March 29, 1982, 52.

Kryzanek, M.J. *Leaders, Leadership, and U.S. Policy in Latin America*. Boulder, CO: Westview Press, 1992.

Ku-ying, C. *Lao Tzu Text, Notes, and Comments*. Translated and adapted by Rhett Y.W. Young and Roger T. Ames. San Francisco: Chinese Materials Center, Inc., 1977.

LaFargue, M. *The Tao of the Tao Te Ching*. Albany, NY: State University of New York Press, 1992.

Larson, D. *The Puritan Ethic in United States Foreign Policy*. Princeton, NJ: Van Nostrand, 1966.

Lawson, K. *The Trainer's Handbook of Leadership Development: Tools, Techniques, and Activities*. San Francisco: Pfeiffer, 2011.

Le Joly, E. *We Do It for Jesus: Mother Teresa and Her Missionaries of Charity*. New York: Oxford University Press, 1998.

Ledeen, M.A. *Machiavelli on Modern Leadership: Why Machiavelli's Iron Rules Are as Timely and Important Today as Five Centuries Ago*. New York: Truman Talley Books, 2000.

Leuchter, M., and J.M. Hutton, eds. *Levites and Priests in History and Tradition*. Boston, MA: Brill, 2011.

Lewis, P.H. *Guerillas and Generals: The "Dirty War" in Argentina*. Westport, CT: Praeger, 2002.

Lewis, R.D. *When Cultures Collide: Leading Across Cultures*, 3rd edn. Boston, MA: Nicholas Brealey International, 2006.

Liebert, H., G.L. McDowell, and T.L. Price, eds. *Executive Power in Theory and Practice*. New York: Palgrave Macmillan, 2012.

Linton, M. *Choosing Terror: Virtue, Friendship, and Authenticity in the French Revolution*. New York: Oxford University Press, 2013.

Lippy, C.H., R. Choquette, and S. Poole. *Christianity Comes to the Americas, 1492–1776*. New York: Paragon House, 1992.

Lowney, C. *A Vanished World: Muslims, Christians, and Jews in Medieval Spain*. New York: Oxford University Press, 2006.

Lynch, J. *Argentine Caudillo: Juan Manuel de Rosas*. Wilmington, DE: SR Books, 2001.

Lynch, J. *New Worlds: A Religious History of Latin America*. New Haven, NJ: Yale University Press, 2012.

Lyons, M. *Napoleon Bonaparte and the Legacy of the French Revolution*. New York: St. Martin's Press, 1994.

McCabe, J. *Charlie Chaplin*. Garden City, NY: Doubleday, 1978.

McDonald, J.H. "Paraphrase of the *Tao Te Ching*." Public Domain, 1996. http://www.wright-house.com/religions/taoism/tao-te-ching.html.

McDowell, S. *Apostle of Liberty: The World-Changing Leadership of George Washington*. Nashville, TN: Cumberland House Publishing, 2007.

McFaul, T.R. *The Future of Peace and Justice in the Global Village: The Role of the World Religions in the Twenty-First Century*. Westport, CT: Praeger, 2006.

McGregor, D. "The Human Side of Enterprise." *Management Review*, 46, 11 (1957): 22–24, 88–89, 91.

McMahon, W.W. *Higher Learning, Greater Good: The Private and Social Benefits of Higher Education*. Baltimore, MD: Johns Hopkins University Press, 2009.

Machiavelli, N. *The Prince*. New York: Modern Library, 1950.

The Making of an Epic: Mohammed the Messenger of God, directed by Moustapha Akkad. Filmco International Productions, 1976. DVD.

Mallett, M., and N. Mann, eds. *Lorenzo the Magnificent: Culture and Politics*. London: Warburg Institute, University of London, 1996.

Maltby, R. "Made for Each Other: The Melodrama of Hollywood and the House Committee on Un-American Activities," in Philip Davies and Brian Neve, eds. *Cinema, Politics and Society in America*. Manchester: Manchester United Press, 1981.

Malunga, C. *Understanding Organizational Leadership Through Ubuntu*. London: Adonis and Abbey, 2009.

Man, J. *The Leadership Secrets of Genghis Khan*. London: Transword Digital, 2010.

Mangaliso, M.P. "Building Competitive Advantage from *Ubuntu*: Management Lessons From South Africa." *Academy of Management Executive*, 15, 3 (2001): 23–33.

Manning, P. "The Enslavement of Africans: A Demographic Model." *Canadian Journal of African Studies*, 15, 3 (1981): 499–526.

Manning, P. *Slavery and African Life: Occidental, Oriental, and African Slave Trades*. Cambridge: Cambridge University Press, 1990.

Mansbach, R. and E. Rhodes, eds. *Introducing Globalization: Analysis and Readings*. Thousand Oaks, CA: CQ Press, 2013.

Mapadimeng, M. "*Ubunto/Botho*, The Work Place and the Two Economies." *Journal of Development Studies*, 37, 2 2007: 257–271.

Marx, K. *The Eighteenth Brumaire of Louis Bonaparte.* Toronto: Norman Bethune Institute, 1977.

Masciarelli, F. *The Strategic Value of Social Capital: How Firms Capitalize on Social Assets.* Cheltenham: Edward Elgar, 2011.

Maslow, A.H. "A Theory of Human Motivation." *Psychological Review*, 50, 4 (1943): 370–396.

Mathisen, R.W. *Ancient Mediterranean Civilizations: From Prehistory to 640 CE.* New York: Oxford University Press, 2012.

Matyszak, P. *Chronicle of the Roman Republic: The Rulers of Ancient Rome from Romulus to Augustus.* New York: Thames & Hudson, 2003.

Maurice, C.E. *The Revolutionary Movement of 1848–9 in Italy, Austria-Hungary, and Germany.* New York: Haskell House Publishers, 1969.

Mbiti, J.S. *African Religions and Philosophy.* London: Heinemann, 1969.

Meltzer, M. *Francisco Pizarro: The Conquest of Peru.* New York: Benchmark Books, 2003.

Meredith, M. *The Fate of Africa: A History of the Continent Since Independence*, rev. edn. New York: Public Affairs, 2011.

The Message, directed by Moustapha Akkad. Beverley Hills, CA: Anchor Bay Entertainment/Filmco International Productions, 1976. DVD.

Metcalfe, B.D., and F. Mimouni. *Leadership Development in the Middle East.* Cheltenham: Edward Elgar, 2011.

"Mexico." The Hofstede Centre. Accessed April 26, 2014. http://geert-hofstede.com/mexico.html.

Mill, J.S. *Utilitarianism.* Mineola, NY: Dover Publications, 2007.

Miller, A., and H. Ibsen. *An Enemy of the People.* New York: Penguin Books, 1970.

Mir, A.M. "Leadership in Islam." *Journal of Leadership Studies*, 4, 3 (2010): 69–72.

Mohammed, S.N. *Communication and the Globalization of Culture: Beyond Tradition and Borders.* Lanham, MD: Lexington Books, 2011.

Moore, R.I. *The War on Heresy.* Cambridge, MA: Belknap Press of Harvard University Press, 2012.

Morgan, G. *Images of Organizations*, updated edn. Los Angeles: Sage, 2006.

Morgan, M.H. *Lost History: The Enduring Legacy of Muslim Scientists, Thinkers, and Artists.* Washington, DC: National Geographic Society, 2007.

Morgan, P., and Lawton, C.A. *Ethical Issues in Six Religious Traditions.* Edinburgh: Edinburgh University Press 1996.

Morrison, M. *The Other Side of the Card: Where Your Authentic Leadership Story Begins.* New York: McGraw-Hill, 2007.

Morrison, T., and W.A. Conaway. *Kiss, Bow or Shake Hands. Latin America: How to do Business in 18 Latin American Countries.* Avon, MA: Adams Media, 2007.

Muir, D.E. *Machiavelli and His Times.* Westport, CT: Greenwood Press, 1976.

Nanus, B. *Visionary Leadership: Creating a Compelling Sense of Direction for Your Organization.* San Francisco: Jossey-Bass, 1992.

Narasimbaial, S. "Hermann Hesse's 'Siddhartha': Between Rebellion and Regeneration." *Literary Criterion*, 16 (1981): 50–66.

Nellis, E. *Shaping the New World: African Slavery in the Americas, 1500–1888.* North York, Ontario, Canada: University of Toronto Press, 2013.

Néret, G. *Eugène Delacroix: 1798–1863; The Prince of Romanticism*, translated by Chris Miller. London: Taschen, 1999.

New York Herald. "Dvořák on His New Work." December 15, 1893.

Nielson, R., H.S. Ferraro, and J.A. Marrone. *Leading With Humility*. London: Routledge, 2013.

"The Nobel Prize in Literature 1967." Nobel Prize. Last modified 2014. http://www. nobelprize.org/nobel_prizes/literature/laureates/1967.

"The Nobel Peace Prize for 2006." Nobelprize.org. Last modified October 13, 2006. http://www.nobelprize.org/nobel_prizes/peace/laureates/2006/press.html.

Northouse, P. *Leadership: Theory and Practice*, 6th edn. Los Angeles: Sage Publications, 2012.

Nuccetelli, S. *Latin American Thought: Philosophical Problems and Arguments*. Boulder, CO: Westview Press, 2002.

Nuccetelli, S., O. Schutte, and O. Bueno, eds. *A Companion to Latin American Philosophy*. Malden, MA: Wiley-Blackwell, 2010.

Nurmela, R. *The Levites: Their Emergence as a Second-Class Priesthood*. Atlanta, GA: Scholars Press, 1998.

Odahl, C.M. *Constantine and the Christian Empire*. New York: Routledge, 2004.

Olson-Buchanan, J., L.K. Bryan, L.F. Thompson, eds. *Using Industrial Organizational Psychology for the Greater Good: Helping Those Who Help Others*. London: Routledge, 2013.

Österling, A. "Award Ceremony Speech." Speech, Amsterdam, 1967. Nobel Prize. http://www.nobelprize.org/nobel_prizes/literature/laureates/1967/press.html.

Outram, D. *The Enlightenment*. New York: Cambridge University Press, 2013.

Paparchontis, K. *100 World Leaders Who Shaped World History*. San Mateo, CA: Bluewood Books, 2001.

Parameshwar, S. "Inventing Higher Purpose Through Suffering: The Transformation of the Transformational Leader." *Leadership Quarterly*, 17 (2006): 454–474.

Paslick, R.H. "Dialectic and Non-Attachment: The Structure of Hermann Hesse's 'Siddhartha'." *Symposium*, XXVII, Spring (1973): 64–75.

Pastor, R. *U.S. Foreign Policy Toward Latin America and the Caribbean*. Princeton, NJ: Princeton University Press, 1992.

Pearch, C.L., and J.A. Conger. *Shared Leadership: Reframing the Hows and Whys of Leadership*. Thousand Oaks, CA: Sage, 2003.

Peck, R. "Condemned to Choose, but What? Existentialism in Selected Works by Fugard, Brint, and Gordimer." *Research in African Literatures*, 23, 3 (1992): 67–84.

Perea, N.S. *The Caudillo of the Andes: Andrés de Santa Cruz*. New York: Cambridge University Press, 2011.

Perruci, G. "Millennials and Globalization: The Cross-Cultural Challenge of Intra-generational Leadership." *Journal of Leadership Studies*, 5, 3 (2011): 82–87.

—— "Leadership Education Across Disciplines: The Social Science Perspective." *Journal of Leadership Studies*, 7, 4 (2014): 43–47.

Perruci, G., and R.M. McManus. "The State of Leadership Studies." *Journal of Leadership Studies*, 6, 3 (2012): 49–54.

Philbrick, N. *The Mayflower and the Pilgrims' New World*. New York: G.P. Putnam's Sons, 2008.

Phillips, D.T. *Martin Luther King, Jr., on Leadership: Inspiration and Wisdom for Challenging Times*. New York: Warner Books, 2001.

Phillips, T. *Niccolo' Machiavelli's* The Prince: *A 52 Brilliant Ideas Interpretation*. Oxford: Infinite Ideas, 2008.

Pilbeam, P. *The 1830 Revolution in France*. London: Macmillan, 1991.

Pissarro, J., and S. Rachum. *Camille Pissarro: Impressionist Innovator.* Jerusalem: Israel Museum, 1994.

Plain, N. *Louis XVI, Marie-Antoinette and the French Revolution.* New York: Benchmark Books, 2002.

Pobee, J. "Aspects of African Traditional Religion." *Sociological Analysis,* 37, 1 (1976): 1–18.

Pohl, J., and C.M. Robinson. *Aztecs and Conquistadores: The Spanish Invasion and the Collapse of the Aztec Empire.* New York: Osprey Publishing, 2005.

Post, R.M. "Racism in Athol Fugard's *'Master Harold' . . . and the Boys.*" *World Literature Written in English,* 30, 1 (1990): 97–102.

Pratkanis, A.R., and E. Aronson. *Age of Propaganda: The Everyday Use and Abuse of Persuasion.* New York: W.H. Freeman/Holt & Co., 2002.

Prendergast, C. *The Fourteenth of July.* London: Profile Books, 2008.

"The Private Life of a Masterpiece." Disc 3. *Masterpieces 1800–1850.* DVD. Directed by Judith Winnan, Lucie Donahue, Michael Burke, Mick Gold, and Clare Lynch. London: BBC Home Entertainment, 2008.

Putnam, R.D. *Bowling Alone: The Collapse and Revival of American Community.* New York: Simon & Schuster, 2000.

Putnam, R.D. "Bowling Alone: America's Declining Social Capital," in M.J. Gannon, ed. *Cultural Metaphors: Readings, Research Translations, and Commentary.* Thousand Oaks, CA: Sage, 2001.

Putnam, R.D., and L.M. Feldstein. *Better Together: Restoring the American Community.* New York: Simon & Schuster, 2003.

Putterman, E. *Rousseau, Law and the Sovereignty of the People.* New York: Cambridge University Press, 2010.

Quelch, J.A., and K.E. Jocz. *Greater Good: How Good Marketing Makes for Better Democracy.* Boston, MA: Harvard Business Press, 2007.

Rahula, W. *What the Buddha Taught.* New York: Grove Press, 1959.

Rainey, L.D. *Confucius and Confucianism: The Essentials.* Hoboken, NY: Wiley-Blackwell, 2010.

Rawlings, H. *The Spanish Inquisition.* Malden, MA: Blackwell Publishing, 2006.

Ray, T., S. Clegg, and R.A. Gordon. "A New Look at Dispersed Leadership: Power, Knowledge and Context," in J. Storey, ed. *Leadership in Organizations.* London: Routledge, 2004.

Rees, J.C., and S. Spignesi. *George Washington's Leadership Lessons.* Hoboken, NJ: Wiley, 2007.

Reid, R.J. *A History of Modern Africa: 1800 to the Present,* 2nd edn. Hoboken: NJ: Wiley Blackwell, 2012.

Reid, T.R. *Confucius Lives Next Door: What Living in the East Teaches Us About Living in the West.* New York: Vintage Books, 1999.

Rejai, M., and K. Phillips. *Concepts of Leadership in Western Political Thought.* Westport, CT: Praeger, 2002.

Riggio, R.E., I. Chaleff, and J. Lipman-Blumen. *The Art of Followership: How Great Followers Create Great Leaders and Organizations.* San Francisco: Jossey-Bass, 2008.

Roberts, D., ed. *Student Leadership Programs in Higher Education.* Carbondale, IL: American College Personnel Association, 1981.

Roberts, W. *The Leadership Secrets of Attila the Hun.* New York: Grand Central Publishing, 2007.

Robinson, D. *Chaplin: His Life and Art.* New York: McGraw-Hill, 1985.

Rodgers, E., C.R. Bradley, and S. Ward. "Poetic Forms of Leadership Pedagogy: Rediscovering Creative Leadership through the Arts." *Journal of Leadership Studies*, 3, 4 (2010): 91–96.

Rondinelli, D.A. and J.M. Heffron, eds. *Leadership for Development: What Globalization Demands of Leaders Fighting for Change.* Sterling, VA: Kumarian Press, 2009.

Rost, J.C. *Leadership for the Twenty-First Century.* Westport, CN: Praeger, 1991.

Rotberg, R.I. *Transformative Political Leadership: Making a Difference in the Developing World.* Chicago: University of Chicago Press, 2012.

Roth, J.D., ed. *Constantine Revisited: Leithart, Yoder, and the Constantinian Debate.* Eugene, OR: Pickwick Publications, 2013.

Rousseau, J. *The Social Contract,* translated by G.D.H. Cole. Buffalo, NY: Prometheus Books, 1988.

Rowlands, G. *The Financial Decline of a Great Power: War, Influence, and Money in Louis XIV's France.* Oxford: Oxford University Press, 2012.

Ruben, B.D. *What Leaders Need to Know: A Leadership Competencies Scorecard.* Washington, DC: National Association of College and University Business Officers, 2006.

Sandoval, E. "The Metaphoric Style in Politically Censored Theater." Diss., Concordia University, 1986.

Sarpong, P. *Ghana in Retrospect: Some Aspects of Ghanaian Culture.* Accra-Tema: Ghana Publishing Corporation, 1974

Sashkin, M. "Transformational Leadership Approaches: A Review and Synthesis," in J. Antonkis, A.T. Cianciolo, and R.J. Sternberg, eds. *The Nature of Leadership.* Thousand Oaks, CA: Sage, 2004.

Savitz, A.W., and K. Weber. *The Triple Bottom Line: How Today's Best-Run Companies are Achieving Economic, Social, and Environmental Success – And How You Can Too.* San Francisco: Jossey-Bass, 2014.

Schein, E.H. *Organizational Culture and Leadership,* 4th edn. San Francisco: Jossey-Bass, 2010.

Scherer, B.L. "A Narrative of Heroism in Crisis." *Wall Street Journal,* December 20, 2013: C13.

Schludermann, B., and Finlay, R. "Mythical Reflections of the East in Hermann Hesse." *Mosaic,* 2 (1969): 97–111.

Schoultz, L. *National Security and United States Policy Toward Latin America.* Princeton, NJ: Princeton University Press, 1987.

Schutte, A. *Philosophy for Africa.* Cape Town: University of Cape Town Press, 1993.

Scurr, R. *Fatal Purity: Robespierre and the French Revolution.* New York: Metropolitan Books, 2006.

Sellnow, D., and T. Sellnow. "John Corigliano's 'Symphony No. 1' as a Communicative Medium for the AIDS Crisis." *Communication Studies,* 44, 2 (1993): 87–101.

Senge, P. *The Fifth Discipline, The Art and Practice of the Learning Organization,* rev. edn. New York: Doubleday/Random House, 2006.

Shamir, B., R. Pillai, M.C. Bligh, and M. Uhl-Bien. *Follower-Centered Perspectives on Leadership: A Tribute to the Memory of James R. Meindl.* Greenwich, CN: Information Age Publishing, 2007.

Shaw, L. "Time and Structure of Hermann Hesse's 'Siddhartha'." *Symposium,* XI (1957): 202–224.

Shillington, K. *History of Africa,* 3rd edn. Basingstroke: Palgrave Macmillan, 2012.

Siemann, W. *The German Revolution of 1848–49,* translated by C. Banerji. New York: St. Martin's Press, 1998.

Slavicek, L.C. *Mother Teresa: Caring for the World's Poor*. New York: Chelsea House, 2007.

Smith, A. *An Inquiry into the Nature and Causes of the Wealth of Nations*. London: W. Strahan & T. Cadell, 1776.

Smith, H. *The World's Religions: Our Great Wisdom Traditions*. San Francisco: HarperCollins, 1958/1991.

Smith, H.J. "The Shareholders vs. The Stakeholders Debate." *MIT Sloan Management Review*, 44.4 (2003): 85–90.

Smith, W.W., Jr. *Confucianism in Modern Japan: A Study of Conservatives in Japanese Intellectual History*, 2nd edn. Tokyo: Hokuseido Press, 1973.

Sommer, M. *The Complete Roman Emperor: Imperial Life at Court and on Campaign*. London: Thames & Hudson, 2010.

Sonn, T. "Islam and Economics," in J. Neusner, ed. *Religious Belief and Economic Behavior*. Atlanta, GA: Scholars Press Issues, 1999.

Soboul, A. *The French Revolution, 1787–1799: From the Storming of the Bastille to Napoleon*, translated by Alan Forrest and Colin Jones. Boston, MA: Unwin Hyman, 1989.

Spielvogel, J.J. *Western Civilization*. Boston, MA: Wadsworth, Cengage Learning, 2012.

Spindler, G. and J.E. Stockard, eds. *Globalization and Change in Fifteen Cultures: Born in One World, Living in Another*. Belmont, CA: Thomson/Wadsworth, 2007.

Spitz, L.W. *The Protestant Reformation, 1517–1559*. St. Louis, IL: CPH, 2001.

Stearns, P.N. *The Industrial Revolution in World History*. Boulder, CO: Westview Press, 2013.

Stelzig, E.L. *Hermann Hesse's Fictions of the Self: Autobiography and the Confessional Imagination*. Princeton, NJ: Princeton University Press, 1988.

Sternberg, R.J., ed. *Wisdom: It's Nature, Origins, and Development*. New York: Cambridge University Press, 1990.

Stevens, E.P. "Marianismo: The Other Face of Machismo in Latin America," in A. Minas, ed. *Gender Basics: Feminist Perspectives on Women and Men*. Belmont, CA: Wadsworth/ Thomson Learning, 2000.

Strathern, P. *The Medici: Godfathers of the Renaissance*. London: Jonathan Cape, 2003.

Takahashi, M., and W.F. Overton. "Cultural Foundations of Wisdom: An Integrated Development Approach," in R.J. Sternberg and J. Jordan, eds. *A Handbook of Wisdom: Psychological Perspectives*. New York: Cambridge University Press, 2005.

Tan, C. *Search Inside Yourself*. New York: HarperOne, 2012.

Taylor, F.W. *The Principles of Scientific Management*. New York: Harper & Brothers, 1913.

Terry, R.W. *Authentic Leadership: Courage in Action*. San Francisco: Jossey-Bass, 1993.

Thompson, K. *Auguste Comte: The Foundation of Sociology*. New York: Wiley, 1975.

Tombs, R. *The Paris Commune, 1871*. New York: Longman, 1999.

Tomlinson, G. *The Singing of the New World: Indigenous Voice in the Era of European Contact*. New York: Cambridge University Press, 2009.

Tubbs, S.L. *Keys to Leadership: 101 Steps to Success*. Boston, MA: McGraw-Hill Custom Publishing, 2005.

Tutu, D.M. *No Future Without Forgiveness*. New York: Image/Doubleday, 1999.

Tzu, C. *The Complete Works of Chuang Tzu*, translated by B. Watson. New York: Columbia University Press, 1968.

Urban, D.V. "Tolstoy's Presence in Fugard's 'Master Harold' . . . and the Boys': Sam's Pacifist Christian Perseverance and a 'Case of Illness'." *REN*, 62, 4 (2010): 311–326.

Van Norden, B.W. *Introduction to Classical Chinese Philosophy*. Indianapolis, IN: Hackett, 2011.

Vance, N. *The Victorians and Ancient Rome*. Cambridge, MA: Blackwell Publishers, 1997.

Vandenbroucke, R. *Truths The Hand Can Touch*. New York: Theater Communications Group, 1985.

Verma, K.D. "The Nature of Perception of Reality in Hermann Hesse's 'Siddhartha'." *South Asian Review*, 11–12 (1988): 1–10.

Viroli, M. *Machiavelli*. New York: Oxford University Press, 1998.

Waddock, S. *The Difference Makers: How Social and Institutional Entrepreneurs Created the Corporate Responsibility Movement*. Sheffield: Greenleaf Publishing, 2008.

Wald, K.D., and A. Calhoun-Brown, *Religion and Politics in the United States*. Lanham, MD: Rowman & Littlefield Publishers, 2011.

Walder, D. *Athol Fugard*. Gordonville, VA: St. Martin's Press, 1990.

Walumbwa, F.O., B.J. Avolio, W.L. Gardner, T.S. Wernsing, and S.J. Peterson. "Authentic Leadership Development and Validation of a Theory-based Measure." *Journal of Management*, 34 (2008): 89–126.

Walumbwa, F.O. and George O. Ndege, "Cultural Mythology and Global Leadership in Kenya," in E.H. Kessler and D.J. Wong-Mingji, *Cultural Mythology and Global Leadership*. Cheltenham: Edward Elgar, 2009.

Watson, B. *The Complete Works of Chang Tzu*. New York: Columbia University Press, 1968.

Watson, B. *Chuang Tzu: Basic Writings*, 3rd edn. New York: Columbia University Press, 2003.

Weales, G. "Fugard Masters the Code." *Twentieth Century Literature*, 39, 4 (1993): 503–516.

Weber, M. *The Theory of Social and Economic Organization*. London: Oxford University Press, 1947.

—— *The Protestant Ethic and the Spirit of Capitalism*, translated by Stephen Kalberg. London: Routledge, 1930/2012.

Welsh, K. *African Dance*, 2nd edn. New York: Chelsea House Publishers, 2010.

Wheatley, M.J. *Leadership and the New Science: Discovering Order in a Chaotic World*, 3rd edn. San Francisco: Berrett-Koehler Publishers, 2006.

Whissen, T.R. "Siddhartha." *Classic Cult Fiction*. New York: Greenwood Press, 1992.

Wiarda, H.J. *Latin American Politics*. New York: Wadsworth, 1995.

Wing, R.L. *The Tao of Power: Lao Tzu's Classic Guide to Leadership, Influence, and Excellence*. Garden City, NY: Doubleday, 1986.

Woodward, Jr., R.L., ed. *Positivism in Latin America, 1850–1900: Are Order and Progress Reconcilable?* Lexington, MA: Heath, 1971.

Wren, J.T. *Inventing Leadership: The Challenge of Democracy*. Northampton, MA: Edward Elgar, 2007.

Wren, J.T., and M.J. Swatez. "The Historical and Contemporary Contexts of Leadership: A Conceptual Model," in J.T. Wren, ed. *The Leader's Companion: Insights on Leadership Through the Ages*. New York: Free Press, 1995.

Wyatt III, L.T. *The Industrial Revolution*. Westport, CT: Greenwood Press, 2009.

Yang, S. "Wisdom Displayed Through Leadership: Exploring Leadership-Related Wisdom." *Leadership Quarterly*, 22 (2011): 616–632.

Zand, D.E. *The Leadership Triad: Knowledge, Trust, and Power*. New York: Oxford University Press, 1997.

Ziolkowski, T. *The Novels of Hermann Hesse: A Study in Theme and Structure*. Princeton, NJ: Princeton University Press, 1965.

van Zyle, E.C., C. Dalglish, M. du Plessis, L. Luer, and E. Pietersen. *Leadership in the African Context*. Cape Town: Juta and Co. Ltd, 2009.

Index